Human–AI Interaction and Collaboration

The integration of artificial intelligence (AI) into information systems will affect the way users interface with these systems. This exploration of the interaction and collaboration between humans and AI reveals its potential and challenges, covering issues such as data privacy, credibility of results, misinformation, and search interactions. Later chapters delve into application domains such as healthcare and scientific discovery.

In addition to providing new perspectives on and methods for developing AI technology and designing more humane and efficient AI systems, the book also reveals the shortcomings of AI technologies through case studies and puts forward corresponding countermeasures and suggestions. This book is ideal for researchers, students, and industry practitioners interested in enhancing human-centered AI systems and insights for future research.

DAN WU is Full Professor at the School of Information Management at Wuhan University. She is also the Director of the Human–Computer Interaction and User Behavior Research Center at Wuhan University. She is the editor-in-chief of *Aslib Journal of Information Management* and has served as Director at Large of ASIS&T. She has received multiple research grants, including from the National Key R&D Program of China.

SHAOBO LIANG is Associate Professor at the School of Information Management at Wuhan University. He was supported by the Young Elite Scientists Sponsorship Program by CAST. He has served as Chair-Elect of the Asia Chapter of ASIS&T and as a member of the iNext Group of iSchool AP. His research interests include human–computer interaction, user information-seeking behavior, and mobile interaction behavior.

This book offers a comprehensive exploration of the dynamic interaction and collaboration between humans and AI across various domains. It tackles both the opportunities and challenges presented by AI, highlighting its potential to enhance productivity, ethical considerations, and its role in shaping the future of industries such as healthcare and education. A valuable resource for anyone interested in understanding the multifaceted impact of AI.

Chuanfu Chen, *Senior Professor of Humanities and Social Sciences, Wuhan University, China*

Human–AI Interaction and Collaboration

Edited by

DAN WU
Wuhan University, China

SHAOBO LIANG
Wuhan University, China

Shaftesbury Road, Cambridge CB2 8EA, United Kingdom

One Liberty Plaza, 20th Floor, New York, NY 10006, USA

477 Williamstown Road, Port Melbourne, VIC 3207, Australia

314–321, 3rd Floor, Plot 3, Splendor Forum, Jasola District Centre,
New Delhi – 110025, India

103 Penang Road, #05-06/07, Visioncrest Commercial, Singapore 238467

Cambridge University Press is part of Cambridge University Press & Assessment,
a department of the University of Cambridge.

We share the University's mission to contribute to society through the pursuit of
education, learning and research at the highest international levels of excellence.

www.cambridge.org
Information on this title: www.cambridge.org/9781009587853

DOI: 10.1017/9781009587877

© Cambridge University Press & Assessment 2026

This publication is in copyright. Subject to statutory exception and to the provisions
of relevant collective licensing agreements, no reproduction of any part may take
place without the written permission of Cambridge University Press & Assessment.

When citing this work, please include a reference to the DOI 10.1017/9781009587877

First published 2026

Cover image: Grid pattern of abstract human head silhouettes filled with layers of
AI letters. © Daryl Solomon / Photodisc / Getty Images.

A catalogue record for this publication is available from the British Library

*A Cataloging-in-Publication data record for this book is available from the Library of
Congress*

ISBN 978-1-009-58785-3 Hardback

Cambridge University Press & Assessment has no responsibility for the persistence
or accuracy of URLs for external or third-party internet websites referred to in this
publication and does not guarantee that any content on such websites is, or will
remain, accurate or appropriate.

For EU product safety concerns, contact us at Calle de José Abascal, 56, 1°,
28003 Madrid, Spain, or email eugpsr@cambridge.org

Contents

List of Contributors		page ix
Preface		xv

1 Introduction — 1
Dan Wu, Guoye Sun, and Shaobo Liang
- 1.1 Background — 1
- 1.2 Research Implications — 5
- 1.3 Structure of the Book — 8

2 User Interaction for Human–AI Interaction and Collaboration — 14
Dan Wu and Qingyue Guo
- 2.1 Introduction — 14
- 2.2 From Human–Computer Interaction to Human–AI Interaction and Collaboration — 15
- 2.3 A Framework of Human–AI Interaction and Collaboration — 19
- 2.4 Interaction Quality in Human–AI Interaction and Collaboration — 21
- 2.5 Interaction Mode in Human–AI Interaction and Collaboration — 27
- 2.6 Future Directions and Challenges — 31

3 Privacy Identification of Human–Generative AI Interaction — 43
Dan Wu and Guoye Sun
- 3.1 Introduction — 43
- 3.2 Related Concepts — 45
- 3.3 Construction of Privacy Type Model — 53
- 3.4 Application Value of Privacy Type Model — 71
- 3.5 Summary — 76

4	**Credibility Assessment of Human–Generative AI Interaction**		82
	Yuxiang Chris Zhao, Shijie Song, and Yutian Jing		
	4.1	Introduction	82
	4.2	The Concept of AI Credibility	83
	4.3	Measures of AI Credibility in Human–Generative AI Interaction	86
	4.4	Influences on Credibility Assessment in Human–Generative AI Interaction	88
	4.5	Challenges in Credibility Assessment of Human–Generative AI Interaction	91
	4.6	Ways to Enhance the Credibility Assessment in Human–Generative AI Interaction	92
	4.7	Domains of Credibility Assessment in Human–Generative AI	93
	4.8	Future Research Agenda	96
	4.9	Conclusion	98
5	**AI-supported Crowdsourcing for Knowledge Sharing**		110
	Chei Sian Lee, Dion Hoe-Lian Goh, Hang Guo, Kok Khiang Lim, and Qian Wu		
	5.1	Introduction	110
	5.2	Background on AI-supported Crowdsourcing	113
	5.3	Systematic Review of AI-supported Crowdsourcing	116
	5.4	Case Study	122
	5.5	Recommendations	127
6	**AI-supported Search Interaction for Enhancing Users' Understanding**		135
	Shaobo Liang and Chenrui Shi		
	6.1	Introduction	135
	6.2	Literature Review	137
	6.3	Research Design	139
	6.4	Findings	143
	6.5	Discussion and Conclusion	149
7	**AI for Human and Misinformation Interactions: A Case of Social Media**		153
	Nannan Huang, Xiuzhen Zhang, and Jia Tina Du		
	7.1	Introduction	153
	7.2	Literature Review	155
	7.3	Methodology and Data	157

		7.4	Results	165
		7.5	Discussion	168
		7.6	Conclusion	170
8		**Effective Human–AI Collaborative Intelligence**		**175**
		Zhuoren Jiang and Xiaozhong Liu		
		8.1	Introduction	175
		8.2	Technical Foundations of Human–AI Collaboration	179
		8.3	Practical Applications and Case Studies	193
		8.4	Future Directions	200
		8.5	Conclusion	204
9		**Human–AI Collaboration for Identifying Health Information Wants**		**213**
		Zhuochun Li, Zhimeng Luo, Ning Zou, Bo Xie, and Daqing He		
		9.1	Introduction	213
		9.2	Literature Review	216
		9.3	Background	219
		9.4	Human–AI Collaboration for HIW Identifications	222
		9.5	Experiments	224
		9.6	Results	228
		9.7	Discussions	231
		9.8	Conclusions	233
10		**Human–AI Collaboration for Scientific Discovery**		**239**
		Shuo Zhao, Yang Liu, Jiayu Wan, Tan Tang, and Xin Li		
		10.1	Introduction	239
		10.2	Human–AI Collaboration in Mathematics	245
		10.3	Human–AI Collaboration in Physics	248
		10.4	Human–AI Collaboration in Chemistry	251
		10.5	Human–AI Collaboration in Life Science	255
		10.6	Summary	259
11		**Challenges of Generative AI on Human–AI Interaction and Collaboration**		**268**
		Shaobo Liang and Yiting Cai		
		11.1	User-level Challenges	268
		11.2	Algorithm Optimization Challenges	271
		11.3	Psychological Game in Human–AI Interaction and Collaboration	275
		11.4	Countermeasures	278

12 Conclusion 284
Dan Wu, Guoye Sun, and Shaobo Liang
    12.1   Key Findings in Human–AI Interaction
           and Collaboration 284
    12.2   Future Challenges 289
    12.3   Prospects for Coping Strategies 291

Contributors

The contributors are listed in alphabetical order:

Yiting Cai is a master's student at Wuhan University in China, where she received her bachelor's degree from the School of Information Management. Her research focuses on digital addiction and human–AI interaction, particularly the impact of generative AI on user behavior and experience.

Jia Tina Du is head of the School of Information and Communication Studies at Charles Sturt University. Her research explores human information behavior and emerging technologies. She has published more than 130 papers and received numerous awards, including the Australian Research Council DECRA, the Young Tall Poppy Science Award, and recognition as Australia's field leader in Library & Information Science.

Dion Hoe-Lian Goh is a professor at Nanyang Technological University, Singapore, where he is the Associate Chair for Graduate and Continuing Education in the Wee Kim Wee School of Communication and Information. His major areas of research are in gamification techniques for shaping user perceptions and motivating behavior, mobile information sharing and seeking, and crowdsourcing.

Hang Guo is the co-founder and designer of Zhongxun. He is an expert in user experience and was the recipient of the Good Design Award (G-Mark) in 2017. The award recognized the conceptual unity between user, function, and machine learning technology in the design of Zhongxun. He received a Master of Science in Human–Computer Interaction from the University of Michigan and a Bachelor of Engineering from the National University of Singapore.

Qingyue Guo is a PhD candidate at the School of Information Management, Wuhan University. Her research focuses on human–computer interaction in the context of artificial intelligence, employing a user-centered approach. She serves as an editor of *Documentation, Information & Knowledge*, a member of ASIS&T, and a reviewer for multiple academic journals.

Daqing He is a professor at the Department of Informatics and Networked Systems, School of Computing and Information at the University of Pittsburgh, and the director of the Information Retrieval, Integration and Synthesis (iRiS) lab. His research interests include natural language processing, information retrieval, adaptive systems, and data management. His research is supported by NSF, NIH, Amazon, DARPA, UPMC Enterprise, ALISE/OCLC, the University of Pittsburgh, and other agencies.

Nannan Huang is pursuing a PhD at RMIT University. Her research interests include bias in opinion summarization.

Zhuoren Jiang is a tenure-track assistant professor at the Department of Information Resources Management, School of Public Affairs, Zhejiang University. He also serves as a consultant (visiting professor) of Alibaba DAMO Academy.

Yutian Jing is a PhD candidate in the School of Information Management at Nanjing University, China. Her research interests span human–computer interaction, user information behavior, and the management and utilization of online information resources.

Chei Sian Lee is a professor at the Wee Kim Wee School of Communication and Information at the Nanyang Technological University in Singapore, where she is also the associate chair for faculty. She is actively involved in research on issues related to everyday human–computer interaction and everyday information practices that facilitate collaboration, learning, and social interactions. More broadly, her research focuses on designing and leveraging everyday digital technology and emerging AI innovations to influence behavior change for the benefit of the public good.

Xin Li is a professor in Electrical & Computer Engineering (ECE) at Duke University and serves as the Associate Vice-Chancellor for Graduate Studies and Research at Duke Kunshan University. He received his PhD in ECE from

Carnegie Mellon University in 2005. His research interests include integrated circuits, signal processing, and data analytics. He was the deputy editor-in-chief of IEEE TCAD. He was an associate editor of IEEE TCAD, IEEE TBME, ACM TODAES, IEEE D&T, and IET CPS. He was the general chair of ISVLSI and FAC. He received the NSF CAREER Award in 2012 and six Best Paper Awards from IEEE TCAD, DAC, ICCAD, and ISIC. He is a fellow of IEEE.

Zhuochun Li is a PhD student of information science at the School of Computing and Information, University of Pittsburgh. His research interests include natural language processing (NLP) and machine learning.

Shaobo Liang is an associate professor at the School of Information Management, Wuhan University. His research interests include human–computer interaction, user information-seeking behavior, mobile search behavior, and cross-device search. He was supported by the Young Elite Scientists Sponsorship Program by CAST. He served as a member of the ASIS&T Asia Chapter committee, a member of the iNext Group of iSchool AP, and an editorial member of *Aslib Journal of Information Management*. He has received multiple research grants, including from the National Natural Science Foundation of China.

Kok Khiang Lim is a PhD candidate at the Wee Kim Wee School of Communication and Information at Nanyang Technological University in Singapore. His research interests lie in the intersections between behavioral economics and informal online learning and incorporating data analytics to uncover trends and derive insights.

Xiaozhong Liu is an associate professor of Computer Science and Data Science at the Worcester Polytechnic Institute. He was previously an associate professor at the School of Informatics, Computing and Engineering at Indiana University Bloomington. His research interests include natural language processing (NLP), text/graph mining, information retrieval/recommendation, metadata, and computational social science.

Yang Liu is an adjunct associate professor at Duke Kunshan University. He received his PhD from Michigan Technological University and did post-doctoral research at Carnegie Mellon University and at Duke University. His research involves cyber-physical systems, smart manufacturing, renewable energy, and smart supply chain.

Zhimeng Luo is a PhD student of information science at the School of Computing and Information, University of Pittsburgh, and an affiliated researcher with the Information Retrieval, Integration and Synthesis (iRiS) lab at the Department of Informatics and Networked Systems. His research interests include natural language processing (NLP), information extraction, summarization, and their applications in health informatics.

Chenrui Shi is a master's student at Wuhan University in China, where he received his bachelor's degree from the School of Information Management. His research focuses on human–computer interaction, especially interactions with AI in public libraries.

Shijie Song is an associate professor at the Department of Marketing, Business School of Hohai University, China. His research focuses on information systems, human–computer interaction, and health informatics. His work has appeared in journals including *Information Processing & Management*, *Internet Research*, the *Journal of Documentation*, and the *Journal of Medical Internet Research*.

Guoye Sun is a PhD candidate at the School of Information Management, Wuhan University. Her research interests include human–computer interaction and user information behavior, with a particular focus on privacy in human–computer interaction.

Tan Tang is an assistant professor at the School of Art and Archaeology, Zhejiang University. He received his PhD at the College of Computer Science and Technology from Zhejiang University in 2021. His research interests include information visualization, visual analytics, and human–AI collaboration. He was a program community member of IEEE VIS, IEEE PacificVis, and ChinaVis. He received the Best Paper Honorable Mention Award from IEEE VIS 2021 and ChinaVis 2022.

Jiayu Wan is an associate professor at the Global Institute of Future Technology (GIFT), Shanghai Jiao Tong University (SJTU). He is also the executive director of the Future Battery Research Center of GIFT, SJTU. he obtained his PhD from the University of Maryland, College Park, under the supervision of Liangbing Hu, and did postdoctoral research at Stanford University, working with Professors Yi Cui and Zhenan Bao. His research interests are primarily energy storage, ultrafast synthesis, and their intersection with AI, and he has authored over 90 journal articles. He has been recognized among the Emerging Investigators or Rising Stars of the *Journal of Materials Chemistry A* (RSC), *Energy & Fuels* (ACS), and *Green Chemistry* (RSC), and was also selected for the Dorothy M. and Earl S. Hoffman Award by the American Vacuum Society.

Dan Wu is a professor at the School of Information Management, Wuhan University, and director of the Human–Computer Interaction and User Behavior Research Center, Wuhan University. She is the editor-in-chief of *Aslib Journal of Information Management* and has served as director at large of ASIS&T. Her research interests include human–computer interaction, user information behavior, information organization and retrieval, and smart libraries. She has received multiple research grants, including the National Key R&D Program of China, the National Social Science Fund Major Project, and the National Natural Science Foundation Major Research Program Project.

Qian Wu is an assistant professor at Shanghai Jiao Tong University, China. Her research interest lies in human–computer interaction and computational sociology, exploring (1) the impact of linguistic cues on human–AI collaborations, (2) the psychological influences of visual cues, and (3) the methodological transformations and governance challenges in the digital era.

Bo Xie is a professor in the Schools of Nursing and Information at the University of Texas at Austin. Her research interests cover the design, implementation, and evaluation of eHealth interventions for older adults. She is a fellow of the Gerontological Society of America and has led federally funded interdisciplinary research on aging, health, and technology, with over 100 publications.

Xiuzhen Zhang is a professor of data science at RMIT University. Her research interests include data science and machine learning, text mining, and social media analysis. She has published extensively on these topics. Her research has been supported by the Australian Research Council, the Victoria state government, and industry partners.

Shuo Zhao is a senior research scientist at the Data Science Research Center, Duke Kunshan University. He received his PhD in Communication and Information Systems from the University of the Chinese Academy of Sciences in 2016. His research interests include deep learning, machine learning, and digital signal processing.

Yuxiang Chris Zhao is a professor in the School of Information Management at Nanjing University, China. His research centers on interdisciplinary studies related to human–computer interaction, health informatics, the social impact of emerging technologies, and digital humanities. He has been named in Stanford University's World's Top 2% Scientists 2024 list. His recognitions include the ASIS&T Best Poster Award, iConference Best Poster Nomination Award, ESI Highly Cited Paper, and JASIST Highly Cited Paper. He is serving as Asia Chapter Chair (2024–2025) of ASIS&T.

Ning Zou is a PhD candidate in Library and Information Science at the School of Computing and Information, University of Pittsburgh, and an affiliated researcher with the Information Retrieval, Integration and Synthesis (iRiS) lab at the Department of Informatics and Networked Systems. Her research focuses on consumer health informatics and human–data interaction.

Preface

This book systematically explores the dynamics of human–AI interaction and collaboration across various domains, addressing both opportunities and challenges posed by AI technology. It begins with an introduction to the background and importance of human–AI collaboration, followed by an examination of design principles and user-centric methods for improving collaboration through optimized interaction experiences. The book delves into privacy and credibility concerns within generative AI applications, proposing methods to identify user privacy and assess credibility.

Further chapters focus on AI's role in enhancing crowdsourcing knowledge sharing, and how AI can improve users' search experience and understanding. The discussion extends to AI's involvement in both the spread and control of misinformation, highlighting strategies for mitigating its impact.

Additionally, the book explores the practical applications of human–AI collaborative intelligence in industries such as healthcare, manufacturing, and scientific research. Case studies demonstrate AI's potential in improving work efficiency, solving complex problems, and facilitating personalized health services.

In its later chapters, the book tackles the challenges generative AI faces in real-world applications, offering suggestions for improvement. It concludes with a summary of the key insights and future research directions, aiming to provide academia and industry with valuable guidance to promote the development and responsible application of AI technology.

1
Introduction

Dan Wu, Guoye Sun, and Shaobo Liang

1.1 Background

In the technological wave of the twenty-first century, artificial intelligence (AI), as a transformative technology, is rapidly reshaping our society, economy, and daily life. Since the concept of AI was first proposed, this field has experienced many technological innovations and application expansions. Artificial intelligence has experienced three booms in the past half century and has developed rapidly. In the 1960s, marked by the Turing test, the application of knowledge reasoning systems and other technologies set off the first boom. Computer scientists at that time began to explore how to let computers simulate human intelligence. Early AI research focused on rule systems and logical reasoning. The rise of expert systems and artificial neural networks brought a second wave of enthusiasm (McDermott, 1982). The third boom is marked by deep learning and big data, especially the widespread application of artificial intelligence-generated content represented by ChatGPT. During this period, AI technology shifted from traditional rule systems to methods that relied on algorithms to learn patterns from data. The rise of deep learning enabled AI to achieve significant breakthroughs in areas such as image recognition and natural language processing.

The rapid development of AI not only improves the efficiency of data processing, pattern recognition, and automated operations, but also brings unprecedented convenience, and its application scenarios are also constantly expanding. In the medical field, AI can assist doctors in diagnosis and treatment through big data analysis and machine learning algorithms, thereby improving the quality and efficiency of medical services. For example, AI can analyze medical images to detect diseases such as cancer early and provide patients with more timely treatment. In the field of education, AI uses personalized learning systems to provide customized teaching plans based on students' learning progress and interests, thereby improving students' learning effects. In the financial field, AI helps financial institutions conduct risk management and investment decisions through risk analysis and intelligent investment advisory and improves the safety and profitability of financial services. As it develops today, artificial intelligence is largely oriented by commercial needs and integrated with industry. It covers all aspects of human life and plays an important role in society, which has also triggered a series of thoughts.

As AI is widely used in all aspects of human society, especially in high-risk, high-impact fields such as autonomous driving (Muhammad et al., 2021), criminal justice, and medical diagnosis (Park & Han, 2018), there is an increasing demand for transparency in the development and application of AI-related technologies (Zhu et al., 2018). Most users, especially the general public, do not have enough knowledge to understand the mechanisms behind AI decision-making, which has a negative impact on the credibility of AI systems (Xu et al., 2019). As early as 1991, Buckland and Florian discussed "intelligent systems" and "artificial intelligence." They noted that human expertise and task complexity may be a substitute or supplement for the use of artificial intelligence. They also discussed "computer-entrusted" and "computer-assisted" systems and argued that systems and human intelligence should enhance each other. The information field has long been interested in the social changes associated with rapidly growing technological capabilities.

Human–Computer Interaction (HCI), as an important branch of computer science, studies how to design and optimize the interaction between humans and computers. Initially, human–computer interaction research mainly focused on command line interface and graphical user interface (GUI) designs. With the advancement of technology, the field of HCI has gradually expanded to emerging interaction technologies such as touch screens, voice recognition, virtual reality (VR), and augmented reality (AR). Especially in recent years, with the development of natural language processing technology, the modes of human–computer interaction have become more natural and intuitive. For example, the emergence of intelligent voice assistants such as Siri, Alexa, and Google Assistant allows users to communicate with devices through voice, lowering the threshold for technology use. Human–computer interaction not only focuses on the implementation of technology but also pays attention to user experience and psychological factors in the interaction process. Researchers are committed to understanding user needs and optimizing interaction design to improve system ease of use and user satisfaction.

On the other hand, Human–AI Collaboration (HAIC) describes the cooperation model between humans and AI systems when they jointly complete tasks. This collaboration model emphasizes that humans and AI systems leverage their respective strengths to jointly solve problems. For example, in the medical field, AI systems can analyze large amounts of medical data and provide diagnostic suggestions to doctors, who in turn provide clinical experience and patient background information. Effective human–machine collaboration can give full play to the computing power of AI and human expertise, thereby improving the accuracy and efficiency of decision-making.

The development of artificial intelligence technology has brought new challenges to human–computer interaction (HCI) and AI collaboration (HAIC). A major challenge is ensuring that AI systems are designed with human users in mind. This involves not only making AI systems technically proficient, but also ensuring that they are user-friendly, ethical and able to build trust with their users. As AI systems become more ubiquitous and influential, addressing these challenges becomes increasingly important to achieve successful and beneficial human–machine collaboration. In *Human–AI Interaction and Collaboration*, we explore the multifaceted dynamics between individuals and artificial intelligence. The potential applications of human–machine collaboration are endless, from increasing productivity in the workplace to revolutionizing healthcare, education, and entertainment. However, these opportunities come with ethical considerations, transparency issues, and the need for responsible designs.

The first is the issue of ethics and responsibility. Whether AI systems can treat all users fairly and equitably during the decision making process and whether its decision-making mechanism is transparent are issues that directly affect users' trust in AI (Xu et al., 2019). For example, in the field of criminal justice, AI systems are used to predict crime risks and sentencing decisions but, if their algorithms are biased, they may lead to unfair sentences. Secondly, there are privacy and security issues. When AI technology processes large amounts of data, how to protect user privacy and avoid data leakage are also issues that need to be solved urgently. For example, in fields such as smart homes and smart medical care, a large amount of user data is collected and analyzed. If this data is abused or leaked, it will pose a serious threat to user privacy.

In order to deal with these challenges and problems, researchers have proposed many new methods and theories. For example, the concept of human-centered artificial intelligence (HAI) emphasizes that the design and application of AI should be aimed at enhancing and empowering humans (Shneiderman, 2022). By incorporating user needs and experiences into the design and development process of AI systems, the acceptability and user satisfaction of AI systems can be improved. In addition, the development of explainable AI (XAI) technology also provides new ideas for solving the transparency and trust issues of AI systems. By providing clear and understandable explanations, users can understand the decision-making process of the AI system, thereby increasing trust in the AI system.

Although HAI is a relatively new field in artificial intelligence, it has attracted considerable attention around the world. The next frontier of AI is not only technological but also humanistic, as AI aims to augment and empower humans rather than replace them (Shneiderman, 2022). HAI is considered multidisciplinary and interdisciplinary, but it is ultimately achieved through human–AI interaction (Wang et al., 2019), which is fundamentally an information processing task. Since information and interaction are the basic elements of human–AI interaction, experts in related fields have begun to explore the research perspective of information science in HAI (Liao et al., 2020). By efficiently processing and analyzing large amounts of information, artificial intelligence technology has great potential in supporting knowledge management and the development of next-generation decision support environments (Olan et al., 2022). AI technology will also impact health information management professionals (Stanfill & Marc, 2019).

Exploring the interaction between artificial intelligence and information science is beneficial because the exchange of knowledge brings technological changes and breakthroughs to both parties. For example, intelligent systems such as search, recommendation, and analysis and prediction can achieve human-centered contexts by considering humans' information behavior in acquiring, managing, and utilizing information in more new contexts (Konstan & Terveen, 2021). At the same time, HAI has deeply affected the present and future of information science and human information society (Bryson & Theodorou, 2019). In the information age, by further exploring the new role of users and information ethics in HAI situations, we will create more efficient and intelligent human–AI interactions and develop artificial intelligence that is more transparent, better able to solve human problems, and serve the human information society, making a contribution (Shneiderman, 2020). This also points to the question: To what extent can/should we "hand over" intelligence to technologies that process information and build knowledge? Where is the line between human-centered information processing and AI-based information processing?

This book aims to explore the challenges and ethical considerations related to privacy in artificial intelligence. We also envisioned a pattern where information flows seamlessly and enhances collaboration between humans and machines. In this dynamic landscape, the need for explainable AI becomes a key factor. The need to demystify complex algorithms and decision-making processes increases user trust and promotes a deeper understanding of AI systems. Furthermore, as we explore this complex field, trustworthiness assessment becomes critical – establishing benchmarks to assess the reliability and completeness of AI-generated information. The book also highlights the important role of artificial intelligence in scientific research and knowledge discovery, as well as its impact on social media.

1.2 Research Implications

This book is dedicated to systematically exploring the complex interaction and collaboration dynamics between humans and artificial intelligence (AI), revealing its potential and challenges in different application fields. Through in-depth research on these topics, we expect to provide new perspectives and methods for academia and industry to promote the development and application of AI technology. This book is designed for a diverse audience, including researchers, practitioners, and students interested in the fields of artificial intelligence, human–computer interaction, and related disciplines. Academics will find valuable insights and methodologies for future research, while industry professionals can gain practical knowledge to enhance the design and implementation of AI systems. Additionally, students will benefit from the comprehensive overview of current trends and challenges in human–AI collaboration, equipping them with the necessary tools to engage in this evolving field.

First of all, the research significance of this book is to deepen the understanding of human–AI interaction and collaboration. The advancement of AI technology has made the complexity of the human–machine relationship more and more prominent, involving many aspects such as user experience, technology applications, privacy protection, and ethical issues. In today's digital era, User Experience (UX) has become a key factor in measuring the success of technology systems. Good human–AI interaction design can significantly improve user satisfaction and efficiency. By studying user needs and behavior patterns, a system can be designed that better meets user expectations. For example, in a smart home system, users may want to control home appliances through natural language rather than through cumbersome interface operations. In-depth user research can help design a system that is more in line with actual needs and improve the overall user experience. By systematically exploring the theory and practice of human–AI interaction, this book provides a valuable reference for designing more humane and efficient AI systems. For example, studying user needs and behavior patterns can help design systems that meet user expectations, thereby improving user experience. Traditional AI systems tend to focus on technical implementation and ignore user experience. However, this book provides strategies on how to optimize the interaction process through in-depth analysis of user interaction behavior. This will not only improve user satisfaction, but also increase the frequency of system use, thereby promoting the popularization and application of technology.

Secondly, this book focuses on the important role of AI in scientific research and knowledge discovery. AI technology does not only accelerate the scientific research process and promote the dissemination and sharing of knowledge, but also helps researchers discover new research directions and methods. For example, in the field of natural language processing, AI can discover new research hotspots and trends by analyzing a large amount of literature and data, and guide researchers to conduct innovative research. The application of AI in social media has also had a profound impact on information dissemination and user behavior. Social media is an important platform for information dissemination, and its data analysis and processing are of great significance for understanding user behavior and information flow. Through specific case analysis, this book explores the applications and challenges of AI technology in these fields and puts forward corresponding countermeasures and suggestions, thereby promoting the further development of scientific research and knowledge discovery.

Privacy protection and information credibility are another important research area of this book. Although the application of generative AI technology has brought many conveniences, it has also caused serious privacy leak issues. When users interact with generative AI systems, they inevitably share data, which may be used for model training and leaked in future outputs. The book delves deeply into how to protect user privacy in the design and application of AI systems, including strategies such as privacy classification and identification, optimizing training data, and limiting generated content. In addition, the assessment of information credibility is also a key issue in AI applications. By examining system properties (such as transparency, explainability, and user feedback mechanisms) and user-related factors (such as algorithm literacy, sociocultural background, and prior experience), this book provides methods and techniques for improving information credibility assessment to ensure the reliability and accuracy of information generated by AI systems provide theoretical support and practical guidance.

Research on human–machine collaboration is of great significance to a wide range of fields and applications. In fields such as healthcare, education, finance, and more, effective collaboration between humans and AI systems can significantly improve outcomes and productivity. For example, in healthcare, AI systems can assist doctors by analyzing medical data and providing diagnostic recommendations, while doctors can provide clinical expertise and patient background. By optimizing the human–machine collaboration model, more efficient medical services can be achieved. In the financial field, AI can analyze market trends, provide investment advice, and help decision-makers make strategic decisions, and human managers can use this information to make strategic decisions. Understanding how to optimize these collaborations can help achieve more efficient problem solutions and drive practical applications of technology and social progress, which is critical to realizing the full potential of artificial intelligence technology.

At the same time, research on human–AI interaction and collaboration is critical to solving ethical and social issues related to artificial intelligence. This book focuses on the potential of AI technology to solve ethical and social issues. With the widespread application of AI technology, ethical issues such as privacy, data security, and algorithm fairness have gradually emerged, and concerns about privacy, fairness, and transparency have become increasingly important. How to embed ethical considerations in system design to ensure the fairness and transparency of AI systems is an important issue at present. This book studies how to prevent bias in algorithms and reduce possible unfairness in the actual application of AI systems, and explores how to protect user privacy and ensure data security, thereby ensuring the trustworthiness of AI systems. These research results are of great significance in ensuring that AI technology is used in a responsible and ethical manner and in cultivating public trust and acceptance of AI.

In addition, this book also explores the role of AI technology in promoting technological innovation. Research on human–AI interaction and collaboration can open up new research areas and market opportunities. For example, the application of AI technology in fields such as autonomous driving, smart homes, and virtual reality has achieved technological progress through continuous optimization of human–AI interaction and collaboration models. Continued research in this area contributes to a broader understanding of how AI technologies can be used to enhance human capabilities and improve quality of life. By exploring how AI systems can complement and enhance human capabilities, researchers can uncover new opportunities for innovation and advancement. Therefore, this research not only contributes to technological progress but also to promoting social change and improving human well-being.

Finally, the research significance of this book also lies in improving complex decision-making processes. In complex decision-making scenarios, such as emergency management, human–machine collaboration can combine the computing power of AI and human judgment to improve decision-making quality and efficiency. For example, AI systems can analyze large amounts of data and provide real-time decision support, while human experts can make judgments and adjustments based on actual conditions. Studying the optimization of human–machine collaboration models can significantly improve the decision-making process and increase the timeliness and accuracy of responses.

To sum up, this book not only reveals the application potential and challenges of AI technology, but also provides new perspectives and methods for solving these problems. By systematically exploring the multi-dimensional dynamics of human–AI interaction and collaboration, this book provides valuable reference for academia and industry and promotes the development and application of AI technology. These research results have a profound impact on improving user experience, promoting technology applications, solving ethical and social issues, promoting technological innovation, and improving decision-making processes.

1.3 Structure of the Book

This book consists of twelve chapters, each of which revolves around different aspects of human–AI interaction and collaboration. The logic is rigorous and progressive, so as to comprehensively explore the multi-dimensional dynamics of this complex field (Figure 1.1).

Chapter 1, as an introduction, first introduces the background and importance of human–AI interaction and collaboration and analyzes the current application status of AI technology and the challenges it faces. Through a literature review, we explore the application and impact of AI in different fields and put forward the research significance and objectives of this book. The introduction lays the foundation for the whole book, so that readers can have a comprehensive understanding of the basic concepts and research status of human–AI interaction and collaboration.

Chapter 2 focuses on the design principles and application scenarios of user interaction and human–AI collaboration. From the user's perspective, the basic theories and methods of human–AI interaction and collaboration are explored. By analyzing the design principles and methods in different application scenarios, it is revealed how to improve the efficiency and effectiveness of human–AI collaboration by optimizing the user interaction experience.

Chapter 3 explores the privacy identification problem in generative AI interaction in depth. With the development of generative AI technology,

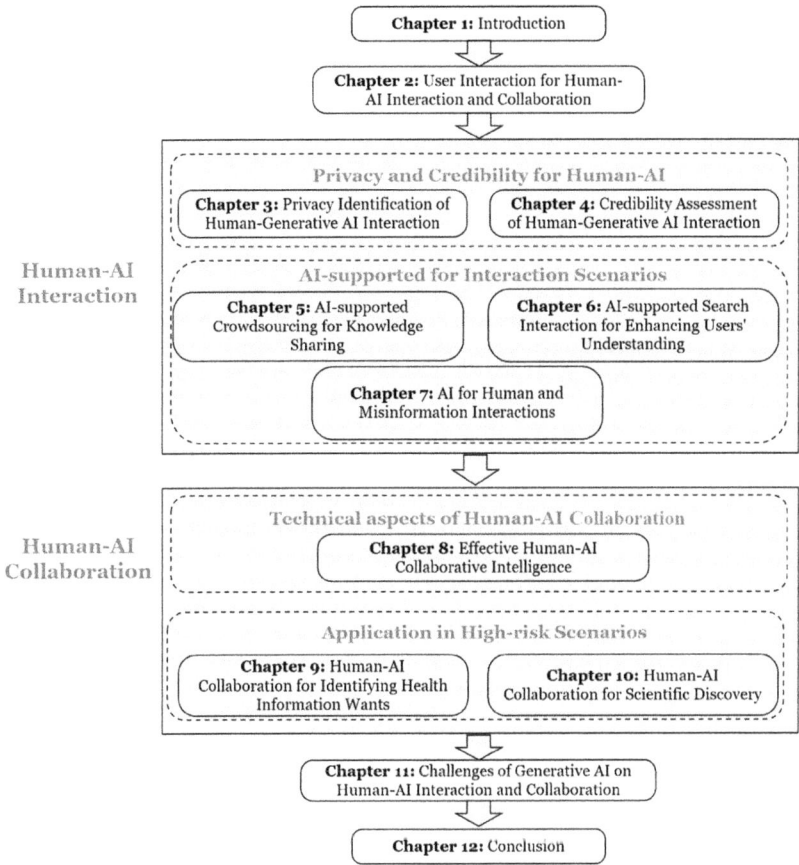

Figure 1.1 Structure of the book

privacy and security issues have become more prominent. In this chapter, we will analyze the challenges faced by generative AI in privacy leakage and explore solutions to identify user privacy. For example, in the fields of smart home and smart healthcare, the application of generative AI technology requires processing a large amount of user data. If the data is abused or leaked, it will pose a serious threat to user privacy. Therefore, studying how to identify user privacy in different interaction scenarios and providing support for avoiding data leakage is an important content of this chapter.

Chapter 4 discusses the credibility assessment methods of generative AI information and the challenges it faces. With the widespread application of generative AI technology, the credibility assessment of information has become particularly important. In this chapter, we will analyze the credibility assessment methods of generative AI information and explore its actual effects in different application scenarios. For example, in the field of news, generative AI technology can be used to generate news reports, but how to ensure the authenticity and accuracy of the generated news reports is an urgent problem to be solved. By exploring the credibility assessment methods of generative AI information, we hope to provide new ideas and methods for improving the credibility of information.

Chapter 5 describes the application of AI in enhancing crowdsourcing knowledge sharing and explores the role of motivation in it through case studies. Crowdsourcing knowledge sharing is one of the important application areas of AI technology. By bringing together the wisdom and power of a large number of users, many complex problems can be solved. In this chapter, we will analyze the application of AI in crowdsourcing knowledge sharing and explore how to motivate users to participate in crowdsourcing knowledge sharing activities through motivation design. For example, on crowdsourcing knowledge sharing platforms such as online encyclopedias and question-and-answer platforms, by designing a reasonable incentive mechanism, users can be motivated to contribute high-quality content and improve the efficiency and quality of knowledge sharing on the platform.

Chapter 6 studies how AI can improve users' understanding ability through search interaction. Search is one of the important ways to obtain information, and the development of AI technology has brought new possibilities for search interaction. In this chapter, we will explore the application of AI in search interaction and analyze how to improve users' understanding ability by optimizing the search experience. For example, by designing an intelligent search engine, personalized search results can be provided based on users' search behavior and preferences to help users quickly find the information they need. By exploring the application of AI technology in search interaction, we hope to provide new ideas and methods for improving users' search experience.

Chapter 7 analyzes the role of AI in the spread of misinformation and explores strategies to effectively deal with the spread of misinformation. With the popularity of social media and the Internet, the spread of misinformation has become a serious problem. The role of AI technology in the spread of misinformation has both positive and negative effects. In this chapter, we will analyze the role of AI in the spread of misinformation and explore how to effectively deal with the spread of misinformation through technical means and strategies. For example, by designing an intelligent filtering system, we can identify and filter misinformation and reduce its spread; by designing an intelligent recommendation system, we can recommend reliable information sources to users and improve their information literacy.

Chapters 8–10 focus on effective human–AI collaborative intelligence and its practical applications in different fields. Chapter 8 explores the technology and application of human–AI collaborative intelligence and evaluates its actual effect in improving work efficiency and solving complex problems. For example, in the manufacturing and service industries, human–AI collaborative intelligence technology can improve production efficiency and service quality; in the field of scientific research, human–AI collaborative intelligence technology can accelerate the progress of scientific research and promote the dissemination and sharing of knowledge. Chapter 9 studies the application of AI in identifying health information needs, especially helping and supporting caregivers. Health information needs are one of the important application areas of AI technology. By analyzing users' health information needs, personalized health services can be provided to improve users' health outcomes. In this chapter, we will explore the application of AI in identifying health information needs and analyze its potential in improving the quality and efficiency of health services. Chapter 10 explores the application of AI in scientific research and analyzes its potential in promoting scientific discovery and knowledge dissemination. Scientific research is one of the important application areas of AI technology. Through AI technology, the process of scientific research can be accelerated and new research directions and methods can be discovered. In this chapter, we will explore the application of AI in scientific research and analyze its potential in promoting scientific discovery and knowledge dissemination.

Chapter 11 analyzes the challenges faced by generative AI in current applications and proposes suggestions for improvement. By exploring the problems and solutions of generative AI technology in practical applications, we hope to provide readers with deep insights and practical suggestions. For example, in the field of automated writing and content generation, the application of generative AI technology has made significant progress, but how to ensure the quality and credibility of generated content is an urgent problem to be solved. In this chapter, we will analyze the challenges faced by generative AI in current applications and propose suggestions for improvement to promote the development and application of generative AI technology.

Finally, Chapter 12 summarizes the views of the whole book, reviews the main contents of each chapter, and proposes suggestions for future research and practice. Through a comprehensive exploration of the complex field of human–AI interaction and collaboration, we hope to provide academia and industry with new perspectives and methods to promote the development and applications of AI technology.

Through the above chapter structure, this book systematically explores the multi-dimensional dynamics of human–AI interaction and collaboration, revealing the application potential and challenges of AI in different fields. We hope that, through the research of this book, we can provide readers with a comprehensive and in-depth understanding and valuable reference and promote the widespread application and development of AI technology in society.

Acknowledgments

This work was supported by National Natural Science Foundation of China (No. 92370112) and the Innovative Research Group Project of Hubei Provincial Natural Science Foundation (No. 2023AFA012).

References

Bryson, J. J., & Theodorou, A. (2019). How Society Can Maintain Human-Centric Artificial Intelligence. In M. Toivonen & E. Saari (eds.), *Human-Centered Digitalization and Services* (pp. 305–323). Springer Nature. https://doi.org/10.1007/978-981-13-7725-9_16

Buckland, M. K., & Florian, D. (1991). Expertise, Task Complexity, and Artificial Intelligence: A Conceptual Framework. *Journal of the Association for Information Science and Technology*, *42*(9), 635–643. https://doi.org/10.1002/(SICI)1097-4571(199110)42:9%3C635::AID-ASI2%3E3.0.CO;2-L

Konstan, J., & Terveen, L. (2021). Human-Centered Recommender Systems: Origins, Advances, Challenges, and Opportunities. *AI Magazine*, *42*(3), Article 3. https://doi.org/10.1609/aimag.v42i3.18142

Liao, Q. V., Gruen, D., & Miller, S. (2020). Questioning the AI: Informing Design Practices for Explainable AI User Experiences. *Proceedings of the 2020 CHI Conference on Human Factors in Computing Systems*, 1–15. https://doi.org/10.1145/3313831.3376590

McDermott, J. (1982). R1: A Rule-based Configurer of Computer Systems. *Artificial Intelligence*, *19*(1), 39–88. https://doi.org/10.1016/0004-3702(82)90021-2

Muhammad, K., Ullah, A., Lloret, J., Ser, J. D., & de Albuquerque, V. H. C. (2021). Deep Learning for Safe Autonomous Driving: Current Challenges and Future Directions. *IEEE Transactions on Intelligent Transportation Systems*, *22*(7), 4316–4336. https://doi.org/10.1109/TITS.2020.3032227

Olan, F., Ogiemwonyi Arakpogun, E., Suklan, J., Nakpodia, F., Damij, N., & Jayawickrama, U. (2022). Artificial Intelligence and Knowledge Sharing: Contributing Factors to Organizational Performance. *Journal of Business Research*, *145*, 605–615. https://doi.org/10.1016/j.jbusres.2022.03.008

Park, S. H., & Han, K. (2018). Methodologic Guide for Evaluating Clinical Performance and Effect of Artificial Intelligence Technology for Medical Diagnosis and Prediction. *Radiology*, *286*(3), 800–809. https://doi.org/10.1148/radiol.2017171920

Shneiderman, B. (2020). Human-Centered Artificial Intelligence: Reliable, Safe & Trustworthy. *International Journal of Human–Computer Interaction, 36*(6), 495–504. https://doi.org/10.1080/10447318.2020.1741118

Shneiderman, B. (2022). *Human-Centered AI.* Oxford University Press.

Stanfill, M. H., & Marc, D. T. (2019). Health Information Management: Implications of Artificial Intelligence on Healthcare Data and Information Management. *Yearbook of Medical Informatics, 28,* 56–64. https://doi.org/10.1055/s-0039-1677913

Wang, D., Yang, Q., Abdul, A., & Lim, B. Y. (2019). Designing Theory-Driven User-Centric Explainable AI. *Proceedings of the 2019 CHI Conference on Human Factors in Computing Systems,* 1–15. https://doi.org/10.1145/3290605.3300831

Xu, F., Uszkoreit, H., Du, Y., Fan, W., Zhao, D., & Zhu, J. (2019). Explainable AI: A Brief Survey on History, Research Areas, Approaches and Challenges. In J. Tang, M.-Y. Kan, D. Zhao, S. Li, & H. Zan (eds.), *Natural Language Processing and Chinese Computing* (pp. 563–574). Springer International Publishing. https://doi.org/10.1007/978-3-030-32236-6_51

Zhu, J., Liapis, A., Risi, S., Bidarra, R., & Youngblood, G. M. (2018). Explainable AI for Designers: A Human-Centered Perspective on Mixed-Initiative Co-Creation. *2018 IEEE Conference on Computational Intelligence and Games (CIG),* 1–8. https://doi.org/10.1109/CIG.2018.8490433

2
User Interaction for Human–AI Interaction and Collaboration

Dan Wu and Qingyue Guo

2.1 Introduction

Artificial intelligence (AI) has progressively gained autonomy and anthropomorphic traits as it advances toward "intelligence." For instance, AI may assist humans in decision-making by utilizing gathered data; Intelligent voice assistants like Siri, Alexa, Cortana, etc., possess human-like intonation qualities and can engage in conversations with humans, thereby alleviating feelings of loneliness. The field of human–computer interaction is undergoing a transformation due to the integration of AI technology. This transformation is leading to the emergence of human–AI interaction and collaboration as the next direction of development.

The emergence of intelligent manufacturing, intelligent transportation, intelligent medical care, intelligent education, and other scenarios involving human–AI interaction has led to the question of whether people can establish effective interaction and collaborative relationships with AI. Humans, in their role as users and participants of intelligent systems, communicate their requirements. The behavior and decision-making of the intelligent system will be significantly influenced by human intention, willingness, and feedback. Hence, it is imperative to examine the future direction of AI with a focus on human-centric principles. This chapter seeks to provide a comprehensive understanding of the field of human–AI interaction and collaboration through looking at user interaction. It takes a multidisciplinary viewpoint, incorporating insights from information science, computer science, psychology, and other relevant disciplines. Additionally, it aims to investigate potential future research directions in this field.

2.2 From Human–Computer Interaction to Human–AI Interaction and Collaboration

2.2.1 Origin: Human–Computer Interaction

The interaction between human and artificial intelligence is a manifestation of the progress in human–computer interaction throughout the era of artificial intelligence. To begin with, it is important to comprehend the meaning of human–computer interaction and its origins. Human–computer interaction (HCI) is an academic discipline that investigates different types of interactions between humans and computers (Pargman et al., 2019). It involves the study of how individuals design, develop, and utilize interactive computer systems, as well as the potential impact of computers on individuals, organizations, and societies (Myers et al., 1996). It is a multidisciplinary field that incorporates techniques and approaches from various disciplines (Jiang et al., 2024; S. Kim, 1995), including computer science, information science, psychology, sociology, and design. During the process of conducting research, it frequently involves examining methods to assist users in completing activities and improving their access to information, as well as facilitating more convenient interactions for users (Myers et al., 1996). Some instances include techniques for optimizing input and output devices to enhance interaction, efficient information transfer, and controlling and mastering computer behavior. Additionally, it includes designing, testing, and evaluating tools for user interfaces, as well as the principles developers should adhere to when creating human–computer interaction tools. HCI research has been described as "a field of truly constructive problem solving" (Oulasvirta & Hornbæk, 2016) because it explores multiple fields of practice through interdisciplinary collaboration to provide solutions to the problems that humans face when interacting with different types of computer systems.

Human–computer interaction is a topic that has emerged as a result of the development of computers, tracing its origins back to the establishment of the ACM Special Interest Group on Social and Behavioral Computing (SIGSOC) in 1969 (Borman, 1996). The initial focus of SIGSOC was on the advancement of computing from a social science standpoint. With the development of the research, SIGSOC has progressively redirected its research emphasis toward investigating user requirements and behavioral traits. In 1982, SIGSOC underwent a name change and transformed into the ACM Special Interest Group on Computer–Human Interaction (SIGCHI). The first SIGCHI conference was held in Boston in 1983. Subsequently, the conference underwent a name modification and is now known as the ACM SIGCHI Conference on Human Factors in Computer Systems (CHI). It is currently recognized as the foremost meeting in the subject of human–computer interaction. Subsequently, HCI began on a golden period of advancement.

Human–computer interaction is intricately connected to the field of "Human Factors" and may be described as "Human–Tool Interaction" (Grudin, 2018). Some researchers (Harrison et al., 2011; Sun et al., 2020) have proposed that the research paradigm of human–computer interaction can be divided into three paradigms. The first paradigm focuses on the relationship between physical systems and human, which is based on Human Factors. The second paradigm studies the cognitive process in human–computer information interaction, which is based on information processing. The third paradigm focuses on the situational factors of human–computer interaction and believes that intelligent technology enhances the perception and cognitive ability of machines. It can actively initiate interactive behaviors by sensing user needs, emphasizing the integration of human, machines, and the environment. Due to the incorporation of artificial intelligence technology, the third paradigm of human–computer interaction introduces new difficulties and possibilities to the area, making it complex and unclear. "Human–AI Interaction" has evolved into a state-of-the-art subject in HCI (Amershi et al., 2019).

2.2.2 Development: Human–AI Interaction

The field known as "Human–AI Interaction" researches and develops solutions for improving communication and collaboration between human and AI systems. The goal of human–AI interaction is to develop AI systems that are easy to use, reliable, morally sound, and advantageous for people. The chronicle of human–AI contact commences with the advent of AI. During the 1950s and 1960s, researchers in the field of artificial intelligence successfully created the initial AI systems capable of executing complex tasks like playing chess, demonstrating theorems, and translating languages. Individuals could engage with artificial intelligence systems through the act of playing checkers at that time. During the 1970s and 1980s, scientists created artificial intelligence systems capable of emulating human cognitive processes and achieving more authentic interactions, including speech recognition, computer vision, and natural language understanding. Nevertheless, these systems encounter difficulties in terms of reliability and explainability, and are frequently condemned as black boxes. Since the 1990s, deep learning has made significant progress. Artificial intelligence has exhibited exceptional proficiency in activities such as image processing, natural language processing, and game playing, and has even outperformed human talents in certain domains. New patterns have also been formed as a result of the interaction between humans and artificial intelligence. These new patterns include recommendation systems, voice assistants, conversational agents, and other similar systems. However, there are also concerns regarding privacy, security, morality, and ethics that are associated with artificial intelligence.

Within the field of human–AI interaction, researchers are consistently investigating new approaches to enhance the capabilities of artificial intelligence. For instance, they examine ways to make artificial intelligence systems more transparent and explainable in order to make it easier for people to comprehend how the system operates and the outcomes of its operation. The needs of users and the input they provide are also taken into consideration by researchers, who are continually investigating ways to develop artificial intelligence systems that are more responsive. Researchers are also considering how to develop suitable indicators to evaluate the influence that artificial intelligence systems have on users, society, and the environment. Therefore, human–AI interaction involves multiple disciplines such as computer science, psychology, sociology, design, and ethics, and has interdisciplinary research characteristics. Researchers use methods such as user research, prototyping, and evaluation to create user-centered artificial intelligence systems. By doing so, they want to amplify and enhance human capabilities.

The field of human–AI interaction has introduced new challenges due to the unique characteristics of AI systems, including situational awareness, adaptive learning, autonomous decision-making, and active interaction. These challenges include addressing issues such as the allocation of human–computer initiative, situational adaptation, and active response modes, which are not typically encountered in traditional HCI fields. When AI is introduced into the context of society, AI that assumes a social role should possess anthropomorphic characteristics such as language proficiency, emotion detection, and cognitive abilities (Spatola et al., 2022). However, this also presents new challenges in the study of human–AI interaction.

2.2.3 New Motivation: Human–AI Collaboration

Human–AI collaboration is when humans and AI each use their own strengths to jointly complete a task. The purpose is to establish a synergistic relationship between the two to contribute to the completion of tasks in various fields (Cañas, 2022). During the collaborative process, humans and artificial intelligence transfer information, comprehend each other's objectives through interaction, and coordinate tasks and advancement following appropriate communication, finally accomplishing tasks proficiently. Studies indicate that the collaboration between humans and AI yields superior outcomes compared to situations when either people or AI work alone (Kahn et al., 2020). Artificial intelligence thrives in the domain of computing, which involves the rapid processing of data and tasks using predetermined algorithms and rules. Despite significant developments in machine learning, deep learning, and neural networks, artificial intelligence remains short in cognitive capacity, domain knowledge, creative thinking, and moral judgment when compared to humans. The collaboration between humans and artificial intelligence involves the integration of human perception and the computational capabilities of artificial intelligence to deliver novel solutions to complex challenges.

The aim of human–AI collaboration is to enhance the level and efficacy of overall job accomplishment by assembling a team consisting of humans and AI. Furthermore, it is imperative to take into account the human–AI interaction experience and situational awareness in specific scenarios (Kitchin & Baber, 2016), as well as the division of roles of the AI system in the workflow. Given that AI systems serve as collaborators, it is essential to address the matter of trust between humans and AI. Additionally, it is important to investigate the psychological models and changes in emotions experienced by humans throughout the collaboration process. An additional significant problem that arises during the process of carrying out tasks is the question of how to combine the practical experience and expertise of human workers with the results of calculations performed by artificial intelligence. When both humans and artificial intelligence created information, the next step should be to concentrate on effectively transferring that information. In addition, the focus of human–AI collaboration is also on the development of an effective interactive interface and approach.

The study of Human–AI interaction prioritizes the improvement of interaction methods and interface design of artificial intelligence systems, with a strong emphasis on enhancing the user experience. In contrast, human–AI collaboration encompasses a broader scope of research. Human–AI collaboration focuses on using the strengths of each to effectively accomplish job tasks. In practical situations, AI can be utilized in collaborative decision-making environments, where it works alongside humans to offer insights, evaluate data, and participate in decision-making processes (Deshpande et al., 2020; D. Wang et al., 2019). In the field of human-centered collaborative automated driving, AI can help human drivers with navigation and traffic management by evaluating sensor data (Xing et al., 2021). Within the field of artistic production, the advancement of generative artificial intelligence allows designers to employ artificial intelligence modeling for the purpose of generating stimulating samples that can enhance their creativity (Jeon et al., 2021). Overall, the relationship and collaboration between humans and artificial intelligence should prioritize humans, empower human workers to take control, and utilize AI to its fullest potential without excessive dependence (Buçinca et al., 2021).

2.3 A Framework of Human–AI Interaction and Collaboration

With the growing autonomy of AI, it assumes a novel role in systems of human–computer interaction. Artificial intelligence technology has transformed machines from being simple assistants to become possible collaborators in human collaboration (Seeber et al., 2020). Researchers have seen this trend of transformation and have conducted investigations into research areas such as human–AI interaction (Amershi et al., 2019), human–AI teamwork (Seeber et al., 2020), and human–AI symbiosis (Nagao, 2019). A conceptual framework of joint cognitive systems was proposed by Xu and Gao (2024) as part of the framework research of human–AI interaction. This framework was intended to reveal the interaction between human–AI collaborative teams, drawing from Erik Hollnagel and David Woods's joint cognitive systems theory, Mica Endsley's situation awareness cognitive engineering theory, and the widely used agent theory in the AI communities (Xu & Gao, 2024). The framework defines the human–AI team as a joint cognitive system consisting of two cognitive agents. The team achieves the complementarity of human biological intelligence and computer intelligence through their collaboration and interaction.

Interaction is essential in the topic of human–AI interaction. Hornbæk et al. (2019) conducted a comprehensive analysis of the articles published at the CHI conference during the last thirty-five years. The analysis focused on the key issues in the field of HCI, especially looking at the features of interaction style and interaction quality. Interaction style generally refers to a variety of factors, including the type of input/output, the technology that is utilized during the interaction, or the media that is used for the interaction. Different types of interactions, such as mobile interaction, touch screen interaction, cross-device interaction, and virtual reality interaction, are examples of interaction styles that are frequently associated with the way they take place. The quality of interaction is connected to the emotions and thoughts of individuals, and it is typically expressed in the user experience, which includes features such as the utility, usability, efficiency, and other aspects of interaction.

The research in human–AI interaction aims to investigate the relationship and behavioral patterns that exist between humans and AI. We have developed

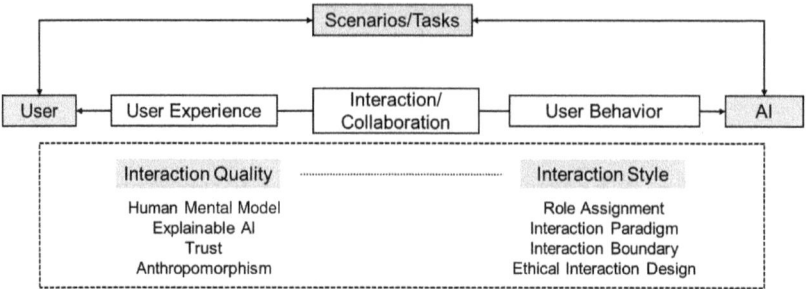

Figure 2.1 The framework of Human–AI Interaction and Collaboration (HAII&C)

a study framework for the interaction and collaboration between humans and AI based on prior studies (Figure 2.1). Similar to researchers who explore HCI in the field of artificial intelligence, humans and AI are considered to be the two primary subjects of the research. The two are connected through interaction and collaboration in a variety of scenarios and tasks. In the context of human–AI collaboration research, we expand the traditional human–computer interaction framework and refer to Hornbæk's research (Hornbæk et al., 2019) to separate it into two aspects: interaction quality and interaction mode. The quality of interaction is most closely linked to the user's interactive experience. Driven by the idea of "human-centered AI" (GDPi, 2018; Xu, 2019), human perception of artificial intelligence is placed in an important position. The aspect of interaction quality includes various human-related subjects, including user psychological models of human–AI collaborative teams, the ability to explain AI interaction behaviors and outcomes, human trust in AI team members, and human emotional awareness of AI. The interaction mode is associated with the technology of artificial intelligence interaction and user behavior in the interaction process. The attributes of artificial intelligence, including situational awareness, autonomous decision-making, and adaptive learning, introduce new aspects to the way of interaction, which encompass the allocation of roles for AI in interactions, the methods of interacting with AI, the boundaries of human–AI interaction, and the design of interaction in innovative interactive contexts.

Based on this Human–AI Interaction and Collaboration (HAII&C) framework, this book reviews the current research status of related issues and points out future development directions. The literature review is a qualitative study that examines current literature and highlights research topics. While it may not be exhaustive, it should be enough to identify the main challenges and prospects in the present domain. These findings will call for increased attention from researchers toward the topic of human–AI interaction and collaboration; and offer strategic suggestions for future initiatives in human–AI interaction.

2.4 Interaction Quality in Human–AI Interaction and Collaboration

The quality of user interaction is inextricably linked to the user experience. In contrast to traditional research on HCI, which has focused on system usability and ease of use, research on human–AI interaction has emerged as a new area of enquiry in the context of emerging technologies. In situations where an AI is engaged in a collaborative task as a helper or team member, it is pertinent to ascertain whether humans are able to accurately assess the AI capabilities and work with it in an efficient manner.

The question thus arises as to whether humans are more tolerant of AI performance or whether they set more exacting standards for AI. To what extent do humans trust AI, and to what extent do they trust their human colleagues? What is the human perception of the reliability of the results provided by AI? As AI becomes increasingly involved in human activities, these questions will continue to emerge and drive further discussion among researchers. This discussion encompasses a range of topics, including users' mental models in human–AI interactions and collaborations, interpretable AI, users' trust in AI, and AI anthropomorphism.

2.4.1 Human Mental Model of AI

The ability to construct an accurate mental model of AI will influence human use of AI (Steyvers & Kumar, 2023). A mental model of AI consists of human beliefs about AI and expectations about interacting with AI. In general, a mental model is a simplified perception of the world developed by humans, according to which humans process information and make predictions (Barnes, 1944). The more accurate the mental model people construct of the AI, the more likely the AI will be used correctly (Bansal et al., 2019). If a user constructs the wrong mental model, it can lead to inappropriate trust and reliance on the AI (Steyvers & Kumar, 2023), creating barriers to human–AI collaboration.

Collaborative work emphasizes shared mental models (SMMs) among human teams (Merry et al., 2021), which require team members to have consistent perceptions of both the team and the task, and this mental model can better facilitate effective collaboration. In the context of human–AI interaction, researchers explore the content of human perceptions when using AI as a potential object of collaboration. The researcher introduces the cognitive science approach to the field of human–AI interaction and discusses the concept of user perception of AI through the user's perceptual image of the AI entity (Hwang & Won, 2022). Improving our understanding of how humans perceive their AI teammates is an important foundation for our understanding of human–AI teams in general, and Kelly et al. (2023) proposes a framework based on Item Response Theory (IRT) to model users' perceptions, and apply this framework to the real world to observe human perceptions of the AI, as well as the perceptions of other teammates.

Individuals' perceptions of phenomena are invariably influenced by a multitude of factors. It is hypothesized that interactive explanations, affective associations, and cognitive biases will exert an influence on users' mental models of AI. Nevertheless, empirical evidence indicates that, in the context of adaptive in-vehicle systems, the provision of interactive explanations does not markedly enhance system comprehensibility and fails to facilitate the optimization of users' mental models, when compared to text-based explanatory approaches (Graefe et al., 2023). The researchers posit that participants may exhibit greater cognitive proficiency in scenarios involving AI-based driving systems, necessitating comprehensive investigations across diverse scenarios. Pataranutaporn et al. (2023) found that users' mental models of AI will influence their perceptions, experiences, and interactions. Furthermore, it was discovered that users tend to construct mental models using their past views and expectations of the experience. Consequently, different users will perceive trustworthiness, empathy, and validity differently when confronted with the same AI. During the interaction, if the AI responds to the user's emotions in a manner that evokes a sense of empathy, the user will respond with a similar empathetic response. This raises the question for developers as to whether it is preferable to conceptualize the AI as an emotional entity or as an algorithmic system devoid of emotional capacity. The understanding and perception of AI by humans is frequently distorted by cognitive biases. Rastogi et al. (2022) employed a mathematical approach to model these biases and devised a time-based de-anchoring strategy based on the constructed framework. Their study demonstrated that the time-allocation strategy can effectively mitigate the anchoring bias and enhance the efficacy of human–AI collaboration.

The mental model is not a fixed entity; rather, it will undergo gradual transformation as a result of the interaction and collaboration between humans and AI. To illustrate, in the context of a team voting process conducted in collaboration with AI, the performance of the AI system will have a significant impact on the confidence of the human team members in their ability to make decisions collectively with the AI. When the AI system demonstrates poor performance, the confidence of the human team members in the AI system tends to decline rapidly (M. Hu et al., 2025). Cao et al. (2023) demonstrated that, in AI-assisted human decision-making, users were more likely to adhere to the AI's recommendations when presented with a longer time frame for decision-making. This finding elucidates the impact of time pressure at different stages of the decision-making process on human cognition. Similarly, the accumulation of experience gives rise to alterations in mental models. In the course of playing games with AI players, Villareale et al. (2022) identified two distinct approaches to the development of mental models by players. The first is based on observational learning, whereby players observe the actions of others in the game. The second is based on the construction of mental models using a priori experience, whereby players draw upon their existing knowledge and understanding to interpret and make sense of the game. The formation of mental models is a complex process that is influenced by a number of factors and exhibits dynamic behavior. These insights provide valuable guidance for researchers engaged in the field of human–AI interaction and collaboration.

2.4.2 Human-Centered Explainable AI

Explainable Artificial Intelligence (XAI) has emerged as a prominent research area in recent years, driven primarily by the ongoing discourse surrounding "black box" algorithms and the imperative for transparency. It has been demonstrated that systems that are opaque can result in comprehension issues for users, which in turn can impair the efficacy of human–machine collaboration. The concepts of "explainability," "transparency," and "interpretability" are often intertwined. The terms "interpretability" and "transparency" are often used interchangeably. Indeed, "explainability" and "interpretability" are reflections of the transparency of a system. "Explainability" emphasizes that the logic of a system can be understood by humans from a human perspective (Rosenfeld & Richardson, 2019), whereas "interpretability" focuses on the results from an output perspective. Researchers in the HCI community have placed a particular emphasis on explainability, which is more closely related to the user during human–AI collaboration.

The provision of more detailed and comprehensive explanations will enhance the transparency of AI, which will facilitate the identification of AI biases, mitigate the influence of AI biases on human judgments (T.-Y. Hou et al., 2024), and enable users to discern AI failures through such explanatory mechanisms (Cabrera et al., 2023). To gain a deeper understanding of the concept of explainability, researchers have initiated a detailed examination of the user requirements for interpretability in diverse contexts. C. Chen and Zheng (2023) demonstrated that consumers have a greater need for explainability in AI recommendations in utilitarian scenarios, such as those pertaining to healthcare. Users are more interested in acquiring information that is genuinely useful than in the intricacies of a technical system. Furthermore, they seek to utilize the information for the enhancement of their own abilities (S. S. Y. Kim et al., 2023). Malandri et al. (2023) even based their study on user needs, with the objective of developing a system that incorporates user knowledge and experience into the AI interpreter, thereby enhancing the utility of the explainability. The choice of explanation strategy also presents a trade-off between advantages and disadvantages, which must be considered in the context of the specific application scenario. B. Wang et al. (2024) established three distinct explainability strategies: global explainability, comparative explainability, and deductive explainability. Global explainability is more appropriate for tasks that require significant cognitive effort, whereas comparative explainability is better suited to daily scenarios that involve higher social presence and trust. In scenarios that require rapid interaction with the AI, it is advisable for the AI system design to consider reducing the mental effort required by the user by employing global or deductive explainability.

The explainability of human–AI interaction is also not as high as it should be. The provision of excessive explanatory information can result in information overload for the user (Westphal et al., 2023). The provision of explanations to users may result in the perception of increased task complexity. Ribera and Lapedriza (2019) proposed the concept of "user-centered explainable AI," which entails the delivery of an optimal amount of high-quality information that is pertinent to the user. In a user-centered study, it was discovered that, when the explanation provided by the AI is in contradiction with the user's decision, the user will experience negative emotions and express dissatisfaction with the AI (Ebermann et al., 2023). The degree of alignment between user perception and the provided explanation will influence the efficacy of the latter. We put forth the proposition that AI should be permitted to engage in discourse with users, wherein they may elucidate their reasoning processes and proffer tailored explanations contingent on the cognitive capabilities of disparate users.

2.4.3 Trust between AI and Humans

The current state of AI systems does not yet allow for the development of a fully reliable decision-support system. As a result, trust becomes a significant factor in human–AI interaction. The concept of trust in AI refers to the extent to which humans can rely on the technology when faced with uncertainty during human–AI interaction and collaboration. It is important to note that trust is a double-edged sword, and excessive trust can lead to users reducing their workloads by delegating tasks to the AI (Harbarth et al., 2025), which can ultimately result in less efficient collaborative work. Moreover, an understanding of the fundamental principles governing the system can mitigate the tendency of users to place excessive trust and complacency in its capabilities. It is, therefore, essential to establish a suitable trust relationship between humans and AI, also known as calibrated trust, in order to optimize the collaborative performance of AI. The question of human trust in AI remains a topic of ongoing debate among researchers. It was found that humans will demonstrate a higher level of trust when they collaborate with AI compared to when they engage in human collaboration (Jain et al., 2022). Conversely, Georganta and Ulfert (2024) posited that humans exhibit diminished perceptions of trustworthiness and emotional interpersonal trust in AI when it is introduced as a novel member of the team, relative to human teammates. This disparate outcome also exemplifies, from a particular standpoint, that the trust between humans and AI is a multifaceted matter that may be influenced by a convergence of assorted types of elements.

Indeed, researchers are also investigating the factors that influence the level of trust that individuals place in AI systems. These factors include aspects such as user education, past experiences, user biases, and perceptions of automation (Asan et al., 2020). K. Hou et al. (2023) developed a model that suggests that there are three main factors that influence the level of trust that individuals place in AI systems: interaction characteristics, environmental characteristics, and personal characteristics. Interaction characteristics include factors such as perceived anthropomorphism, perceived rapport, and perceived enjoyment. Environmental characteristics include factors such as peer influence and facilitating conditions. Personal characteristics include factors such as self-efficacy. The findings of this study indicate that the interaction will be an important factor of trust that is established between humans and AI team members. In regard to personal characteristics, Tutul et al. (2023) yielded analogous results, indicating that user openness is positively correlated with trust. The more open and accepting a user is, the more likely he or she is to trust the AI's decisions. In order to foster appropriate trust in AI, G. Zhang et al. (2022) proposed a "deception strategy" to calibrate trust. This strategy involved users being unaware that they were working with AI. However, the results demonstrated that this approach did not enhance the average performance of teamwork. It is, therefore, recommended that future research should also explore how to appropriately calibrate human trust in AI and improve the joint performance of humans and AI.

2.4.4 Anthropomorphism and Emotional Support

Anthropomorphism can be defined as the tendency to attribute human characteristics, motives, intentions, or emotions to nonhuman subjects, whether actual or imagined (Epley et al., 2007). The anthropomorphic characteristics of AI encompass both the physical and psychological attributes of human beings (M. Zhang et al., 2021). The term "physical" is used to describe the face or body of a person, whereas "psychological" refers to the mind or personality. The uncanny valley theory posits that anthropomorphism exerts inconsistent effects on users (Gursoy et al., 2019). At higher levels of anthropomorphism, positive effects are observed within a certain range, including increased human trust in automated systems, enjoyment of interacting with AI assistants (A. Kim et al., 2019), and the quality of interactions with AI systems (Xie et al., 2024). However, at some point, the practice of anthropomorphization may prove detrimental to the user. Anthropomorphization has the potential to foster a sense of intimacy between humans and machines, thereby enhancing the emotional experience of users. However, in the context of human–AI interaction and collaboration, this intimacy may intensify the user's perception of the intrusion of their personal information, leading to a heightened sense of privacy invasion (Chi et al., 2020).

Through a series of investigations, researchers have endeavored to elucidate the processes by which anthropomorphism influences the efficacy of HCI. This includes the examination of the influence of psychological distance on user perceptions of AI-based assistants (Li & Sung, 2021). Lee et al. (2021) posit that emotional support enhances interactant satisfaction with communication, urging designers to prioritize the emotional and empathetic responses of AI over functional considerations. To gain further insight into the impact of anthropomorphism on interaction, Xie et al. (2023) employ the smart home as a case study, delineating anthropomorphism into four dimensions: visual, identity, emotional, and auditory cues. The findings indicate that emotional and auditory cues exert a pronounced positive influence on interaction satisfaction, whereas visual and identity cues exhibit a relatively minimal effect. Furthermore, the incorporation of emotional cues, such as humor, can directly influence the user's perception of the interaction content. It is important to note that the study of Xie et al. (2023) focuses on smart home voice assistants. Given the specific characteristics of this technology, users are likely to be influenced by the task environment, demonstrating a tendency to prioritize the sound and interaction content during the interaction. It is thus imperative to conduct further investigations in other scenarios. In order to more accurately ascertain users' emotional satisfaction, Shin et al. (2021) employ a methodology designated as Kansei engineering (alternatively referred to as affective engineering) to quantify the influence of voice-based intelligent systems with disparate dialogical styles on users' emotional satisfaction during interactions. Research on the anthropomorphization and emotional characterization of AI can provide insights to advance the development of the "emotional quotient (EQ)" in AI systems and facilitate harmonious human–AI interaction.

2.5 Interaction Mode in Human–AI Interaction and Collaboration

Interaction mode primarily signifies the manner or conduct of human beings when engaging with technology in the setting of artificial intelligence technology assistance. In the context of technological advancement in the age of smart devices, the environment of interaction has undergone a significant transformation, evolving from the traditional WIMP (window, icon, menu, pointing) paradigm to a multimodal interaction that supports a range of modalities, including speech, vision, and gesture. In light of these developments, researchers have conducted studies on effective interaction paradigms in the new environment. In the context of specific interaction processes, the advancement of AI capabilities and autonomy has led to a shift in the role of AI, which is no longer constrained to a supporting role but has the potential to assume a more prominent position. Concurrently, the enhanced autonomy of AI has prompted scholars to examine the boundaries of interaction and interaction ethics, thereby creating new avenues for HCI research.

2.5.1 Role Assignment in Collaboration

The collaboration between human and AI can be an effective method for leveraging the strengths of machines, including accuracy, speed, and flexibility. The integration of these strengths with human traits can be a powerful approach for addressing complex problems. It has been demonstrated that AI can facilitate disease assessment by pathologists (Lindvall et al., 2021), provide assistance with the writing of second language texts (Zou & Huang, 2024), and automate data analysis (D. Wang et al., 2019) with a view to enhancing productivity. In these task scenarios, the AI is primarily engaged in a supportive role. Indeed, there are various types of role assignments involved in human–AI collaboration. Scholtz (2003) defines five roles for humans in their interactions with robots, based on the level of automation: the Supervisor, the Operator, the Teammate, the Bystander, and the Mechanic. In light of the distinctions inherent to the collaborative process between humans and AI, Jiang et al. (2024) postulated four distinct models of human–AI collaboration: assisted intelligence, augmented intelligence, cooperative intelligence, and autonomous intelligence. This classification of collaboration modes is primarily based on the varying degrees of human control and supervision involved in collaborative tasks. Further distinction can be made between the dominant roles of human and AI, leading to the classification of collaboration modes as human-led (including assistive and augmentative intelligence), collaboration modes in which humans and AI divide the work (which can be categorized as a complete or incomplete division of labor), and AI-led collaboration modes (in which AIs dominate the assignment of tasks).

In response to the division of different roles, scholars have conducted research on the work efficiency of human–AI collaboration. In contexts where humans occupy a dominant role, some studies have revealed that dominant individuals derive a sense of power (P. Hu et al., 2022) from treating AIs as subordinates (Sadeghian & Hassenzahl, 2022). This sense of power is manifested in the user commanding the AI assistant to perform the desired actions, which the AI then accomplishes to the best of its ability. This perceived sense of power can result in humans exhibiting overconfidence and optimism, which in turn reduces the perception of potential risks associated with AI. The aforementioned perception of risk can also affect human attitudes toward AI. Consequently, individuals occupying decision-making roles may exhibit a greater reluctance to embrace AI in comparison to their less influential counterparts (Jain et al., 2022). There is a paucity of research examining the phenomenon of AI assuming a dominant position. One study, however, did identify a preference among some collaborators for the independence and speed afforded by an AI leader. This suggests that, in scenarios where time is of the essence, the assignment of the leader role to AI may prove advantageous (Lobo et al., 2024). The AI-dominated collaboration model may offer enhanced efficiency and could become the prevailing model for human–AI collaboration in certain domains. This shift may also encourage a more profound level of research in human–AI collaboration.

2.5.2 Effective Intelligent Interaction Paradigm

The advancement of AI has prompted a shift in the manner of human–machine interaction, whereby the objective is to convey the desired outcome to the machine rather than to instruct it on the means to achieve that outcome. Historically, HCI research has undergone a significant transformation, evolving from batch processing to command-based interaction design. Batch processing interactions typically do not entail a back-and-forth between the user and the machine. Instead, the user specifies the entire workflow and then delegates it to the machine for execution. In the command-based interaction paradigm, the user and the computer take turns executing commands, with text and graphical user interfaces emerging in the process. While the majority of contemporary generative AI tools engage with users through a user interface, they are capable of performing tasks based on the user's intent and represent the current intention-based interaction paradigm. It is possible that this paradigm will persist and evolve for an extended period.

In accordance with the intention-guided paradigm, researchers conduct a further analysis of the interaction paradigm and verify its validity. To illustrate, J. Fan et al. (2018) put forth a framework for software research that encompasses interface paradigms, interaction design principles, and mental models. In particular, the study by Desolda et al. (2024) examines the enhancement of interaction effects through the implementation of three distinct interaction strategies: clarification, negotiation, and reconfiguration. To illustrate these concepts, the authors utilize a healthcare environment as a case study. Nevertheless, this interaction remains user interface centric. In the context of multimodal and pervasive computing, the development of methods for interacting with users in natural ways, such as through vision, hearing, and gesture, represents a promising avenue of research. By analyzing the user's gaze, it is able to discern the user's implied points of interest and project human intentions (Newn et al., 2019). Zhao and Bao (2023) developed a story generation tool to support multimodal interactions by recognizing the user's gestures in conjunction with an image generation model. The utilization of sensors can also assist AI in acquiring further information, including determining the location of an object, extracting intricate data from speech, and recognizing user gazes and gestures of interest (Paul et al., 2023). In conclusion, the design of multimodal fusion interaction paradigms for AI systems will become a significant issue in the future of human–AI interaction and collaboration.

2.5.3 Human-Controlled Interaction Boundary

AI is typically met with greater skepticism than humans, and examining interactions centered on human control may help alleviate concerns. Haupt et al. (2025) indicate that texts generated by interactions in which the AI acts as the author but ultimate control is in the hands of humans will acquire a higher level of credibility, reflecting human concerns about control. Control is a fundamental human need, whereby humans seek to oversee the process and outcome of events (C. Y. Chen et al., 2016). When their need for control is threatened, they experience frustration or helplessness. Moreover, the majority of AI systems are "black box" models, rendering them vulnerable. In the event of a system malfunction, the loss of human control will impede operators' ability to comprehend the system's operation (Sarter & Woods, 1995). However, it is not always the case that humans have a strong desire for control. In the context of education, one study revealed that teachers are inclined to collaborate with AI in order to alleviate the burden of pairing students (Yang et al., 2021). This reflects a desire to leverage the autonomy of AI in certain scenarios or tasks, thereby enhancing the efficiency of collaboration. It is, therefore, recommended that the future focus of research be on the allocation of control in human–AI interaction and collaboration, as well as the delineation of the boundaries of these interactions.

In future research, it would be beneficial to explore methods of maximizing the autonomy of AI while maintaining human control. Autonomy represents a significant aspect of AI technology. However, research on system autonomy within the HCI community remains in its nascent stages. Further research is required to assess the applicable scenarios and degree of manifestation of AI autonomy, as well as the relationship between autonomy and safety, reliability, and accountability. As an illustration, while contemporary self-driving automobiles may be autonomous (Biondi et al., 2019), it is crucial to recognize the potential risks and concurrently investigate the boundaries of human–AI interaction to guarantee that humans can assume control of the vehicle in emergencies and to develop human-controllable AI.

2.5.4 Ethical Interaction Design

The ethical design of artificial intelligence has been the subject of considerable research and practical application. In a significant development, UNESCO released the inaugural global standard on AI ethics, the Ethics of Artificial Intelligence (Ethics of Artificial Intelligence | UNESCO, n.d.). This document proposes a series of key principles to enhance privacy and data protection, transparency and interpretability, responsibility and accountability, and fairness and nondiscrimination in the development of AI. Additionally, prominent technology companies such as Google (Google AI Principles, n.d.), IBM, and Microsoft have published ethical principles for the development of AI systems. Nevertheless, there is still a considerable distance to travel before ethical principles can be upheld in human–AI interaction and collaboration.

In order to achieve this objective, researchers in the HCI community are investigating methods for incorporating transparent design principles into automated systems, with the aim of facilitating the tracing back of system error data (Santoni de Sio & van den Hoven, 2018). Presently, researchers are training and optimizing the behavior of AI by incorporating users into the design and testing process. This allows for the training and optimization of AI's behavior through user interaction and feedback data, with the aim of improving the results provided by AI and aligning them with human value needs. Furthermore, the interaction between humans and AI must be governed by ethical standards. To this end, accountability, authorization, and supervision should be implemented to regulate human interactions. Moreover, those working in the HCI field may wish to consider incorporating additional ethical cues into the interaction to remind human operators of the legitimacy of the interaction process (van Diggelen et al., 2021). In sum, the formation of ethical human–AI interaction and collaboration necessitates not only the engineering of reliable technology but also the guidance of human behavior to foster a sustainable human–AI collaboration environment.

2.6 Future Directions and Challenges

2.6.1 Building A Complete Cognitive Framework for Human–AI Interaction

In recent years, there has been a significant increase in research interest on the application of AI for decision-making and prediction. It is widely acknowledged that AI has the potential to greatly aid people in practical tasks. Optimally, both humans and AI will reap the benefits of engaging in human–AI interaction and collaboration. However, in large-scale communication and cooperation between humans and AI, people need to face a challenging problem: how to make AI compatible with human values, cognitive laws, and morality and ethics, so as to form a complete cognitive framework to ensure trust and reliability in human–AI interactions.

The comprehensive cognitive framework encompasses fundamental topics ranging from user perception to value ethics. From a micro perspective, individuals might have biases or mistrust toward AI based on their intrinsic perceptions, which can hinder the collaboration between humans and AI. In addition, if the design principles of the AI do not align with the cognitive laws of humans, the AI's behaviors may confuse humans and lead them to discontinue its usage. Aside from the limitations imposed on the utilization of AI as a result of distrust, an excessive reliance on AI might also prompt humans to unquestioningly adopt the choice outcomes furnished by AI throughout the collaborative procedure, so potentially resulting in erroneous judgments. The field of artificial intelligence has seen a transition from the use of small models to the utilization of large models. AI large models include a diverse array of Internet data into their training sets, which may include erroneous information, disinformation, and biased information. Consequently, these inaccuracies can significantly impact the effectiveness of the AI during human–AI interaction, posing a substantial risk. At the moment, the lack of ability to precisely understand the user's cognitive patterns and alert the human at the appropriate moment would be a significant disadvantage. The instantaneous, complexity, and flexibility of user cognition also present major challenges for human–AI interaction. The ability to precisely comprehend the user's cognitive, emotional, and demand shifts in human–AI interaction will significantly influence the efficacy of AI.

From a broad perspective, such as considering human values, the contemporary world can be described as a pluralistic society. AI as a global topic will be viewed differently in different cultures. Further discussion is required among researchers to harmonize the value system supporting AI with the cultural values of human society. This includes addressing concerns related to protecting privacy, evaluating reliability, monitoring risks, and other relevant issues in the context of global AI governance. Attaining consensus within the human community will establish a foundation to uphold the cognitive framework for human–AI collaboration. According to this, AI can enhance human cognition and comprehension of decision support, aiding humans in developing a more precise grasp of AI and consequently enabling more accurate utilization of AI (Bansal et al., 2019).

In the future, we can investigate the topics that follow: understanding how humans perceive the capabilities of AI, including their ability to determine what AI is capable of and what it is not; examining how humans evaluate the privacy protection and security of AI, specifically whether sharing information during interactions and collaborations with AI presents a risk to information security; human assessment of AI reliability and trustworthiness, in which scenarios the results provided by AI will be more trustworthy and how the level of trust for AI-generated results will change during the changes in trust in the results generated by the AI over a long period of interaction and collaboration; and human perceptions of the risks and threats of AI, such as the hazards that inappropriate use will bring to the practice. Through the comprehensive depiction of human social values as well as the individual user's cognitive system, it promotes the formation of a complete cognitive framework for human–AI interaction and collaboration, which can guide the design of interaction and optimize functions, so as to enable AI to better empower human beings, and improve the efficiency of the future human–AI collaborative society.

2.6.2 Supporting Adaptive Learning in Human–AI Collaboration

The degree of intelligence exhibited by AI systems in collaborative work with humans is significantly influenced by their capacity to autonomously learn, considering both user requirements and expert knowledge. Improving the AI's capacity for adaptive learning will be a crucial research topic in the domain of human–AI interaction and collaboration.

There are now two well-established paradigms in the field of AI: connectionism and symbolicism. Deep neural networks are the most frequently utilized among connectionist AI models in contemporary times. Deep neural networks are trained to acquire perceptual capabilities by learning from data in existing environments, and subsequently utilize these capabilities to make decisions when presented with new information in different contexts. This perceptive competence is dependent on an enormous amount of training data. In future complex scenarios of human–AI collaboration, it will be difficult for the AI to perform better without pre-prepared training data. In the meantime, the training and computation of neural networks are opaque, making it challenging to figure out the meaning of the parameters and the rationale behind the outcomes. Among the currently common methods in symbolist AI are nonmonotonic reasoning. The technique assumes that the processing at the perceptual level has been finalized and that the information in the given circumstance has been transformed into coherent knowledge. Humans utilize this knowledge to engage in logical reasoning in order to get valid conclusions or results. This approach is reliant on knowledge and requires the involvement of human specialists to maintain a knowledge foundation that supports logical thinking. symbolicism and connectionism AI approach problem-solving from distinct angles. Human–AI collaboration have the potential to combine symbolic and associative AI, thereby utilizing the respective advantages of each approach. Integrating human expertise and supervision into machine learning workflows effectively combines human and machine intelligence, enabling human specialists to directly enhance model performance.

The process of human–AI interaction and collaboration is frequently characterized by its dynamic and flexible nature. Aside from integrating expert knowledge into model training to enhance the model's overall performance, it is also crucial to consider the intelligent system's ability to adapt to different learning scenarios. Nevertheless, the existing AI technology requires further enhancement in terms of autonomy and particularly its capacity for learning. It ought to try to advance toward autonomous continuous learning and acquiring knowledge through user interaction. Sekmen and Challa (2013) revealed that adaptive learning mechanisms can enable machine intelligence to consistently and independently update user models, acquire knowledge about the preferences and behaviors of communicating with users, and modify its own behaviors accordingly. This leads to improved and friendly interactions. These adaptive learning robots are highly favored by users.

By integrating user knowledge, adaptive learning in human–AI collaboration can enhance the friendliness of AI interaction behaviors and approaches. Future research can focus on investigating efficient methods for human–AI collaboration in circumstances with abundant information. For example, conducting insightful research in fields that possess rich expert knowledge, such as healthcare, education, and finance. And from an information science perspective, it provides insights for data and knowledge fusion to support the optimization of machine learning. We can hope that this will lead the way for AI to achieve previously unimaginable levels of self-learning and facilitate more harmonious human–AI partnerships.

2.6.3 Complementing the Strengths of Humans and AI

An important goal in human–AI collaboration is to achieve complementarity (Kelly et al., 2023) and, in doing so, to obtain good performance beyond that of humans alone or AI alone doing the work (Donahue et al., 2022). This is similar to the division of tasks in a human team, but it is important to note that this is the ideal situation. Collaboration between human and AI does not always result in better performance than either people or AI working alone. In fact, research shows that human decision-makers are unable to improve the team overall efficacy when working with AI, and that AI can attain optimal performance when left to its own devices (Green & Chen, 2019). Nevertheless, we should have expectations for the future of human–AI collaboration. From this study, we should realize that collaborative work between humans and AI in practice is complex, and how to truly complement the strengths of humans and AI is a major challenge for future development.

As AI is undergoing a period of rapid development, the application of large models presents a multitude of possibilities for AI. The "black box" and opaque operational process make it challenging for humans to accurately predict the collaborative behavior of AI, which can result in unexpected outcomes that may negatively impact the overall performance of the team. To achieve effective integration of human and AI capabilities, it is essential to first identify the respective strengths of humans and AI in different task scenarios. This requires an analysis of the unique contributions that humans and AI can make as standalone entities, as well as an exploration of the ways in which their respective insights can be combined to create a more comprehensive and valuable knowledge base. Given the intricate nature of human knowledge, it is imperative to categorize the knowledge that humans may generate in diverse contexts, establish methodologies for knowledge organization, and integrate the findings of AI data analysis with this knowledge to develop a new knowledge base that can assist in decision-making processes. Furthermore, it is essential to investigate how humans perceive and evaluate the capabilities of AI in diverse contexts. During human–AI collaboration, the AI has become a teammate with a human-like role. In practical scenarios, humans can discern the potential advantages and supplementary functions of AI through the provision of explanatory data and instructions by AI. Furthermore, humans are guided by AI to achieve a genuine complementarity between humans and AI. The realization of complementarity between humans and AI necessitates a focus on the collaborative and communicative aspects between these two entities. As AI develops, it will gradually gain autonomy and initiative. It will be able to judge the support that human intelligence can provide in the current task through proactive situational awareness. It will then be able to provide feedback and suggestions to human beings, seek human help, and stimulate human creativity and initiative in this way. Accordingly, the establishment of a two-way communication channel in human–AI collaboration is a crucial element in attaining complementary advantages.

In practical situations, effective interaction and collaboration between two entities can be facilitated by a comprehensive understanding of human intent and the capabilities of AI. In the context of interaction scenarios, it is of great importance to investigate the ways in which AI can be utilized to enhance human intelligence. This can be achieved, for instance, by facilitating the collection, organization, and sharing of information and expertise through the introduction of AI participation in crowdsourcing efforts. Furthermore, in the process of human access to knowledge, it is essential to explore the ways in which AI can enhance an interactive search, improve human understanding of various domains, and satisfy the needs and cognitive abilities of different users. In collaboration scenarios, the utilization of AI capabilities in an aging society is a promising area of research. Potential applications include the modeling of health-related domain knowledge to assist in the creation of AI models that can collaborate with caregivers to complete care tasks and reach intelligent care. In the field of scientific discovery, the introduction of sophisticated AI tools can facilitate collaboration with human experts through interactive AI to drive scientific innovation acceleration. It can be posited that future research will be situated at the crossroads of humans and AI, facilitating the integration of disparate subject matter, and drawing upon the strengths of both to achieve efficacious collaboration.

References

Amershi, S., Weld, D., Vorvoreanu, M., Fourney, A., Nushi, B., Collisson, P., Suh, J., Iqbal, S., Bennett, P. N., Inkpen, K., Teevan, J., Kikin-Gil, R., & Horvitz, E. (2019). Guidelines for Human–AI Interaction. *Proceedings of the 2019 CHI Conference on Human Factors in Computing Systems*, 1–13. https://doi.org/10.1145/3290605.3300233

Asan, O., Bayrak, A. E., & Choudhury, A. (2020). Artificial Intelligence and Human Trust in Healthcare: Focus on Clinicians. *Journal of Medical Internet Research*, 22(6), e15154. https://doi.org/10.2196/15154

Bansal, G., Nushi, B., Kamar, E., Lasecki, W. S., Weld, D. S., & Horvitz, E. (2019). Beyond Accuracy: The Role of Mental Models in Human–AI Team Performance. *Proceedings of the AAAI Conference on Human Computation and Crowdsourcing*, 7, 2–11. https://doi.org/10.1609/hcomp.v7i1.5285

Barnes, W. H. F. (1944). The Nature of Explanation. *Nature*, 153(3890), 605–605. https://doi.org/10.1038/153605a0

Biondi, F., Alvarez, I., & Jeong, K.-A. (2019). Human–System Cooperation in Automated Driving. *International Journal of Human–Computer Interaction*, 35(11), 917–918. https://doi.org/10.1080/10447318.2018.1561793

Borman, L. (1996). SIGCHI: The Early Years. *ACM SIGCHI Bulletin*, 28(1), 4–6. https://doi.org/10.1145/249170.249172

Buçinca, Z., Malaya, M. B., & Gajos, K. Z. (2021). To Trust or to Think: Cognitive Forcing Functions Can Reduce Overreliance on AI in AI-assisted Decision-making. *Proceedings of the ACM on Human–Computer Interaction, 5(CSCW1)*, 188:1–188:21. https://doi.org/10.1145/3449287

Cabrera, Á. A., Perer, A., & Hong, J. I. (2023). Improving Human–AI Collaboration with Descriptions of AI Behavior. *Proceedings of the ACM on Human–Computer Interaction*, 7(CSCW1), 136:1–136:21. https://doi.org/10.1145/3579612

Cañas, J. J. (2022). AI and Ethics When Human Beings Collaborate with AI Agents. *Frontiers in Psychology*, 13. https://doi.org/10.3389/fpsyg.2022.836650

Cao, S., Gomez, C., & Huang, C.-M. (2023). How Time Pressure in Different Phases of Decision-Making Influences Human–AI Collaboration. *Proceedings of the ACM on Human–Computer Interaction*, 7(CSCW2), 277:1–277:26. https://doi.org/10.1145/3610068

Chen, C., & Zheng, Y. (2023). When Consumers Need More Interpretability of Artificial Intelligence (AI) Recommendations? The Effect of Decision-making Domains. *Behaviour & Information Technology*. https://doi.org/10.1080/0144929X.2023.2279658

Chen, C. Y., Lee, L., & Yap, A. J. (2016). Control Deprivation Motivates Acquisition of Utilitarian Products. *Journal of Consumer Research*, ucw068. https://doi.org/10.1093/jcr/ucw068

Chi, O. H., Denton, G., & Gursoy, D. (2020). Artificially Intelligent Device Use in Service Delivery: A Systematic Review, Synthesis, and Research Agenda. *Journal of Hospitality Marketing & Management*, *29*(7), 757–786. https://doi.org/10.1080/19368623.2020.1721394

Deshpande, K. V., Pan, S., & Foulds, J. R. (2020). Mitigating Demographic Bias in AI-based Resume Filtering. *Adjunct Publication of the 28th ACM Conference on User Modeling, Adaptation and Personalization*, 268–275. https://doi.org/10.1145/3386392.3399569

Desolda, G., Dimauro, G., Esposito, A., Lanzilotti, R., Matera, M., & Zancanaro, M. (2024). A human–AI Interaction Paradigm and Its Application to Rhinocytology. *Artificial Intelligence in Medicine*, 102933. https://doi.org/10.1016/j.artmed.2024.102933

van Diggelen, J., Barnhoorn, J., Post, R., Sijs, J., van der Stap, N., & van der Waa, J. (2021). Delegation in Human–Machine Teaming: Progress, Challenges and Prospects. In D. Russo, T. Ahram, W. Karwowski, G. Di Bucchianico, & R. Taiar (eds.), *Intelligent Human Systems Integration 2021* (pp. 10–16). Springer International Publishing. https://doi.org/10.1007/978-3-030-68017-6_2

Donahue, K., Chouldechova, A., & Kenthapadi, K. (2022). Human–Algorithm Collaboration: Achieving Complementarity and Avoiding Unfairness. *2022 ACM Conference on Fairness, Accountability, and Transparency*, 1639–1656. https://doi.org/10.1145/3531146.3533221

Ebermann, C., Selisky, M., & Weibelzahl, S. (2023). Explainable AI: The Effect of Contradictory Decisions and Explanations on Users' Acceptance of AI Systems. *International Journal of Human–Computer Interaction*. www.tandfonline.com/doi/abs/10.1080/10447318.2022.2126812

Epley, N., Waytz, A., & Cacioppo, J. T. (2007). On Seeing Human: A Three-Factor Theory of Anthropomorphism. *Psychological Review*, *114*(4), 864–886. https://doi.org/10.1037/0033-295X.114.4.864

Ethics of Artificial Intelligence | UNESCO. (n.d.). Retrieved July 30, 2024, from www.unesco.org/en/artificial-intelligence/recommendation-ethics

Fan, J., Tian, F., Dai, G., Du, Y., & Liu, Z. (2018). Thoughts on Human–Computer Interaction in the Age of Artificial Intelligence. *SCIENTIA SINICA Informationis*, *48*(4), 361–375. https://doi.org/10.1360/N112017-00221

Georganta, E., & Ulfert, A.-S. (2024). My Colleague Is an AI! Trust Differences between AI and Human Teammates. *Team Performance Management: An International Journal*, *30*(1/2), 23–37. https://doi.org/10.1108/TPM-07-2023-0053

Google AI Principles. (n.d.). Google AI. Retrieved July 30, 2024, from https://ai.google/responsibility/principles/

Graefe, J., Rittger, L., Carollo, G., Engelhardt, D., & Bengler, K. (2023). Evaluating the Potential of Interactivity in Explanations for User-Adaptive In-Vehicle Systems: Insights from a Real-World Driving Study. In V. G. Duffy, H. Krömker, N. A. Streitz, & S. Konomi (eds.), *HCI International 2023: Late Breaking Papers* (pp. 294–312). Springer Nature Switzerland. https://doi.org/10.1007/978-3-031-48047-8_19

Green, B., & Chen, Y. (2019). The Principles and Limits of Algorithm-in-the-Loop Decision Making. *Proceedings of the ACM on Human–Computer Interaction*, *3* (CSCW), 1–24. https://doi.org/10.1145/3359152

Grudin, J. (2018). From Tool to Partner: The Evolution of Human–Computer Interaction. *Extended Abstracts of the 2018 CHI Conference on Human Factors in Computing Systems*, 1–3. https://doi.org/10.1145/3170427.3170663

Gursoy, D., Chi, O. H., Lu, L., & Nunkoo, R. (2019). Consumers Acceptance of Artificially Intelligent (AI) Device Use in Service Delivery. *International Journal of Information Management*, *49*, 157–169. https://doi.org/10.1016/j.ijinfomgt.2019.03.008

Harbarth, L., Gößwein, E., Bodemer, D., & Schnaubert, L. (2025). (Over)Trusting AI Recommendations: How System and Person Variables Affect Dimensions of Complacency. *International Journal of Human–Computer Interaction*, *41*(1), 391–410. https://doi.org/10.1080/10447318.2023.2301250

Harrison, S., Sengers, P., & Tatar, D. (2011). Making Epistemological Trouble: Third-Paradigm HCI as Successor Science. *Interacting with Computers*, *23*(5), 385–392. https://doi.org/10.1016/j.intcom.2011.03.005

Haupt, M., Freidank, J., & Haas, A. (2025). Consumer Responses to Human–AI Collaboration at Organizational Frontlines: Strategies to Escape Algorithm Aversion in Content Creation. *Review of Managerial Science*, *19*, 377–413. https://doi.org/10.1007/s11846-024-00748-y

Hornbæk, K., Mottelson, A., Knibbe, J., & Vogel, D. (2019). What Do We Mean by "Interaction"? An Analysis of 35 Years of CHI. *ACM Transactions on Computer–Human Interaction*, *26*(4), 27:1–27:30. https://doi.org/10.1145/3325285

Hou, K., Hou, T., & Cai, L. (2023). Exploring Trust in Human–AI Collaboration in the Context of Multiplayer Online Games. *Systems*, *11*(5), Article 5. https://doi.org/10.3390/systems11050217

Hou, T.-Y., Tseng, Y.-C., & Yuan, C. W. (Tina). (2024). Is This AI Sexist? The Effects of a Biased AI's Anthropomorphic Appearance and Explainability on Users' Bias Perceptions and Trust. *International Journal of Information Management*, *76*, 102775. https://doi.org/10.1016/j.ijinfomgt.2024.102775

Hu, M., Zhang, G., Chong, L., Cagan, J., & Goucher-Lambert, K. (2025). How Being Outvoted by AI Teammates Impacts Human–AI Collaboration. *International Journal of Human–Computer Interaction*, *41*, 4049–4066. https://doi.org/10.1080/10447318.2024.2345980

Hu, P., Lu, Y., & Wang, B. (2022). Experiencing Power over AI: The Fit Effect of Perceived Power and Desire for Power on Consumers' Choice for Voice Shopping. *Computers in Human Behavior*, *128*, 107091. https://doi.org/10.1016/j.chb.2021.107091

Hwang, A. H.-C., & Won, A. S. (2022). AI in Your Mind: Counterbalancing Perceived Agency and Experience in Human–AI Interaction. *CHI Conference on Human Factors in Computing Systems Extended Abstracts*, 1–10. https://doi.org/10.1145/3491101.3519833

Jain, R., Garg, N., & Khera, S. N. (2022). Effective Human–AI Work Design for Collaborative Decision-making. *Kybernetes*, *52*(11), 5017–5040. https://doi.org/10.1108/K-04-2022-0548

Jeon, Y., Jin, S., Shih, P. C., & Han, K. (2021). FashionQ: An AI-Driven Creativity Support Tool for Facilitating Ideation in Fashion Design. *Proceedings of the 2021 CHI Conference on Human Factors in Computing Systems*, 1–18. https://doi.org/10.1145/3411764.3445093

Jiang, T., Sun, Z., Fu, S., & Lv, Y. (2024). Human–AI Interaction Research Agenda: A User-centered Perspective. *Data and Information Management*, 100078. https://doi.org/10.1016/j.dim.2024.100078

Kahn, L. H., Savas, O., Morrison, A., Shaffer, K. A., & Zapata, L. (2020). Modelling Hybrid Human–Artificial Intelligence Cooperation: A Call Center Customer Service Case Study. *2020 IEEE International Conference on Big Data (Big Data)*, 3072–3075. https://doi.org/10.1109/BigData50022.2020.9377747

Kelly, M., Kumar, A., Smyth, P., & Steyvers, M. (2023). Capturing Humans' Mental Models of AI: An Item Response Theory Approach. *2023 ACM Conference on Fairness, Accountability, and Transparency*, 1723–1734. https://doi.org/10.1145/3593013.3594111

Kim, A., Cho, M., Ahn, J., & Sung, Y. (2019). Effects of Gender and Relationship Type on the Response to Artificial Intelligence. *Cyberpsychology, Behavior, and Social Networking*, *22*(4), 249–253. https://doi.org/10.1089/cyber.2018.0581

Kim, S. (1995). Interdisciplinary Cooperation. In R. M. Baecker, J. Grudin, W. A. S. Buxton, & S. Greenberg (eds.), *Readings in Human–Computer Interaction* (pp. 304–311). Morgan Kaufmann. https://doi.org/10.1016/B978-0-08-051574-8.50033-9

Kim, S. S. Y., Watkins, E. A., Russakovsky, O., Fong, R., & Monroy-Hernández, A. (2023). "Help Me Help the AI": Understanding How Explainability Can Support Human–AI Interaction. *Proceedings of the 2023 CHI Conference on Human Factors in Computing Systems*, 1–17. https://doi.org/10.1145/3544548.3581001

Kitchin, J., & Baber, C. (2016). A Comparison of Shared and Distributed Situation Awareness in Teams through the Use of Agent-based Modelling. *Theoretical Issues in Ergonomics Science*, *17*(1), 8–41. https://www.tandfonline.com/doi/abs/10.1080/1463922X.2015.1106616

Lee, C. T., Pan, L.-Y., & Hsieh, S. H. (2021). Artificial Intelligent Chatbots as Brand Promoters: A Two-stage Structural Equation Modeling–Artificial Neural Network Approach. *Internet Research*, *32*(4), 1329–1356. https://doi.org/10.1108/INTR-01-2021-0030

Li, X., & Sung, Y. (2021). Anthropomorphism Brings Us Closer: The Mediating Role of Psychological Distance in User–AI Assistant Interactions. *Computers in Human Behavior*, *118*, 106680. https://doi.org/10.1016/j.chb.2021.106680

Lindvall, M., Lundström, C., & Löwgren, J. (2021). Rapid Assisted Visual Search: Supporting Digital Pathologists with Imperfect AI. *26th International Conference on Intelligent User Interfaces*, 504–513. https://doi.org/10.1145/3397481.3450681

Lobo, I., Koch, J., Renoux, J., Batina, I., & Prada, R. (2024). When Should I Lead or Follow: Understanding Initiative Levels in Human–AI Collaborative Gameplay. *Designing Interactive Systems Conference*, 2037–2056. https://doi.org/10.1145/3643834.3661583

Malandri, L., Mercorio, F., Mezzanzanica, M., & Nobani, N. (2023). ConvXAI: A System for Multimodal Interaction with Any Black-box Explainer. *Cognitive Computation*, *15*(2), 613–644. https://doi.org/10.1007/s12559-022-10067-7

Merry, M., Riddle, P., & Warren, J. (2021). A Mental Models Approach for Defining Explainable Artificial Intelligence. *BMC Medical Informatics and Decision Making*, *21*(1), 344. https://doi.org/10.1186/s12911-021-01703-7

Myers, B., Hollan, J., Cruz, I., Bryson, S., Bulterman, D., Catarci, T., Citrin, W., Glinert, E., Grudin, J., & Ioannidis, Y. (1996). Strategic Directions in Human–Computer Interaction. *ACM Computing Surveys*, *28*(4), 794–809. https://doi.org/10.1145/242223.246855

Nagao, K. (2019). Symbiosis between Humans and Artificial Intelligence. In K. Nagao (ed.), *Artificial Intelligence Accelerates Human Learning: Discussion Data Analytics* (pp. 135–151). Springer. https://doi.org/10.1007/978-981-13-6175-3_6

Newn, J., Singh, R., Velloso, E., & Vetere, F. (2019). Combining Implicit Gaze and AI for Real-time Intention Projection. *Adjunct Proceedings of the 2019 ACM International Joint Conference on Pervasive and Ubiquitous Computing and Proceedings of the 2019 ACM International Symposium on Wearable Computers*, 324–327. https://doi.org/10.1145/3341162.3343786

Oulasvirta, A., & Hornbæk, K. (2016). HCI Research as Problem-Solving. *Proceedings of the 2016 CHI Conference on Human Factors in Computing Systems*, 4956–4967. https://doi.org/10.1145/2858036.2858283

Pargman, D. S., Eriksson, E., Bates, O., Kirman, B., Comber, R., Hedman, A., & van den Broeck, M. (2019). The Future of Computing and Wisdom: Insights from Human–Computer Interaction. *Futures*, *113*, 102434. https://doi.org/10.1016/j.futures.2019.06.006

Pataranutaporn, P., Liu, R., Finn, E., & Maes, P. (2023). Influencing Human–AI Interaction by Priming Beliefs about AI Can Increase Perceived Trustworthiness, Empathy and Effectiveness. *Nature Machine Intelligence*, *5*(10), 1076–1086. https://doi.org/10.1038/s42256-023-00720-7

Paul, S. K., Nicolescu, M., & Nicolescu, M. (2023). Enhancing Human–Robot Collaboration through a Multi-Module Interaction Framework with Sensor Fusion: Object Recognition, Verbal Communication, User of Interest Detection, Gesture and Gaze Recognition. *Sensors*, *23*(13), Article 13. https://doi.org/10.3390/s23135798

Rastogi, C., Zhang, Y., Wei, D., Varshney, K. R., Dhurandhar, A., & Tomsett, R. (2022). Deciding Fast and Slow: The Role of Cognitive Biases in AI-assisted Decision-making. *Proceedings of the ACM on Human–Computer Interactions*, *6*(CSCW1), 83:1–83:22. https://doi.org/10.1145/3512930

Ribera, M., & Lapedriza, À. (2019, March 2). *Can We Do Better Explanations? A Proposal of User-centered Explainable AI*. IUI Workshops. www.semanticscholar.org/paper/Can-we-do-better-explanations-A-proposal-of-AI-Ribera-Lapedriza/60758a8b15d843ed4f731b4eaa7832be8a7a7e13

Rosenfeld, A., & Richardson, A. (2019). Explainability in Human–Agent Systems. *Autonomous Agents and Multi-Agent Systems*, *33*(6), 673–705. https://doi.org/10.1007/s10458-019-09408-y

Sadeghian, S., & Hassenzahl, M. (2022). The "Artificial" Colleague: Evaluation of Work Satisfaction in Collaboration with Non-human Coworkers. *27th International Conference on Intelligent User Interfaces*, 27–35. https://doi.org/10.1145/3490099.3511128

Santoni de Sio, F., & van den Hoven, J. (2018). Meaningful Human Control over Autonomous Systems: A Philosophical Account. *Frontiers in Robotics and AI*, *5*. https://doi.org/10.3389/frobt.2018.00015

Sarter, N. B., & Woods, D. D. (1995). How in the World Did We Ever Get into That Mode? Mode Error and Awareness in Supervisory Control. *Human Factors: The Journal of the Human Factors and Ergonomics Society*, *37*(1), 5–19. https://doi.org/10.1518/001872095779049516

Scholtz, J. (2003). Theory and Evaluation of Human Robot Interactions. *Proceedings of The 36th Annual Hawaii International Conference on System Sciences, 2003*, 10 pp. https://doi.org/10.1109/HICSS.2003.1174284

Seeber, I., Bittner, E., Briggs, R. O., de Vreede, T., de Vreede, G.-J., Elkins, A., Maier, R., Merz, A. B., Oeste-Reiß, S., Randrup, N., Schwabe, G., & Söllner, M. (2020). Machines as Teammates: A Research Agenda on AI in Team Collaboration. *Information & Management*, *57*(2), 103174. https://doi.org/10.1016/j.im.2019.103174

Sekmen, A., & Challa, P. (2013). Assessment of Adaptive Human–Robot Interactions. *Knowledge-Based Systems*, *42*, 49–59. https://doi.org/10.1016/j.knosys.2013.01.003

Shin, J.-G., Choi, G.-Y., Hwang, H.-J., & Kim, S.-H. (2021). Evaluation of Emotional Satisfaction Using Questionnaires in Voice-Based Human–AI Interaction. *Applied Sciences*, *11*(4), Article 4. https://doi.org/10.3390/app11041920

Spatola, N., Marchesi, S., & Wykowska, A. (2022). Different Models of Anthropomorphism across Cultures and Ontological Limits in Current Frameworks: The Integrative Framework of Anthropomorphism. *Frontiers in Robotics and AI*, *9*. https://doi.org/10.3389/frobt.2022.863319

Stanford GDPi. (2018, July 9). Human-Centered AI: Building Trust, Democracy and Human Rights by Design. *Stanford's GDPi*. https://medium.com/stanfords-gdpi/human-centered-ai-building-trust-democracy-and-human-rights-by-design-2fc14a0b48af

Steyvers, M., & Kumar, A. (2023). Three Challenges for AI-Assisted Decision-Making. *Perspectives on Psychological Science*, *19*(5), 17456916231181102. https://doi.org/10.1177/17456916231181102

Sun, X., Zhang, Y., Qin, J., Li, J., & Wang, S. (2020). Review on Human–Intelligent System Collaboration. *Packaging Engineering*, *41*(18), 1–11. https://doi.org/10.19554/j.cnki.1001-3563.2020.18.001

Tutul, A. A., Chaspari, T., Levitan, S. I., & Hirschberg, J. (2023). Human–AI Collaboration for the Detection of Deceptive Speech. *2023 11th International Conference on Affective Computing and Intelligent Interaction Workshops and Demos (ACIIW)*, 1–4. https://doi.org/10.1109/ACIIW59127.2023.10388114

Villareale, J., Harteveld, C., & Zhu, J. (2022). "I Want To See How Smart This AI Really Is": Player Mental Model Development of an Adversarial AI Player. *Proceedings of the ACM on Human–Computer Interactions*, *6*(CHI PLAY), 219:1–219:26. https://doi.org/10.1145/3549482

Wang, B., Yuan, T., & Rau, P.-L. P. (2024). Effects of Explanation Strategy and Autonomy of Explainable AI on Human–AI Collaborative Decision-making. *International Journal of Social Robotics*, *16*(4), 791–810. https://doi.org/10.1007/s12369-024-01132-2

Wang, D., Weisz, J. D., Muller, M., Ram, P., Geyer, W., Dugan, C., Tausczik, Y., Samulowitz, H., & Gray, A. (2019). Human–AI Collaboration in Data Science: Exploring Data Scientists' Perceptions of Automated AI. *Proceedings of the ACM on Human–Computer Interactions*, *3*(CSCW), 211:1–211:24. https://doi.org/10.1145/3359313

Westphal, M., Vössing, M., Satzger, G., Yom-Tov, G. B., & Rafaeli, A. (2023). Decision Control and Explanations in Human–AI Collaboration: Improving User Perceptions and Compliance. *Computers in Human Behavior*, *144*, 107714. https://doi.org/10.1016/j.chb.2023.107714

Xie, Y., Zhao, S., Zhou, P., Lu, L., Liang, C., & Jiang, L. (2024). Estimating the Impact of "Humanizing" AI Assistants. *International Journal of Human–Computer Interaction*, *40*(24), 8876–8889. https://doi.org/10.1080/10447318.2023.2291614

Xie, Y., Zhu, K., Zhou, P., & Liang, C. (2023). How Does Anthropomorphism Improve Human–AI Interaction Satisfaction: A Dual-Path Model. *Computers in Human Behavior*, *148*, 107878. https://doi.org/10.1016/j.chb.2023.107878

Xing, Y., Lv, C., Cao, D., & Hang, P. (2021). Toward Human–Vehicle Collaboration: Review and Perspectives on Human-centered Collaborative Automated Driving. *Transportation Research Part C: Emerging Technologies*, *128*, 103199. https://doi.org/10.1016/j.trc.2021.103199

Xu, W. (2019). Toward Human-centered AI: A Perspective from Human–Computer Interaction. *Interactions*, *26*(4), 42–46. https://doi.org/10.1145/3328485

Xu, W., & Gao, Z. (2024). Applying HCAI in Developing Effective Human–AI Teaming: A Perspective from Human–AI Joint Cognitive Systems. *Interactions*, *31*(1), 32–37. https://doi.org/10.1145/3635116

Yang, K. B., Lawrence, L., Echeverria, V., Guo, B., Rummel, N., & Aleven, V. (2021). Surveying Teachers' Preferences and Boundaries Regarding Human–AI Control in Dynamic Pairing of Students for Collaborative Learning. In T. De Laet, R. Klemke, C. Alario-Hoyos, I. Hilliger, & A. Ortega-Arranz (eds.), *Technology-Enhanced Learning for a Free, Safe, and Sustainable World* (pp. 260–274). Springer International Publishing. https://doi.org/10.1007/978-3-030-86436-1_20

Zhang, G., Raina, A., Brownell, E., & Cagan, J. (2022). The Impact of a Strategy of Deception about the Identity of an Artificial Intelligence Teammate on Human Designers. *Volume 3B: 48th Design Automation Conference (DAC)*, V03BT03A017. https://doi.org/10.1115/DETC2022-88535

Zhang, M., Gursoy, D., Zhu, Z., & Shi, S. (2021). Impact of Anthropomorphic Features of Artificially Intelligent Service Robots on Consumer Acceptance: Moderating Role of Sense of Humor. *International Journal of Contemporary Hospitality Management*, *33*(11), 3883–3905. https://doi.org/10.1108/IJCHM-11-2020-1256

Zhao, Y., & Bao, X. (2023). Narratron: Collaborative Writing and Shadow-playing of Children Stories with Large Language Models. *Adjunct Proceedings of the 36th Annual ACM Symposium on User Interface Software and Technology*, 1–6. https://doi.org/10.1145/3586182.3625120

Zou, M., & Huang, L. (2024). The Impact of ChatGPT on L2 Writing and Expected Responses: Voice from Doctoral Students. *Education and Information Technologies*, *29*, 13201–13219. https://doi.org/10.1007/s10639-023-12397-x

3

Privacy Identification of Human–Generative AI Interaction

Dan Wu and Guoye Sun

3.1 Introduction

At the end of 2022, OpenAI released ChatGPT, a large language model chatbot created using the GPT-3.5 model, sparking a heated public discussion about generative artificial intelligence (GenAI). In February 2023, Microsoft updated Bing to integrate the AI technology behind the OpenAI, and the craze continued. Users can now speak into the search box and get targeted answers to their questions. This is where the new generative AI technology comes into play, which has brought the discussion about generative AI to a peak. Due to the surge in large language models and the increase in computing power, more and more such generative AI products have appeared on the open market. These include Google's Bard, Baidu's Wenxin Yiyan, Anthropic's Claude, and others. Generative AI represents a new generation of AI driven by large language models, allowing humans to control AI to create text, images, videos, and more.

It has demonstrated remarkable capabilities, for example, passing college-level exams (Choi et al., 2021), and has achieved remarkable results even in areas that are considered unsuitable for machines, such as creativity (Chen et al., 2023). Generative AI based on large language models has been widely used in various scenarios with its powerful advantages, including, for example, educational work (Baidoo-anu & Ansah, 2023), code writing (Dwivedi et al., 2023), and medical health (Cascella et al., 2023). It can be easily accessed through a web interface, which has led to its widespread adoption by humans. Further, the interaction between humans and generative AI has gradually increased and deepened. The most obvious evidence is the number of users of ChatGPT, which is the fastest product to reach 100 million users in history and is still growing rapidly (Porter, 2023). It should be noted that, although such transformative tools have brought great help to human work and life, critical and inevitable privacy issues have also emerged.

The essence of generative AI is to try to imitate human capabilities and produce content closely related to humans through large-scale learning and training data. With the widespread application of this technology, the problem of privacy leakage has become increasingly prominent and needs to be solved urgently. This is because its interaction with humans is based on the collection and processing of human data, which itself poses the risk of privacy leakage. On the one hand, these large language models rely heavily on massive data sets for training, which usually come from public Internet resources, social media, and even private communication records (Brown et al., 2020). Due to the diversity and extensiveness of data sources, the protection of data security and privacy has become extremely complicated. On the other hand, when users use generative AI, they will share various types of data with the system, such as text, voice, images, etc. After being collected, these data may continue to be used for model training to further improve the performance of the system. This training process may cause personal data to be accidentally leaked in future outputs. Specifically, the risk of privacy leakage is closely related to the inherent operating mechanism of generative AI. In the process of content generation, users' sensitive information may be inadvertently embedded in the generated results, posing a threat to user privacy (Carlini et al., 2021).

To this end, both the industry and academia have proposed some methods to solve the privacy leakage of generative AI, including methods to optimize the boundary constraints of data and generated content. After the training data is optimized, researchers will be obliged to ensure that the data does not contain any sensitive information, and to minimize the risks of privacy dimensions such as data screening and cleaning through technical means. Generative AI developers can set content filters, sensitive information identifiers, etc., so that the generated results do not contain the user's personal data. These measures have alleviated the risk of privacy leakage to a certain extent, but the defects are still large.

Therefore, solving the problem of privacy leakage of generative AI in the future requires the joint efforts of developers and users. On the one hand, the developers of generative AI should adhere to the principle of privacy protection during the development and training process, exclude sensitive content during data training, and also perform privacy protection processing in the generated results. On the other hand, users should be given clear guidance to let them understand the operating mechanism of generative AI to improve their awareness of privacy-related issues. In the process of interaction between generative AI and users, they should know what types of information will be obtained and how they should act to protect privacy.

In this chapter, we focus on identifying the privacy involved, and establish a privacy type model for human-generative AI interaction by focusing on the exchange of privacy information during the interaction between users and generative AI. We will start with a theoretical review to explore the issues and existing methods of privacy protection in generative AI. Subsequently, we will establish a privacy type model to describe in detail the privacy types and scenarios that may be involved in human-generative AI interaction. Through the classification and analysis of various privacy types, we can understand the privacy risks of generative AI in different application scenarios. Finally, we will explore the value and importance of the privacy type model in practical applications. Generative AI has broad application potential in knowledge sharing, search, management of health information, scientific discovery, etc. The privacy type model can be further utilized in these fields to better protect user privacy and improve the credibility and user satisfaction of generative AI. The research in this chapter, on the one hand, lays a theoretical foundation for subsequent privacy research in human-generative AI interaction and, on the other hand, it also provides specific references for the application practice of privacy protection measures. Specifically, this chapter systematically identifies privacy in the interaction between humans and generative AI, and proposes a scientific and effective privacy type model, hoping to provide reference and guidance for users and developers, ensure user privacy security, and promote the healthy development of generative AI technology, thereby achieving a more secure and reliable human–AI interaction environment.

3.2 Related Concepts

3.2.1 Privacy Leakage in Generative AI

The privacy leakage problem in generative AI has become a research hotspot in academia and industry. This section will explore the privacy leakage problem in generative AI from two aspects: data source and operation mechanism, combining existing research and practice.

Data Source

Generative AI models are large-scale and involve massive amounts of data from various sources, much of which may be related to private information. The diversity and breadth of data are the basis for generative AI to generate high-quality content, but it also brings about the problem of privacy leakage. The data collection and processing process links generative AI with privacy issues and the root of these issues is that the source of data directly affects the security of user privacy. This section explores how the source of data creates privacy issues in the interaction between people and generative AI. The vast majority of data required for generative AI systems is trained using data extracted from the Internet, social media platforms and other public domain sources, which means that it is difficult to determine whether there is any form of sensitive information in the training data.

Internet data can be said to be one of the most widely used data sources in the training process of generative AI models, and a large part of it is created by Internet users. For example, GPT-3 is trained using data from the wider Internet, including Wikipedia, news articles, etc. (Brown et al., 2020). Often, this data may contain sensitive personal information, such as names. Unless this information is filtered in advance, the model may inadvertently embed this information when training content. Social media data is a key type of Internet data that enriches the data source of generative AI. User interactions on social media are very rich, from public posts on blogs to comments on social media, which are reused without permission. Direct use of this data in model training will leak private information (Carlini et al., 2021).

In addition, another important source of generative AI training data is public datasets, which are published by scientific research institutions, governments or enterprises and open to academic research and technology development. But, at the same time, publicly released datasets also contain some private information. For example, in the widely used ImageNet dataset, some images present personal information, including facial expressions and geographic locations (Deng et al., 2009). Since the dataset is already in the public domain, the risk of privacy leakage increases during data sharing and reuse.

Another important source of data is that generative AI collects user data input in real-time during the interaction process. This data is not only used to provide customized services but also to continuously enhance and optimize the model. Human contact with generative AI is information-intensive, including chat records, voice interactions, and search records. If not protected, this type of information may be maliciously exploited or leaked, posing serious privacy risks. In order to reduce data leakage, data related to user interactions must be stored and sent using extremely strict security methods. However, most generative AI systems are not well protected in this regard. For example, if the user's voice data is not protected during transmission, it may be stolen by a man-in-the-middle attack. In addition, when data is transmitted to a cloud server without proper access control, hackers may exploit weaknesses to obtain sensitive information from users. Although public datasets, online crawled data, user interaction data, etc. provide valuable training data, generative AI systems face new privacy challenges in terms of data sources.

Operation Mechanism

Generative AI is increasingly being used in fields such as healthcare (Leonard, 2023), finance (Estrada, 2023), and emotional counseling (Kimmel, 2023). When using generative AI in these fields, individuals often disclose sensitive information, such as their medical data, financial status, or emotional harm. Users expose more private information when using generative AI due to three characteristics of its working mechanism, namely content integration, question–answer interactivity, and tool anthropomorphism (Wu & Sun, 2023). These three characteristics distinguish privacy issues in user-generated AI interactions from privacy issues in other environments.

In terms of content integration, generative AI can receive structured text input from users and generate integrated answers in a unified format, showing the value association between semantic parts, thereby guiding users to include various private information when creating content. In terms of question–answer interaction, generative AI can have multiple rounds of dialogue with users and provide answers that are closer to the dialogue context and user needs based on the retrieval context and intent. This feature greatly increases users' trust in the output of generative AI, but the immediacy and continuity of this association also make privacy issues complex and changeable. In terms of tool anthropomorphism, generative AI often adds anthropomorphic and emotional expressions to conversational discourse. By imitating the naturalness of human discourse, generative AI can often help users let down their psychological defenses and make it easier to input private information (Lu et al., 2022).

The Impact of Privacy Leakage

Diverse data sources and operational processes make it easier and more complex for humans to leak privacy when interacting with generative AI, exposing users to a series of new privacy issues (Peris et al., 2023). The new privacy challenges in user interactions with generative AI mainly stem from two factors. On the one hand, there are classic privacy issues such as data leakage and the use or sale of personal information (Kshetri, 2023). Due to computing resource limitations and content review requirements, most popular generative AI based on large language models are run using cloud services. Cyber attackers can exploit vulnerabilities in developers' systems to access users' personal accounts and conversation history data (Carlini et al., 2021). For example, ChatGPT was exposed to the leakage of some users' names, email addresses, payment addresses, and credit card numbers (Golda et al., 2024).

On the other hand, previous studies have found that large language models remember information in training data and leak this information in response to specific prompts (C. Zhang et al., 2023). Since generative AI based on large language models currently uses user data to train models regularly, there is a risk that generative AI will output user privacy information to others. This means that private information entered by a specific user may be remembered by the model and leaked when responding to prompts from others. Although language models are used in classical AI, such as Siri, their applications are more limited, such as smart home control (Shalaby et al., 2020). The openness of generative AI allows users to leak more private information, and the scale and intensity of such harms are likely to increase further compared to classical AI. For example, the knowledge provided by researchers to a large language model may be incorporated into the model, and generative AI can provide it to others without verifying the original source (Van Dis et al., 2023). Existing research has shown that the training data of the model can be inferred from the generated text (Song et al., 2017). This attack method highlights how generative models leak training data while generating content.

Privacy leakage in generative AI not only threatens personal privacy and leads to the abuse of personal information but may also have adverse effects on enterprises and society. If corporate personnel fail to protect corporate-related privacy when using generative AI, technical or trade secrets may be leaked, resulting in economic losses to the company (Maddison, 2023). Large scale privacy leaks may cause the public to lose trust in generative AI and hinder the development and use of new technologies. Therefore, understanding how to deal with new privacy challenges in the interaction between users and generative AI is crucial for developers to enhance the interaction experience between people and generative AI from the perspective of human–computer interaction.

3.2.2 Privacy Protection Methods

In Section 3.2.1, we discussed in detail the privacy leakage issues in generative AI, emphasizing the privacy risks and challenges faced by humans in the process of interacting with the system. In order to effectively deal with these issues, researchers and engineers have developed a variety of privacy protection methods. This section will comprehensively review the existing privacy protection methods, mainly involving data restrictions and user participation, and explore their advantages and disadvantages and practical application effects.

Restriction of Data

In the training process of large-scale language models, data restriction aims to reduce the potential risk of privacy leakage in the model training process by improving the selection and processing of data. It is an important means to ensure the privacy protection of generative AI models during the training process.

Data anonymization is a common privacy protection strategy that protects privacy by removing or blurring personal identity information. However, anonymization cannot completely guarantee that data will not be re-identified. For example, studies have shown that social media data may include users who use pseudonyms or usernames, but attackers can find users' real names or even other personal information through natural language processing technology (Fire et al., 2014). Individual identities can also be reidentified by combining multiple de-identified data sets (Narayanan & Shmatikov, 2008). This de-anonymization technology shows that, although the data may be processed before being released, it is still possible for attackers to extract sensitive information from the anonymized data through data re-identification technology. It is difficult to completely protect user privacy by relying solely on anonymization processing.

In order to further improve the privacy protection effect of training data, differential privacy technology is introduced into data processing. Differential privacy effectively prevents over-reliance on and potential leakage of training data by introducing noise during model training, ensuring that, even if an attacker has external information, personal information cannot be recovered from the processed data (Abadi et al., 2016). For example, some studies have enhanced privacy through differential privacy stochastic gradient descent, while also allowing the generated data to maintain high availability to support multiple visual tasks (Dockhorn et al., 2023). Although it can provide strong privacy protection in theory, in practical applications, how to effectively introduce noise while ensuring the usefulness of data remains a challenge. Differential privacy still faces challenges such as high computational complexity and the balance between noise and data analysis accuracy in practical applications. Its effectiveness depends on the way noise is introduced and the specific characteristics of the data. If noise is introduced improperly, it may affect the validity of the data and the performance of the model (Dwork & Roth, 2014).

In order to prevent generative AI from leaking user privacy information in generated content, methods to restrict generated content have also emerged. These methods mainly reduce the risk of sensitive information leakage by introducing constraints or adopting special generation strategies during the generation process. Generative adversarial networks are widely used in content generation for generative AI. In order to protect privacy, researchers have proposed privacy-enhanced generative adversarial networks. For example, a study used a diffusion autoencoder to generate semantically meaningful perturbations, thereby facilitating the protected face to be recognized as another person (Liu et al., 2023). However, the introduction of privacy-preserving constraints may also affect the quality and diversity of generated content. How to strike a balance between protecting privacy and maintaining content quality remains an important research topic.

Privacy by Design

The lack of transparency in the working mechanism of generative AI is particularly prominent compared to traditional information acquisition tools. The list of links provided by traditional search engines allows users to choose trusted sources of results, while the training data and working principles of large language models are little known (Stokel-Walker, 2023). This opacity makes it difficult for users to prevent privacy leaks (Li et al., 2024). Therefore, it is particularly important to let users understand how the private information they input is collected, processed and disseminated for privacy protection.

In this context, the concept of privacy-inclusive design has been applied in some human–computer interaction research (Wong & Mulligan, 2019). Privacy-inclusive design refers to embedding privacy protections into products at the initial design stage, which has been incorporated into the EU's General Data Protection Regulation and the US Federal Trade Commission's policy recommendations. Traditional legal and regulatory means usually rely on ex-post penalties to implement privacy protection, while privacy-inclusive design provides a proactive approach to build privacy protection into the design process.

One of the main purposes of privacy-inclusive design is to provide information and support for privacy decisions. System design can help users make privacy-related choices and operations during use. To this end, existing research has been devoted to improving the design of privacy statements, from visual design to text content to presentation time (Kelley et al., 2010). In addition, some studies have explored the design of user privacy controls, visual and interaction design, and architecture (Jancke et al., 2001), or encouraged users to participate in privacy behaviors through the design of privacy prompts (Chang et al., 2016), thereby supporting user decision-making.

In these designs, privacy issues are conceptualized as information problems or insufficient tools for users. Therefore, the design of informing and supporting privacy decisions focuses on providing users with relevant information to encourage them to make more privacy-protecting decisions or providing tools and methods that enable them to more easily resolve privacy issues in practice. This implicitly assumes that, if users receive the right information or have the right tools, they will be able to participate in human–AI interactions in a more privacy-protecting way.

The Shortcomings of Privacy Protection Methods

Although there are many privacy protection methods, such as data anonymization, differential privacy, and privacy-incorporated design, these methods still have many shortcomings in practical applications in addition to their inherent flaws. First, although they can cope with privacy leakage issues in static data analysis and model training to a certain extent, there is an urgent need for real-time privacy identification and protection in dynamic scenarios where users interact with generative AI. There is currently a lack of private information identification mechanisms during user input and interaction, making it difficult for generative AI systems to effectively avoid the leakage of sensitive information.

Secondly, different types of private information have significant differences in sensitivity and protection needs. Existing privacy protection methods are often generic and lack differentiated protection for different types of private information. For example, the General Data Protection Regulation has stricter protection requirements for specific types of information such as health data and financial data. This shows that health data and financial data are much more sensitive than general types of data and unified protection measures may affect the former. Therefore, existing privacy protection methods need to be further optimized to better cope with the protection needs of different types of private information.

Third, transparency of privacy protection measures is the basis for user trust. Although existing privacy protection methods cover certain user participation, they often lack transparency, making it impossible for users to understand how the system handles their data. This not only increases the risk of privacy leaks, but also reduces users' trust in the system. By increasing the transparency of privacy protection measures and allowing users to understand how the system handles and protects their data, it can enhance user trust and promote the widespread use of the system.

Given the shortcomings of existing privacy protection methods, we aim to perform more granular type identification of private information in generative AI systems. This can provide a basis for developing more sophisticated and effective privacy protection methods in the future. By identifying different types of private information and understanding which private information is more sensitive to users, more targeted and effective protection measures can be designed. For example, stronger encryption technology and strict access control can be used for certain types of data, while relatively loose protection measures can be used for other types of data. This can protect sensitive data while ensuring that the use of non-sensitive data is not subject to excessive restrictions. The model can better balance privacy protection and user experience, thereby enhancing the user experience.

In addition, different types of private information have different requirements in laws and regulations. Identifying privacy types helps ensure that generative AI systems comply with corresponding legal and regulatory requirements when processing data and avoid legal risks. At the same time, by clearly classifying privacy types and protecting them in a targeted manner, the transparency of generative AI systems can be improved, giving users a clearer understanding of what information is collected and how it is protected. This transparency can enhance users' trust in the system and promote wider acceptance and use.

3.2.3 Context Integrity Theory

In recent years, norm-based privacy theories have received increasing attention. As one of them, the contextual integrity theory has been widely used to identify privacy violations in various contexts. This theory recognizes that people interact in different contexts, and each context contains specific expectations about "what types of information to share with whom under what circumstances." Its core concept is that the protection of privacy depends not only on the protection of the data itself, but also on the flow and use rules of data in specific contexts (Nissenbaum, 2004). The contextual integrity theory emphasizes that privacy is not just the nondisclosure or the nonpublicity of data, but the flow of data in appropriate contexts according to appropriate norms and expectations. Privacy management thus becomes a process of negotiating the social norms and expectations held by individuals. This theory provides a new perspective for our research, identifying the types of privacy involved in the interaction between humans and generative AI by considering the dissemination and use of private data in different contexts.

Specifically, the contextual integrity theory points out that different contexts shape the information flow norms in different scenarios, and these norms determine what kind of information use behavior is appropriate. Context-related information norms are composed of three categories: information subject, information type, and transmission principle (Nissenbaum, 2004). The appropriateness of information flow depends on the examination of five elements in the three categories of norms: information sender, information receiver, subject involved in the information, information type, and flow conditions or constraints.

Contextual context integrity theory is often used to explore privacy norms in different environments, such as the Internet of Things (Apthorpe et al., 2019) and education (Shvartzshnaider et al., 2016). The five elements of the theory provide a method to study the subtle effects of information on privacy in a specific context. When one or more of these five elements do not meet the norms and expectations of individuals, privacy violations occur. Specifically, contexts (such as interaction contexts) are social spaces of privacy expectations involving multiple participants, including information senders, receivers, and individuals or groups as information subjects; the type of shared information (such as location information) and transmission principles (rules for how information is transmitted between participants) also need to be considered.

This study applies the contextual integrity theory to the interaction between humans and generative AI and maps five elements to specific elements in the context: the sender of information is the individual user who interacts with generative AI; the receiver of information includes the large language model of generative AI (direct receiver), its developers, operators, and other users (indirect receiver); the subjects involved in the information include individual users, other individuals, or groups; the information type is the various types of information input by the user, which is reflected in the context of privacy disclosure as the privacy type disclosed by the user; and the transmission principle is the condition or constraint in the flow of private information.

Through these detailed contextual elements, this study evaluates the privacy disclosure in the interaction between humans and generative AI, focusing on the possible application scenarios of the interaction, and using this as a theoretical basis to identify privacy types.

3.3 Construction of Privacy Type Model

3.3.1 Construction Principles of Privacy Type Model

In the process of building the privacy type model, this chapter is based on multiple dimensions and methods and follows a series of detailed and scientific principles. These principles are not only reasonable in theory but also highly operational and adaptable in practical applications. The following are the main principles followed in this study when building the privacy type model.

Contextual Principle

The contextual principle emphasizes that the way humans interact with generative AI and the types of private information involved may differ significantly in different contexts. Therefore, when building a privacy type model, it must be based on different interaction scenarios to provide a reference for the identification of privacy types. This principle ensures that the privacy-type model is suitable for the complex and varied practical applications of generative artificial intelligence. In privacy research, the concept of context has been widely used. Based on the contextual integrity theory, this chapter identified common interaction contexts for generative artificial intelligence, through content analysis and a literature review, and explored the common types of private information in each context. In order to comprehensively understand the privacy needs in different contexts, this study analyzed a variety of interaction contexts. In an educational context, private information may include student grades, etc.; in a medical context, private information may involve diagnostic records, etc. This classification helps this study to conduct specific analysis and identification of different contexts when building a privacy type model.

Developmental Principle

The developmental principle advocates continuous evaluation and optimization. At each stage of model construction, this study conducted detailed data analysis, supplemented by user interviews at certain stages, and continuously adjusted and optimized the privacy classification based on feedback. In order to ensure the dynamic adaptability and continuous improvement capabilities of the model, this study adopted an iterative approach during the construction process. At each iterative stage, this study will conduct a detailed evaluation, fully compare and analyze various data to ensure the accuracy and applicability of the model, and continuously improve the privacy classification. In addition, supplemented by user interviews at certain stages, this study was able to continuously adjust and optimize the privacy classification based on the real feedback of users on the privacy classification. For example, LDA topic modeling was used to verify the rationality of the privacy classification and ultimately determine the privacy type.

Openness Principle

The openness principle emphasizes the open feedback of users in the process of privacy information classification. Studies have shown that users' privacy needs and expectations change over time or in different situations, so the model needs to have a certain degree of flexibility (Wong & Mulligan, 2019). This study allows users to label information based on the privacy type model initially identified in this study. Users can not only label information based on the privacy type provided by the model, but also other types of privacy information. In the follow-up, this study will further understand users' views and expectations on privacy classification through open interviews and adjust and optimize the model. This process ensures that the privacy classification model is always open to various types of data and feedback during construction.

3.3.2 Data Sampling Strategy

Dataset

This study focused on using ShareGPT-related datasets in the process of building a privacy type model. ShareGPT is a Chrome extension that supports users to share chat records with ChatGPT. The ShareGPT-CN dataset[1] used in this study is public data based on the ShareGPT extension. ChatGPT is a typical representative of generative artificial intelligence. As a large-scale dataset containing 38,558 chat records between users and ChatGPT, it provides an excellent reference for this study to identify the privacy involved in the interaction between humans and generative artificial intelligence. Since the original chat records of ShareGPT involve multiple languages, and the follow-up of this study involves inviting some Chinese generative artificial intelligence users to annotate data, in order to facilitate user participation, the ShareGPT-CN dataset selected in this study is a version that has been translated from the original chat records into Chinese.

This dataset includes both user questions and ChatGPT answers. Each chat record between a user and ChatGPT may involve one round of conversation or multiple rounds, but each chat record is identified by a unique ID, which facilitates this study to identify a specific conversation set. It is worth mentioning that ShareGPT-related datasets have been widely used for model training and fine-tuning in previous studies, and their availability and quality have been well-proven in academic research (Mu et al., 2023; Ouyang et al., 2023; The Vicuna Team, 2023; H. Zhang et al., 2023; Z. Zhang et al., 2024). The conversations in the ShareGPT-CN dataset cover a variety of life scenarios and information needs, providing a rich corpus for the privacy identification task of this study.

Preliminary Judgment of Large Language Model

In the process of building a privacy-type model, the data needs to be preliminarily screened to identify conversation data containing private information. To achieve this goal, this study used the Llama-2-7b model[2] to conduct a preliminary analysis of the conversation data set between users and ChatGPT in the ShareGPT-CN dataset. The main purpose of this step is to preliminarily screen and identify the user conversation data set through the powerful analysis capabilities of the large language model to find out the data that may contain private information. This stage not only lays the foundation for

---

[1] https://huggingface.co/datasets/FreedomIntelligence/ShareGPT-CN
[2] https://llama.meta.com/llama2/

subsequent data analysis, but also effectively improves the efficiency of private information identification. The Llama2 series of large language models was released by Meta in 2023. This is a set of pre-trained and fine-tuned generative text models trained on 2 trillion tokens. Among them, Llama-2-7b has a scale of 7 billion parameters. The model is based on the Transformer architecture and is designed and trained to understand and generate natural language. The Llama model performs well in multiple natural language processing tasks, including text generation, text classification, question-answering systems, etc. These features make it an ideal choice for identifying private information.

In this study, the Llama-2-7b model is used to determine whether the conversation dataset between users and ChatGPT in the ShareGPT-CN dataset involves privacy. These conversation data contain the interactive content between users and ChatGPT, which is diverse and complex. By making a preliminary judgment on these data, the Llama-2-7b model can identify data texts containing potential privacy information, laying the foundation for subsequent detailed analysis. Based on the privacy identification instructions and the privacy information features learned during the training process, the Llama-2-7b model analyzes and judges each piece of data in the ShareGPT-CN dataset, automatically identifying and marking data that may contain privacy information. According to the recognition results of the Llama-2-7b model, the dataset is divided into two categories, one is the data judged by the model to contain privacy information, and the other is the data judged by the model to not contain privacy information. Through the preliminary judgment of Llama-2-7b, this study obtained a conversation dataset containing private information, including 3,460 chat records between users and ChatGPT, and the chat records in the remaining ShareGPT-CN dataset were classified as data that does not contain private information.

Although the Llama-2-7b model showed strong private information recognition capabilities in the preliminary judgment stage, this process still has some limitations. First, the model's judgment depends on its training data and algorithm. For certain types of private information, the model may not accurately recognize it. Secondly, the model's automated judgment lacks human review and may result in misjudgment. Therefore, the preliminary judgment results need to be further verified and corrected through subsequent research. In other words, the judgment of the Llama-2-7b model at this stage is only a preliminary screening and cannot be used as the final result. These data, marked as possibly containing private information, need further human review and confirmation. This study preliminarily regards the 3,460 chat records containing private information as data texts involving privacy-related users and ChatGPT, and further analyzes them in subsequent research. It can be said

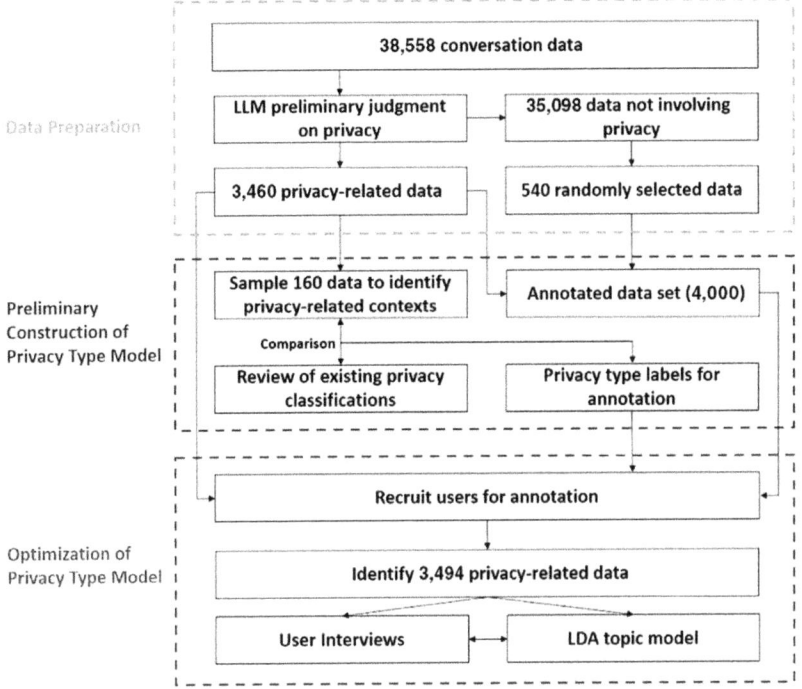

Figure 3.1 Overall research steps

that these preliminary judgment results reduce the workload for subsequent experiments, making the experimental process such as user labeling more targeted and efficient. In the following subsections, this study will describe in detail the specific methods and results of how to further analyze these data to build a privacy type model. The overall research steps are shown in Figure 3.1.

3.3.3 Privacy-related Contexts Identification

When building a privacy type model, identifying the interaction context between humans and generative AI is a crucial step. This process not only helps to more comprehensively understand the privacy needs of users in different contexts, but also provides basic support for the refined design of the privacy type model. Since this study hopes to analyze the contexts involved in the disclosure of privacy information, this study sampled the privacy information judged by the Llama-2-7b model. This study qualitatively coded 40 chat records randomly selected from 3,460 chat records containing privacy information each time. When sampling to the fourth batch, no new typical contexts appeared. Therefore, this study finally qualitatively coded the data of 160 chat records, and we believe that the coded data had reached saturation.

Qualitative coding is guided by the contextual integrity theory. When identifying the contexts involving privacy in the interaction between humans and generative AI, it focuses on the sender, subject, and type of information involved in the chat records to better judge the context of the conversation. Through the analysis of chat record data, this study extracted six types of privacy-related situations in the interaction between humans and generative AI. These situations cover the main interactions between users and generative AI in life, study, work, and other fields. The following will quote relevant texts in the data and explain the six types of situations in combination with existing research. In order to minimize the potential harm to the privacy of relevant individuals or groups in the dataset, we deleted all private information in the cited data and replaced it with the specific information type corresponding to the text.

Study and Education Consultation

Study and education consultation is one of the common scenarios in which users use generative AI. Existing studies have shown that users often use generative AI for complex learning or research that traditional search engines cannot help with, including learning new languages (Wolf & Maier, 2024). In this scenario, the senders of information are mainly students, who may use generative AI to assist them in improving their learning methods, acquiring academic resources, and writing relevant applications.

For example, a user proposed in a conversation with ChatGPT:

> I am looking for an internship in *** (work direction) this summer. I hope to rewrite this introduction into a better summary of myself: As a *** (school name) *** (grade) *** (major) student ... I am interested in using *** (expertise) to focus on *** (tool name) for *** (skills).

Daily Life Consultation

In daily life consultation scenarios, users interact with generative AI in a wide range of areas, including various matters in daily life, such as cooking suggestions, time management, travel recommendations, etc. (Dwivedi et al., 2023).

For example, a user asked in a conversation with ChatGPT:

> Today, I need to pick up my child from school at *** (specific time), arrange and make a meal plan, buy groceries, write an article, shoot a YouTube video, mow the

lawn, pick up my child from school at *** (specific time), and have dinner with friends at *** (specific time). Make a schedule for me. Show it in a table.

Another user asked:

Can you help me plan the activities to do during a week-long vacation in *** (specific location)? We will land in *** (specific location) at *** (specific time) and depart from *** (specific location) again at *** (specific time). We will bring *** (pets) and rent *** (rental items). We will spend most of the nights in a house in *** (specific location) and want to spend one night in *** (specific location). During this week, we want to spend time with *** (pets) on the beach and visit *** (specific location).

Financial Consumption Consultation

Financial consumption consultation mainly involves the interaction between users and generative AI in financial management and consumption decisions. Users may seek advice or information from generative AI in financial-related scenarios, such as financial management advice, budget planning, and consumption advice (Dwivedi et al., 2023).

For example, a user asked in a conversation with ChatGPT:

*** (another person in a relationship) and I are both nearly *** (age). We want to invest for our retirement. We live in *** (specific area). We have about *** (specific amount) of income each year. Is there any good investment guide? How much money do we need to invest and what methods do we choose to have enough money in retirement?

Another user asked:

I have a debt that is due in *** (specific month) for *** (specific amount). If I pay it in advance, I only have to pay *** (specific amount) today. Considering the *** (country name) financial market, which is more worthwhile? Pay in advance to get a discount? Or invest the money so that it generates income before the due date?

Health and Medical Consultation

Health and medical consultation is another important context for users to interact with generative AI. Users may consult generative AI about health issues, disease prevention, treatment plans, etc., in health and medical related contexts.

For example, a user asked in a conversation with ChatGPT:

Make me a muscle-building diet plan with *** (specific number) calories and sufficient protein. I am *** (specific height), weigh *** (specific weight), work out *** (specific time)/day in the gym, and hope to gain weight to *** (specific weight).

> I hope this diet plan can be applied to pre-prepared meals, which means it can be kept in the refrigerator/freezer for a week.

Another user asked:

> My *** (body index) has always been above *** (specific number). Except for *** (food name), I have completely quit *** (food name). I don't feel *** (symptoms), and my *** (body index) is usually *** (condition). But I suspect that I may not drink enough water every day. My height is *** (specific height), weight is *** (specific weight), and blood pressure is usually *** (blood pressure range). Considering all this, why does my *** (body index) still remain above *** (specific number)?

Social and Emotional Consultation

Users often seek advice or support from generative AI in social and emotional contexts. Studies have shown that users may use ChatGPT to brainstorm when giving gifts to others, or consult ChatGPT when preparing emails or greeting cards for them (Wolf & Maier, 2024). In such contexts, users interact with generative AI on interpersonal relationships, emotional distress, and other aspects.

For example, a user asked in a conversation with ChatGPT:

> What should I buy for my lab colleague as a secret Christmas gift? The gift should be relatively cheap. He was born in *** (city name) and grew up in *** (city name). He received *** (degree) in *** (school name) and is now studying *** (major) *** (degree) in *** (school name). His research involves *** (research direction). He likes *** (music genre), especially *** (album name). He recently lost *** (item name) at the airport on his way back from *** (conference name). He likes *** (specific hobby).

Another user made a request:

> Write an email in *** (language) to my *** (relationship with the user) *** (other person's name). I am *** (own name). Explain to her in a calm and matter-of-fact way that I will no longer contact her. I will only contact her if something very serious happens to *** (relationship with the user).

Work Affairs Consultation

Users may seek advice or information in the context of career development and work task management. For example, a user asked in a conversation with ChatGPT:

> My name is *** (my name), currently living in *** (city name) as *** (occupation). My best friend and business partner is *** (other person's name), a *** (occupation). We both run a *** (group direction) group called *** (group name),

working with *** (occupation) *** (other person's name). Can you help me write a thoughtful and compassionate email to an investor interested in a startup in *** (location)?

Another user requested:

Please help write an opening statement for *** (city name) *** (court name) *** (case number). I represent the plaintiff *** (other person's name). *** (other person's name) was injured in *** (specific incident) and is now suing the company where *** (occupation) works.

3.3.4 Preliminary Construction of Privacy Type Model

Existing Privacy Classifications

The classification of privacy in laws, regulations, and relevant literature is an important reference for building the privacy type model. When analyzing privacy issues in the process of human interaction with generative artificial intelligence, understanding and following existing privacy classification policies can not only ensure the legality and compliance of the privacy type model, but also make it better to meet social needs.

Some laws and regulations involve specific interpretations and regulations on different types of privacy information. These laws and regulations are usually formulated by governments or certain institutions within a region to regulate the collection, storage, use, and sharing of data. The EU's General Data Protection Regulation is one of the most stringent data protection laws in the world and has detailed requirements for the processing of personal data. The General Data Protection Regulation defines personal data as "any information related to an identified or identifiable (directly or indirectly) natural person." China's Personal Information Protection Law also has clear provisions on the processing of personal information, with special emphasis on the protection of sensitive personal information. It points out that sensitive personal information is "various information related to an identified or identifiable natural person recorded electronically or otherwise." The California Privacy Rights Act of the United States has set high transparency and responsibility requirements for the collection and processing of personal data to ensure that users' privacy rights are protected. It points out that personal sensitive information refers to information that identifies, relates to, describes a specific individual or family, can be reasonably associated with a specific individual or family directly or indirectly, or may be reasonably associated with a specific consumer or family. There are also some other countries' relevant laws that explain privacy information. Switzerland's Federal Data Protection Act and Brazil's General Data Protection Act both point out that personal privacy information is information related to an identified or identifiable natural person. The above laws and regulations, as well as the US Department of Homeland Security's "Sensitive Personally Identifiable Information Protection Manual" and the US National Institute of Standards and Technology's "Guidelines for Confidentiality Protection of Personally Identifiable Information" all provide more specific enumeration or description of the types of information involved in privacy. In addition, a large number of academic studies have conducted detailed classification and analysis of privacy types. These studies provide theoretical support for the construction of the privacy type model. Combined with these laws, regulations and literature research, this study summarizes the existing privacy classifications (see Table 3.1).

Table 3.1 *Summary of existing privacy classifications*

Laws and Regulations/ Literature	Privacy Classifications
Federal Act on Data Protection, 2023[a]	Sensitive information such as religious belief information; health information; ethnicity information; genetic information; biometric information; legal information; social assistance information, etc.
China's Personal Information Protection Law, 2021[b]	Sensitive information such as biometrics, religious beliefs, specific identities, medical health, financial accounts, whereabouts, and personal information of minors under the age of fourteen
California Privacy Rights Act, 2020[c]	Identity information; biometric information; consumption information; work information; location data; online activity information; education information; personal information related to inferred individual traits, psychological tendencies, preferences, beliefs and abilities, as well as sensitive information such as health information
Brazilian General Data Protection Law, 2020[d]	Sensitive information such as racial information; religious belief information; social identity information; health information; genetic information, etc.
General Data Protection Regulation, 2018[e]	Personal identifiers; physiological and psychological; psychological information; genetic information; economic information; cultural information; social identity information, etc.
Handbook on the Protection of Sensitive Personally Identifiable Information, 2017[f]	Personal identification number; financial account number; biometrics; citizenship or immigration status; medical information; ethnicity or religious beliefs; personal email; address; account passwords; date of birth; criminal record; mother's maiden name

Table 3.1 (*cont.*)

Laws and Regulations/ Literature	Privacy Classifications
Guide to Protecting the Confidentiality of Personally Identifiable Information, 2010[g]	Name; personal identification number; address information; electronic asset information; telephone number; personal characteristics; information identifying an individual's property; personal information related to or linkable to any of the above
Chua et al. (2021)	Life behavior information; socioeconomic information; whereabouts information; financial information; authentication information; medical and health information
Rumbold and Pierscionek (2018)	Information about human–computer interactions; demographic data; behavior, thoughts and opinions; overt individual characteristics; medical or health care data
Milne et al. (2017)	Basic demographic data; personal preferences; contact information; social interactions; financial information; security identifiers
Robinson (2017)	Contact information; payment information; life history; financial/medical information; work-related information; online account information
Finn et al. (2013)	Privacy of personal identity; privacy of behavior and actions; privacy of personal communications; privacy of data and images; privacy of thoughts and feelings; privacy of location and space; privacy of interactions (including group privacy)
Leon et al. (2013)	Browsing Information; Computer Information; Demographic Information; Location Information; Personally Identifiable Information
Smith et al. (2011)	Employment information; identity information; consumer information; medical information; financial information; behavioral information
Phelps et al. (2000)	Demographic characteristics; lifestyle characteristics (including media habits); shopping/purchasing habits; financial data; personal identifiers

[a] www.fedlex.admin.ch/eli/cc/2022/491/en
[b] www.gov.cn/xinwen/2021-08/20/content_5632486.htm
[c] https://thecpra.org/
[d] https://lgpd-brazil.info/
[e] https://gdpr.eu/tag/gdpr/
[f] www.dhs.gov/publication/handbook-safeguarding-sensitive-personally-identifiable-information
[g] https://csrc.nist.gov/pubs/sp/800/122/final

It can be seen that privacy classifications in different fields and backgrounds have their own unique focus and protection needs. When constructing a privacy type model, it is necessary to comprehensively consider these classification perspectives and protection requirements to ensure the comprehensiveness and applicability of the model. Based on this, this study merged the same or similar privacy types in different laws, regulations or literature in the existing privacy classifications. Subsequently, this study identified more than three similar items as generally recognized privacy types and sorted out the types based on the information content involved in the covered similar items. Finally, this study identified nine privacy types, including online activity information, education information, health information, preference information, location information, financial consumption information, personal identity information, social relationship information, and work information.

Comparison of Existing Classifications and Identified Contexts

The construction of the privacy type model needs to refer to the existing privacy classification and combine it with specific interaction scenarios to ensure that the model can cover all common types of privacy information. This study has identified nine privacy types through legal regulations and literature analysis. Next, these privacy types will be compared with the identified actual interaction scenarios to determine whether the identified privacy types cover the common privacy information in these scenarios.

In terms of learning and education consultation, users use generative artificial intelligence to seek advice or information in learning and education-related scenarios, which may involve privacy information such as the user's or related individuals' educational background (such as school name, major), learning needs (such as specific learning goals, academic interests), and academic performance (such as test scores, course grades). The privacy protection requirements for this scenario are relatively high, because educational information is usually highly personal and directly related to an individual's learning performance and potential future career development. Among the nine identified privacy types, educational information and personal identity information can better cover the privacy information involved in this scenario.

In terms of daily life consultation, this scenario may involve individual living habits (such as daily schedules), location information (such as the individual's geographical location, places often visited), personal preferences (such as dietary preferences, travel preferences), etc. Once this information is leaked, it may cause the user or the relevant individual's life to be disturbed or even cause security risks. Among the nine identified privacy types, location information and preference information can better cover the privacy information involved in this scenario.

In terms of financial consumption consultation, this scenario may involve the user's financial status (such as bank accounts, investment status), consumption records (such as shopping lists, transaction records), financial planning (such as monthly budgets, long-term financial goals) information, etc. The information related to financial consumption scenarios is extremely sensitive, and any information leakage may lead to economic losses and security risks. Therefore, privacy protection in this scenario is crucial. Among the nine identified privacy types, financial consumption information and online activity information can better cover the privacy information involved in this scenario.

In terms of health and medical consultation, this scenario may involve the user's health status (such as medical history, diagnosis results), medical records (visit records, drug use), health habits (such as exercise plans), etc. The privacy protection requirements for health information are very strict, because the disclosure of such information may have a serious impact on the privacy and mental health of users, and also involve legal and ethical issues. Among the nine identified privacy types, health information and personal identity information can better cover the privacy information involved in this context.

In terms of social-emotional counseling, this type of context may involve the user's social relationships (such as friends, family, etc.), emotional state (such as mental health, emotional problems), private interactions (such as private communication content with others), and so on. The privacy information in this context is usually sensitive, and often involves the personal identity information of other individuals with whom the user has a social relationship, and its disclosure may have an impact on the social and emotional life of the user or the people around him. Among the nine identified privacy types, social relationship information and preference opinion information can better cover the privacy information involved in this context.

In terms of work affairs consultation, this type of scenario may involve the user's career information (such as work experience, career planning), project details (such as project progress, task allocation), company information (such as company strategy, team structure), etc. The privacy protection of work affairs information is more important to the user's career development and company interests, and the leakage of related information may lead to occupational risks and the leakage of commercial secrets. Among the nine identified privacy types, work information can better encompass the privacy information involved in this scenario.

It can be seen that the nine privacy types determined based on the existing privacy classification basically cover the privacy information involved in different interaction scenarios. Therefore, this study takes these nine privacy types as the core, preliminarily constructs a privacy type model, and identifies the common types of privacy information in each scenario. In the next step, the privacy type model will be optimized and verified through user labeling experiments to ensure its accuracy and effectiveness in practical applications.

3.3.5 Optimization of Privacy Type Model

User Annotation Experiment

Based on the privacy judgment results of the Llama-2-7b model on the data set, this study conducted a user labeling experiment, allowing users to browse specific conversation data and label the privacy types contained in it according to the initially constructed privacy type model. The user labeling experiment is a method of identifying private information through manual review and subjective judgment, which can make up for the shortcomings of large models in the identification of complex private information. It is a further confirmation and refinement of the preliminary judgment results of the large model, and also a verification and optimization of the initially constructed privacy type model. Through the labeling and classification of data by actual users, this study can more accurately identify and classify private information. The work at this stage will combine the subjective judgment of users and the automated analysis of large language models to further improve the accuracy and practicality of the privacy type model.

Specifically, in terms of the selection of labeled data, this study selected all data that the model believes contains private information from the judgment results of the Llama-2-7b model, involving chat records of 3,460 users with ChatGPT. At the same time, this study randomly selected 540 pieces of data from the remaining data that the model believes does not contain private information and integrated them to form 4,000 pieces of data. Subsequently, this study used the Easydata data annotation service platform provided by Baidu to recruit users to annotate these data, asking users to annotate the text in each piece of data that they believe to be private information, and using labels to classify these texts into ten categories. These ten categories include the nine privacy categories in the privacy type model initially constructed in this study. At the same time, in order to prevent the existence of information that some users believe to be private but does not belong to the nine privacy categories in the privacy type model, this study added a tenth category to the annotation label, namely other privacy-related information.

This study recruited twelve users with experience in using generative artificial intelligence from college students. These users came from different majors and grades, covering students who are pursuing bachelor's degrees, master's degrees and doctoral degrees, with diverse professional backgrounds and perspectives. They use generative artificial intelligence almost every day, indicating that they have relatively rich experience in using generative artificial intelligence and are a potential group that discloses privacy in the process of interacting with it. Before officially starting the annotation experiment, it was necessary to conduct systematic training for the participating users. Therefore, after the recruitment, this study trained the users who participated in the annotation, introduced the platform used for annotation, explained the specific annotation process, and provided detailed privacy type classification instructions and examples to ensure that they understood the definition of privacy and the connotation of the ten labels involved in the annotation, and had a unified understanding and judgment in the annotation process.

Subsequently, this study divided the twelve users into three groups, with four users in each group, and assigned the same 4,000 data to users in different groups. Each user in each group was responsible for annotating 1,000 data. Through such data allocation, each piece of data was independently annotated by three users, which facilitated cross-validation based on the annotation results of multiple people to improve the accuracy and reliability of the annotation results. During the annotation process, users reviewed and annotated the assigned data one by one. The annotation work mainly involves two steps. The first step is to determine whether a piece of data contains privacy information. The second step is to further annotate the specific type of privacy according to the preset label if it contains privacy information.

Annotation Result Analysis

After completing the user labeling experiment, this study analyzed the labeling results. By combining user labeling and the judgment results of the large model, a basis can be provided for the optimization of the privacy type model. First, this study sorted out the labeling results of three users who labeled the same data and recorded whether each data contained private information and the specific privacy category. The labeling results of the three users were compared with the judgment results of the large model, and the consistency was calculated. If three or more of the four results (the judgment results of the large model and the labeling results of the three users) believed that the data involved private information, it was determined to be data containing privacy, with a total of 3,494 pieces. Subsequently, for the data containing private information, the specific privacy categories involved and the distribution of each category of private information were counted to understand the proportion and frequency of different categories of private information in the data set. For example, this study found that work information and personal identity information were categories with higher frequency, while health information and financial consumption information were relatively rare. At the same time, this study analyzed the consistency of user labeling results to understand the degree of consistency of users in labeling different categories of private information. In the annotation of work information and health information, the consistency is high, while in the annotation of preference opinion information and online activity information, the consistency is low, indicating that these categories of privacy information are more subjective and complex.

After completing the systematic analysis of the annotation results, this study entered the verification and adjustment stage of the privacy type model. The main goal of this stage is to optimize and refine the privacy categories based on user feedback and LDA topic modeling analysis, so as to build a more accurate, comprehensive, and practical privacy type model. Based on the analysis results of the annotation data, this study first conducted user interviews to gain an in-depth understanding of the users' specific experiences, problems encountered, and suggestions during the annotation process. The purpose of this link is to further improve and optimize the privacy type model through the subjective feedback of users.

Through the integration and analysis of user feedback, this study identified the following aspects that need to be adjusted. First, some users proposed improvement suggestions for the names and definitions of some privacy categories by replacing the wording. For example, the "opinion" in the category of preference opinion information cannot well summarize future plans, personal beliefs, and other contents; the personal belongings mentioned in some data are closely related to financial consumption information, but it is difficult to simply summarize them with the category of financial consumption information. Second, users also pointed out that they found some privacy information categories that were not covered by the nine privacy type labels, and they classified them into other privacy-related information. For example, some data mentioned the human or natural environment around them. Based on this, this study adjusted the nine privacy categories in the privacy type model to work information, location environment information, health information, preference and thought information, online activity information, social relationship information, personal identity information, property consumption information, and education information.

In order to further verify and optimize the privacy classification model, this study introduced the Latent Dirichlet Allocation (LDA) topic modeling technology. LDA topic modeling is a commonly used text analysis method that can effectively classify and summarize large-scale text data by identifying potential topics in text. First, this study selected 3,494 data that were finally determined to contain privacy information and performed data preprocessing, including text cleaning and stop word removal. Subsequently, this study used the LDA topic modeling algorithm to train the preprocessed data to determine the optimal number of topics.

This study determined that the optimal number of topics was nine, through consistency analysis, as shown in Figure 3.2. Finally, this study parsed the topics output by the LDA model to identify the main content of each topic. The

Table 3.2 *LDA topic modeling results*

Topic	High frequency words	Corresponding privacy type
Topic 1	Website, Email, Campaign, Page, Test, Tip, Platform, Marketing, Tool, Database	Online activity information
Topic 2	Students, courses, learning, research, conferences, attending, professional, community, education, teachers	Education information
Topic 3	Exercise, doctor, health, pain, muscle, suffer, treatment, care, calories, medicine	Health information
Topic 4	Idea, video, ad, like, model, campaign, title, feature, type, language	Preference and thought information
Topic 5	Travel, miles, attractions, solar, path, meals, immigration, company, history, menu	Location and environment information
Topic 6	Pay, assess, fees, services, items, legal, categories, check, style, unique	Property and consumption information
Topic 7	Name, industry, scene, weekly, birthday, weight, children, establishment, Muslim, email	Personal identity information
Topic 8	Media, social, client, account, form, Instagram, friends, post, script, designer	Social relationship information
Topic 9	Work, company, team, project, product, position, sales, manager, management, profession	Work information

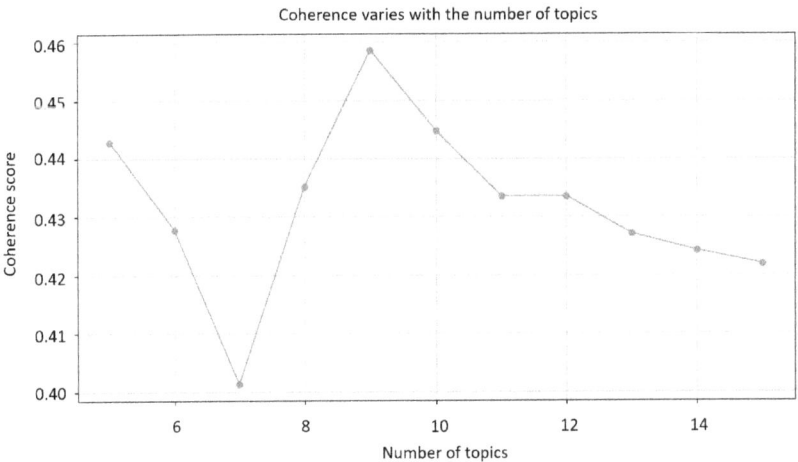

Figure 3.2 Relationship between coherence score and number of topics modeled by LDA

main words in the nine topic categories output by the LDA model are shown in Table 3.2. Figure 3.3 shows an example of visualization of high-frequency words in Topic 1.

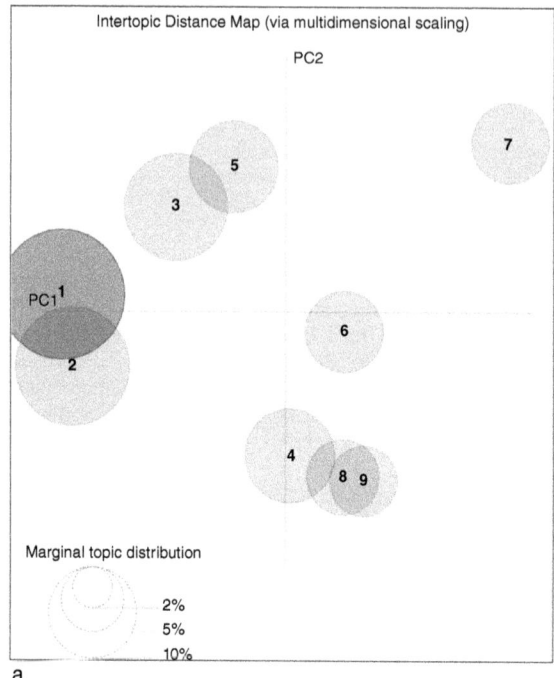

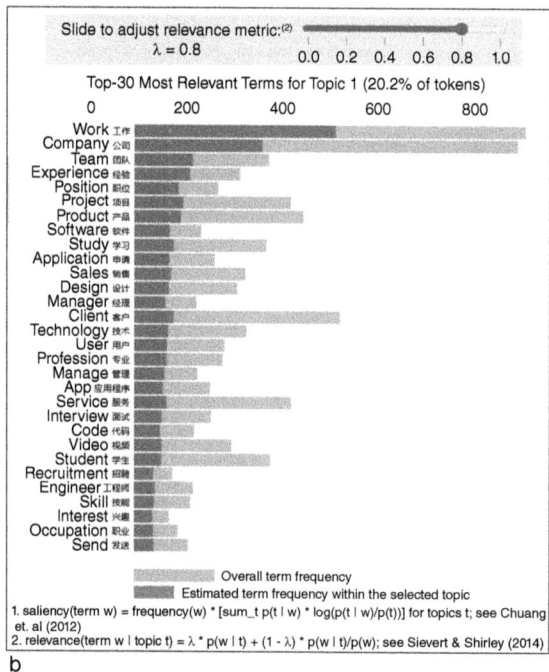

Figure 3.3 Visualization results of LDA model for privacy text

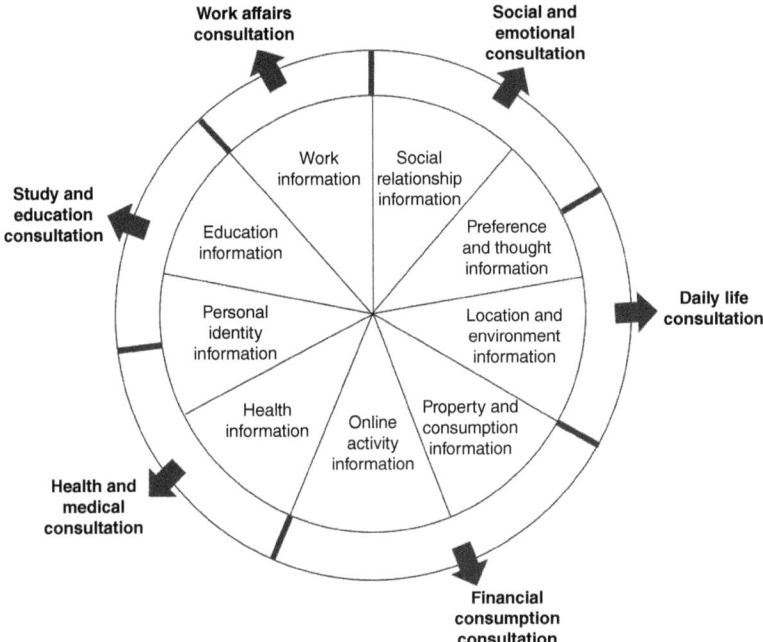

Figure 3.4 Privacy type model

It can be seen that the results of the LDA topic modeling analysis are consistent with the privacy types determined in this study, both in terms of quantity and the main content involved in each topic. Through this series of verification steps, this study finally determined the optimized privacy type model, as shown in Figure 3.4, which provides a solid foundation for privacy protection in the interaction between humans and generative artificial intelligence.

3.4 Application Value of Privacy Type Model

The application value of the privacy type model in the interaction between humans and generative AI is reflected in many aspects, especially in the fields of knowledge sharing, search, misinformation processing, health information management, and scientific discovery. With the widespread application of generative AI in these fields, privacy protection issues have become increasingly important. The privacy type model can not only help developers and users better understand and deal with privacy risks but also improve the credibility and user satisfaction of generative AI. This section will discuss in detail the potential application value of the privacy type model in the discussed fields.

3.4.1 Application Value in the Field of Knowledge Sharing

On knowledge sharing platforms, generative AI is often used for personalized knowledge recommendation, providing customized knowledge content by analyzing user behavior data and interest preferences. Knowledge sharing platforms bring together a large amount of user-generated content and interaction records, which are very important for providing personalized services and improving platform functions. However, these data also contain users' personal information and learning habits, which may lead to privacy leakage if not handled properly. The privacy type model can help platforms identify and classify these data, take different protection measures according to their sensitivity, and ensure user privacy security. For example, the model can distinguish between general behavior data and data containing personal identity information and take more stringent protection measures for the latter.

In the intelligent question-answering system, users may ask questions involving personal privacy, such as career planning and health issues. The privacy type model can monitor and identify this sensitive information in real-time, remind users in time, and take protective measures to avoid privacy leakage. At the same time, the platform can formulate corresponding privacy policies and user education content based on the privacy type model to enhance users' privacy protection awareness.

In addition, AI-supported crowdsourcing platforms promote knowledge sharing by gathering the wisdom of the masses. However, when participants contribute knowledge, they often need to provide personal information, which may lead to privacy leakage. The privacy type model can help identify and classify different types of privacy data to ensure that the privacy of participants is effectively protected during the knowledge sharing process. For example, in a crowdsourcing platform, the privacy type model can help automatically identify sensitive information, such as personal identity information and preference information, and take corresponding protective measures. At the same time, motivation plays an important role in crowdsourcing platforms, driving participants to actively contribute knowledge. The privacy type model can help understand and manage the privacy motivations of participants. For example, some participants may want to remain anonymous when sharing knowledge, while others may be willing to disclose their identities to obtain more reputation rewards. By applying the privacy type model, crowdsourcing platforms can provide personalized privacy protection measures based on the privacy preferences of different participants, thereby enhancing the enthusiasm and participation of participants.

3.4.2 Application Value in the Field of Information Search

The application of generative AI in search engines can provide personalized search results based on the user's search history and behavior data. These data usually contain the user's search preferences and interests, which may lead to privacy leakage if not handled properly.

Specifically, search engines collect a large amount of user search behavior data, which is very important for optimizing search algorithms and improving search quality. However, these data also contain a large amount of personal privacy information. The privacy type model can help search engines identify and classify these data, and take different protection measures according to their sensitivity to ensure user privacy security. For example, the model can help distinguish between general search data and data containing personal preferences. For search behavior data involving personal preferences, stricter data encryption and access control measures can be adopted.

The query terms entered by users on search engines may sometimes contain sensitive information, such as medical conditions, financial information, etc. The privacy type model can help identify these sensitive query terms and take corresponding privacy protection measures in the search results. For example, for query terms involving medical conditions, anonymized search results can be provided to avoid exposing users' privacy information.

3.4.3 Application Value in the Field of Misinformation Processing

The application of generative AI in misinformation detection can help identify and filter false information. However, during the detection process, it may be necessary to analyze a large amount of user data, including user-published content and interaction records. These data usually contain users' personal information and social relationships, which may lead to privacy leakage if not handled properly. Privacy type models can help identify and classify these data to ensure that sensitive information is properly protected. For example, the model can help distinguish between general published content and content containing personally identifiable information and take stricter protection measures for the latter.

When tracing the chain of false information propagation, it may be necessary to analyze interaction records and propagation paths involving multiple users. These data usually contain users' social relationships and interactive behaviors. Privacy type models can help identify and classify these data, and take different protection measures according to their sensitivity to ensure user privacy security. For example, for data involving social relationships, stricter data encryption and access control measures can be adopted.

In the process of correcting misinformation, generative AI may need to interact with users to collect user feedback and opinions. These interactive data usually contain users' personal information and opinions, which may lead to privacy leakage if not handled properly. Privacy type models can help distinguish between general feedback data and data containing personally identifiable information and take stricter protection measures for the latter.

In addition, on social media, AI can identify and handle false information through sentiment analysis. However, sentiment analysis usually requires the collection and analysis of a large amount of user data, which brings privacy risks. Privacy-type models can help AI systems protect user privacy when performing sentiment analysis. For example, privacy-type models can identify users' sensitive emotional expressions and anonymize these expressions to prevent user privacy leaks.

3.4.4 Application Value in the Field of Health Information Management

The application of generative AI in the field of health information includes online health consultation, disease prediction, etc. These applications involve a large amount of patient privacy data, such as medical history, diagnosis results, and treatment plans. Privacy type models can help identify and classify this data.

Specifically, in telemedicine services, doctors and patients may communicate in real-time through generative AI to provide medical advice and consulting services. In this case, patients may inadvertently disclose private information during the conversation. Privacy type models can analyze the content of the conversation in real-time, identify potential privacy risks, and warn or take protective measures when necessary to protect the privacy of patients.

When providing nursing services, caregivers usually need to obtain patients' health information. Generative AI can help optimize nursing services by analyzing the information behavior of caregivers. However, this also means that the operation behavior of caregivers and the health data of patients may be collected and analyzed, bringing privacy risks. Privacy type models can help identify and manage privacy data in the information behavior of caregivers, ensuring that user privacy is effectively protected during the information behavior analysis process.

In addition, medical institutions and research institutions usually collect a large amount of health data for scientific research and public health monitoring. However, these data also contain a large amount of personal privacy information, which may lead to privacy leakage if not handled properly. The privacy type model can help identify and classify this data, and take different protection measures according to its sensitivity to ensure patient privacy. For example, for health data involving personally identifiable information, stricter data encryption and access control measures can be adopted.

3.4.5 Application Value in the Field of Scientific Discovery

The application of generative AI in scientific research includes data analysis, model prediction, and so on. These applications usually involve a large amount of research data and experimental records, which may contain personal privacy information of research participants. Specifically, scientific research usually requires sharing research data to promote cooperation and verification of results. However, these shared data also contain a large amount of personal privacy information, which may lead to privacy leakage if not handled properly. Privacy type models can help identify and classify these data and take different protection measures according to their sensitivity. For example, for shared data involving personal identity information, data anonymization and strict access control measures can be adopted. When disseminating scientific research results, researchers may need to display and discuss data and results involving personal privacy information. Privacy type models can help identify and classify these data to ensure that sensitive information is properly protected. For example, the model can help researchers shield or anonymize personal privacy information during the presentation process to ensure the privacy security of research participants.

In addition, when conducting scientific research collaboration, researchers usually need to share and communicate scientific research data. AI can help optimize the scientific research collaboration process by analyzing scientific research collaboration behavior. However, this also means that the collaborative behavior and scientific research data of researchers may be collected and analyzed, bringing privacy risks. Privacy type models can help identify and manage privacy data in scientific research collaboration and ensure that privacy is effectively protected during the collaboration process.

In addition to its application value in specific fields, privacy type models also have general application directions, including personalized privacy protection and cross-domain privacy protection. With the development of AI technology, personalized privacy protection has become possible. Privacy type models can help understand and manage users' privacy preferences and provide personalized privacy protection measures. For example, privacy type models can dynamically adjust the encryption level and anonymization degree of data according to users' privacy preferences to provide personalized privacy protection services. With the widespread application of AI in different fields, cross-domain privacy protection has become increasingly important. Privacy type models can help identify and manage data privacy in different fields and provide a unified privacy protection framework. For example, privacy type models can formulate general privacy protection strategies and technical means based on the characteristics of data in different fields to ensure that data is effectively protected during cross-domain applications.

In summary, the application value of privacy type models in generative artificial intelligence and human interaction is reflected in many aspects. By applying privacy type models in fields such as knowledge sharing, information search, error information processing, health information management, and scientific discovery, different types of data can be effectively identified and classified. With the continuous development of generative AI technology, privacy-type models can be applied and promoted in more fields, providing users with safer and more reliable services.

3.5 Summary

This chapter explores the privacy issues in the interaction between humans and generative AI and proposes a systematic privacy type model, which aims to provide guidance for developers and users to ensure user privacy security. By analyzing the sources and operating mechanisms of privacy leakage in detail, the key issues in privacy protection are identified, and the existing privacy protection methods and their shortcomings are introduced. On this basis, the establishment of the privacy type model provides a theoretical basis and practical guidance for the privacy protection of generative AI in different application fields.

The application value of the privacy type model is reflected in many aspects, including knowledge sharing, information search, misinformation processing, health information management and scientific discovery. In these fields, the privacy type model can help identify and classify different types of data and provide reference for taking corresponding privacy protection measures, thereby reducing the risk of privacy leakage and improving the credibility and user satisfaction of generative AI. The privacy type model not only provides a systematic privacy protection framework for developers and users, but also lays a solid foundation for the healthy development of generative AI.

However, there are still many challenges in privacy protection. First of all, privacy protection needs to balance the relationship between data utilization and user privacy. Finding a balance between providing personalized services and protecting user privacy is a key issue in privacy protection. Secondly, with the development of technology, privacy protection technology also needs to be continuously updated and improved to cope with new privacy threats. Finally, privacy protection requires the joint efforts of all sectors of society, including the participation of policymakers, technology developers, users, etc., to jointly promote the development of privacy protection.

Future research can further explore the specific implementation methods and effect evaluation of the privacy type model in different application scenarios, explore the combination of the privacy type model with other privacy protection technologies, and improve the overall level of privacy protection. At the same time, it is also necessary to strengthen the cultivation of user privacy protection awareness, guide users to actively participate in privacy protection, and jointly build a safe and reliable generative AI application environment. In short, the proposal and application of the privacy type model further clarify the key information types involved in privacy protection, provide a reference for privacy protection in the interaction between humans and generative artificial intelligence, and provide strong support for the healthy development of generative AI.

Acknowledgments

This work was supported by the National Natural Science Foundation of China (No. 92370112) and the Innovative Research Group Project of Hubei Provincial Natural Science Foundation (No. 2023AFA012).

References

Abadi, M., Chu, A., Goodfellow, I., McMahan, H. B., Mironov, I., Talwar, K., & Zhang, L. (2016). Deep Learning with Differential Privacy. *Proceedings of the 2016 ACM SIGSAC Conference on Computer and Communications Security*, 308–318. https://doi.org/10.1145/2976749.2978318

Apthorpe, N., Varghese, S., & Feamster, N. (2019). Evaluating the Contextual Integrity of Privacy Regulation: Parents' {IoT} Toy Privacy Norms Versus {COPPA}, 123–140. www.usenix.org/conference/usenixsecurity19/presentation/apthorpe

Baidoo-anu, D., & Ansah, L. O. (2023). Education in the Era of Generative Artificial Intelligence (AI): Understanding the Potential Benefits of ChatGPT in Promoting Teaching and Learning. *Journal of AI*, 7(1), 52–62. https://doi.org/10.61969/jai.1337500

Brown, T., Mann, B., Ryder, N., Subbiah, M., Kaplan, J. D., Dhariwal, P., Neelakantan, A., Shyam, P., Sastry, G., Askell, A., Agarwal, S., Herbert-Voss, A., Krueger, G.,

Henighan, T., Child, R., Ramesh, A., Ziegler, D., Wu, J., Winter, C., ... Amodei, D. (2020). Language Models are Few-Shot Learners. *Advances in Neural Information Processing Systems, 33*, 1877–1901. https://proceedings.neurips.cc/paper/2020/hash/1457c0d6bfcb4967418bfb8ac142f64a-Abstract.html

Carlini, N., Tramèr, F., Wallace, E., Jagielski, M., Herbert-Voss, A., Lee, K., Roberts, A., Brown, T., Song, D., Erlingsson, Ú., Oprea, A., & Raffel, C. (2021). Extracting Training Data from Large Language Models. *30th USENIX Security Symposium*, 2633–2650. www.usenix.org/conference/usenixsecurity21/presentation/carlini-extracting

Cascella, M., Montomoli, J., Bellini, V., & Bignami, E. (2023). Evaluating the Feasibility of ChatGPT in Healthcare: An Analysis of Multiple Clinical and Research Scenarios. *Journal of Medical Systems, 47*(1), 33. https://doi.org/10.1007/s10916-023-01925-4

Chang, D., Krupka, E. L., Adar, E., & Acquisti, A. (2016). Engineering Information Disclosure: Norm Shaping Designs. *Proceedings of the 2016 CHI Conference on Human Factors in Computing Systems*, 587–597. https://doi.org/10.1145/2858036.2858346

Chen, L., Sun, L., & Han, J. (2023). A Comparison Study of Human and Machine-Generated Creativity. *Journal of Computing and Information Science in Engineering, 23*(051012). https://doi.org/10.1115/1.4062232

Choi, J. H., Hickman, K. E., Monahan, A. B., & Schwarcz, D. (2021). ChatGPT Goes to Law School. *Journal of Legal Education, 71*, 387.

Chua, H. N., Ooi, J. S., & Herbland, A. (2021). The Effects of Different Personal Data Categories on Information Privacy Concern and Disclosure. *Computers & Security, 110*, 102453. https://doi.org/10.1016/j.cose.2021.102453

Deng, J., Dong, W., Socher, R., Li, L.-J., Li, K., & Fei-Fei, L. (2009). ImageNet: A Large-scale Hierarchical Image Database. *2009 IEEE Conference on Computer Vision and Pattern Recognition*, 248–255. https://doi.org/10.1109/CVPR.2009.5206848

Dockhorn, T., Cao, T., Vahdat, A., & Kreis, K. (2023). Differentially Private Diffusion Models [arXiv preprint]. arXiv:2210.09929. https://doi.org/10.48550/arXiv.2210.09929

Dwivedi, Y. K., Kshetri, N., Hughes, L., Slade, E. L., Jeyaraj, A., Kar, A. K., Baabdullah, A. M., Koohang, A., Raghavan, V., Ahuja, M., Albanna, H., Albashrawi, M. A., Al-Busaidi, A. S., Balakrishnan, J., Barlette, Y., Basu, S., Bose, I., Brooks, L., Buhalis, D., ... Wright, R. (2023). Opinion Paper: "So What if ChatGPT Wrote It?" Multidisciplinary Perspectives on Opportunities, Challenges and Implications of Generative Conversational AI for Research, Practice and Policy. *International Journal of Information Management, 71*, 102642. https://doi.org/10.1016/j.ijinfomgt.2023.102642

Dwork, C., & Roth, A. (2014). The Algorithmic Foundations of Differential Privacy. *Foundations and Trends® in Theoretical Computer Science, 9*(3–4), 211–407. https://doi.org/10.1561/0400000042

Estrada, S. (2023, March 1). A Startup CFO used ChatGPT to Build an FP&A tool: Here's How It Went. *Fortune*. https://fortune.com/2023/03/01/startup-cfo-chatgpt-finance-tool/

Finn, R. L., Wright, D., & Friedewald, M. (2013). Seven Types of Privacy. In S. Gutwirth, R. Leenes, P. de Hert, & Y. Poullet (eds.), *European Data Protection:*

Coming of Age (pp. 3–32). Springer Netherlands. https://doi.org/10.1007/978-94-007-5170-5_1

Fire, M., Goldschmidt, R., & Elovici, Y. (2014). Online Social Networks: Threats and Solutions. *IEEE Communications Surveys & Tutorials, 16*(4), 2019–2036. https://doi.org/10.1109/COMST.2014.2321628

Golda, A., Mekonen, K., Pandey, A., Singh, A., Hassija, V., Chamola, V., & Sikdar, B. (2024). Privacy and Security Concerns in Generative AI: A Comprehensive Survey. *IEEE Access, 12*, 48126–48144. https://doi.org/10.1109/ACCESS.2024.3381611

Jancke, G., Venolia, G. D., Grudin, J., Cadiz, J. J., & Gupta, A. (2001). Linking Public Spaces: Technical and Social Issues. *Proceedings of the SIGCHI Conference on Human Factors in Computing Systems*, 530–537. https://doi.org/10.1145/365024.365352

Kelley, P. G., Cesca, L., Bresee, J., & Cranor, L. F. (2010). Standardizing Privacy Notices: An Online Study of the Nutrition Label Approach. *Proceedings of the SIGCHI Conference on Human Factors in Computing Systems*, 1573–1582. https://doi.org/10.1145/1753326.1753561

Kimmel, D. (2023, May 16). ChatGPT Therapy Is Good, But It Misses What Makes Us Human. *Columbia University Department of Psychiatry*. www.columbiapsychiatry.org/news/chatgpt-therapy-is-good-but-it-misses-what-makes-us-human

Kshetri, N. (2023). Cybercrime and Privacy Threats of Large Language Models. *IT Professional, 25*(3), 9–13. https://doi.org/10.1109/MITP.2023.3275489

Leon, P. G., Ur, B., Wang, Y., Sleeper, M., Balebako, R., Shay, R., Bauer, L., Christodorescu, M., & Cranor, L. F. (2013). What Matters to Users? Factors That Affect Users' Willingness to Share Information with Online Advertisers. *Proceedings of the Ninth Symposium on Usable Privacy and Security*, 1–12. https://doi.org/10.1145/2501604.2501611

Leonard, A. (2023, September 16). "Dr. Google" Meets Its Match in Dr. ChatGPT. *NPR*. www.npr.org/sections/health-shots/2023/09/16/1199924303/chatgpt-ai-medical-advice

Li, J., Cao, H., Lin, L., Hou, Y., Zhu, R., & El Ali, A. (2024). User Experience Design Professionals' Perceptions of Generative Artificial Intelligence. *Proceedings of the CHI Conference on Human Factors in Computing Systems*, 1–18. https://doi.org/10.1145/3613904.3642114

Liu, J., Lau, C. P., & Chellappa, R. (2023). DiffProtect: Generate Adversarial Examples with Diffusion Models for Facial Privacy Protection [arXiv preprint]. arXiv:2305.13625. https://doi.org/10.48550/arXiv.2305.13625

Lu, L., McDonald, C., Kelleher, T., Lee, S., Chung, Y. J., Mueller, S., Vielledent, M., & Yue, C. A. (2022). Measuring Consumer-perceived Humanness of Online Organizational Agents. *Computers in Human Behavior, 128*, 107092. https://doi.org/10.1016/j.chb.2021.107092

Maddison, L. (2023, April 4). Samsung Workers Made a Major Error by Using ChatGPT. *TechRadar*. www.techradar.com/news/samsung-workers-leaked-company-secrets-by-using-chatgpt

Milne, G. R., Pettinico, G., Hajjat, F. M., & Markos, E. (2017). Information Sensitivity Typology: Mapping the Degree and Type of Risk Consumers Perceive in Personal

Data Sharing. *Journal of Consumer Affairs*, *51*(1), 133–161. https://doi.org/10.1111/joca.12111

Mu, Y., Zhang, Q., Hu, M., Wang, W., Ding, M., Jin, J., Wang, B., Dai, J., Qiao, Y., & Luo, P. (2023). EmbodiedGPT: Vision-Language Pre-Training via Embodied Chain of Thought. *Advances in Neural Information Processing Systems*, *36*, 25081–25094. https://proceedings.neurips.cc/paper_files/paper/2023/hash/4ec43957eda1126ad4887995d05fae3b-Abstract-Conference.html

Narayanan, A., & Shmatikov, V. (2008). Robust De-anonymization of Large Sparse Datasets. *2008 IEEE Symposium on Security and Privacy (Sp 2008)*, 111–125. https://doi.org/10.1109/SP.2008.33

Nissenbaum, H. (2004). Privacy as Contextual Integrity Symposium: Technology, Values, and the Justice System. *Washington Law Review*, *79*(1), 119–158.

Ouyang, S., Wang, S., Liu, Y., Zhong, M., Jiao, Y., Iter, D., Pryzant, R., Zhu, C., Ji, H., & Han, J. (2023). The Shifted and The Overlooked: A Task-oriented Investigation of User-GPT Interactions [arXiv preprint]. arXiv:2310.12418. https://doi.org/10.48550/arXiv.2310.12418

Peris, C., Dupuy, C., Majmudar, J., Parikh, R., Smaili, S., Zemel, R., & Gupta, R. (2023). Privacy in the Time of Language Models. *Proceedings of the 16th ACM International Conference on Web Search and Data Mining*, 1291–1292. https://doi.org/10.1145/3539597.3575792

Phelps, J., Nowak, G., & Ferrell, E. (2000). Privacy Concerns and Consumer Willingness to Provide Personal Information. *Journal of Public Policy & Marketing*, *19*(1), 27 41. https://doi.org/10.1509/jppm.19.1.27.16941

Porter, J. (2023, November 6). ChatGPT Continues to Be One of the Fastest-Growing Services Ever. *The Verge*. www.theverge.com/2023/11/6/23948386/chatgpt-active-user-count-openai-developer-conference

Robinson, C. (2017). Disclosure of Personal Data in Ecommerce: A Cross-national Comparison of Estonia and the United States. *Telematics and Informatics*, *34*(2), 569–582. https://doi.org/10.1016/j.tele.2016.09.006

Rumbold, J. M. M., & Pierscionek, B. K. (2018). What Are Data? A Categorization of the Data Sensitivity Spectrum. *Big Data Research*, *12*, 49–59. https://doi.org/10.1016/j.bdr.2017.11.001

Shalaby, W., Arantes, A., GonzalezDiaz, T., & Gupta, C. (2020). Building Chatbots from Large Scale Domain-specific Knowledge Bases: Challenges and Opportunities. *2020 IEEE International Conference on Prognostics and Health Management (ICPHM)*, 1–8. https://doi.org/10.1109/ICPHM49022.2020.9187036

Shvartzshnaider, Y., Tong, S., Wies, T., Kift, P., Nissenbaum, H., Subramanian, L., & Mittal, P. (2016). Learning Privacy Expectations by Crowdsourcing Contextual Informational Norms. *Proceedings of the AAAI Conference on Human Computation and Crowdsourcing*, *4*, 209–218. https://doi.org/10.1609/hcomp.v4i1.13271

Smith, H. J., Dinev, T., & Xu, H. (2011). Information Privacy Research: An Interdisciplinary Review. *MIS Quarterly*, *35*(4), 989–1015. https://doi.org/10.2307/41409970

Song, C., Ristenpart, T., & Shmatikov, V. (2017). Machine Learning Models that Remember Too Much. *Proceedings of the 2017 ACM SIGSAC Conference on Computer and Communications Security*, 587–601. https://doi.org/10.1145/3133956.3134077

Stokel-Walker, C. (2023). AI Chatbots Are Coming to Search Engines: Can You Trust the Results? *Nature*. https://doi.org/10.1038/d41586-023-00423-4

Van Dis, E. A. M., Bollen, J., Zuidema, W., van Rooij, R., & Bockting, C. L. (2023). ChatGPT: Five Priorities for Research. *Nature*, *614*(7947), 224–226. https://doi.org/10.1038/d41586-023-00288-7

The Vicuna Team. (2023, March 30). Vicuna: An Open-Source Chatbot Impressing GPT-4 with 90%* ChatGPT Quality. *LMSYS Org*. https://lmsys.org/blog/2023-03-30-vicuna

Wolf, V., & Maier, C. (2024). ChatGPT Usage in Everyday Life: A Motivation-Theoretic Mixed-methods Study. *International Journal of Information Management*, *79*, 102821. https://doi.org/10.1016/j.ijinfomgt.2024.102821

Wong, R. Y., & Mulligan, D. K. (2019). Bringing Design to the Privacy Table: Broadening "Design" in "Privacy by Design" Through the Lens of HCI. *Proceedings of the 2019 CHI Conference on Human Factors in Computing Systems*, 1–17. https://doi.org/10.1145/3290605.3300492

Wu, D., & Sun, G. (2023). The Credibility of the Results of Generative Intelligent Search. *Journal of Library Science in China*, *49*(6), 51–67. https://doi.org/10.13530/j.cnki.jlis.2023048

Zhang, C., Ippolito, D., Lee, K., Jagielski, M., Tramer, F., & Carlini, N. (2023). Counterfactual Memorization in Neural Language Models. *Advances in Neural Information Processing Systems*, *36*, 39321–39362.

Zhang, H., Chen, J., Jiang, F., Yu, F., Chen, Z., Li, J., Chen, G., Wu, X., Zhang, Z., Xiao, Q., Wan, X., Wang, B., & Li, H. (2023). HuatuoGPT, towards Taming Language Model to Be a Doctor [arXiv preprint]. arXiv:2305.15075. https://doi.org/10.48550/arXiv.2305.15075

Zhang, Z., Jia, M., Lee, H.-P. (Hank), Yao, B., Das, S., Lerner, A., Wang, D., & Li, T. (2024). "It's a Fair Game," or Is It? Examining How Users Navigate Disclosure Risks and Benefits When Using LLM-Based Conversational Agents. *Proceedings of the CHI Conference on Human Factors in Computing Systems*, 1–26. https://doi.org/10.1145/3613904.3642385

4

Credibility Assessment of Human–Generative AI Interaction

Yuxiang Chris Zhao, Shijie Song, and Yutian Jing

4.1 Introduction

With the rapid development of artificial intelligence, Human–AI Interaction (HAII) has gradually become the focus of Human–Computer Interaction (HCI) and its related cross-fields (Amershi et al., 2019). The emergence of ChatGPT indicates that generative artificial intelligence (GAI) based on the large language model (LLM) has entered a new stage of development. Particularly, a deep learning model is employed to generate human-like content; that is, AI-Generated Content (AIGC) in response to complex and diverse prompts (Lim et al., 2023). Human interaction with GAI will greatly enhance people's productivity and creativity, and further penetrate all aspects of the public's life (De Freitas et al., 2023). However, while bringing benefits to people, GAI will inevitably raise a series of technical, socio-cultural, and ethical issues, among which, the credibility of GAI remains a research concern worth attention in the new era (Longoni et al., 2022).

Credibility was originally defined as 'believability' or perceived information quality from the perspective of information recipients but credibility is not necessarily equal to objective information quality (Flanagin & Metzger, 2017). Many researchers agree that the concept of credibility is multidimensional, including the components such as trustworthiness, expertise, objectivity (Choi & Stvilia, 2015). As technology advances and times move forward, credibility studies also need to pay close attention to the depth of interaction between people and information, digital artifacts, and socio-cultural environments (Shin, 2022). The credibility problem in the traditional mass media era is not comparable to that in the Internet era. Similarly, credibility issues in the era of GAI are facing more challenges brought on by new technologies, new businesses, and new environments (Huschens et al., 2023), and therefore credibility research needs to keep up with the times and be critically examined.

The credibility assessment and judgment of AI has become an important topic in the research of explainable AI (Wagle et al., 2021). While AI technology injects vitality into social development, it also triggers negative problems such as technological black box (Castelvecchi, 2016), algorithmic discrimination (Shin, 2022), dissemination of misinformation (Zhou et al., 2023), and echo chambers (Jeon et al., 2024); in particular, the rapid development of GAI in recent years has created a series of concerns among the public about privacy, employment opportunities, and the loss of control, which in turn affects the trust between people and technology, as well as the adoption and use of GAI by individuals and organizations (Wach et al., 2023). Therefore, the credibility assessment of GAI aims to alleviate people's concerns about new technologies represented by ChatGPT to a certain extent, and advocate the development of human-centered AI, which promotes a harmonious symbiotic relationship between humans and the new generation of AI. For example, Johnson et al. (2023) suggested that verifying the reliability of the content generated by ChatGPT is conducive to further designing models to improve the robustness of an AI system, thus increasing the credibility of users' perception of AI.

In view of this, the topic of credibility in human–generative AI interaction needs to be further explored. Although there have been reviews of credibility research in the algorithmic era in recent years (Alrubaian et al., 2018), studies specifically addressing credibility issues from the GAI perspective remain limited. So far, there have been some studies focusing on the topic of credibility in user's adoption and use of GAIs, and some studies have specifically explored the trust and reliability of GAIs empirically in various contexts. Therefore, the aim of this chapter is to present a clear picture of the current state of credibility research in human–generative AI interaction by analyzing the relevant literature dispersed across various disciplines and to provide a holistic review of measurement instruments, influencing factors, challenges, emerging technologies and optimization methods for the assessment of AIGC credibility. Finally, the chapter also proposes several directions for further investigation with respect to the limitations of AIGC credibility assessment.

4.2 The Concept of AI Credibility

4.2.1 What Is Credibility?

Credibility is a multifaceted construct that pertains to the degree to which an entity – be it information, an individual, or a system – is perceived as trustworthy and reliable in a specific context (Rieh & Danielson, 2007). The foundational definition of credibility often revolves around the term "believability," signifying the extent to which stakeholders are willing to trust and rely on a given source or system (Fogg & Tseng, 1999). However, credibility encompasses a broader array of dimensions beyond mere believability. Credibility is often complex and multidimensional, encompassing a comprehensive evaluation of various characteristics or factors, such as reliability, accuracy, expertise, authority, objectivity, and appeal (Fogg & Tseng, 1999; McCroskey & Young, 1981; Rieh, 2002). From the perspective of the subject being assessed, researchers have classified credibility into categories like advertisement credibility, review credibility, and media credibility (Cheung et al., 2012; Cotte et al., 2005). Furthermore, Flanagin and Metzger (2007) subdivided credibility into content credibility, source credibility, and design credibility.

Credibility is a key factor for individuals, corporations, governments, and the media in maintaining a good reputation, and it also influences public trust in the broader social structure (Tseng & Fogg, 1999). Whether in information dissemination, investment decisions, or policy formulation, credibility often becomes a benchmark for evaluating the success and effectiveness of these activities. As such, credibility has become increasingly important across various sectors, from news reporting (Hofeditz et al., 2021) and scientific research (Alam & Mohanty, 2022) to business marketing (Khan & Mishra, 2024) and smart healthcare (Aliyeva & Mehdiyev, 2024; Stevens & Stetson, 2023). However, in the age of AI – marked by the rapid proliferation of emerging technologies, the lack of algorithmic transparency, the risks of bias and manipulation, and the globalized, decentralized digital environment – the task of maintaining and enhancing AI credibility presents both significant opportunities and substantial challenges.

There are several similarities between the concept of credibility and the concept of human-centered AI, as both emphasize the important position of users in shaping perceived experience. Some researchers suggest that the design of human-centered AI should pay attention to the influence of AI on people and put the user experience at the center (Shneiderman, 2020; Xu, 2019). Furthermore, traditional human–computer interaction is actively evolving toward human–generative AI interaction, and the original credibility dimension can no longer fully cover and reflect the connotation of AI credibility. Therefore, it is necessary to revisit the conceptualization of AI credibility in the context of human–generative AI interaction. The integrated framework of credibility evaluation (Hilligoss & Rieh, 2008), dominance-interpretation theory (Fogg, 2003), credibility MAIN model (Sundar, 2008), and other related theories lay a theoretical foundation for expanding the conceptual map of AIGC credibility.

4.2.2 Main Dimensions of AI Credibility

It is necessary to consider the characteristics of the AI when constructing the concept of AIGC credibility. Shin (2022) suggests that the credibility of AIGC should be mapped with some characteristics of AI in a broader scope. At present, researchers generally agree that human-centered AI should be Explainable AI (Capel & Brereton, 2023), which can be embodied in the characteristics of AI, such as fairness, accountability, transparency, and interpretability. This section elaborates and expands on AI credibility based on the primary dimensions of explainable AI. Table 4.1 summarizes the main dimensions and corresponding concepts of AI credibility.

Firstly, the reliability and security of AI systems are paramount, as users expect stable performance and data integrity even in complex or uncertain situations. For example, in the healthcare domain, the accuracy of AIGC will affect patients trust (Johnson et al., 2023). Secondly, transparency and intelligibility are key dimensions of AI credibility, helping users understand the logic and reasoning behind AI decisions, thus reducing fear or distrust of "black box" models (Shin, 2023). Thirdly, accountability refers to the presence of clear responsibility mechanisms in AI systems, ensuring that issues can be

Table 4.1 *Main dimensions of AI credibility*

Dimension	Description	References
Reliability	The ability of AI to consistently deliver accurate and stable results under various conditions – including flexibility, accessibility, and timeliness – also encompasses the system's robustness when faced with data changes, failures, or stress. Reliability is crucial in assessing AI credibility, as users expect the system to maintain stable performance even in complex, uncertain, or extreme situations.	Bedué and Fritzsche (2022); Hayashi and Wakabayashi (2017)
Fairness	Fairness in AI credibility requires that the system not only avoids overt biases but also possesses the ability to detect and correct hidden biases. To ensure AI credibility, developers must rigorously control for bias throughout model design, data collection, training, and testing processes.	Mehrabi et al. (2021); Sambasivan et al. (2021)
Accountability	A key component of AI credibility is ensuring clear accountability when errors or failures occur. Whether involving developers, operators, or users, the responsibility framework for AI systems must be well-defined to ensure that issues can be traced back to their source and corrective actions taken.	Busuioc (2021); Hallowell et al. (2022)

Table 4.1 (*cont.*)

Dimension	Description	References
Transparency	Transparency in AI refers not only to the explainability and comprehensibility of the system's decision-making processes but also to the transparency of information, such as data sources and algorithm choices, and the transparency of processes, like records of system updates or adjustments. A transparent AI system enables users to understand how data is collected, processed, and analyzed, allowing them to better grasp and trust the decision-making flow of the AI.	Ehsan et al. (2021); Vössing et al. (2022)
Security	Security and robustness ensure that AI systems do not make erroneous decisions in abnormal situations, such as when faced with malicious inputs or adversarial attacks, thereby safeguarding user trust.	Hu et al. (2021)
Ethic	AI decisions must not only be technically accurate but also align with social, ethical, and moral standards. By addressing issues such as privacy protection, eliminating algorithmic bias, and considering the impact on vulnerable groups, AI systems can enhance user trust.	Reinhardt (2023)
Intelligibility	From the user's perspective, AI outputs need to be understandable, and its decisions must provide clear explanations to practitioners without a technical background. This allows users to maintain trust in the results while utilizing AI.	Lim et al. (2019)

traced, corrected, and prevented from recurring – an essential aspect of building and maintaining user trust (Hallowell et al., 2022). Lastly, fairness and ethics represent two extended dimensions of AI credibility, reflecting the importance of social values and human cultural norms in AI applications. Enhancing AI credibility requires not only technological advancements but also the establishment of strict ethical and fairness standards, ensuring that AI systems make more responsible decisions within various social contexts (Zhang & Zhang, 2023).

4.3 Measures of AI Credibility in Human–Generative AI Interaction

Measuring and evaluating AI credibility is a crucial aspect of achieving trustworthy and human-centered AI systems. Through a review of the literature, we classify the measurement of AI credibility into subjective assessments from a user-centric perspective and relatively objective measurements using technical methods.

On the one hand, the user-centered subjective measurement approach primarily refers to measure users' perceived credibility of AI products through questionnaires, focusing on specific research situations and research questions (Xiang et al., 2023). For example, in order to evaluate the perceived credibility of students on ChatGPT, Tossell et al. (2024) used the updated multidimensional measure of trust (MDMT), version 2 questionnaire. The measurement dimensions include reliability, ability, morality, transparency, and kindness (Ullman & Malle, 2019). In addition, Tossell et al. (2024) used 7-point Likert scales to evaluate students' trust in ChatGPT, and the measurement items were adapted from the surveys used in military training (Dzindolet et al., 2003) and autonomous driving research (Tenhundfeld et al., 2020). Uzir et al. (2023) used the form of questionnaire, which included two dimensions of privacy and security, and measured the perceived credibility of smart watches by elderly consumers.

In addition, some researchers assess the users' perceived AI credibility from other dimensions. For example, measuring the propensity of users relying on agents in future situations is one of the initial methods used to assess the credibility (Kohn et al., 2021; Momen et al., 2023; Monfort et al., 2018). Because trust comes from the drive of rational factors and the stimulation of positive emotions, or the comprehensive effect of the two, Chen and Park (2021) divide users' trust in intelligent personal assistants into cognitive trust (e.g., usefulness, reliability, honesty and integrity of AI) and emotional trust (e.g., safety, comfort and satisfaction of AI).

On the other hand, relatively objective measurements using technical methods can assist researchers and developers in quantifying and evaluating AI system credibility, thereby enhancing its reliability and safety in practical applications. For example, automated methods may assess an AI system's responsiveness and explainability (Lin et al., 2021), test model performance on specific tasks (Huang et al., 2024), and develop quantitative metrics to evaluate the robustness of deep neural networks (Ruan et al., 2019). Some researchers also use machine learning techniques to assess AI system explainability (Yang, 2019), employ blockchain technology to enhance data credibility (Distefano et al., 2021). Some frameworks such as DeepTrust (Cheng et al., 2020) and credibility metrics models (Uslu et al., 2021) are proposed to measure AI system reliability.

Overall, while numerous studies have highlighted the need to improve the credibility of AI systems, relatively few have explored the quantitative assessment of AI credibility, in particular the contextualized measurement of AIGC credibility and the refinement of credibility dimensions in human–generative AI interaction.

4.4 Influences on Credibility Assessment in Human–Generative AI Interaction

Early research on information credibility assessment identified information sources, cues, and affordances as key factors influencing users' perceived credibility. Since then, numerous studies on the credibility of HCI have highlighted the impact of technical signifiers in the interaction environment on users' credibility assessment (Liao & Mak, 2019). For instance, when users search for health information on short video platforms, social media indicators positively influence their perception of credibility (Song et al., 2021). As HCI evolves into human–generative AI interaction, AI credibility assessment not only involves technical aspects such as system components and algorithm optimization, but also focuses on the practical performance of AI systems across diverse application scenarios and users' trust perceptions in human–generative AI interaction. Therefore, recent research trends toward a comprehensive consideration of various factors affecting AI credibility assessment, including data, system, algorithm and user factors in addition to information factors. Specific details and examples are provided in Table 4.2.

4.4.1 Date and Information-related Attributes

In terms of data factors, data quality significantly impacts the credibility of medical AI. Issues such as data errors and omissions, the lack of standardized metadata, and the prevalence of unstructured data can undermine technical reliability, negatively affecting the credibility of medical AI (Zhang & Zhang, 2023). Additionally, aspects of the AI data process (e.g., data design, data archiving and data evaluation) also influence the credibility of the AI model (Liang et al., 2022).

As for information, the content quality is a key factor influencing users' perception of AI credibility. For instance, users' overall trust in an AI system largely depends on its ability to provide accurate, authentic, complete, and timely information to support their tasks (Kim et al., 2021). Moreover, it has been found that content generated by ChatGPT often lacks completeness, which can easily mislead users and diminish its credibility (Van Bulck & Moons, 2024).

Table 4.2 *Influencing factors of AI credibility*

Dimensions	Categories	Examples
Date and information	Data quality	Data acquisition, data processing and data storage (Hu et al., 2021; Liang et al., 2022; Zhang & Zhang, 2023)
	Information source	News organizations/media with cognitive authority (Kim & Kim, 2020)
	Information content	Accuracy, authenticity, completeness, and timeliness (Kim et al., 2021; Van Bulck & Moons, 2024)
System	System interpretability	Audit integrity (Raji et al., 2020), trust calibration (Zhang et al., 2020), agency transparency (Araujo et al., 2020), explanatory element types (Ha & Kim, 2024; Pareek et al., 2024)
	System attribute characteristics	System reliability (Hayashi & Wakabayashi, 2017), system (service) quality (Chen et al., 2023), model performance (Zhang et al., 2021)
	AI anthropomorphism	AI anthropomorphism features (Chen & Park, 2021), AI voice features (Kim et al., 2022), AI warmth and ability (Chandra et al., 2022)
Algorithm	Algorithm complexity	Complexity degree of algorithm (Lehmann et al., 2022)
	Algorithm transparency	Algorithmic interpretability (Chen, 2024; Grimmelikhuijsen, 2023; Markus et al., 2021), algorithm reliability (Durán & Jongsma, 2021)
	Algorithm security	Algorithm errors (Schmitt et al., 2021)
	Fairness of algorithm	Algorithm bias (Bernagozzi et al., 2021; Winkle et al., 2021)
User	Interactive experience	Perceptual interactive experience (Zhuang et al., 2024)
	Individual ability	Algorithm literacy (Shin, 2022)
	Sociocultural contexts	Social and cultural environment (Chien et al., 2018)

4.4.2 System-related Attributes

For the system, explanation directly affects the transparency of AI, which in turn positively correlates with AI credibility. For example, research has shown that providing users with text-based explanations can enhance their trust in explainable AI systems more effectively than visual explanations (Ha & Kim, 2024). Additionally, the security and reliability of AI systems impact users' perceived credibility. For instance, the service quality of AI chatbots positively influences customer loyalty by enhancing perceived value, cognitive trust, and emotional trust (Chen et al., 2023).

The anthropomorphism of AI is supported by its strong comprehension and innovative capabilities (Pelau et al., 2021), enabling AI systems to grasp the nuances of human–generative AI interaction. The anthropomorphic traits of AI enhance users' trust, making AI systems with human-like expression styles more approachable and trustworthy (Chen & Park, 2021; L. Lu et al., 2022; Wang & Zhao, 2023). For instance, AI instructors with human-like voices tend to achieve higher perceived credibility among students than those with robotic voices (Kim et al., 2022). However, humans generally possess greater social appeal, competence, and credibility compared to robots (Beattie et al., 2020; Edwards et al., 2018; Finkel & Krämer, 2022).

4.4.3 Algorithm-related Attributes

In the realm of algorithms, specific characteristics such as fairness, accountability, transparency, and explainability are closely linked to trust and performance expectations (Shin, 2023). Algorithm transparency can significantly influence users' trust in the information provided by the algorithm (Grimmelikhuijsen, 2023; Yeomans et al., 2019), as well as their confidence in algorithmic outcomes and decision-makers, ultimately impacting their interactive experiences and decision-making processes (Cadario et al., 2021). However, when the complexity of an algorithm falls below users' expectations, increased transparency can actually diminish perceived credibility (Lehmann et al., 2022). Additionally, algorithmic bias can undermine users' trust in AI systems, with gender bias being a particularly prominent issue in human–generative AI interaction (Bernagozzi et al., 2021; Winkle et al., 2021).

4.4.4 User-related Attributes

In the early years of theories of information credibility, it was widely accepted that the user's understanding, judgment, and cognitive processing of information clues or components would have a significant impact on the evaluation of information credibility during interaction with the computer (Fogg, 2003). In the context of human–generative AI intelligence interaction, the interaction experience between users and AI systems also influences their evaluation of AI credibility. For example, older adults have had positive experiences watching short medical videos created by large language models, which has enhanced their trust in medical care (Zhuang et al., 2024).

From the user's perspective, algorithm literacy is a key factor influencing the credibility assessment of AI, which represents an advanced stage of both information and digital literacy, manifesting a profound understanding of AI (Shin et al., 2022). It is indispensable in forecasting user decisions in human–generative AI interaction (Shin, 2022). In addition, social and cultural backgrounds also influence the evaluation of AI credibility (Chien et al., 2018). This aligns with sociocultural perspectives, which suggests that people's evaluation of credibility are constrained by their particular cultural, systemic, and historical backgrounds (Mansour & Francke, 2017).

4.5 Challenges in Credibility Assessment of Human–Generative AI Interaction

The challenges in assessing AI credibility encompass issues related to transparency, ethics, security, privacy, and rights, as detailed in Table 4.3. AI models generally use complex algorithms such as machine learning and deep learning, so users cannot understand the process of AI decision-making in a direct way (Hamon et al., 2021). For example, "black box" problems are common in AI systems in healthcare, characterized by a lack of interpretability and potential biases. This situation can clash with clinicians' and patients' expectations for a clear logical chain, thereby undermining trust in AI (Esmaeilzadeh, 2024). Additionally, as the amount of explanatory information provided by AI systems increases, especially in time-sensitive situations, managing information overload and identifying the most relevant details becomes a significant challenge (Ehsan et al., 2021).

Secondly, moral and ethical issues, such as gender bias (Winkle et al., 2021) and moral conflicts (Morley et al., 2020), must be thoroughly considered in assessing AI credibility. These issues often arise from algorithmic bias. Data

Table 4.3 *Challenges in credibility assessment of human–generative AI interaction*

Challenges	Examples
Transparency issue	Lack of explanatory (Ehsan et al., 2021; Esmaeilzadeh, 2024), technical black box (Schoenherr et al., 2023)
Moral and ethical issues	Gender prejudice (Winkle et al., 2021), moral conflict (Morley et al., 2020)
Security and privacy issues	Algorithm deviation and error (Kaissis et al., 2020), data abuse (Kaissis et al., 2020), privacy violation (Mou & Meng, 2024)
Power and responsibility issues	Responsibility attribution (Leo & Huh, 2020)
Other risk issues	Misinformation dissemination (Esmaeilzadeh, 2020; Molina & Sundar, 2022), cognitive biases (Ehsan et al., 2021), weakening of human autonomy (Abbass, 2019; Ernst, 2020)

security and privacy are also major challenges in AI credibility assessment. The inherent fragility of algorithms can lead to incorrect decisions when processing data, directly impacting the stability and security of AI systems (Zhang & Zhang, 2023). Additionally, using extensive data sets for credibility evaluation raises substantial privacy and security concerns. If data is misused, it can severely threaten user privacy and security (Kaissis et al., 2020). For example, users' normative behaviors and reactions may be exploited by intelligent machines (Leong & Selinger, 2019) and their designers for monitoring, tracking, or fraudulent activities (Shahriar et al., 2023), posing a serious threat to personal privacy and potentially resulting in significant privacy violations.

Besides the above challenges, there is also an important issue of how to clarify the attribution of responsibility when AI systems fail or cause harm to users. In particular, this issue is critical and urgent when AI applications directly affect the health and safety of patients (Esmaeilzadeh, 2020), and solving this problem requires a combination of technical, legal, and ethical considerations.

It is important to recognize that misplaced or inappropriate trust in GAI can lead to a variety of potential consequences and risks, including the spread of misinformation (Molina & Sundar, 2022), cognitive biases (Ehsan et al., 2021), and reduced human autonomy (Abbass, 2019). For instance, AIGC, while fueling efficient content creation, also risks the spread of disinformation (Shusas, 2024).

4.6 Ways to Enhance the Credibility Assessment in Human–Generative AI Interaction

Due to the complexity and opacity of AI systems, users often find it difficult to understand and trust their decision-making processes and outcomes. Therefore, exploring new methods and technical solutions to enhance the credibility evaluation of AI systems is crucial. Currently, a key approach is to calibrate AI system trust and robustness using advanced technologies. Techniques such as machine learning (Carvalho et al., 2019), deep learning (Chander et al., 2024), federated learning (P. Chen et al., 2022; Lo et al., 2022), and Shapley Additional Explanations (SHAP) (Sabharwal et al., 2024; Trindade Neves et al., 2024) are used to improve model transparency and system explanation. Toreini et al. (2020) proposed four technologies to enhance AI credibility: Fairness, Explanatory Ability, Auditability, and Safety (FEAS), which should be considered throughout all stages of the system life cycle.

The human–computer collaborative decision-making design method integrates system decision-making with human experience and cross-domain knowledge, aiming to enhance both the credibility and operational efficiency of AI systems. This approach includes measures such as optimizing configurations or designs to improve user–AI collaboration (Jain et al., 2023), incorporating domain-specific knowledge to interpret local data errors in AI-assisted decision-making (Zhang et al., 2020) and enabling users to provide feedback to algorithms (Molina & Sundar, 2022). These strategies can significantly enhance AI system credibility and ensure its reliable use across various application scenarios. Researchers urge various institutions – including government bodies, accounting firms, insurance companies, non-governmental organizations, civil society organizations, professional groups, and research institutions – to collaborate in exploring new ways to improve the credibility of human-centered AI and advance interpretable AI (Arnold et al., 2019; Shneiderman, 2020).

In addition to the above technical approaches, some important theoretical frameworks have also been proposed to ensure the reliability of AI system reliability assessment from multiple dimensions. For example, the algorithmic audit framework can be applied to the whole life cycle of AI system assessment (Raji et al., 2020). The AI Public Trust Model (Knowles & Richards, 2021) and the AI Trust, Risk and Security Management (AI TRiSM) framework (Habbal et al., 2024) aim to improve the trustworthiness and reliability of AI; Context-cognitive frameworks for Explainable AI (SAFE-AI) (Sanneman & Shah, 2022), confidence measures frameworks (van der Waa et al., 2020) for explainability, and multidimensional interpretative matrices (Hamon et al., 2021) can be used to assess the explainable behavior of AI systems.

Some auxiliary evaluation classifications are proposed to solve the ethical problems brought by the credibility of AI. For example, the interpretable classification of evaluation system (Sokol & Flach, 2020), the "dishonest personification" classification of AI robot (Leong & Selinger, 2019), and the visual evaluation classification of gender bias in AI systems (Bernagozzi et al., 2021). These auxiliary evaluations can alleviate, to varying degrees, the diverse socio-cultural and technological ethical dilemmas raised by human–generative AI interaction, and help users make better use of GAI.

4.7 Domains of Credibility Assessment in Human–Generative AI

With the rapid advancement and widespread application of AI technology, credibility issues in human–generative AI interaction have become increasingly significant across various industries, including healthcare, finance,

Table 4.4 *Domains of credibility assessment for human–generative AI*

Domains	Examples
Health	Smart medical care (Aliyeva & Mehdiyev, 2024; Hallowell et al., 2022; Stevens & Stetson, 2023; Yokoi et al., 2021), health information (Van Bulck & Moons, 2024; Zalzal et al., 2024), AI health product adoption (Sebastian et al., 2023)
Financial industry	Investment forecasting (Sabharwal et al., 2024), credit risk (Candello et al., 2023)
Communicate	Intelligent customer service, intelligent voice (Shin, 2022), interpersonal communication (Hohenstein & Jung, 2020)
Media communication	Automated journalism (Hofeditz et al., 2021; Kim & Kim, 2020; Z. Lu et al., 2022; Tandoc Jr et al., 2020)
Traffic	Self-driving (Lee & Kolodge, 2020; Stettinger et al., 2024)
Education	Online learning and teaching (Alam & Mohanty, 2022; M. Chen et al., 2022; Tossell et al., 2024; Vincent-Lancrin & Van der Vlies, 2020), subject education (Cukurova et al., 2020)
Philosophy	Ethics (Durán & Jongsma, 2021; Lee, 2022), morality (Giroux et al., 2022)
Law	Judicial assistance (Hayashi & Wakabayashi, 2017), legal rules (Shank, 2021)
Marketing	Consumer experience (Alboqami, 2023; Khan & Mishra, 2024), consumer's purchase intentions (Uzir et al., 2023), consumer's willingness to use (Yue & Li, 2023)
Others	Online translation (Bernagozzi et al., 2021)

services, and education. Specific application scenarios such as smart healthcare, autonomous driving, investment forecasting, and intelligent customer service highlight these concerns, as detailed in Table 4.4. This underscores the need for heightened attention to AI credibility within both industry and academia. Addressing these issues is crucial for fostering effective interactions between users and AI technology and advancing the development of trustworthy AI.

Research on AI credibility assessment in the healthcare sector primarily focuses on several key areas. Firstly, as AI applications in disease prediction, diagnosis, treatment, and health management become increasingly prevalent (Holzinger et al., 2019; Zahlan et al., 2023), ensuring the credibility of AI outcomes is crucial. Trust in medical AI is considered foundational for the adoption of smart healthcare. Studies have shown that clinicians' acceptance of AI is influenced by AI credibility (Stevens & Stetson, 2023), and there are also differences in how patients perceive trust in both their doctors and AI medical systems (Yokoi et al., 2021). Secondly, recent research has concentrated on the impact of transparency and explainability of medical models on AI credibility (Albahri et al., 2023), particularly addressing issues such as the "black box" nature of algorithms that can lead to distrust or even aversion among patients (Zhang & Zhang, 2023). Finally, AI systems and tools such as ChatGPT (Van Bulck & Moons, 2024), AI chatbots (Weeks et al., 2023), and AI medical devices (Fehr et al., 2022) are central to assessing AI credibility in the healthcare field. Future research needs to focus on enhancing credibility through human–AI collaboration, addressing privacy, ethical, and responsibility issues in medical practice, and improving AI's decision-making capabilities.

Research on the AI credibility in education primarily focuses on students' perceived trust in AI and the exploration of human–AI collaboration in online learning models. Students' trust in AI teaching tools may affect the effectiveness of online education, and such studies are usually analyzed using user experiments. For instance, the perceived credibility of AI instructors is influenced by AI voice features and their social presence (Kim et al., 2022). Additionally, personal perceptions and communication styles influence how students perceive the credibility of AI graders in the classroom (Abendschein et al., 2024). Researchers are also exploring how to foster a collaborative relationship between AI systems and human educators, rather than relying solely on AI or using it as a supplementary tool, to enhance teaching outcomes (M. Chen et al., 2022; Tossell et al., 2024). Meanwhile, large language models like ChatGPT present significant risks for higher education, including the spread of misinformation, a potential decline in students' critical thinking abilities, and a reduction in the credibility of educational research evidence (M. Chen et al., 2022; Cukurova et al., 2020).

The evaluation of AI credibility in the marketing field is predominantly based on empirical research, supplemented by qualitative methods such as interviews. The primary focus of these studies is the impact of credibility on consumers' AI experience and their willingness to purchase AI products. The perceived quality of user experience is a key factor influencing the credibility of AI systems. When consumers use AI products or platforms, their trust in the AI is shaped by the system's interaction experience, the accuracy of its recommendations, the credibility of its sources, and its anthropomorphic characteristics (Alboqami, 2023; Khan & Mishra, 2024; Kim et al., 2021). Moreover, consumers' perceived credibility of AI has a significant impact on both their intention to use AI and their actual purchasing behavior (Uzir et al., 2023). Traditional models like the Technology Acceptance Model (TAM) and the Stimulus-Organism-Response (S-O-R) theory provide a theoretical foundation for AI credibility research, though there is a need to extend these theories in the context of human–generative AI interaction (Cheng et al., 2022; Wang et al., 2023).

In the financial sector, AI credibility assessment has garnered significant attention from scholars, particularly in areas such as market volatility, credit risk evaluation, and fraud detection. Recent research has focused on developing more interpretable models, aiming to enable financial professionals to better understand and validate the reasoning behind AI-driven decisions, thereby enhancing transparency and trust in decision-making processes (Edunjobi & Odejide, 2024; Sabharwal et al., 2024).

4.8 Future Research Agenda

The issue of credibility as a cross-cutting research area has been the subject of extensive and sustained attention. In the new context of human—generative AI interaction, credibility research will continue to derive new propositions with the development of technology, changes in scenarios, updating of measurement approaches, and adaptive use of theories.

4.8.1 Reconceptualizing the AI Credibility

Compared to the earlier years of website credibility and the social media credibility in the Web 2.0 era, the research object of AI credibility has changed considerably and the emergence of some technologies rich in intelligent features may have made some new changes to the concept of credibility. For example, the credibility perception and evaluation of AIGC is quite different from the previous credibility measurement of user-generated content (UGC), and the production and dissemination of information content is not comparable in terms of speed, scale, and degree of influence. In addition, the GAI era on digital artifact and the embodiment of intelligences need to be further incorporated into the conceptual kernel of AI credibility. Further, the traditional credibility research conducted based on individuals urgently needs to break through toward a collectivist perspective, especially with the development of crowdsourcing, citizen science, and crowd science, the concept of AI credibility needs to take into account the characteristics of collectiveness in order to better construct the measurements of credibility in the interactions of different groups of people with GAI.

4.8.2 Examining Technological Advancement in GAI Credibility

Advances in algorithm have created a complex digital environment in which credibility assessment has become even more difficult. People no longer rely only on information cues (e.g., author, credentials, news source, etc.) to make a judgment of credibility. Instead, they make a holistic assessment of the platform, the source, the content, and even the judgments of other users. In this view, how to use algorithm-driven new technologies to improve human capabilities such as decision-making, problem-solving, situational learning, and work performance will be important future research topics. With the development of GAI, misinformation and disinformation (e.g., fake news, fake videos, fake pictures) could be intentionally created and quickly spread by various social bots. How to combat the dark side of AIGC will be an important topic for future research. While the dark side creates critical problems, the bright side of algorithmic affordances creates promising opportunities for credibility research. We can observe that GAI could be a powerful tool for filtering misinformation, combating fake news, and supporting laypeople's credibility judgment. While analyzing large-scale data to understand credibility judgment patterns utilizing deep learning and computational methods, it will be important to incorporate much previous credibility research in which individuals' multiple dimensions of credibility assessment are characterized and identified.

4.8.3 Evolution of Credibility Measures in Human–Generative AI Interaction

We found that a variety of methodological approaches have been taken to investigate credibility issues. Traditional credibility research methods, such as interviews, focus groups, case studies, ethnography, grounded theory, and content analysis, as well as quantitative research methods, such as surveys, experiments, network analyses, sentiment analyses, and data-mining techniques, are often used in combination to assess credibility. Recently, various algorithmic techniques have been developed to detect falseness or inaccuracy of information. We call for more mixed-methods analyses in future AI credibility studies, especially in combining the characteristics of the algorithms themselves as well as the characteristics of the people interacting with the algorithms and using multi-source data to carry out AI credibility measurements. Furthermore, credibility researchers could examine AI credibility judgments from neuro-information science perspectives while using EEG/FMRI techniques to do in-depth studies on interaction effects between information cues and judgments.

4.8.4 Building a Human-centered Theoretical Lens of AI Credibility

The development of technology and the richness of research objects place new demands on extending the theory of credibility. Some of the traditional dimensions of the concept of credibility, trustworthiness, expertise, authority, and objectivity, may no longer be sufficient in the context of GAI. The anonymity and "authorless" character of the next-generation Internet increases when machine learning and GAI play the role of content creators and gatekeepers of information dissemination. Therefore, future research needs to enrich and deepen the theoretical foundation of credibility by building and testing new dimensions of AIGC credibility by drawing extensively on relevant theories from different disciplines. Some concepts of AI credibility that are considered core dimensions of human judgment, such as fairness, openness, inclusiveness, and diversity, can be integrated into the development of machine learning and AI algorithms. Given that people will increasingly conduct holistic credibility assessments in the context of GAI, humanistic elements will be an important point for future AI credibility constructs.

In addition, the ethical and moral issues surrounding the assessment of AI credibility are complex and multifaceted, involving data privacy, attribution of responsibility, transparency and interpretability during system design, testing, and feedback. Current research lacks a clear mechanism for attributing responsibility and does not adequately address the details of user consent in the collection and use of feedback data. Future research should take a humanistic approach by establishing a clear regulatory framework for AI credibility assessment, strengthening accountability mechanisms, and ensuring rigorous ethical scrutiny of user feedback collected through surveys and other approaches.

4.9 Conclusion

Credibility has always been a central topic of concern for information-related fields, and the intelligent era has brought new opportunities and challenges to the assessment of credibility. With the dual empowerment of digital and intelligent technologies, future credibility assessment of AI should focus on diverse human–generative AI interaction scenarios (Appelganc et al., 2022), with the goal of developing trustworthy AI (Peckham, 2024). This undoubtedly puts forward higher requirements for theoretical and methodological tools for credibility assessment. Today, the credibility of GAI faces a series of ethical, information security, and data governance challenges. This review outlines the conceptual connotation of AI credibility and analyzes the main dimensions of GAI. In terms of research content, the main measures, influencing factors, challenges, and emerging approaches to AI credibility assessment are reviewed. We advocate researchers to strengthen interdisciplinary dialogue, exchange, and cooperation in the future, further enrich the theoretical lens, and innovate assessment methods, expand the application scenarios of

GAI credibility assessment, and pay attention to the role of human–generative AI interaction experience in credibility assessment.

Acknowledgment

The study is jointly supported by the National Natural Science Foundation of China (Grant numbers 72374104, 72204076).

References

Abbass, H. A. (2019). Social Integration of Artificial Intelligence: Functions, Automation Allocation Logic and Human–Autonomy Trust. *Cognitive Computation, 11*(2), 159–171.

Abendschein, B., Lin, X., Edwards, C., Edwards, A., & Rijhwani, V. (2024). Credibility and Altered Communication Styles of AI Graders in the Classroom. *Journal of Computer Assisted Learning, 40*(4), 1766–1776.

Alam, A., & Mohanty, A. (2022). Facial Analytics or Virtual Avatars: Competencies and Design Considerations for Student–Teacher Interaction in AI-powered Online Education for Effective Classroom Engagement. *International Conference on Communication, Networks and Computing* (pp. 252–265). Springer.

Albahri, A. S., Duhaim, A. M., Fadhel, M. A., Alnoor, A., Baqer, N. S., Alzubaidi, L., Albahri, O. S., Alamoodi, A. H., Bai, J., & Salhi, A. (2023). A Systematic Review of Trustworthy and Explainable Artificial Intelligence in Healthcare: Assessment of Quality, Bias Risk, and Data Fusion. *Information Fusion, 96*, 156–191.

Alboqami, H. (2023). Trust Me, I'm an Influencer! Causal Recipes for Customer Trust in Artificial Intelligence Influencers in the Retail Industry. *Journal of Retailing and Consumer Services, 72*, 103242.

Aliyeva, K., & Mehdiyev, N. (2024). Uncertainty-Aware Multi-criteria Decision Analysis for Evaluation of Explainable Artificial Intelligence Methods: A Use Case from the Healthcare Domain. *Information Sciences, 657*, 119987.

Alrubaian, M., Al-Qurishi, M., Alamri, A., Al-Rakhami, M., Hassan, M. M., & Fortino, G. (2018). Credibility in Online Social Networks: A Survey. *IEEE Access, 7*, 2828–2855.

Amershi, S., Weld, D., Vorvoreanu, M., Fourney, A., Nushi, B., Collisson, P., Suh, J., Iqbal, S., Bennett, P. N., & Inkpen, K. (2019). Guidelines for Human–AI Interaction. *Proceedings of the 2019 Chi Conference on Human Factors in Computing Systems* (pp. 1–13). ACM.

Appelganc, K., Rieger, T., Roesler, E., & Manzey, D. (2022). How Much Reliability Is Enough? A Context-specific View on Human Interaction with (Artificial) Agents from Different Perspectives. *Journal of Cognitive Engineering and Decision Making, 16*, 207–221.

Araujo, T., Helberger, N., Kruikemeier, S., & De Vreese, C. H. (2020). In AI We Trust? Perceptions about Automated Decision-making by Artificial Intelligence. *AI & Society, 35*(3), 611–623.

Arnold, M., Bellamy, R. K., Hind, M., Houde, S., Mehta, S., Mojsilović, A., Nair, R., Ramamurthy, K. N., Olteanu, A., & Piorkowski, D. (2019). FactSheets: Increasing Trust in AI sServices through Supplier's Declarations of Conformity. *IBM Journal of Research and Development*, *63*(4/5), 6:1–6:13.

Beattie, A., Edwards, A. P., & Edwards, C. (2020). A Bot and a Smile: Interpersonal Impressions of Chatbots and Humans using Emoji in Computer-mediated Communication. In S. Nah, J. E. McNealy, J. H. Kim, & J. Joo (eds.), *Communicating Artificial Intelligence (AI)* (pp. 41–59). Routledge.

Bedué, P., & Fritzsche, A. (2022). Can We Trust AI? An Empirical Investigation of Trust Requirements and Guide to Successful AI Adoption. *Journal of Enterprise Information Management*, *35*(2), 530–549.

Bernagozzi, M., Srivastava, B., Rossi, F., & Usmani, S. (2021). Gender Bias in Online Language Translators: Visualization, Human Perception, and Bias/Accuracy Tradeoffs. *IEEE Internet Computing*, *25*(5), 53–63.

Busuioc, M. (2021). Accountable Artificial Intelligence: Holding Algorithms to Account. *Public Administration Review*, *81*(5), 825–836.

Cadario, R., Longoni, C., & Morewedge, C. K. (2021). Understanding, Explaining, and Utilizing Medical Artificial Intelligence. *Nature Human Behaviour*, *5*(12), 1636–1642.

Candello, H., Soella, G. M., Sanctos, C. S., Grave, M. C., & De Brito Filho, A. A. (2023). "This Means Nothing to Me": Building Credibility in Conversational Systems. *Proceedings of the 5th International Conference on Conversational User Interfaces* (pp. 1–6). ACM.

Capel, T., & Brereton, M. (2023). What is Human-centered about Human-centered AI? A Map of the Research Landscape. *Proceedings of the 2023 CHI Conference on Human Factors in Computing Systems* (pp. 1–23). ACM.

Carvalho, D. V., Pereira, E. M., & Cardoso, J. S. (2019). Machine Learning Interpretability: A Survey on Methods and Metrics. *Electronics*, *8*(8), 832.

Castelvecchi, D. (2016). Can We Open the Black Box of AI? *Nature News*, *538*(7623), 20.

Chander, B., John, C., Warrier, L., & Gopalakrishnan, K. (2024). Toward Trustworthy Artificial Intelligence (TAI) in the Context of Explainability and Robustness. *ACM Computing Surveys*, *57*(6), 1–49.

Chandra, S., Shirish, A., & Srivastava, S. C. (2022). To Be or Not to Be ... Human? Theorizing the Role of Human-like Competencies in Conversational Artificial Intelligence Agents. *Journal of Management Information Systems*, *39*(4), 969–1005.

Chen, C. (2024). How Consumers Respond to Service Failures Caused by Algorithmic Mistakes: The Role of Algorithmic Interpretability. *Journal of Business Research*, *176*, 114610.

Chen, M., Liu, F., & Lee, Y.-H. (2022). My Tutor Is an AI: The Effects of Involvement and Tutor Type on Perceived Quality, Perceived Credibility, and Use Intention. *International Conference on Human–Computer Interaction* (pp. 232–244). Springer.

Chen, P., Du, X., Lu, Z., Wu, J., & Hung, P. C. (2022). Evfl: An Explainable Vertical Federated Learning for Data-oriented Artificial Intelligence Systems. *Journal of Systems Architecture*, *126*, 102474.

Chen, Q., Lu, Y., Gong, Y., & Xiong, J. (2023). Can AI Chatbots Help Retain Customers? Impact of AI Service Quality on Customer Loyalty. *Internet Research*, *33*(6), 2205–2243.

Chen, Q. Q., & Park, H. J. (2021). How Anthropomorphism Affects Trust in Intelligent Personal Assistants. *Industrial Management & Data Systems*, *121*(12), 2722–2737.

Cheng, M., Nazarian, S., & Bogdan, P. (2020). There Is Hope after All: Quantifying Opinion and Trustworthiness in Neural Networks. *Frontiers in Artificial Intelligence*, *3*, 54.

Cheng, X., Zhang, X., Cohen, J., & Mou, J. (2022). Human vs. AI: Understanding the Impact of Anthropomorphism on Consumer Response to Chatbots from the Perspective of Trust and Relationship Norms. *Information Processing & Management*, *59*(3), 102940.

Cheung, C. M.-Y., Sia, C.-L., & Kuan, K. K. (2012). Is this Review Believable? A Study of Factors Affecting the Credibility of Online Consumer Reviews from an ELM Perspective. *Journal of the Association for Information Systems*, *13*(8), 2.

Chien, S.-Y., Lewis, M., Sycara, K., Liu, J.-S., & Kumru, A. (2018). The Effect of Culture on Trust in Automation: Reliability and Workload. *ACM Transactions on Interactive Intelligent Systems (TiiS)*, *8*(4), 1–31.

Choi, W., & Stvilia, B. (2015). Web Credibility Assessment: Conceptualization, Operationalization, Variability, and Models. *Journal of the Association for Information Science and Technology*, *66*(12), 2399–2414.

Cotte, J., Coulter, R. A., & Moore, M. (2005). Enhancing or Disrupting Guilt: The Role of Ad Credibility and Perceived Manipulative Intent. *Journal of Business Research*, *58*(3), 361–368.

Cukurova, M., Luckin, R., & Kent, C. (2020). Impact of an Artificial Intelligence Research Frame on the Perceived Credibility of Educational Research Evidence. *International Journal of Artificial Intelligence in Education*, *30*(2), 205–235.

De Freitas, J., Agarwal, S., Schmitt, B., & Haslam, N. (2023). Psychological Factors underlying Attitudes toward AI Tools. *Nature Human Behaviour*, *7*(11), 1845–1854.

Distefano, S., Di Giacomo, A., & Mazzara, M. (2021). Trustworthiness for Transportation Ecosystems: The Blockchain Vehicle Information System. *IEEE Transactions on Intelligent Transportation Systems*, *22*(4), 2013–2022.

Durán, J. M., & Jongsma, K. R. (2021). Who Is Afraid of Black Box Algorithms? On the Epistemological and Ethical Basis of Trust in Medical AI. *Journal of Medical Ethics*, *47*(5), 329–335.

Dzindolet, M. T., Peterson, S. A., Pomranky, R. A., Pierce, L. G., & Beck, H. P. (2003). The Role of Trust in Automation Reliance. *International Journal of Human–Computer Studies*, *58*(6), 697–718.

Edunjobi, T. E., & Odejide, O. A. (2024). Theoretical Frameworks in AI for Credit Risk Assessment: Towards Banking Efficiency and Accuracy. *International Journal of Scientific Research Updates*, *7*(1), 92–102.

Edwards, C., Edwards, A., & Omilion-Hodges, L. (2018). Receiving Medical Treatment Plans from a Robot: Evaluations of Presence, Credibility, and Attraction. *Companion of the 2018 ACM/IEEE International Conference on Human–Robot Interaction* (pp. 101–102). ACM.

Ehsan, U., Liao, Q. V., Muller, M., Riedl, M. O., & Weisz, J. D. (2021). Expanding Explainability: Towards Social Transparency in AI Systems. *Proceedings of the 2021 CHI Conference on Human Factors in Computing Systems* (pp. 101–102). ACM.

Ernst, C. (2020). Artificial Intelligence and Autonomy: Self-determination in the Age of Automated Systems. *Regulating Artificial Intelligence*, 53–73.

Esmaeilzadeh, P. (2020). Use of AI-based Tools for Healthcare Purposes: A Survey Study from Consumers' Perspectives. *BMC Medical Informatics and Decision Making*, 20, 1–19.

Esmaeilzadeh, P. (2024). Challenges and Strategies for Wide-scale Artificial Intelligence (AI) Deployment in Healthcare Practices: A Perspective for Healthcare Organizations. *Artificial Intelligence in Medicine*, 151, 102861.

Fehr, J., Jaramillo-Gutierrez, G., Oala, L., Gröschel, M. I., Bierwirth, M., Balachandran, P., Werneck-Leite, A., & Lippert, C. (2022). Piloting a Survey-based Assessment of Transparency and Trustworthiness with Three Medical AI Tools. *Healthcare*, 10(10), 1923.

Finkel, M., & Krämer, N. C. (2022). Humanoid Robots–Artificial. Human-like. Credible? Empirical Comparisons of Source Credibility Attributions between Humans, Humanoid Robots, and Non-human-like Devices. *International Journal of Social Robotics*, 14(6), 1397–1411.

Flanagin, A. J., & Metzger, M. J. (2007). The Role of Site Features, User Attributes, and Information Verification Behaviors on the Perceived Credibility of Web-based Information. *New Media & Society*, 9(2), 319–342.

Flanagin, A. J., & Metzger, M. J. (2017). Digital Media and Perceptions of Source Credibility in Political Communication. In K. Kenski & K. H. Jamieson (eds.), *The Oxford Handbook of Political Communication* (pp. 417–436). Oxford University Press.

Fogg, B. J. (2003). Prominence–Interpretation Theory: Explaining How People Assess Credibility Online. *CHI'03 Extended Abstracts on Human Factors in Computing Systems* (pp. 722–723). ACM.

Fogg, B. J., & Tseng, H. (1999). The Elements of Computer Credibility. *Proceedings of the SIGCHI Conference on Human Factors in Computing Systems* (pp. 80–87). ACM.

Giroux, M., Kim, J., Lee, J. C., & Park, J. (2022). Artificial Intelligence and Declined Guilt: Retailing Morality Comparison between Human and AI. *Journal of Business Ethics*, 178(4), 1027–1041.

Grimmelikhuijsen, S. (2023). Explaining Why the Computer Says No: Algorithmic Transparency Affects the Perceived Trustworthiness of Automated Decision-making. *Public Administration Review*, 83(2), 241–262.

Ha, T., & Kim, S. (2024). Improving Trust in AI with Mitigating Confirmation Bias: Effects of Explanation Type and Debiasing Strategy for Decision-Making with Explainable AI. *International Journal of Human–Computer Interaction*, 40(24), 8562–8573.

Habbal, A., Ali, M. K., & Abuzaraida, M. A. (2024). Artificial Intelligence Trust, Risk and Security Management (AI trism): Frameworks, Applications, Challenges and Future Research Directions. *Expert Systems with Applications*, 240, 122442.

Hallowell, N., Badger, S., Sauerbrei, A., Nellåker, C., & Kerasidou, A. (2022). "I Don't Think People Are Ready to Trust These Algorithms at Face Value": Trust and the

Use of Machine Learning Algorithms in the Diagnosis of Rare Disease. *BMC Medical Ethics, 23*(1), 112.

Hamon, R., Junklewitz, H., Malgieri, G., Hert, P. D., Beslay, L., & Sanchez, I. (2021). Impossible Explanations? Beyond Explainable AI in the GDPR from a COVID-19 Use Case Scenario. *Proceedings of the 2021 ACM Conference on Fairness, Accountability, and Transparency* (pp. 549–559). ACM.

Hayashi, Y., & Wakabayashi, K. (2017). Can AI Become Reliable Source to Support Human Decision Making in a Court Scene? *Companion of the 2017 ACM Conference on Computer Supported Cooperative Work and Social Computing* (pp. 195–198). ACM.

Hilligoss, B., & Rieh, S. Y. (2008). Developing a Unifying Framework of Credibility Assessment: Construct, Heuristics, and Interaction in Context. *Information Processing & Management, 44*(4), 1467–1484.

Hofeditz, L., Mirbabaie, M., Holstein, J., & Stieglitz, S. (2021). *Do You Trust an AI-Journalist? A Credibility Analysis of News Content with AI-Authorship*. ECIS.

Hohenstein, J., & Jung, M. (2020). AI as a Moral Crumple Zone: The Effects of AI-mediated Communication on Attribution and Trust. *Computers in Human Behavior, 106*, 106190.

Holzinger, A., Langs, G., Denk, H., Zatloukal, K., & Müller, H. (2019). Causability and Explainability of Artificial Intelligence in Medicine. *Wiley Interdisciplinary Reviews: Data Mining and Knowledge Discovery, 9*(4), e1312.

Hu, Y., Kuang, W., Qin, Z., Li, K., Zhang, J., Gao, Y., Li, W., & Li, K. (2021). Artificial Intelligence Security: Threats and Countermeasures. *ACM Computing Surveys (CSUR), 55*(1), 1–36.

Huang, Y., Sun, L., Wang, H., Wu, S., Zhang, Q., Li, Y., Gao, C., Huang, Y., Lyu, W., & Zhang, Y. (2024). Position: TrustLLM: Trustworthiness in Large Language Models. *International Conference on Machine Learning* (pp. 20166–20270). PMLR.

Huschens, M., Briesch, M., Sobania, D., & Rothlauf, F. (2023). Do You Trust ChatGPT?: Perceived Credibility of Human and AI-Generated Content. [arXiv preprint]. arXiv:2309.02524.

Jain, R., Garg, N., & Khera, S. N. (2023). Effective Human–AI Work Design for Collaborative Decision-making. *Kybernetes, 52*(11), 5017–5040.

Jeon, Y., Kim, J., Park, S., Ko, Y., Ryu, S., Kim, S.-W., & Han, K. (2024). HearHere: Mitigating Echo Chambers in News Consumption through an AI-based Web System. *Proceedings of the ACM on Human–Computer Interaction, 8*(CSCW1), 1–34.

Johnson, D., Goodman, R., Patrinely, J., Stone, C., Zimmerman, E., Donald, R., Chang, S., Berkowitz, S., Finn, A., & Jahangir, E. (2023). Assessing the Accuracy and Reliability of AI-generated Medical Responses: An Evaluation of the Chat-GPT Model. *Research Square*.

Kaissis, G. A., Makowski, M. R., Rückert, D., & Braren, R. F. (2020). Secure, Privacy-Preserving and Federated Machine Learning in Medical Imaging. *Nature Machine Intelligence, 2*(6), 305–311.

Khan, A. W., & Mishra, A. (2024). AI Credibility and Consumer–AI Experiences: A Conceptual Framework. *Journal of Service Theory and Practice, 34*(1), 66–97.

Kim, J., Giroux, M., & Lee, J. C. (2021). When Do You Trust AI? The Effect of Number Presentation Detail on Consumer Trust and Acceptance of AI Recommendations. *Psychology & Marketing, 38*(7), 1140–1155.

Kim, J., Merrill Jr, K., Xu, K., & Kelly, S. (2022). Perceived Credibility of an AI Instructor in Online Education: The Role of Social Presence and Voice Features. *Computers in Human Behavior, 136*, 107383.

Kim, S., & Kim, B. (2020). A Decision-making Model for Adopting AI-generated News Articles: Preliminary Results. *Sustainability, 12*(18), 7418.

Knowles, B., & Richards, J. T. (2021). The Sanction of Authority: Promoting Public Trust in AI. *Proceedings of the 2021 ACM Conference on Fairness, Accountability, and Transparency* (pp. 262–271). ACM.

Kohn, S. C., De Visser, E. J., Wiese, E., Lee, Y.-C., & Shaw, T. H. (2021). Measurement of Trust in Automation: A Narrative Review and Reference Guide. *Frontiers in Psychology, 12*, 604977.

Lee, J. D., & Kolodge, K. (2020). Exploring Trust in Self-driving Vehicles through Text Analysis. *Human Factors, 62*(2), 260–277.

Lee, S. S. (2022). Philosophical Evaluation of the Conceptualisation of Trust in the NHS' Code of Conduct for Artificial Intelligence-driven Technology. *Journal of Medical Ethics, 48*(4), 272–277.

Lehmann, C. A., Haubitz, C. B., Fügener, A., & Thonemann, U. W. (2022). The Risk of Algorithm Transparency: How Algorithm Complexity Drives the Effects on the Use of Advice. *Production and Operations Management, 31*(9), 3419–3434.

Leo, X., & Huh, Y. E. (2020). Who Gets the Blame for Service Failures? Attribution of Responsibility toward Robot versus Human Service Providers and Service Firms. *Computers in Human Behavior, 113*, 106520.

Leong, B., & Selinger, E. (2019). Robot Eyes Wide Shut: Understanding Dishonest Anthropomorphism. *Proceedings of the Conference on Fairness, Accountability, and Transparency* (pp. 299–308). ACM.

Liang, W., Tadesse, G. A., Ho, D., Fei-Fei, L., Zaharia, M., Zhang, C., & Zou, J. (2022). Advances, Challenges and Opportunities in Creating Data for Trustworthy AI. *Nature Machine Intelligence, 4*(8), 669–677.

Liao, M.-Q., & Mak, A. K. (2019). "Comments are Disabled for This Video": A Technological Affordances Approach to Understanding Source Credibility Assessment of CSR Information on YouTube. *Public Relations Review, 45*(5), 101840.

Lim, B. Y., Yang, Q., Abdul, A. M., & Wang, D. (2019). Why These Explanations? Selecting Intelligibility Types for Explanation Goals. *IUI Workshops*.

Lim, W. M., Gunasekara, A., Pallant, J. L., Pallant, J. I., & Pechenkina, E. (2023). Generative AI and the Future of Education: Ragnarök or Reformation? A Paradoxical Perspective from Management Educators. *The International Journal of Management Education, 21*(2), 100790.

Lin, Y.-S., Lee, W.-C., & Celik, Z. B. (2021). What Do You See? Evaluation of Explainable Artificial Intelligence (XAI) Interpretability through Neural Backdoors. *Proceedings of the 27th ACM SIGKDD Conference on Knowledge Discovery & Data Mining* (pp. 1027–1035). ACM.

Lo, S. K., Liu, Y., Lu, Q., Wang, C., Xu, X., Paik, H.-Y., & Zhu, L. (2022). Toward Trustworthy AI: Blockchain-based Architecture Design for Accountability and Fairness of Federated Learning Systems. *IEEE Internet of Things Journal, 10*(4), 3276–3284.

Longoni, C., Fradkin, A., Cian, L., & Pennycook, G. (2022). News from Generative Artificial Intelligence Is Believed Less. *Proceedings of the 2022 ACM Conference on Fairness, Accountability, and Transparency* (pp. 97–106). ACM.

Lu, L., McDonald, C., Kelleher, T., Lee, S., Chung, Y. J., Mueller, S., Vielledent, M., & Yue, C. A. (2022). Measuring Consumer-perceived Humanness of Online Organizational Agents. *Computers in Human Behavior, 128*, 107092.

Lu, Z., Li, P., Wang, W., & Yin, M. (2022). The Effects of AI-based Credibility Indicators on the Detection and Spread of Misinformation under Social Influence. *Proceedings of the ACM on Human–Computer Interaction, 6* (CSCW2), 1–27.

Mansour, A., & Francke, H. (2017). Credibility Assessments of Everyday Life Information on Facebook: A Sociocultural Investigation of a Group of Mothers. *Information Research, 22*(2).

Markus, A. F., Kors, J. A., & Rijnbeek, P. R. (2021). The Role of Explainability in Creating Trustworthy Artificial Intelligence for Health Care: A Comprehensive Survey of the Terminology, Design Choices, and Evaluation Strategies. *Journal of Biomedical Informatics, 113*, 103655.

McCroskey, J. C., & Young, T. J. (1981). Ethos and Credibility: The Construct and Its Measurement after Three Decades. *Communication Studies, 32*(1), 24–34.

Mehrabi, N., Morstatter, F., Saxena, N., Lerman, K., & Galstyan, A. (2021). A Survey on Bias and Fairness in Machine Learning. *ACM Computing Surveys (CSUR), 54*(6), 1–35.

Molina, M. D., & Sundar, S. S. (2022). When AI Moderates Online Content: Effects of Human Collaboration and Interactive Transparency on User Trust. *Journal of Computer-mediated Communication, 27*(4), zmac010.

Momen, A., De Visser, E., Wolsten, K., Cooley, K., Walliser, J., & Tossell, C. C. (2023). Trusting the Moral Judgments of a Robot: Perceived Moral Competence and Humanlikeness of a GPT-3 enabled AI. In *Proceedings of the 56th Hawaii International Conference on System Sciences* (pp. 501–510). IEEE.

Monfort, S. S., Graybeal, J. J., Harwood, A. E., McKnight, P. E., & Shaw, T. H. (2018). A Single-item Assessment for Remaining Mental Resources: Development and Validation of the Gas Tank Questionnaire (GTQ). *Theoretical Issues in Ergonomics Science, 19*(5), 530–552.

Morley, J., Machado, C. C., Burr, C., Cowls, J., Joshi, I., Taddeo, M., & Floridi, L. (2020). The Ethics of AI in Health Care: A Mapping Review. *Social Science & Medicine, 260*, 113172.

Mou, Y., & Meng, X. (2024). Alexa, It Is Creeping over Me: Exploring the Impact of Privacy Concerns on Consumer Resistance to Intelligent Voice Assistants. *Asia Pacific Journal of Marketing and Logistics, 36*(2), 261–292.

Pareek, S., van Berkel, N., Velloso, E., & Goncalves, J. (2024). Effect of Explanation Conceptualisations on Trust in AI-assisted Credibility Assessment. *Proceedings of the ACM on Human–Computer Interaction CSCW*.

Peckham, J. B. (2024). An AI Harms and Governance Framework for Trustworthy AI. *Computer, 57*(3), 59–68.

Pelau, C., Dabija, D.-C., & Ene, I. (2021). What Makes an AI Device Human-like? The Role of Interaction Quality, Empathy and Perceived Psychological

Anthropomorphic Characteristics in the Acceptance of Artificial Intelligence in the Service Industry. *Computers in Human Behavior, 122*, 106855.

Raji, I. D., Smart, A., White, R. N., Mitchell, M., Gebru, T., Hutchinson, B., Smith-Loud, J., Theron, D., & Barnes, P. (2020). Closing the AI Accountability Gap: Defining an End-to-End Framework for Internal Algorithmic Auditing. *Proceedings of the 2020 Conference on Fairness, Accountability, and Transparency* (pp. 33–44). ACM.

Reinhardt, K. (2023). Trust and Trustworthiness in AI Ethics. *AI and Ethics, 3*(3), 735–744.

Rieh, S. Y. (2002). Judgment of Information Quality and Cognitive Authority in the Web. *Journal of the American Society for Information Science and Technology, 53*(2), 145–161.

Rieh, S. Y., & Danielson, D. R. (2007). Credibility: A Multidisciplinary Framework. *Annual Review of Information Science and Technology, 41*(1), 307–364.

Ruan, W., Wu, M., Sun, Y., Huang, X., Kroening, D., & Kwiatkowska, M. (2019). Global Robustness Evaluation of Deep Neural Networks with Provable Guarantees for the Hamming Distance. *IJCAI-19*.

Sabharwal, R., Miah, S. J., Wamba, S. F., & Cook, P. (2024). Extending Application of Explainable Artificial Intelligence for Managers in Financial Organizations. *Annals of Operations Research*, 1–31.

Sambasivan, N., Arnesen, E., Hutchinson, B., Doshi, T., & Prabhakaran, V. (2021). Re-imagining Algorithmic Fairness in India and Beyond. *Proceedings of the 2021 ACM Conference on Fairness, Accountability, and Transparency* (pp. 315–328). ACM.

Sanneman, L., & Shah, J. A. (2022). The Situation Awareness Framework for Explainable AI (SAFE-AI) and Human Factors Considerations for XAI Systems. *International Journal of Human–Computer Interaction, 38*(18–20), 1772–1788.

Schmitt, A., Wambsganss, T., Söllner, M., & Janson, A. (2021). *Towards a Trust Reliance Paradox? Exploring the Gap Between Perceived Trust in and Reliance on Algorithmic Advice*. ICIS.

Schoenherr, J. R., Abbas, R., Michael, K., Rivas, P., & Anderson, T. D. (2023). Designing AI Using a Human-centered Approach: Explainability and Accuracy toward Trustworthiness. *IEEE Transactions on Technology and Society, 4*(1), 9–23.

Sebastian, G., George, A., & Jackson Jr, G. (2023). Persuading Patients Using Rhetoric to Improve Artificial Intelligence Adoption: Experimental Study. *Journal of Medical Internet Research, 25*, e41430.

Shahriar, S., Allana, S., Hazratifard, S. M., & Dara, R. (2023). A Survey of Privacy Risks and Mitigation Strategies in the Artificial Intelligence Life Cycle. *IEEE Access, 11*, 61829–61854.

Shank, C. E. (2021). Credibility of Soft Law for Artificial Intelligence: Planning and Stakeholder Considerations. *IEEE Technology and Society Magazine, 40*(4), 25–36.

Shin, D. (2022). How Do People Judge the Credibility of Algorithmic Sources? *AI & Society*, 1–16.

Shin, D. (2023). Embodying Algorithms, Enactive Artificial Intelligence and the Extended Cognition: You Can See as Much as You Know About Algorithm. *Journal of Information Science, 49*(1), 18–31.

Shin, D., Rasul, A., & Fotiadis, A. (2022). Why am I Seeing This? Deconstructing Algorithm Literacy through the Lens of Users. *Internet Research, 32*(4), 1214–1234.

Shneiderman, B. (2020). Bridging the Gap between Ethics and Practice: Guidelines for Reliable, Safe, and Trustworthy Human-centered AI Systems. *ACM Transactions on Interactive Intelligent Systems (TiiS), 10*(4), 1–31.

Shusas, E. (2024). Designing Better Credibility Indicators: Understanding How Emerging Adults Assess Source Credibility of Misinformation Identification and Labeling. In *Companion Publication of the 2024 ACM Designing Interactive Systems Conference* (pp. 41–44).

Sokol, K., & Flach, P. (2020). Explainability Fact Sheets: A Framework for Systematic Assessment of Explainable Approaches. *Proceedings of the 2020 Conference on Fairness, Accountability, and Transparency* (pp. 56–67). ACM.

Song, S., Zhao, Y. C., Yao, X., Ba, Z., & Zhu, Q. (2021). Short Video Apps as a Health Information Source: An Investigation of Affordances, User Experience and Users' Intention to Continue the Use of TikTok. *Internet Research, 31*(6), 2120–2142.

Stettinger, G., Weissensteiner, P., & Khastgir, S. (2024). *Trustworthiness Assurance Assessment for High-Risk AI-Based Systems*. IEEE Access.

Stevens, A. F., & Stetson, P. (2023). Theory of Trust and Acceptance of Artificial Intelligence Technology (TrAAIT): An Instrument to Assess Clinician Trust and Acceptance of Artificial Intelligence. *Journal of Biomedical Informatics, 148*, 104550.

Sundar, S. S. (2008). *The MAIN Model: A Heuristic Approach to Understanding Technology Effects on Credibility*. MacArthur Foundation Digital Media and Learning Initiative.

Tandoc Jr, E. C., Yao, L. J., & Wu, S. (2020). Man vs. Machine? The Impact of Algorithm Authorship on News Credibility. *Digital Journalism, 8*(4), 548–562.

Tenhundfeld, N. L., de Visser, E. J., Ries, A. J., Finomore, V. S., & Tossell, C. C. (2020). Trust and Distrust of Automated Parking in a Tesla Model X. *Human Factors, 62*(2), 194–210.

Toreini, E., Aitken, M., Coopamootoo, K., Elliott, K., Zelaya, C. G., & Van Moorsel, A. (2020). The Relationship between Trust in AI and Trustworthy Machine Learning Technologies. *Proceedings of the 2020 Conference on Fairness, Accountability, and Transparency* (pp. 272–283). ACM.

Tossell, C. C., Tenhundfeld, N. L., Momen, A., Cooley, K., & de Visser, E. J. (2024). Student Perceptions of ChatGPT Use in a College Essay Assignment: Implications for Learning, Grading, and Trust in Artificial Intelligence. *IEEE Transactions on Learning Technologies*.

Trindade Neves, F., Aparicio, M., & de Castro Neto, M. (2024). The Impacts of Open Data and eXplainable AI on Real Estate Price Predictions in Smart Cities. *Applied Sciences, 14*(5), 2209.

Tseng, S., & Fogg, B. J. (1999). Credibility and Computing Technology. *Communications of the ACM, 42*(5), 39–44.

Ullman, D., & Malle, B. F. (2019). Measuring Gains and Losses in Human–Robot Trust: Evidence for Differentiable Components of Trust. *2019 14th ACM/IEEE International Conference on Human-Robot Interaction (HRI)* (pp. 618–619). IEEE.

Uslu, S., Kaur, D., Rivera, S. J., Durresi, A., Durresi, M., & Babbar-Sebens, M. (2021). Trustworthy Acceptance: A New Metric for Trustworthy Artificial Intelligence Used in Decision Making in Food–Energy–Water Sectors. *International Conference on Advanced Information Networking and Applications* (pp. 208–219). Springer International Publishing.

Uzir, M. U. H., Bukari, Z., Al Halbusi, H., Lim, R., Wahab, S. N., Rasul, T., Thurasamy, R., Jerin, I., Chowdhury, M. R. K., & Tarofder, A. K. (2023). Applied Artificial Intelligence: Acceptance-Intention-Purchase and Satisfaction on Smartwatch Usage in a Ghanaian Context. *Heliyon*, 9(8).

Van Bulck, L., & Moons, P. (2024). What if Your Patient Switches from Dr. Google to Dr. ChatGPT? A Vignette-based Survey of the Trustworthiness, Value, and Danger of ChatGPT-generated Responses to Health Questions. *European Journal of Cardiovascular Nursing*, 23(1), 95–98.

Vincent-Lancrin, S., & Van der Vlies, R. (2020). Trustworthy Artificial Intelligence (AI) in Education: Promises and Challenges. *OECD Education Working Papers*, 218.

Vössing, M., Kühl, N., Lind, M., & Satzger, G. (2022). Designing Transparency for Effective Human–AI Collaboration. *Information Systems Frontiers*, 24(3), 877–895.

van der Waa, J., Schoonderwoerd, T., van Diggelen, J., & Neerincx, M. (2020). Interpretable Confidence Measures for Decision Support Systems. *International Journal of Human–Computer Studies*, 144, 102493.

Wach, K., Duong, C. D., Ejdys, J., Kazlauskaitė, R., Korzynski, P., Mazurek, G., Paliszkiewicz, J., & Ziemba, E. (2023). The Dark Side of Generative Artificial Intelligence: A Critical Analysis of Controversies and Risks of ChatGPT. *Entrepreneurial Business and Economics Review*, 11(2), 7–30.

Wagle, V., Kaur, K., Kamat, P., Patil, S., & Kotecha, K. (2021). Explainable AI for Multimodal Credibility Analysis: Case Study of Online Beauty Health (mis)-Information. *IEEE Access*, 9, 127985–128022.

Wang, C., Ahmad, S. F., Ayassrah, A. Y. B. A., Awwad, E. M., Irshad, M., Ali, Y. A., Al-Razgan, M., Khan, Y., & Han, H. (2023). An Empirical Evaluation of Technology Acceptance Model for Artificial Intelligence in E-commerce. *Heliyon*, 9(8).

Wang, X., & Zhao, Y. C. (2023). Understanding Older Adults' Intention to Use Patient-accessible Electronic Health Records: Based on the Affordance Lens. *Frontiers in Public Health*, 10, 1075204.

Weeks, R., Sangha, P., Cooper, L., Sedoc, J., White, S., Gretz, S., Toledo, A., Lahav, D., Hartner, A.-M., & Martin, N. M. (2023). Usability and Credibility of a COVID-19 Vaccine Chatbot for Young Adults and Health Workers in the United States: Formative Mixed Methods Study. *JMIR Human Factors*, 10(1), e40533.

Winkle, K., Melsión, G. I., McMillan, D., & Leite, I. (2021). Boosting Robot Credibility and Challenging Gender Norms in Responding to Abusive Behaviour: A Case for Feminist Robots. *Companion of the 2021 ACM/IEEE International Conference on Human–Robot Interaction* (pp. 29–37). ACM.

Xiang, H., Zhou, J., & Xie, B. (2023). AI Tools for Debunking Online Spam Reviews? Trust of Younger and Older Adults in AI Detection Criteria. *Behaviour & Information Technology*, 42(5), 478–497.

Xu, W. (2019). Toward Human-centered AI: A Perspective from Human–Computer Interaction. *Interactions, 26*(4), 42–46.

Yang, Z. (2019). Fidelity: A Property of Deep Neural Networks to Measure the Trustworthiness of Prediction Results. *Proceedings of the 2019 ACM Asia Conference on Computer and Communications Security* (pp. 676–678). ACM.

Yeomans, M., Shah, A., Mullainathan, S., & Kleinberg, J. (2019). Making Sense of Recommendations. *Journal of Behavioral Decision Making, 32*(4), 403–414.

Yokoi, R., Eguchi, Y., Fujita, T., & Nakayachi, K. (2021). Artificial Intelligence Is Trusted Less Than a Doctor in Medical Treatment Decisions: Influence of Perceived Care and Value Similarity. *International Journal of Human–Computer Interaction, 37*(10), 981–990.

Yue, B., & Li, H. (2023). The Impact of Human–AI Collaboration Types on Consumer Evaluation and Usage Intention: A Perspective of Responsibility Attribution. *Frontiers in Psychology, 14*, 1277861.

Zahlan, A., Ranjan, R. P., & Hayes, D. (2023). Artificial Intelligence Innovation in Healthcare: Literature Review, Exploratory Analysis, and Future Research. *Technology in Society*, 102321.

Zalzal, H. G., Abraham, A., Cheng, J., & Shah, R. K. (2024). Can ChatGPT Help Patients Answer Their Otolaryngology Questions? *Laryngoscope Investigative Otolaryngology, 9*(1), e1193.

Zhang, J., & Zhang, Z.-M. (2023). Ethics and Governance of Trustworthy Medical Artificial Intelligence. *BMC Medical Informatics and Decision Making, 23*(1), 7.

Zhang, Y., Liao, Q. V., & Bellamy, R. K. (2020). Effect of Confidence and Explanation on Accuracy and Trust Calibration in AI-assisted Decision Making. *Proceedings of the 2020 Conference on Fairness, Accountability, and Transparency* (pp. 295–305).

Zhang, Z., Genc, Y., Wang, D., Ahsen, M. E., & Fan, X. (2021). Effect of AI Explanations on Human Perceptions of Patient-facing AI-powered Healthcare Systems. *Journal of Medical Systems, 45*(6), 64.

Zhou, J., Zhang, Y., Luo, Q., Parker, A. G., & De Choudhury, M. (2023). Synthetic Lies: Understanding AI-generated Misinformation and Evaluating Algorithmic and Human Solutions. *Proceedings of the 2023 CHI Conference on Human Factors in Computing Systems* (pp. 1–20). ACM.

Zhuang, N., Ma, Z., Zhou, Y., Li, X., Wang, P., Huang, Z., Zhai, S., & Ying, F. (2024). Alleviating Elderly's Medical Communication Issue with Personalized LLM-Generated Short-Form Video. *International Symposium on World Ecological Design* (pp. 763–772). IOS Press.

5
AI-supported Crowdsourcing for Knowledge Sharing

Chei Sian Lee, Dion Hoe-Lian Goh, Hang Guo, Kok Khiang Lim, and Qian Wu

5.1 Introduction

Crowdsourcing involves a diverse group of individuals coming together to address a specific task or problem within an interactive online environment (Estellés-Arolas & González-Ladrón-de-Guevara, 2012). This process is enabled by a digital platform that allows participants or contributors (also known as crowd workers) to collaborate, exchange ideas, and share knowledge, drawing on their combined knowledge and expertise. The collective effort not only helps in solving the task at hand but also harnesses the power of collective intelligence, where the group's shared insights and skills lead to more effective and innovative solutions.

5.1.1 Collective Intelligence from Crowdsourcing

Collective intelligence refers to the shared knowledge or group intelligence that emerges from the collaboration, collective efforts, and contributions of many crowd workers (Lévy, 1999). The phenomenon of creating collective intelligence to solve problems is not new and has been observed on social media sites. For example, on Wikipedia, crowd workers contribute by creating, editing, and updating content on the platform. These volunteers, who come from various backgrounds and locations, share their knowledge and expertise on various topics, ensuring that information is accurate, up-to-date, and accessible to everyone (Lindgren, 2014). Through the collaborative process, they add new articles, enhance existing ones, and verify facts, all while adhering to Wikipedia's guidelines and standards. This collective effort helps maintain Wikipedia as one of the most comprehensive and reliable sources of information on the internet. The crowd workers' knowledge sharing is crucial to the platform's success, as they continuously improve the quality, depth, and breadth of content available to users worldwide.

The collective intelligence from shared knowledge can lead to significant and influential outcomes, including solving major societal problems. Taking Wikipedia as an example again, it has become more than just an information repository; it has evolved into a dynamic platform where complex ideas are discussed, refined, and made accessible to a global audience. The collective intelligence is the aggregated contributions of these crowd workers that can lead to a deeper understanding of critical social issues and the formation of new insights that can inform policymaking, including but not limited to healthcare and education (Yang & Tanaka, 2023).

Indeed, diversity among crowd workers enables crowdsourcing to bring together varied perspectives that can be harnessed to address societal challenges (Brabham, 2012). An example of addressing societal knowledge inequality through crowdsourcing is seen in the efforts of volunteers with diverse language skills who dedicate their time and expertise to translating online course materials on learning platforms (Lee et al., 2024b). Here, the collective intelligence is the shared expertise of the crowd workers, which allows learners worldwide, particularly those whose native language is not English, to access quality educational resources. Another example is Ushahidi (www.ushahidi.com), where the crowdsourcing platform is used for social activism and public accountability to ensure that marginalized populations' voices are heard and their needs are taken care of (Gutierrez, 2019). In the context of Ushahidi, collective intelligence refers to the shared knowledge and problem-solving capabilities that emerge from the collaboration and aggregation of inputs from a diverse group of individuals using the platform. Additionally, widely known crowdsourcing platforms such as Foldit (http://fold.it) and Eyewire (http://eyewire.org) utilize games to engage altruistic participants in solving complex medical and biological problems, from protein folding to neuron mapping. The data generated through these games contribute directly to collective intelligence, showcasing the power of crowdsourcing in scientific discovery. Collectively, these examples highlight the diverse nature of inputs to collective intelligence, spanning playful interactions to expert contributions. Whether through gamified platforms or specialized knowledge, participants from various backgrounds collaborate to address a wide range of complex challenges, demonstrating the versatility and power of collective problem-solving.

5.1.2 Limitations of Human Capacity during Crowdsourcing

While collective intelligence holds immense potential for generating valuable insights and solutions, effectively harnessing it is complex and challenging.

Put differently, the efficiency of crowdsourcing is inherently limited by the human capacity for processing vast amounts of information, a challenge that becomes particularly evident when addressing large-scale societal issues (Vaughan, 2018). Notably, the potential of crowdsourcing to address significant societal issues is limited by several factors. First, the cognitive limitations of crowd workers mean that individuals can only process a certain amount of data before becoming overwhelmed or making errors in judgment (Bell et al., 2023). This is particularly problematic when dealing with complex, large-scale issues that require deep understanding and nuanced solutions. The sheer volume of data and the intricacy of the problems can lead to information overload, reducing the effectiveness of the collective effort.

Second, the reliance on voluntary, unpaid labor introduces additional challenges. While the altruistic nature of crowd workers can drive initial enthusiasm and participation, the lack of financial incentives may lead to burnout, disengagement, and a decline in sustained contributions over time (Goh et al., 2021). Without the motivation provided by compensation, volunteers may prioritize other commitments or lose interest, ultimately affecting the continuity and quality of the work (Lee et al., 2020). This can create gaps in the collaborative process, reducing the overall effectiveness and impact of the crowdsourcing initiative.

It is important to note that, while crowdsourcing can also involve paid contributors who are financially compensated for their efforts, this chapter primarily focuses on the dynamics and limitations of unpaid, volunteer-driven crowdsourcing to solve societal problems. Paid contributors can bring a different set of motivations, work ethics, and sustainability factors, which are not the focus here (Brabham, 2008). Instead, this chapter explores how users and motivational factors influence voluntary knowledge sharing in crowdsourcing efforts aimed at solving complex societal challenges. Through this process, factors such as the challenges of cognitive overload and reliance on unpaid labor that can hinder the long-term success and scalability of crowdsourcing efforts will also be clarified.

5.1.3 Integrating AI into Crowdsourcing

The integration of artificial intelligence (AI) technologies into our everyday life lives has rapidly advanced in recent years. AI now assists humans in decision-making across various fields, such as healthcare, finance, transportation, education, and customer service (Mahotra & Majchrzak, 2024). The emergence of AI has the potential to alleviate the constraints of crowdsourcing and further transform its processes. AI enhances collective intelligence by boosting human capabilities, promoting collaboration, and efficiently processing large volumes of data (Vaughan, 2018). AI's pervasive influence necessitates a thorough understanding of its role in crowdsourcing. We assert that AI-supported crowdsourcing has the potential to improve knowledge sharing and enhance contributions to collective intelligence efforts. Even though there is an expanding body of research on motivations and crowdsourcing, it is still unclear how AI-supported crowdsourcing may affect crowd workers' motives and, ultimately, their participation. Considering crowd workers' perspectives in AI-supported crowdsourcing is crucial for multiple reasons. It enhances engagement by aligning with user motivations and preferences and ultimately improves usability and system design. Additionally, this understanding will help address ethical concerns such as privacy and consent, which can lead to the platform's long-term sustainability and address long-term societal challenges.

5.1.4 Objectives

This chapter is, therefore, motivated by the limited understanding of AI-supported crowdsourcing. It has two main objectives. The first objective is to understand gaps and emerging trends in AI-supported crowdsourcing. We conducted a systematic review to shed light on existing studies that have employed AI during crowdsourcing and understand how AI aids in developing collective intelligence. From the review, we identified themes related to emerging trends, opportunities, and challenges surrounding the use of AI-supported crowdsourcing. Next, we collected empirical data from a real-life AI-supported crowdsourcing platform. Through the analysis of this case study, this chapter aims to shed light on users and motivational factors influencing knowledge sharing in crowdsourcing efforts. The focus of the case study discussion centered on leveraging crowd workers to address complex societal challenges and explored the potential obstacles that may impede the long-term success and scalability of these initiatives. Specifically, we investigated a global societal problem, child trafficking, to understand the user profiles and motives driving the use of AI-supported crowdsourcing to facilitate knowledge sharing.

5.2 Background on AI-supported Crowdsourcing

This chapter defines artificial intelligence (AI) as a system's ability to correctly interpret external data and adapt the data effectively to achieve specific goals and accomplish tasks (Haenlein & Kaplan, 2019). Two aspects of this definition need further discussion. In relation to human–AI interaction, AI makes it possible for machines to learn from experience, adjust to new inputs, and perform human-like tasks (Yang et al., 2020). In relation to data volume, AI enables computers to learn and perform specific tasks by analyzing large volumes of data and identifying patterns within it (Vaughan, 2018). Thus, this definition highlights the synergy between AI and crowdsourcing, combining the strengths of both approaches. Specifically, AI's ability to process and analyze large datasets is combined with human creativity, critical thinking, and diverse perspectives. This integrative perspective of AI and crowdsourcing not only amplifies the strengths of each but also creates new opportunities for innovation and problem-solving on societal challenges.

5.2.1 Differences between AI-supported Crowdsourcing and Traditional Crowdsourcing

Notably, AI-supported crowdsourcing differs significantly from traditional crowdsourcing. Generally, AI-supported crowdsourcing is far more scalable, as it is capable of handling complex and large-scale tasks that would be impractical with traditional crowdsourcing. These differences will be examined across key crowdsourcing components: the process, outcome, and user involvement.

In terms of the crowdsourcing *process*, AI algorithms can automate filtering, sorting, and categorizing large amounts of data, making the process faster and more efficient (Vaughan, 2018). Traditional crowdsourcing, on the other hand, often relies on manual review and analysis of contributions from large numbers of participants, which can be time-consuming and prone to human error.

As for the crowdsourcing *outcome*, AI-supported crowdsourcing can help validate and cross-check crowd workers' contributions, leading to improved accuracy (Mahotra & Majchrzak, 2024). Specifically, AI can detect inconsistencies or errors in the data submitted by human participants, automatically flagging or correcting anomalies based on predefined rules to ensure the integrity and reliability of the information being collected, enhancing the overall quality of crowdsourced outputs

From the *users'* perspective, AI-supported crowdsourcing can tailor the crowdsourcing tasks to individual users based on their skills, preferences, and past performance, making the experience more engaging and relevant. For instance, AI can dynamically adapt to users' progress over time. If a user consistently performs well in certain types of tasks, the system can offer more challenging assignments, fostering a sense of growth and mastery. Ultimately, AI can enhance user experience.

Collectively, prior studies suggest the potential for AI-supported crowdsourcing to be utilized in addressing complex situations and societal problems. Further research is needed to explore and realize this possibility.

5.2.2 Examples of AI-supported Crowdsourcing

There are several noteworthy examples of potential collaborations between AI and crowdsourcing. One is in the healthcare sector, where collaboration between AI and crowdsourcing offers the potential to improve personalized medicine and enhance the effectiveness of treatments. For instance, by combining AI's ability to process complex, high-volume medical data with crowdsourced experiential data from crowdsourcing platforms (e.g., www.patientslikeme.com/) shared by patients, healthcare providers can gain a more holistic understanding of diseases and treatments.

Integrating AI also offers significant value in the broader context of social Q&A sites (e.g., Reddit, Stack Overflow), which are also considered crowdsourcing platforms. Specifically, AI-driven features like chatbots or virtual assistants can engage users more effectively, providing immediate responses and encouraging participation in the community. Furthermore, AI can analyze user interactions and patterns to provide valuable insights into user behavior, trends, and content quality, which can help refine platform strategies and improve user satisfaction. Thus, integrating AI into social Q&A sites can significantly enhance the platform's functionality, user experience, and ability to manage and process information.

In terms of the actual implementation of AI-supported crowdsourcing, one example is Zooniverse, which leverages AI to assist volunteers in analyzing large datasets for scientific research, from identifying galaxies in space to tracking wildlife patterns on Earth (Ceccaroni et al., 2023). Further, recent crowdsourcing research in organizations suggested leveraging the power of AI to more efficiently screen out bad ideas and focus on only good ideas in the crowdsourcing process within ideation (Bell et al., 2023). The collective intelligence generated from contributions is enhanced by AI tools that model and process the data, leading to breakthroughs in research and problem-solving. Bjarnason et al. (2024) also discussed using AI to enhance collective intelligence. They presented an innovative toolkit that leverages AI to enable "smart" crowdsourcing, making the problem-solving approach more scalable, effective, and efficient.

In sum, AI-supported crowdsourcing represents a transformative advancement to enhance the efficiency and accuracy of crowdsourcing processes. By integrating AI's analytical capabilities with the collective intelligence of crowd workers, this approach can address complex challenges more effectively and open new avenues for innovation.

5.2.3 Lack of Research on AI-supported Crowdsourcing

While the above examples have underscored AI's potential to enhance collective intelligence in crowdsourcing, the factors influencing the adoption or non-adoption of AI-supported platforms remain unclear and require further in-depth investigation. Additionally, the literature on AI-supported crowdsourcing is limited. In particular, a holistic understanding of how AI could be applied to facilitate the development of collective intelligence is still lacking, but it is necessary to guide further research on crowdsourcing. More importantly, a user's perspective on AI-supported crowdsourcing and how it can enhance crowdsourcing initiatives for the public good is needed. Section 5.3 addresses these gaps through a systematic review.

5.3 Systematic Review of AI-supported Crowdsourcing

5.3.1 Systematic Review

A systematic review is a rigorous and methodical approach to reviewing and synthesizing existing research on a specific topic. We conducted a systematic review to help identify gaps in the literature and guide future research directions in AI-supported crowdsourcing. The PICO framework (Population, Intervention, Comparison/Control, Outcome) was applied to guide the systematic review (Lee et al., 2024a). The population includes crowd workers, and individuals who participate in crowdsourcing tasks, and datasets contributed through crowdsourcing. Intervention refers to using artificial intelligence or algorithmic methods to facilitate or address crowdsourcing. Comparison/Control involves benchmarking the outcomes. Outcome is the resultant output behavior, perceptions, or processes after interventions. This systematic review also follows the PRISMA guidelines, which include a 27-item checklist and a flowchart to ensure a thorough and transparent review process (Page et al., 2021).

The keywords for the searches were developed based on the research scope. The keywords also encompassed synonyms and alternative spellings, strung together using Boolean operators (OR/AND) to ensure comprehensive searches. The search query was as follows: "crowdsourc*" AND "collab*" AND ("artificial intelligence" OR "AI" OR "generative artificial intelligence" OR "generative AI" OR "GAI" OR "large language model" OR "LLM" OR "machine learning" OR "ML") AND ("societal" OR "welfare"). The searches were conducted in May 2024 across six major databases (Scopus, Web of Science, ACM Digital Library, IEEE Xplore, ScienceDirect, and Google Scholar) between January 2000 and May 2024. In addition, backward and forward citation searches (Bandara et al., 2011) were conducted in May 2024. The search results were captured and managed using a bibliographic management tool, Endnote (Bandara et al., 2011).

The inclusion criteria were: (1) published between January 2000 and May 2024; (2) written in English; (3) published in peer-reviewed journals; (4) available in full-text; (5) related to the scope of this study; and (6) not belonging to any grey literature. The exclusion criteria were: (1) duplicated studies; (2) grey literature (including studies published in preprint or related to the conceptual, working discussion, or literature review); (3) not written in English; and (4) not related to the scope of this study. These criteria were used to screen retrieved records from the databases, as well as during the full-text assessment. Further, PICO was used as an additional selection criterion to ensure the quality of the selected studies.

The five databases' searches produced 190 records, while the backward and forward citation searches identified 11 records (see Figure 5.1). After removing duplicated records (n = 11) and applying the filtering criteria, sixty-four records were further excluded. The remaining records (n = 115) were sought for full-text retrieval for detailed assessment. The final process yielded 6 studies for inclusion in this review after excluding 109 studies not within this review's scope. The limited number of studies currently available indicates that the concept of AI-supported crowdsourcing requires more comprehensive research and investigation to fully understand its potential and implications.

The included studies were analyzed, and data were extracted using six predefined categories. These include the year of publication, study context, sample characteristics, terminology related to the scope of this study, contributions or outcomes, and limitations. Extracted data were then clustered according to common themes for narrative synthesis. Table 5.1 shows a summary of the studies included in this review. Table 5.2 shows a detailed list of the reviewed studies and the terms associated with societal challenges and problem-solving tasks.

5.3.2 Themes from the Systematic Review

The review identified three key themes that highlight both the trends and gaps in AI-supported crowdsourcing: solving complex and challenging issues, lacking practical research, and addressing ethical considerations.

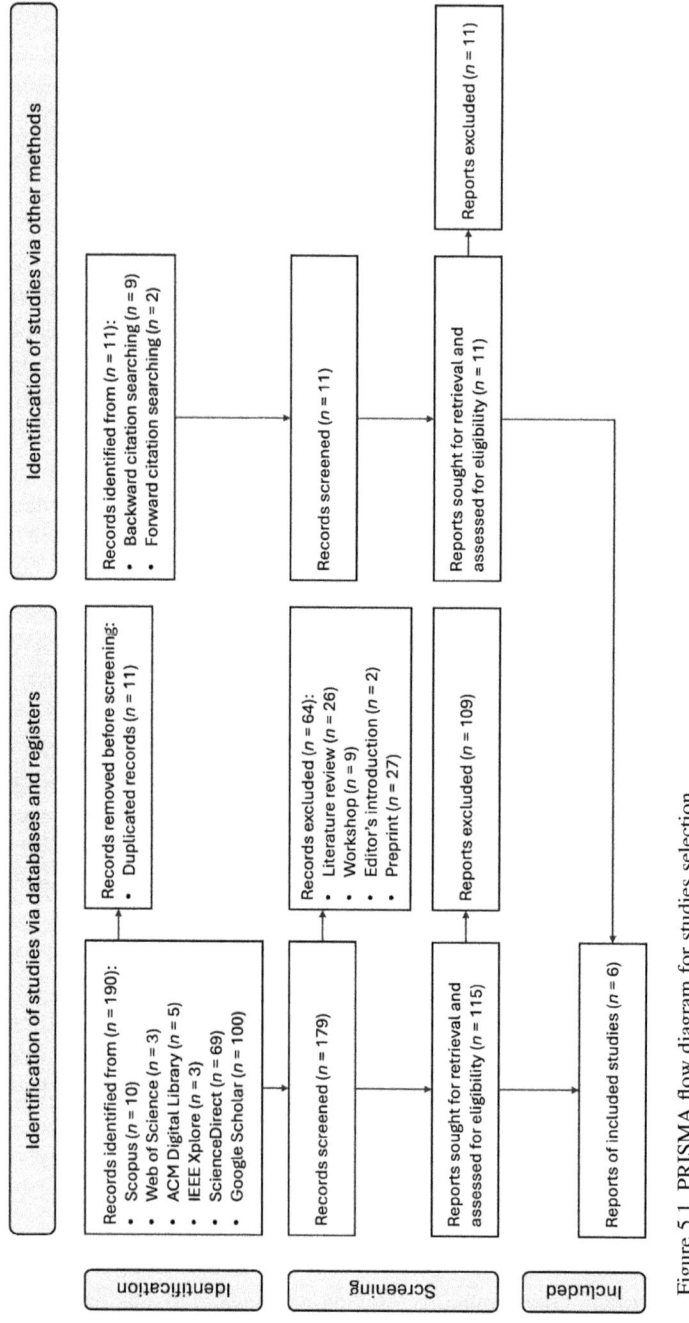

Figure 5.1 PRISMA flow diagram for studies selection

Table 5.1 *Summary of the reviewed studies*

Author / Year	Sample	How does AI support crowdsourcing?
Gimpel et al. (2023)	311 workers	Macro-task crowdsourcing is labor-intensive and complex to facilitate (e.g., sustainable development goals defined by the United Nations), and technology such as AI might overcome these limits. This study evaluates AI affordances and how they could facilitate macro-task crowdsourcing and advance the discourse on facilitation.
Haider et al. (2024)	238 participants from Prolific platform	The increasing prevalence of automatic decision-making systems has raised concerns regarding the fairness of these systems, and the crowdsourced approach to solicit fairness definition are highly context-dependent. This study investigates the hypothesis toward people's fairness perceptions in three societal contexts, each differ on the expected level of risk associated with different types of decision mistakes.
Köhl et al. (2019)	Data from openIDEO platform	Crowdsourcing is increasingly being used to find solutions for pressing wicked problems (e.g., environmental pollution). However, most solutions focus on a few ideas and ignore the large volume of content created by the community. This study applies an automated text-mining technique to analyze the ideas contributed by the community.
Vinella et al. (2022a)	Data for modeling and simulation	Crowdsourcing offers potential solutions to solve complex tasks (e.g., pandemic prevention and emergency response) that require teamwork and collective labor. However, forming project teams from the vast scale of the crowd is a difficult problem. This chapter investigates different ways that crowd teams can be formed from the algorithmic simulation of three team formation models.
Vinella et al. (2022b)	120 participants from Amazon Mechanical Turk	Intense and high-pressure tasks (e.g., environmental disasters) are often solved by teams that are cohesive, adaptable, and prepared, but little is known about how teams of crowdsourced strangers would cooperate and contribute to the teamwork. This study explores which factors matter for team success and perceptions of collaboration quality, as well as how it could support the future work on AI-supported crowdsourcing of remote emergency response teams.
Yu et al. (2019)	Data from the prototype system	Businesses face large fluctuations in manpower demand and require efficient ways to meet the demands. This study proposes an AI-empowered crowdsourcing platform to perform efficient explainable task-worker matching, which aims to address societal challenges (e.g., unfair treatment of workers).

Table 5.2 *Impacts examined in the reviewed studies*

Author	Societal Impact	Description
Gimpel et al. (2023)	Macro-task related to sustainable development goals	Refers to tasks (e.g., sustainable development goals) that are difficult or at times not possible to break down into smaller sub-tasks (Robert, 2019).
Haider et al. (2024)	Events related to societal and cultural context	Refers to social or cultural factors that influence decision-making associated with the events (e.g., perceived risks in requirement prediction).
Köhl et al. (2019)	Wicked problems	Refers to problems (e.g., environmental pollution) which resulted from innumerable causes which are difficult to describe their complete magnitude, and there is no easy way out (Rittel & Webber, 1973; Villarrubia-Gómez et al., 2017).
Vinella et al. (2022a; 2022b)	Complex task	A collective references to macro-task or wicked problems, as well as tasks that are critical, time-bounded, and high pressure (e.g., environmental disaster).
Yu et al. (2019)	Societal challenge with a focus on user profiles	Refers to the problems such as those posed by demographic changes, job securities and wellbeing that require concerted efforts to address it (e.g., ad-hoc work arrangements through untrustworthy agents exposes workers to high risk of exploitation and swindling).
Kokshagina (2022)	Grand challenges related to global problems	Refers as global problems (e.g., COVID-19), characterized as complex, uncertain, and evaluative (Ferraro et al., 2015), that are only effectively addressed through a coordinated and collaborative effort (George et al., 2016) which require technical and societal components to deal with them (Eisenhardt et al., 2016).

By understanding and addressing these themes, researchers and practitioners can enhance crowdsourcing initiatives' effectiveness, efficiency, and ethical standards to solve societal tasks.

A central theme that emerged across the six studies examining integrating AI into crowdsourcing was its potential to tackle complex and challenging societal problems. Although varying in nature, these problems were all characterized by their complexity and the significant obstacles they present, requiring innovative and collaborative approaches to find solutions. These issues ranged from global ones, such as sustainable developmental goals and the COVID-19 pandemic, to localized challenges like demographic changes and emergency responses. Put simply, AI-supported crowdsourcing can enhance collaborative human efforts and solve difficult and complex societal challenges. The review also revealed that successfully leveraging AI requires careful consideration of how to align the AI technology with the specific needs and motivations of the crowd, ensuring that the resulting solutions are not only innovative but also socially and ethically responsible. Therefore, a thorough examination of the motives of crowd workers to understand their needs will be a crucial first step.

Next, although technological advancement has accelerated tremendously in recent years, particularly for AI, the review shows that the integration of AI technology into crowdsourcing platforms has not fully reached its potential to overcome existing limitations, such as task scalability, quality control, and the efficient use of collective intelligence. Indeed, there are challenges related to the ethical use of AI, ensuring transparency, and maintaining trust among users – these are barriers to the implementation of AI-supported crowdsourcing. This suggests that, while AI-supported crowdsourcing holds great promise, much work remains to fully leverage AI's capabilities in solving complex societal problems. Specifically, more practical research on utilizing existing platforms is needed to close this gap and harness the full potential of AI in enhancing crowdsourcing efforts for societal good.

Finally, this review examined two ethical considerations about using AI in crowdsourcing, reflecting the complexity and dual nature of the impact of technology on society. Haider et al. (2024) highlighted the fairness of automatic decision-making systems, as the perception of fairness is highly context-dependent. On the other hand, Yu et al. (2019) suggested exploring how artificial intelligence could be applied to ensure fairness, transparency, and accountability in facilitating crowdsourcing tasks. From a broader perspective, these concerns are interrelated with the transparency and accountability of AI systems. This means that the complexity of AI algorithms can make it difficult for participants to understand how their contributions are being used, raising questions about consent, data privacy, and trust. These ethical concerns may influence the motives of crowd workers, and they need to be addressed.

5.3.3 Summary from the Systematic Review

In summary, integrating AI into crowdsourcing can significantly alter the dynamics of the factors affecting usage. AI introduces new elements into the process that may influence individuals' willingness to share knowledge and contribute to the development of collective intelligence. However, the impact of these AI-supported crowdsourcing elements on participants' profiles and motives has not been fully understood, representing a gap in the literature.

To address this gap, we employed a case study that examined the factors underlying the use of an AI-supported crowdsourcing platform to address a significant societal issue – child trafficking. This is presented in Section 5.4.

5.4 Case Study

Child trafficking is a critical issue that affects societies worldwide. It is a social justice issue that significantly affects human autonomy (Flores, 2009). In the United Kingdom, an estimated 112,853 children are reported missing every year (Global Missing Children's Network, 2023). The number of declared missing children was 359,094 in the United States and more than 25,000 in Africa in 2022 (AfricaNews, 2022; Roush, 2023). Due to the large scale of child trafficking victims, combating it is challenging as limited human capacity and resources are available for tracing suspected trafficked children and providing timely rescue.

To address this issue, crowdsourcing is a feasible option, given its ability to amass a community of users to collectively address a designated task (Assis Neto & Santos, 2018). By connecting willing crowd workers (volunteers) and relevant stakeholders focused on trafficked children, crowdsourcing offers a platform for collaborative rescue efforts (Goh et al., 2018). Nonetheless, it is still hard for human beings to process large amounts of information regarding victims, and it is even harder for them to recognize trafficked children as their appearance changes with age. Due to the limits of human information processing capacity, we examined an AI-supported crowdsourcing platform to combat child trafficking. The study aimed to address one question – will incorporating AI technology affect crowd workers and their motivations to participate?

5.4.1 Motivations of AI-supported Crowdsourcing

Understanding how user motivations interact with AI-supported crowdsourcing platforms can contribute to effective designs by tapping into crowd workers' altruistic desires to help others with their practical, outcome-driven considerations. More broadly, studying motives is essential for the successful implementation of AI-related platforms to solve societal problems. By understanding what drives participation, developers of AI tools can design AI-integrated platforms that appeal to users, ensuring that the platform resonates with users on a deeper level, hence fostering a sense of engagement, ownership, trust, and long-term commitment to the cause.

Further, understanding the motives of potential users helps in designing AI platforms that align with their values and needs. For example, if a platform is intended to address a societal problem, knowing that users are motivated by altruism (wanting to help others) can lead to features that emphasize the social impact of their contributions. On the other hand, if users are driven by utilitarian motives, such as skill development or career advancement, the platform can include elements like certifications, badges, or networking opportunities (Goh et al., 2017).

5.4.2 Introducing Zhongxun

This section introduces Zhongxun, an AI-supported crowdsourcing platform. Zhongxun's AI has three functions: (1) accounting for the effect of aging on children, (2) calculating the similarities between the uploaded children's photos with trafficked children's photos stored in the database, and (3) learning from crowdsourcing users' feedback to improve facial recognition results (Goh et al., 2021). Figure 5.2 illustrates the collaboration between users and Zhongxun's AI in finding missing children. When encountering suspected trafficked children, users can take and upload photos to Zhongxun (see Figure 5.2a). Next, Zhongxun uses its facial recognition algorithm to compare

Figure 5.2 The process of finding trafficked children

the uploaded photos with the stored information of known trafficked children. After that, the matched children and the similarity rates are posted on Zhongxun's official Weibo account of Zhongxun (see Figure 5.2b). Knowledge shared by the user is used to improve the matching results (see Figure 5.2c). Once the matching process is accomplished, notification to relevant parties will be done (e.g., authority and parents of the reported missing children).

5.4.3 Research Participants

An online survey with snowball sampling was conducted to reach Weibo and WeChat users who were interested in participating in this study. In the survey, an introduction to the study was presented, followed by an introduction video about Zhongxun. Next, participants were asked to answer questions assessing (1) their perception of the features of Zhongxun, (2) their intention to share knowledge and contribute to Zhongxun, and (3) their motives for doing so. A total of 407 participants participated in the study. Around 35 percent of the participants were males ($N = 142$), while the rest were females ($N = 265$). Most of the participants (79%) were between 23 and 30 years old.

5.4.4 Construct Operationalization

The scale for measuring voluntary motives, as adapted from Clary et al. (1998), is relevant to the current chapter. It is a comprehensive tool designed to assess the various reasons individuals may have for engaging in volunteer activities. The scale comprises thirty items from six subdimensions, including (1) values function (desire to express values), (2) protective function (protect oneself from negative feelings such as guilt), (3) enhancement function (enhancing personal growth), (4) social function (desire to engage with others), (5) career function (benefits that support personal development), and (6) understanding function (desire to acquire knowledge). Additionally, altruistic and utilitarian motives are incorporated into the motives measurement. Altruistic motives (5 items) are rooted in a desire to help others, contribute to the greater good, or support a cause without expecting personal gain (Bucher et al., 2016) while Utilitarian motives (5 items) are based on practical considerations and the pursuit of specific benefits or outcomes (Bucher et al., 2016). Additionally, demographic information such as age, gender, nationality, country of residence, and experience with crowdsourcing was collected from the participants.

5.4.5 Analysis and Results

Hierarchical regression analysis was conducted to investigate the factors that influenced the use of AI-supported crowdsourcing platforms. The first block comprised demographic variables and prior crowdsourcing experience, followed by altruistic and utilitarian motives in the second block and voluntary motives in the third block.

In terms of demographic variables and prior experience, results suggested that local crowd workers (who lived in China) were more likely to share knowledge on Zhongxun crowdsourcing platform ($\beta = 0.15$, $p = 0.003 < 0.01$) (see Table 5.3). As for the motives (second block), results showed that altruistic motives ($\beta = 0.34$, $p < 0.001$) had statistically significant and positive relationships with the intention to use AI-supported crowdsourcing to share knowledge. In contrast, utilitarian motives had no significant effects. As for the voluntary motives, only the values function ($\beta = 0.22$, $p < 0.001$) was statistically significant and positively related to the intention to use AI-supported crowdsourcing to share knowledge.

5.4.6 Lessons Learnt from the Case Study

The factors and motivations driving knowledge sharing in AI-supported crowdsourcing were uncovered, revealing several key insights and important lessons.

First, the intention to use AI-supported crowdsourcing to share knowledge is influenced by geography. A possible explanation is that, although child trafficking is a global issue, users tend to be more engaged in volunteerism when the issue is geographically closer to them (Mohan et al., 2006). This suggests that contributions from local crowd workers to collective intelligence may be more valuable than those from nonlocal crowd workers, due to their familiarity with the region and its unique context. However, prior research has shown that geography does not always influence participation. One study found that users involved in a mapping project were often more active in tasks located far from their homes, indicating that distance may not be a limiting factor in some crowdsourcing efforts (Baruch et al., 2016). So, the geographical influence on AI-supported crowdsourcing participation may vary depending on the nature of the task, with certain tasks being more accessible or appealing to participants from specific regions due to factors such as cultural context, available resources, technological infrastructure, or local expertise.

Second, altruistic motives positively influence the intention to share knowledge on AI-supported crowdsourcing platforms, as users are often driven by a

Table 5.3 *Results from hierarchy regression analysis (N = 407)*

Independent variable	Standardized beta	t-value
MODEL 1		
Nationality Influence	−0.10	−1.54
Geographical Influence	0.17	2.72**
Age	−0.02	−0.43
Gender	0.00	0.04
Prior Experience	0.12	2.43*
R^2	0.029	
Increase Adjusted R^2	0.029*	
MODEL 2		
Nationality Influence	−0.09	−1.63
Geographical Influence	0.17	3.48**
Age	−0.02	−0.34
Gender	0.07	1.81
Prior Experience	0.06	1.58
Utilitarian Motives	0.06	1.28
Altruistic Motives	0.58	13.86***
R^2	0.383	
Increase Adjusted R^2	0.354***	
MODEL 3		
Nationality	−0.04	−0.80
Geographical Influence	0.15	3.02**
Age	−0.03	−0.63
Gender	0.07	1.75
Prior Experience	0.05	1.37
Utilitarian Motives	0.00	−0.07
Altruistic Motives	0.34	5.41***
Protective Function	−0.06	−1.03
Values Function	0.22	−3.82***
Career Function	0.09	1.20
Social Function	0.00	−0.08
Understanding Function	0.10	1.51
Enhancement Function	0.07	0.97
R^2	0.430	
Increase Adjusted R^2	0.047***	
Total Adjusted R^2	0.430	

Note: * $p < 0.05$, ** $p < 0.01$, *** $p < 0.001$.

sense of social responsibility and a desire to contribute to the greater good. In contrast, utilitarian motives – such as personal gain or efficiency – do not appear to significantly affect this intention, suggesting that the willingness to share knowledge in this context is more strongly associated with intrinsic, rather than extrinsic rewards (e.g., financial compensations). More importantly, AI does not alter deeply ingrained altruistic motives. While AI can facilitate opportunities for altruistic actions (e.g., by enabling easier and more efficient ways to contribute to causes), the underlying motivations for altruism remain rooted in human psychology and social dynamics.

Third, the strong influence of the values function suggests that individuals are more likely to engage in crowdsourcing efforts when they perceive that their participation aligns with their core beliefs and ethical principles. This alignment not only motivates initial involvement but also sustains long-term commitment to the cause, making the values function a critical factor in the success of AI-supported crowdsourcing projects that rely on volunteer contributions. Specifically, the features of Zhongxun (e.g., facial aging and matching algorithms) extend individuals' cognitive capabilities, allowing them to contribute and enhance the collaborative effort. Empirical data from this case study indicates that participants expressed appreciation for AI's cognitive support, provided that the process aligns with their personal values. The alignment of individuals' personal values with the goals of the crowdsourcing initiative is an important factor. Specifically, individuals are driven to contribute based on a sense of moral obligation, social responsibility, or a desire to make a positive impact.

5.4.7 Summary of the Case Study

The empirical analysis of Zhongxun as a case study demonstrates that AI-supported crowdsourcing is a viable approach to addressing societal challenges. Key factors, such as geographical influences, along with motivations like altruism and value functions, are critical to its implementation.

5.5 Recommendations

This chapter examines the use of AI-supported crowdsourcing to solve societal challenges. As technology continues to advance, investigating the role of AI in collaboration with humans becomes essential to effectively integrate this technology into our everyday lives and work (Wang et al., 2020). The findings from the systematic review and case study discussion have implications for practice and research.

5.5.1 Recommendations for Practitioners

This section offers practical contributions to the use of AI-supported crowdsourcing, which are summarized next.

First, practitioners should take into account users' motivations in AI designs. Given that value motivation plays a pivotal role in users' acceptance intentions, designers could use AI to offer timely updates and feedback related to the process of rescuing trafficked children. Highlighting the successful completion of each crowdsourcing task and how the participation contributes to the collective intelligence can help sustain users' engagement and sense of contributing to others' well-being.

Second, while AI development is promising, exciting, and attracting attention, local crowd workers play a crucial role in addressing societal issues within their communities. Put simply, local crowd workers are vital in addressing societal issues within their communities through AI-supported crowdsourcing. The knowledge of local culture, social dynamics, language, and unique challenges enables them to contribute insights and solutions that are deeply relevant to the issues faced by their region. These, in turn, help enhance the effectiveness of the AI models being used. Consequently, effort should be made to match crowd workers with preferred locales. AI should be seen as a complement to these workers, and not a substitute.

Third, designing altruistic features in AI platforms can significantly enhance their appeal to users by aligning with people's innate desire to contribute positively to society. Several approaches are viable. AI can assist users in identifying opportunities where their skills can make a significant impact. Specifically, AI can match users with crowdsourced projects or social causes where their unique expertise or experience can be best applied. Another approach is to utilize AI to recommend causes or tasks that align with the user's preferences, past contributions, or areas of interest. Personalizing these recommendations can increase engagement by ensuring users feel connected to the causes they support.

Fourth, the case study discussion on Zhongxun underscores the relevance of incentivizing the social sharing of good deeds through AI-supported crowdsourcing. Thus, platforms should deploy features that encourage crowd workers to share their altruistic acts and inspire others to join them and contribute, creating a network effect that amplifies social good. Alternatively, stories of individuals who have benefited from altruistic actions or testimonials from those who benefited from the platforms' efforts should be made available. In some cases, altruism may need to be balanced with other forms of motivation, such as recognition. AI tools should be designed to accommodate various motivations for different profiles of crowd workers while ensuring that altruistic contributors are valued and their contributions are integrated effectively into collective intelligence systems.

Finally, it is important to establish clear ethical guidelines that ensure AI-supported crowdsourcing platforms operate in a way that upholds social good.

Users will feel more inclined to engage in crowdsourcing activities if they know their chosen platform aligns with their values and follows ethical practices. While altruism and alignment of values enhance collective intelligence, there is a risk that platforms could exploit altruistic participants by over-relying on volunteer crowd workers. Practitioners must ensure that AI platforms uphold ethical standards by providing transparency in algorithms, safeguarding data privacy and security, and offering appropriate recognition for contributions, while also valuing and respecting the efforts of crowd workers.

5.5.2 Recommendations for Researchers

Here are key recommendations for researchers to advance the field and contribute to impactful research.

First, future research can explore the notion of localized AI-supported crowdsourcing. Local expertise allows AI systems to be customized and adapted to different regions, ensuring that solutions are not one-size-fits-all but tailored to each community's specific needs. This is especially important in domains like healthcare, education, and public services, where regional differences can lead to varying outcomes. By integrating local knowledge, AI systems can be designed to respect cultural norms, legal frameworks, and societal expectations, thereby increasing their acceptance and effectiveness. In particular, local crowd workers can identify and prioritize issues that are of particular importance to their community, such as environmental hazards, public health crises, or infrastructure needs. More importantly, by incorporating local expertise, AI models can be enhanced to recognize specific local conditions, resulting in better predictions and recommendations.

Second, an important area of research is examining crowd workers' commitment to long-term collaboration. A potential area here is developing and building emotional connections among crowd workers, and between them and the platform. This emotional connection fosters a deeper commitment, leading to more sustained involvement in the long run. Participants are more likely to remain engaged if they are emotionally connected and believe their ongoing contributions are crucial to achieving broader societal goals, making long-term research projects more viable and successful. Findings indicate that appropriate incentive structures for voluntary crowdsourcing will be critical.

For instance, AI platforms aimed at crowdsourcing solutions to societal problems might offer recognition or opportunities for personal growth. By understanding user motives, researchers can address potential concerns about trust, privacy, data use, and fairness, which are particularly important in AI systems.

Third, another promising extension of this research involves enhancing AI tools in crowdsourcing to better humanize participation. This can be achieved in several ways. Integrating AI to create feedback loops will be an effective way to continuously improve the platform's ability to promote collective effort. For instance, AI can analyze user engagement patterns, identify what drives successful altruistic projects, and optimize task recommendations and platform features accordingly. Next, research should be conducted on AI tools that accurately measure and quantify the societal impact of altruistic contributions. This may involve creating AI systems that assess the real-world outcomes of crowdsourced tasks, providing users and researchers with data-driven insights into the effectiveness of their efforts.

Fourth, AI-supported crowdsourcing platforms that highlight societal concerns and impact can inspire cross-disciplinary collaborations as researchers from various fields come together with a shared goal. The focus on social outcomes encourages participants from different disciplines – such as data science, biology, public policy, and engineering – to contribute their expertise toward solving complex, multifaceted problems. Specifically, AI-supported platforms can aggregate and analyze large volumes of data contributed by interdisciplinary teams. For example, in a project exploring urban sustainability, an AI system could combine insights from urban planners, economists, environmental scientists, and data scientists to create comprehensive models of urban ecosystems. By synthesizing this data, AI platforms help researchers make sense of complex, multifaceted problems that require input from multiple perspectives. Additionally, AI-supported crowdsourcing platforms can incorporate predictive modeling and simulation tools to help interdisciplinary teams test hypotheses and simulate the impact of various interventions. This is particularly useful across various fields (e.g., medicine, environmental sustainability, urban planning) where AI can model complex systems and provide researchers from different disciplines with actionable insights.

Finally, more user-oriented research is needed to understand crowd workers' segmentations and profiles across different societal challenges. Different users have different reasons for engaging in altruistic behavior (e.g., personal satisfaction, social recognition, or belief in the cause) (Synder et al., 2000). Research into personalizing AI platform interfaces, which aims to enhance user engagement by promoting participation across diverse user groups, will be necessary. By customizing the interface to align with individual profiles, motivations, cultural values, and unique user needs, AI-supported platforms can better cater to contributors' goals.

5.5.3 Summary of the Chapter

This chapter examines the viability of AI-supported crowdsourcing in addressing societal challenges through a systematic review and a case study of a real-world AI-supported crowdsourcing platform. The systematic review highlights the potential of integrating AI to tackle complex societal issues, though research in this area remains limited. The case study further emphasizes that AI can serve as a cognitive extension, complementing human intelligence rather than replacing crowd workers in solving societal problems.

5.6 Conclusion

In conclusion, AI-supported crowdsourcing promotes knowledge sharing among crowd workers to address societal challenges and leveraging AI to facilitate this process can be viewed as a potential solution to prevent the "Tragedy of the Commons." The "Tragedy of the Commons," a concept echoed by economist Hardin (1968), describes a situation where individuals, acting solely in their self-interest without regard for others or the community, ultimately deplete shared resources, negatively affecting everyone in the community (Xia, 2024). Societal challenges, such as climate change, traffic congestion, sustainability, and public health concerns, are often linked to the "Tragedy of the Commons" because they involve the overuse or degradation of shared resources (Spiliakos, 2019). In addressing societal challenges, AI-supported crowdsourcing offers the potential to overcome the "Tragedy of the Commons" by fostering voluntary participation, enhancing coordination, increasing transparency, and aligning individual actions with collective goals for sustainable resource management. Put simply, by harnessing collective intelligence, AI-supported crowdsourcing platforms (together with appropriate governing frameworks) will play important roles in managing shared resources and fostering collaboration to tackle complex societal issues.

References

AfricaNews. (2022). More than 25,000 Minors Still Missing in Africa-ICRC. www.africanews.com/2022/08/30/more-than-25000-minors-still-missing-in-africa-icrc/ (last accessed August 10, 2023).

Assis Neto, F. R., & Santos, C.A.S. (2018). Understanding Crowdsourcing Projects: A Systematic Review of Tendencies, Workflow, and Quality Management. *Information Processing & Management, 54*(4), 490–506.

Bandara, W., Miskon, S., & Fielt, E. (2011). A Systematic, Tool-supported Method for Conducting Literature Reviews in Information Systems. In T. Virpi, N. Joe, R. Matti, & S. Wael (eds.), *ECIS 2011 Proceedings 19th European Conference on Information Systems*, Helsinki, Finland. https://eprints.qut.edu.au/42184/

Baruch, A., May, A., & Yu, D. (2016). The Motivations, Enablers and Barriers for Voluntary Participation in an Online Crowdsourcing Platform. *Computers in Human Behavior*, 64, 923–931.

Bell, J., Pescher, C., Tellis, G. J., & Füller, J. 2023. Can AI Help in Ideation? A Theory-Based Model for Idea Screening in Crowdsourcing Contests. *Marketing Science*, 43(1), 54–72.

Bjarnason, R., Gambrell, D., & Lanthier-Welch, J. (2024). Using Artificial Intelligence to Accelerate Collective Intelligence: Policy Synth and Smarter Crowdsourcing. [arXiv preprint]. arXiv:2407.13960.

Brabham, D. C. (2008). Crowdsourcing as a Model for Problem Solving: An Introduction and Cases. *Convergence*, 14(1), 75–90.

Brabham, D. C. (2012). Motivations for Participation in a Crowdsourcing Application to Improve Public Engagement in Transit Planning. *Journal of Applied Communication Research*, 40(3), 307–328.

Bucher, E., Fieseler, C., & Lutz, C. (2016). What's Mine Is Yours (for a Nominal Fee) – Exploring the Spectrum of Utilitarian to Altruistic Motives for Internet-mediated Sharing. *Computers in Human Behavior*, 62, 316–326.

Ceccaroni, L., Oliver, J. L., Roger, E., Bibby, J., Flemons, P., Michael, K., and Joly, A. (2023), Advancing the Productivity of Science with Citizen Science and Artificial Intelligence, in *Artificial Intelligence in Science: Challenges, Opportunities and the Future of Research*, OECD Publishing.

Clary, E., Snyder, M., Ridge, R. D., Copeland, J., Stukas, A. A., Haugen, J., & Miene, P. (1998). Understanding and Assessing the Motivations of Volunteers: A Functional Approach. *Journal of Personality and Social Psychology*, 74(6), 1516–1530.

Eisenhardt, K. M., Graebner, M. E., & Sonenshein, S. (2016). Grand Challenges and Inductive Methods: Rigor without Rigor Mortis. *Academy of Management Journal*, 59(4), 1113–1123.

Estellés-Arolas, E., & González-Ladrón-de-Guevara, F. (2012). Towards an Integrated Crowdsourcing Definition. *Journal of Information Science*, 38(2), 189–200.

Ferraro, F., Etzion, D., & Gehman, J. (2015). Tackling Grand Challenges Pragmatically: Robust Action Revisited. *Organization Studies*, 36, 363–390.

Flores, V. B. (2009). Human Trafficking: A Reproductive Justice Issue, www.aclu.org/news/civil-liberties/human-trafficking-reproductive-justice-issue (accessed August 7, 2023).

George, G., Howard-Grenville, J., Joshi, A., & Tihanyi, L. (2016). Understanding and Tackling Societal Grand Challenges through Management Research. *Academy of Management Journal*, 59(6), 1880–1895.

Gimpel, H., Graf-Seyfried, V., Laubacher, R., & Meindl, O. (2023). Towards Artificial Intelligence Augmenting Facilitation: AI Affordances in Macro-task Crowdsourcing. *Group Decision and Negotiation*, 32(1), 75–124.

Global Missing Children's Network. (2023). Missing Children's Statistics, *Global Missing Children's Network*, https://globalmissingkids.org/awareness/missing-children-statistics/ (last accessed August 10, 2023)

Goh, D. H.-L., Lee, C. S., & Guo, H. (2018). Finding Trafficked Children through Crowdsourcing. *Proceedings of the Association for Information Science and Technology, 55*(1), 811–812.

Goh, D. H.-L., Lee, C. S., Zhou, Q., and Guo, H. (2021). Finding Trafficked Children through Crowdsourcing: A Usability Evaluation. *Aslib Journal of Information Management, 73*(3), 419–435.

Goh, D. H.-L., Pe-Than, E. P. P., & Lee, C. S. (2017). Perceptions of Virtual Reward Systems in Crowdsourcing Games. *Computers in Human Behavior, 70*, 365–374.

Gutierrez, M. (2019). Maputopias: Cartographies of Communication, Coordination and Action: The Cases of Ushahidi and InfoAmazonia. *GeoJournal, 84*, 101–120.

Haenlein, M., & Kaplan, A. (2019). A Brief History of Artificial Intelligence: On the Past, Present, and Future of Artificial Intelligence. *California Management Review, 61*(4), 5–14.

Haider, C. M. R., Clifton, C., & Yin, M. (2024). Do Crowdsourced Fairness Preferences Correlate with Risk Perceptions? *Proceedings of the 29th International Conference on Intelligent User Interfaces*, 304–324.

Hardin, G. (1968). The Tragedy of the Commons. *Science, 162*(3859), 1243–1248.

Köhl, A., Fuger, S., Lang, M., Füller, J., & Stuchtey, M. (2019). How Text Mining Algorithms for Crowdsourcing Can Help Us to Identify Today's Pressing Societal Issues. Hawaii International Conference on System Sciences, Grand Wailea, Hawaii, USA. https://hdl.handle.net/10125/59509

Kokshagina, O. (2022). Open Covid-19: Organizing an Extreme Crowdsourcing Campaign to Tackle Grand Challenges. *R&D Management, 52*(2), 206–219.

Lee, C. S., Goh, D. H.-L., Zhou, Q., Sin, S.-C. J., & Theng, Y. L. (2020). Integrating Motives and Usability to Examine Community Crowdsourcing. *Proceedings of the Association for Information Science and Technology, 57*(1), e353.

Lee, C. S., Lim, K. K., & Kim, H. K. (2024a). Nudging Public Health Information Behavior towards COVID-19 Preventive Measures: A Systematic Review. *Health Communication*, 29 Feb, 1–12.

Lee, C. S., Yang, Y., Low, K. Y., Chia, H. K., & Ma, L. (2024b). Doing Good for Others or Self: A Study of Crowdsourced Translation on Digital Labor Platforms. *Computers in Human Behavior Reports, 13*, 100373.

Lévy, P. (1999). *Collective Intelligence: Mankind's Emerging World in Cyberspace*. Perseus Books.

Lindgren, S. (2014). Crowdsourcing Knowledge: Interdiscursive Flows from Wikipedia into Scholarly Research. Culture Unbound. *Journal of Current Cultural Research, 6*, 609–627.

Mahotra, A., & Majchrzak, A. (2024). Digital Innovations in Crowdsourcing using AI Tools. *Technovation, 133*, 102997.

Mohan, J., Twigg, L., Jones, K., & Barnard, S. (2006). Fifteen: Volunteering, Geography and Welfare: A Multilevel Investigation of Geographical Variations in Voluntary Action. In C. Milligan & D. Conradson (eds.), *Landscapes of Voluntarism* (pp. 267–284). Policy Press.

Page, M. J., McKenzie, J. E., Bossuyt, P. M., Boutron, I., Hoffmann, T. C., Mulrow, C. D., Shamseer, L., Tetzlaff, J. M., Akl, E. A., Brennan, S. E., Chou, R., Glanville, J., Grimshaw, J. M., Hróbjartsson, A., Lalu, M. M., Li, T., Loder, E. W., Mayo-Wilson, E., McDonald, S., ... Moher, D. (2021). The PRISMA 2020 Statement:

An Updated Guideline for Reporting Systematic Reviews. *Systematic Reviews*, *10*(1), 89.

Rittel, H. W. J., & Webber, M. M. (1973). Dilemmas in a General Theory of Planning. *Policy Sciences*, *4*, 155–169.

Robert, L. P. (2019). Crowdsourcing Controls: A Review and Research Agenda for Crowdsourcing Controls Used for Macro-tasks. In V.-J. Khan, K. Papangelis, I. Lykourentzou, & P. Markopoulos (eds.), *Macrotask Crowdsourcing* (pp. 45–126). Human–Computer Interaction Series. Springer.

Roush, T. (2023). How Bad is Cleveland's "Alarming" Missing Children Trend? Data Suggests an Existing Problem, www.forbes.com/sites/tylerroush/2023/06/03/how-bad-is-clevelands-alarming-missing-children-trend-data-suggests-an-existing-problem/ (last accessed August 10, 2023).

Snyder, M., Clary, E., & Stukas, A. A. (2000). The Functional Approach to Volunteerism, in G. R. Maio & J. M. Olson (eds.), *Why We Evaluate: Functions of Attitudes* (pp. 365–393). Lawrence Erlbaum Associates. https://doi.org/10.13140/2.1.2008.6083

Spiliakos, A. (2019). Tragedy of the Commons: What It Is & 5 Examples, *Harvard Business School Online*, https://online.hbs.edu/blog/post/tragedy-of-the-commons-impact-on-sustainability-issues (last accessed August 14, 2024).

Vaughan, J., W. (2018). Making Better Use of the Crowd: How Crowdsourcing Can Advance Machine Learning Research. *Journal of Machine Learning Research*, *18*, 1–46.

Villarrubia-Gómez, P., Cornell, S. E., & Fabres, J. (2017). Marine Plastic Pollution as a Planetary Boundary Threat: The Drifting Piece in the Sustainability Puzzle. *Marine Policy*, *96*.

Vinella, F. L., Hu, J., Lykourentzou, I., & Masthoff, J. (2022a). Crowdsourcing Team Formation with Worker-centered Modeling. *Frontiers in Artificial Intelligence*, *5*. https://doi.org/10.3389/frai.2022.818562

Vinella, F. L., Odo, C., Lykourentzou, I., & Masthoff, J. (2022b). How Personality and Communication Patterns Affect Online ad-hoc Teams under Pressure. *Frontiers in Artificial Intelligence*, *5*. https://doi.org/10.3389/frai.2022.818491

Wang, D., Churchill, E., Maes, P., Fan, X., Shneiderman, B., Shi, Y., and Wang, Q. (2020). From Human–Human Collaboration to Human–AI Collaboration: Designing AI Systems That Can Work Together with People, in *Extended Abstracts of the 2020 CHI Conference on Human Factors in Computing Systems* (pp. 1–6). Association for Computing Machinery.

Xia, H. (2024). Tragedy of the Commons in Crowd Work-Based Research. *ACM Journal on Responsible Computing*, *1*(1), Article No.:4, 1–25.

Yang, K., & Tanaka, M. (2023). Crowdsourcing Knowledge Production of COVID-19 Information on Japanese Wikipedia in the Face of Uncertainty: Empirical Analysis. *Journal of. Medical Internet Research*, *25*, e45024.

Yang, Q., Steinfeld, A., Rosé, C., & Zimmerman. J. (2020). Re-Examining Whether, Why, and How Human–AI Interaction Is Uniquely Difficult to Design. *Paper presented at the 2020* CHI Conference on Human Factors in Computing Systems, Honolulu, HI, USA, April 25–30. Association for Computing Machinery, 1–13.

Yu, H., Liu, Y., Wei, X., Zheng, C., Chen, T., Yang, Q., & Peng, X. (2019). Fair and Explainable Dynamic Engagement of Crowd Workers. *Paper in Proceedings of the Twenty-Eighth International Joint Conference on Artificial Intelligence*, 6575–6577.

6

AI-supported Search Interaction for Enhancing Users' Understanding

Shaobo Liang and Chenrui Shi

6.1 Introduction

In the era of information explosion, the ability to efficiently access, process, and comprehend vast amounts of data has become crucial for individuals and organizations alike. Traditional search engines, while having made significant strides in information retrieval, often fall short when handling complex queries that require nuanced understanding and contextualization. Users frequently find themselves engaged in multiple iterations of search queries, refining and adjusting their approach to obtain the desired information. This process not only consumes valuable time but also increases cognitive load, potentially hampering effective decision-making and knowledge acquisition (Na & Lee, 2016).

The advent of generative Artificial Intelligence (AI) presents a promising solution to address these limitations. By leveraging advanced natural language processing and contextual understanding capabilities, generative AI has the potential to revolutionize search interactions, offering personalized and contextually relevant content in response to user queries (Ali et al., 2020). This technological leap forward could significantly reduce users' cognitive burden and enhance their efficiency in information retrieval and comprehension. Recent studies have highlighted the transformative potential of AI in search systems. For instance, Yue and Peng (2021) demonstrated that AI-enhanced search interfaces could significantly improve search efficiency and effectiveness in enterprise settings. Similarly, Vuong et al. (2019) found that users reported higher satisfaction when interacting with conversational search systems, which incorporate elements of AI-supported interaction.

However, despite these promising indications, there remains a critical need for comprehensive research to validate the effectiveness of generative AI in real-world search scenarios and to understand its impact on user behavior and cognition. Questions persist regarding the extent to which AI-supported search interactions can truly enhance users' understanding, particularly when dealing with multifaceted or specialized information needs (Huggins-Manley et al., 2022).

To address this research gap, it is crucial to consider theoretical frameworks that can provide insight into user behavior and information seeking processes. Two particularly relevant theories are the Information Gap Theory and the Uses and Gratifications Theory (UGT). The Information Gap Theory, proposed by Loewenstein (1994), suggests that, when individuals become aware of a gap in their knowledge, they are motivated to seek information to fill this gap. In the context of AI-supported search interactions, generative AI has the potential to more efficiently identify and address these information gaps by providing contextually relevant and personalized information, thereby enhancing user understanding and satisfaction (Ullah & Khusro, 2020).

On the other hand, the UGT originally developed in media studies posits that individuals actively choose and use media to satisfy specific needs or goals (Katz et al., 1973; Falgoust et al., 2022). When applied to information seeking behavior, this theory can help explain why users might prefer AI-supported search systems over traditional search engines. If AI-supported systems can better satisfy users' information needs and provide a more gratifying search experience, users may be more inclined to adopt and continue using these systems (Sundar & Limperos, 2013; Hsu et al., 2020). For example, a user engaged in a highly technical search for scientific articles or making purchasing decisions can leverage AI-supported systems to aggregate and summarize multiple sources of information in a more coherent and comprehensible format, thus increasing satisfaction.

The primary objective of this research is to evaluate the impact of AI-supported search interactions on enhancing user understanding, particularly in high-complexity contexts. This chapter will focus on testing two research questions:

RQ1: Whether AI-supported search systems can fill knowledge gaps effectively, thereby improving users' understanding of complex information.
RQ2: Whether users can perceive AI-supported search systems as more useful and easier to use than traditional search engines, and thus are more likely to prefer these systems for future search tasks.

By pursuing these objectives, we seek to contribute valuable insights to both the theoretical understanding and practical application of AI-enhanced search interactions. Our findings could inform the design and optimization of future search systems, potentially leading to more efficient and user-centric information retrieval tools. Through this chapter, we aim to shed light on the transformative potential of AI in search interactions and its role in enhancing users' understanding in an increasingly complex information landscape.

6.2 Literature Review

6.2.1 Applications of Generative AI in Information Retrieval

The integration of generative AI into information retrieval systems has marked a significant advancement in addressing complex information needs. Unlike traditional keyword-based search engines, generative AI models, particularly large language models (LLMs) such as GPT-4, have demonstrated remarkable capabilities in understanding context and generating human-like responses (Zhao et al., 2024). Recent studies have shown that generative AI can significantly enhance search efficiency and user understanding in various ways. Firstly, these models excel at query understanding and expansion. Zamani et al. (2020) demonstrated that AI-powered systems could generate clarifying questions, helping users refine their queries and obtain more precise results. This capability is particularly valuable when users have vague or complex information needs that are difficult to articulate in a single query.

Moreover, generative AI has shown promise in producing comprehensive and contextually relevant summaries of search results. Hao and Cukurova (2023) found that AI-generated summaries could significantly reduce the time users spend sifting through multiple documents, thereby enhancing information absorption and decision-making processes. This is especially beneficial in scenarios requiring the synthesis of information from multiple sources, such as academic research or business intelligence gathering.

The ability of generative AI to engage in multi-turn conversations has also revolutionized the search process. Meng et al. (2023) observed that conversational search systems powered by LLMs could maintain context across multiple queries, allowing for more natural and in-depth exploration of topics. This conversational approach mimics human-to-human interaction, potentially leading to a more intuitive and satisfying search experience.

However, it is crucial to note that the integration of generative AI in search systems is not without challenges. Issues such as hallucination (generating plausible but incorrect information) and bias have been identified as significant concerns (Bender et al., 2021). These challenges underscore the need for a careful system design and the importance of maintaining human oversight in AI-supported search interactions.

6.2.2 Information Gap Theory in AI-supported Search

The Information Gap Theory, as proposed by Loewenstein (1994), provides a valuable framework for understanding user motivation in information-seeking behaviors. This theory posits that when individuals become aware of a gap between what they know and what they want to know, they experience a feeling of deprivation, which motivates them to seek information to close this gap.

In the context of AI-supported search, generative AI has the potential to identify and address these information gaps more efficiently. Jiang et al. (2023) found that AI-powered search systems could infer users' knowledge states and information needs more accurately than traditional systems. By doing so, these systems can provide more targeted and relevant information, effectively bridging the user's knowledge gap.

Moreover, the ability of generative AI to provide explanations and background information alongside search results can significantly enhance user understanding. Yiannakoulias (2024) demonstrated that, when AI systems automatically supplied contextual information, users reported higher levels of topic comprehension and satisfaction. This automatic provision of supplementary information aligns well with the Information Gap Theory, as it proactively addresses potential knowledge gaps that the user may not have initially recognized.

However, it is important to consider potential drawbacks. De Cremer and Kasparov (2022) raised concerns about the risk of over-reliance on AI-generated information, which could potentially narrow users' exploration of diverse viewpoints. This highlights the need for AI-supported search systems to balance efficient information provision with encouraging critical thinking and diverse information seeking.

6.2.3 Uses and Gratifications Theory in AI-supported Systems

The Uses and Gratifications Theory (UGT), originally developed in media studies, has found new relevance in the context of AI-supported information systems. This theory suggests that individuals actively choose and use media to satisfy specific needs or goals (Katz et al., 1973). When applied to AI-supported search systems, UGT can provide insights into user adoption and continued use of these technologies.

Recent studies have identified several gratifications that users seek from AI-supported search systems. Chang et al. (2022) found that, in addition to traditional information-seeking gratifications, users of AI-powered systems reported high levels of "interaction gratification" – the satisfaction derived from engaging with an intelligent system. This suggests that the conversational nature of many AI-supported search interfaces may be intrinsically rewarding for users.

Furthermore, the personalization capabilities of AI systems align well with the UGT framework. Gao and Liu (2023) demonstrated that AI-powered recommendation systems in search interfaces could significantly enhance user satisfaction by providing tailored results. This personalization gratifies users' needs for efficiency and relevance, potentially increasing their likelihood of continued system use. The simplified user interfaces often associated with AI-supported systems also play a role in user gratification. Choi and Drumwright al. (2021) found that users reported higher ease-of-use satisfaction with voice-activated AI search assistants compared to traditional text-based interfaces. This suggests that AI systems' ability to understand natural language queries and provide concise, relevant responses may be particularly gratifying for users seeking quick and effortless information retrieval.

However, it is crucial to consider potential negative gratifications as well. Privacy concerns and the fear of reduced control over information access have been identified as factors that may deter some users from fully embracing AI-supported search systems (Choung et al., 2024). These findings highlight the need for transparent and user-centric design in AI-supported search interfaces to maximize positive gratifications while minimizing potential drawbacks.

In conclusion, the integration of generative AI in information retrieval systems presents significant opportunities for enhancing user understanding and satisfaction. By leveraging the insights from Information Gap Theory and Uses and Gratifications Theory, developers can create AI-supported search systems that not only efficiently bridge knowledge gaps but also provide a gratifying user experience. However, careful consideration must be given to potential challenges, including issues of over-reliance, bias, and privacy concerns. Future research should focus on addressing these challenges while further exploring the potential of AI to revolutionize the search experience.

6.3 Research Design

This chapter employs a mixed-methods approach to investigate the effectiveness of AI-supported search interactions in enhancing users' understanding. Our research design combines quantitative measurements with qualitative insights to provide a comprehensive analysis of user behavior, performance, and perceptions.

6.3.1 Experimental Procedure

The experiment will be conducted in three phases:

(1) Pre-experiment: Participants will complete a simple search task to familiarize themselves with both the traditional search system and the AI-supported search system (New Bing). This phase serves to minimize learning effects and ensure participants are comfortable with both interfaces.
(2) Formal experiment: Participants will be randomly assigned to either the control group (using traditional search) or the experimental group (using AI-supported search). Both groups will complete identical search tasks, with their behavioral data being recorded throughout the process. This between-subjects design allows for a direct comparison of the two search systems while minimizing carry-over effects (Hornbæk & Oulasvirta, 2017).
(3) Post-experimental: Upon completion of the tasks, participants will fill out a questionnaire to provide feedback on their perceptions and experiences with the search systems. This phase is crucial for gathering data related to the Uses and Gratifications Theory (Sundar & Limperos, 2013).

6.3.2 Experiment Tasks

The search tasks are designed to highlight the differences between generative AI and traditional search systems in terms of user understanding and efficiency. Each task is based on real-world scenarios and covers different information needs. These tasks will cover academic research, consumer decision-making, and professional information retrieval. The tasks and corresponding details are presented in the Table 6.1.

The time limits for each task are carefully calibrated to balance the need for thorough exploration with the realities of typical search behaviors (O'Brien et al., 2020).

6.3.3 User Feedback and Questionnaire Design

The post-task questionnaire is designed to capture users' perceptions and experiences. It includes the following dimensions, each using a 5-point Likert scale, as shown in Table 6.2.

Perceived usefulness is a key component of the Technology Acceptance Model (TAM), designed to measure the extent to which a user believes a particular technology enhances their performance in tasks or work-related

Table 6.1 *Experimental tasks design*

Task	Task Description	Task Goals	Time Limit
Academic Search	Search for and summarize key points from academic papers about "The Impact of Climate Change on the Global Economy." Find and summarize at least 3 sources.	Test whether AI can facilitate faster and more accurate retrieval of complex information, helping users form a better understanding of academic material.	30 minutes
Shopping Decision	Search for information comparing smartphone models, user reviews, and prices. Recommend the best phone based on your findings.	Evaluate whether AI can assist in integrating data from multiple sources (reviews, prices) to help users make quicker and more informed purchasing decisions.	15 minutes
Information Access	Search for and summarize recent developments in quantum computing technology. Provide a brief overview and recommend an influential article.	Assess how effectively AI can assist users in retrieving and summarizing information in a technical, specialized field.	10 minutes

Table 6.2 *Questionnaire design*

Objects	Measurement	Constructs
Perceived Usefulness	"Using the AI-supported search system has significantly improved my information retrieval efficiency." "The generative AI search system provided useful information to address my query." "The AI-supported search system enabled me to complete tasks more quickly."	Venkatesh and Davis (2000)
Perceived Ease of Use	"I find the AI-supported search system very easy to use." "I can effortlessly find the information I need through the generative AI." "I find the interface of the generative AI search system intuitive to navigate."	Venkatesh and Bala (2008)
Information Understanding Assessment	"Using the generative AI search system has significantly improved my understanding of the issue." "The AI-supported search helped me better digest and organize information." "I obtained more background information through the generative AI compared to traditional search engines."	Savolainen (2013)
Intention to Use in the Future	"I will prioritize using the generative AI search system for future search tasks." "Based on my experience, I am inclined to recommend the generative AI search system to others." "In the future, using the AI-supported search system will become my default practice."	Venkatesh et al. (2003)

activities (Venkatesh & Davis, 2000). Perceived ease of use assesses the level of difficulty a user experiences when using a particular technology, which is also based on the TAM model (Venkatesh & Bala, 2008). Information understanding assessment evaluates the depth of a user's understanding of tasks or information after using the system, often associated with cognitive load and knowledge acquisition (Savolainen, 2013). Intention to use in the future measures a user's willingness to continue using the AI-supported search system in the future, often linked to user experience and perceived usefulness (Venkatesh et al., 2003).

6.3.4 Behavioral Data Collection

To obtain comprehensive data, we tracked and recorded user behavior through the following methods.

(1) Screen Recording: We used screen recording software to capture users' complete search behavior during the experiment.
(2) Click Path Analysis: We recorded the number of webpages users click on from entering the search query to selecting results, observing their search behavior patterns.
(3) Dwell Time: We tracked the time users spent on each search result page or generated answer, analyzing whether they read and understood the content in depth.
(4) Query Modifications: We recorded the number of times users modified or expanded their search queries, reflecting the difficulties encountered during the search process and information that needs clarification.
(5) Output Quality: We assessed the quality of users' final task outputs through expert scoring or comparison with standard answers.

6.3.5 Participant Characteristics

Fifty participants were selected to ensure diversity in terms of age, gender, and professional background, allowing for generalizable results. Table 6.3 shows a simulated distribution of participants.

Table 6.3 *Participant characteristics*

Age	Participants	Gender (M/F)	Profession
18–24	15	7/8	University Students
25–34	20	10/10	Early Career Professionals
35–44	15	10/5	Mid-Level Professionals

6.4 Findings

6.4.1 Behavioral Results Analysis

Click Path and Task Completion Time Analysis

In the context of information retrieval systems, click path refers to the sequence of clicks users make to navigate through search results, while task completion time measures the total duration users take to complete a task. Analyzing these two variables provides critical insights into user behavior, especially in comparing the effectiveness of traditional search engines versus AI-supported systems (New Bing).

In the research design, participants interacted with both traditional search engines and the AI-enhanced New Bing system. Based on the collected data, we observed the trends illustrated in Figure 6.1.

From the data in Figure 6.1, it is evident that users in the AI-enhanced search group required fewer clicks to reach relevant information across all tasks. This reduction in click path length can be attributed to the contextual understanding of user queries by AI-powered systems, which are able to present more relevant and tailored results earlier in the search process. Natural language processing (NLP) plays a crucial role in interpreting user intent, which reduces the need for multiple refinements or excessive exploration of irrelevant links.

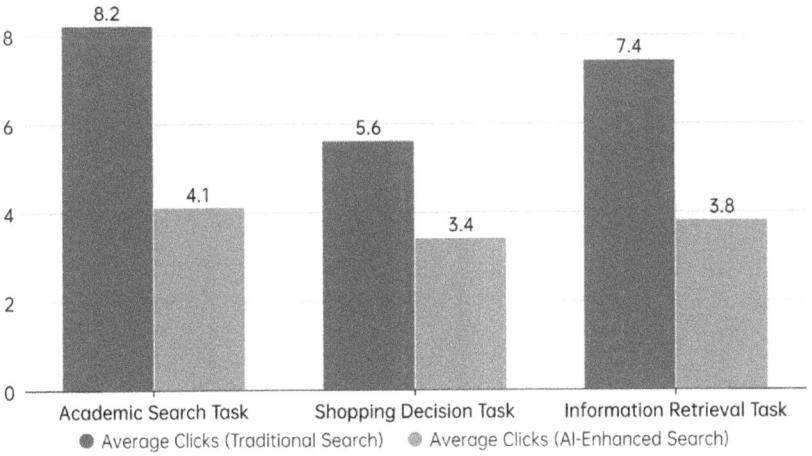

Figure 6.1 Click path analysis

Task Completion Time Analysis

Task completion time serves as a critical metric to assess the efficiency of search systems. It measures how quickly users are able to complete their tasks, which reflects the usability and effectiveness of the system. Results show that AI-enhanced search engines, like New Bing, reduce the time required for users to find relevant information by providing higher quality results upfront. Figure 6.2 summarizes the average task completion times for both groups.

These results clearly demonstrate that users completed tasks significantly faster when using the AI-enhanced system. For example, the academic search task showed a 35 percent reduction in completion time, highlighting the potential of AI-supported systems to expedite information retrieval, particularly for complex, knowledge-based queries.

This time reduction can be attributed to the contextual understanding provided by AI-generated summaries, which allow users to engage with highly relevant information more quickly without the need for excessive query modifications.

The combination of shorter click paths and reduced task completion times indicates that AI-supported search systems are more efficient in delivering relevant content. This efficiency not only enhances user satisfaction but also aligns with the Uses and Gratifications Theory, as users' cognitive and operational needs are met more effectively (Cheng & Jiang, 2020). Furthermore, this aligns with Information Gap Theory, where the system effectively fills users' knowledge gaps more quickly than traditional systems.

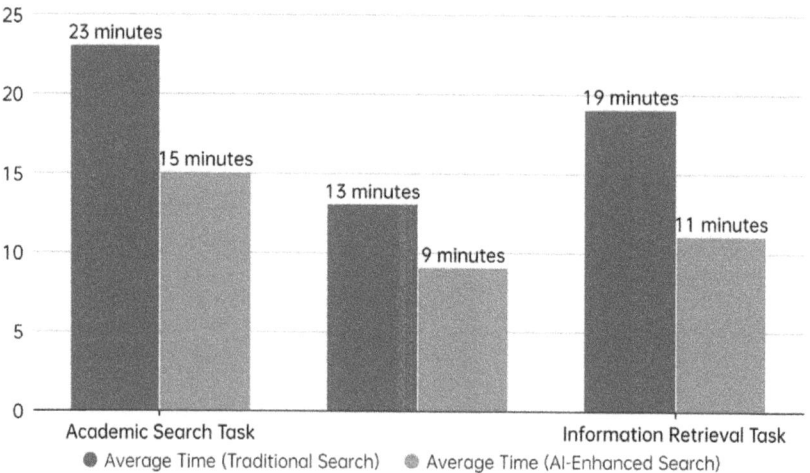

Figure 6.2 Task completion time

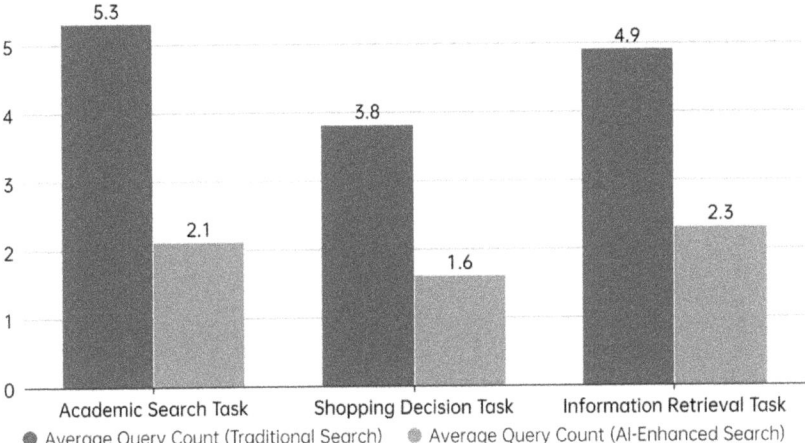

Figure 6.3 Query count analysis

Query Count Analysis

Query count serves as a critical indicator of how effective a search system is at delivering relevant results. Higher query counts may indicate that users need to continuously refine or modify their queries because the system does not fully understand their intent, while lower query counts suggest that the system is able to meet user needs with fewer iterations.

Figure 6.3 shows that participants using the AI-enhanced search system required significantly fewer queries to retrieve relevant information across all tasks. For example, in the academic search task, the average query count for the AI group was less than half of that for the traditional search group (2.1 vs. 5.3). This indicates that the AI system, powered by advanced natural language processing (NLP) and contextual understanding, is more effective at delivering relevant results based on the user's initial query, reducing the need for query reformulation (Pinzolits, 2024).

This reduction in query count demonstrates the efficiency of the AI system in understanding the user's intent and providing tailored results. Generative AI systems can interpret ambiguous queries, generate responses based on context, and offer multiple options from different angles, thereby minimizing the need for users to engage in trial-and-error behavior typical of traditional search engines (Bender et al., 2021).

Time on Page Analysis

Time on page provides a measure of user engagement with the content of search results. Higher time on page typically suggests that users are finding the

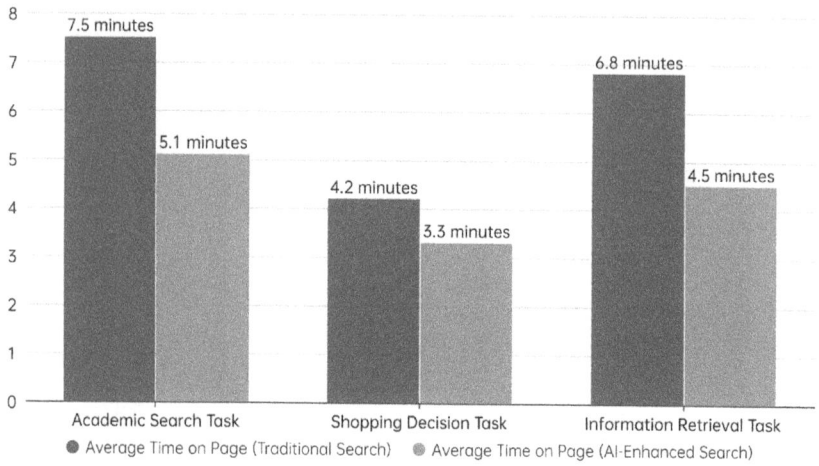

Figure 6.4 Time on page

content relevant and useful enough to spend more time reading or interacting with it. However, an excessively long time on page can also indicate that users are struggling to interpret or process the information.

Figure 6.4 shows that participants spent significantly less time on individual result pages when using the AI-enhanced system. This is particularly evident in the academic search task, where the average time on page dropped from 7.5 minutes in the traditional system to 5.1 minutes in the AI-enhanced system.

This reduction in time on page for the AI group suggests that users were able to find more relevant information faster, without needing to sift through irrelevant or redundant content. AI-generated summaries and contextually relevant results provided by New Bing allowed users to absorb key information quickly, thereby reducing the time spent on each page (Gerlich, 2023). Furthermore, the AI system's ability to synthesize information from multiple sources likely contributed to this reduction in time, as users could easily digest the core findings without having to navigate through multiple lengthy documents.

6.4.2 Perception Data Analysis

In this section, we analyze the perceptual data collected from users regarding their experience with AI-enhanced search systems and traditional search engines. The analysis focuses on three key dimensions: perceived usefulness, perceived ease of use, and future usage intention. In addition to frequency statistics, independent samples t-tests were conducted to examine whether the

Table 6.4 *User's perceived usefulness*

Group	Mean (Traditional Search)	Mean (AI-enhanced Search)	t-value	p-value
Academic Search Task	3.6	4.7	−6.23	< 0.001
Shopping Decision Task	3.9	4.8	−5.88	< 0.001
Information Retrieval Task	3.7	4.6	−6.05	< 0.001

differences between the two systems were statistically significant. The analysis was based on post-task questionnaire responses, using a 5-point Likert scale (1 = Strongly Disagree, 5 = Strongly Agree).

Perceived Usefulness Analysis

Perceived usefulness measures how effectively users believe a system helps them achieve their search objectives. Participants rated their perception of both systems on a Likert scale ranging from 1 (not useful at all) to 5 (very useful). Table 6.4 presents the average perceived usefulness scores for each task.

For the academic search task, the *t*-value of −6.23 with a *p*-value of < 0.001 indicates a statistically significant difference in perceived usefulness between the two systems. Users found the AI-enhanced search system to be substantially more useful in helping them retrieve complex academic content.

Similar statistically significant results were observed for the shopping decision and information retrieval tasks, with *t*-values of −5.88 and −6.05, respectively, and *p*-values all below 0.001. This suggests that participants consistently rated AI-enhanced systems as more useful across various contexts.

These findings highlight the superior ability of AI-enhanced systems to deliver contextually relevant and precise results, improving task completion efficiency and the overall user experience (Gerlich, 2023).

Perceived Ease of Use Analysis

Perceived ease of use evaluates how intuitive and user-friendly the system interface is when performing search tasks. The analysis of perceived ease of use also shows a significant difference favoring the AI-supported system.

In the academic search task, the *t*-value of −7.15 and *p*-value of < 0.001 demonstrate that the AI-enhanced search system was perceived as significantly easier to use. This likely results from the natural language processing (NLP) capabilities of AI systems, which allow users to engage in multi-turn

Table 6.5 *User's perceived ease of use*

Group	Mean (Traditional Search)	Mean (AI-enhanced Search)	t-value	p-value
Academic Search Task	3.5	4.8	−7.15	< 0.001
Shopping Decision Task	4.0	4.7	−4.93	< 0.001
Information Retrieval Task	3.6	4.5	−6.31	< 0.001

Table 6.6 *User's perceived usefulness*

Group	Mean (Traditional Search)	Mean (AI-enhanced Search)	t-value	p-value
Academic Search Task	3.7	4.9	−6.84	< 0.001
Shopping Decision Task	4.1	4.8	−4.75	< 0.001
Information Retrieval Task	3.8	4.7	−5.90	< 0.001

interactions and refine queries contextually, reducing cognitive load (Bender et al., 2021).

The same pattern was found in the shopping decision and information retrieval tasks, where AI-enhanced systems consistently outperformed traditional systems in terms of ease of use, with significant p-values below 0.001.

Future Usage Intention Analysis

Future usage intention assesses users' likelihood of adopting the AI-enhanced search system for future tasks, based on their overall experience. The analysis of future use intention reveals the most pronounced difference between the two systems.

For the academic search task, the t-value of −6.84 and p-value < 0.001 indicate that users are significantly more likely to adopt AI-enhanced systems for future academic searches. The AI system's ability to synthesize and present complex information efficiently contributes to this high future usage intention (Hao & Cukurova, 2023).

The same trend is observed in the shopping decision and information retrieval tasks, where users displayed a strong preference for AI-enhanced systems, as evidenced by statistically significant differences ($p < 0.001$) in future usage intention.

These results align with the Technology Acceptance Model (TAM), which posits that higher perceived usefulness and ease of use lead to greater user adoption of technology (Venkatesh et al., 2003). As AI systems continue to evolve, users are likely to rely more on these tools for tasks that require synthesizing large amounts of information.

6.5 Discussion and Conclusion

This chapter has shed light on the transformative potential of AI-supported search interactions in reshaping users' information seeking behavior and perceptions. Our findings reveal a significant shift in search efficiency, effectiveness, and user satisfaction when comparing AI-supported systems to traditional search methods.

The dramatic reduction in query modifications across all task types – from academic research to consumer decision-making – suggests that AI-supported search is adept at interpreting user intent and providing relevant results from the outset. This efficiency gain is particularly pronounced in complex, information-dense tasks, where the AI's ability to understand context and nuance proves most valuable. The observed increase in dwell time on relevant pages further supports this notion, indicating that users are spending less time reformulating queries and more time engaging with pertinent information.

These behavioral changes have profound implications for our understanding of information seeking processes. Traditional models that emphasize iterative query refinement may need to be revisited in light of the more streamlined search process enabled by AI support.

The consistently positive user perceptions of AI-supported search across dimensions of usefulness, ease of use, and future use intention are particularly striking. These findings strongly support the Technology Acceptance Model and indicate a high likelihood of user adoption and continued use of AI-supported search systems. The marked preference for AI-supported search in future use intention suggests that these systems are not merely efficient, but also provide a more satisfying and gratifying search experience, aligning with the Uses and Gratifications Theory.

From a practical standpoint, these findings underscore the importance of integrating AI capabilities into search systems across various domains. Developers and organizations should prioritize features that reduce the need for query reformulations and support more efficient information retrieval.

However, the varying benefits observed across different task types highlight the need for task-specific optimizations. Interfaces should be designed to capitalize on the increased dwell time, perhaps by providing more in-depth content summaries or related information to support deeper engagement with the material.

While these results are promising, they also open up new avenues for research. The long-term effects of AI-supported search on information seeking behavior and learning outcomes remain to be explored. How different user groups interact with and benefit from these systems is another crucial area for investigation. Moreover, while increased dwell time suggests deeper engagement, future studies should directly assess the quality and depth of information processing and comprehension.

As AI-supported search systems become more prevalent, it is also imperative to consider their ethical implications. Issues of bias in AI algorithms, privacy concerns, and the potential for creating information bubbles need to be thoroughly examined and addressed.

In conclusion, this chapter provides compelling evidence for the effectiveness and user acceptance of AI-supported search interactions. By enhancing search efficiency, promoting deeper engagement with content, and garnering positive user perceptions, these systems have the potential to significantly transform information-seeking behavior.

Acknowledgment

This work was supported by the Natural Science Foundation of Hubei Province (No. 2025AFB770), and "the Fundamental Research Funds for the Central Universities."

References

Ali, M. Y., Naeem, S. B., & Bhatti, R. (2020). Artificial Intelligence Tools and Perspectives of University Librarians: An Overview. *Business Information Review, 37*(3), 116–124.

Bender, E. M., Gebru, T., McMillan-Major, A., & Shmitchell, S. (2021). On the Dangers of Stochastic Parrots: Can Language Models Be Too Big? *Proceedings of the 2021 ACM Conference on Fairness, Accountability, and Transparency* (pp. 610–623).

Chang, Y., Lee, S., Wong, S. F., & Jeong, S. P. (2022). AI-powered Learning Application Use and Gratification: An Integrative Model. *Information Technology & People, 35*(7), 2115–2139.

Cheng, Y., & Jiang, H. (2020). How Do AI-driven Chatbots Impact User Experience? Examining Gratifications, Perceived Privacy Risk, Satisfaction, Loyalty, and Continued Use. *Journal of Broadcasting & Electronic Media*, *64*(4), 592–614.

Choi, T. R., & Drumwright, M. E. (2021). "OK, Google, Why Do I Use You?" Motivations, Post-consumption Evaluations, and Perceptions of Voice AI Assistants. *Telematics and Informatics*, *62*, 101628.

Choung, H., David, P., & Ling, T. W. (2024). *Acceptance of AI-powered Technology in Surveillance Scenarios: Role of Trust, Security, and Privacy Perceptions. Security, and Privacy Perceptions*. http://dx.doi.org/10.2139/ssrn.4724446

De Cremer, D., & Kasparov, G. (2022). The Ethics of Technology Innovation: A Double-edged Sword? *AI and Ethics*, *2*(3), 533–537.

Falgoust, G., Winterlind, E., Moon, P., Parker, A., Zinzow, H., & Madathil, K. C. (2022). Applying the Uses and Gratifications Theory to Identify Motivational Factors behind Young Adult's Participation in Viral Social Media Challenges on TikTok. *Human Factors in Healthcare*, *2*, 100014.

Gao, Y., & Liu, H. (2023). Artificial Intelligence-enabled Personalization in Interactive Marketing: A Customer Journey Perspective. *Journal of Research in Interactive Marketing*, *17*(5), 663–680.

Gerlich, M. (2023). Perceptions and Acceptance of Artificial Intelligence: A Multi-dimensional Study. *Social Sciences*, *12*(9), 502.

Hao, X., & Cukurova, M. (2023, June). Exploring the Effects of "AI-Generated" Discussion Summaries on Learners' Engagement in Online Discussions. In *International Conference on Artificial Intelligence in Education* (pp. 155–161). Springer Nature Switzerland.

Hornbæk, K., & Oulasvirta, A. (2017, May). What Is Interaction? *Proceedings of the 2017 CHI Conference on Human Factors in Computing Systems* (pp. 5040–5052).

Hsu, C. L., Lin, J. C. C., & Miao, Y. F. (2020). Why Are People Loyal to Live Stream Channels? The Perspectives of Uses and Gratifications and Nedia Richness Theories. *Cyberpsychology, Behavior, and Social Networking*, *23*(5), 351–356.

Huggins-Manley, A. C., Booth, B. M., & D'Mello, S. K. (2022). Toward Argument-based Fairness with an Application to AI-enhanced Educational Assessments. *Journal of Educational Measurement*, *59*(3), 362–388.

Jiang, N., Liu, X., Liu, H., Lim, E. T. K., Tan, C. W., & Gu, J. (2023). Beyond AI-powered Context-aware Services: The Role of Human–AI Collaboration. *Industrial Management & Data Systems*, *123*(11), 2771–2802.

Katz, E., Blumler, J. G., & Gurevitch, M. (1973). Uses and Gratifications Research. *The Public Opinion Quarterly*, *37*(4), 509–523.

Loewenstein, G. (1994). The Psychology of Curiosity: A Review and Reinterpretation. *Psychological Bulletin*, *116*(1), 75–98.

Meng, C., Aliannejadi, M., & de Rijke, M. (2023, October). System Initiative Prediction for Multi-turn Conversational Information Seeking. *Proceedings of the 32nd ACM International Conference on Information and Knowledge Management* (pp. 1807–1817).

Na, K., & Lee, J. (2016). When Two Heads Are Better Than One: Query Behavior, Cognitive Load, Search Time, and Task Type in Pairs versus Individuals. *Aslib Journal of Information Management*, *68*(5), 545–565.

O'Brien, H. L., Arguello, J., & Capra, R. (2020). An Empirical Study of Interest, Task Complexity, and Search Behaviour on User Engagement. *Information Processing & Management, 57*(3), 102226.

Pinzolits, R. (2024). AI in Academia: An Overview of Selected Tools and Their Areas of Application. *MAP Education and Humanities, 4*, 37–50.

Savolainen, R. (2013). Approaching the Motivators for Information Seeking: The Viewpoint of Attribution Theories. *Library & Information Science Research, 35*(1), 63–68.

Sundar, S. S., & Limperos, A. M. (2013). Uses and Grats 2.0: New Gratifications for New Media. *Journal of Broadcasting & Electronic Media, 57*(4), 504–525.

Ullah, I., & Khusro, S. (2020). On the Search Behaviour of Users in the Context of Interactive Social Book Search. *Behaviour & Information Technology, 39*(4), 443–462.

Venkatesh, V., & Bala, H. (2008). Technology Acceptance Model 3 and a Research Agenda on Interventions. *Decision Sciences, 39*(2), 273–315.

Venkatesh, V., & Davis, F. D. (2000). A Theoretical Extension of the Technology Acceptance Model: Four Longitudinal Field Studies. *Management Science, 46*(2), 186–204.

Venkatesh, V., Morris, M. G., Davis, G. B., & Davis, F. D. (2003). User Acceptance of Information Technology: Toward a Unified View. *MIS Quarterly, 27*(3), 425–478.

Vuong, T., Saastamoinen, M., Jacucci, G., & Ruotsalo, T. (2019). Understanding User Behavior in Naturalistic Information Search Tasks. *Journal of the Association for Information Science and Technology, 70*(11), 1248–1261.

Yiannakoulias, N. (2024). Spatial Intelligence and Contextual Relevance in AI-driven Health Information Retrieval. *Applied Geography, 171*, 103392.

Yue, G., & Peng, S. (2021, June). Application of Artificial Intelligence in the Academic Search Engine. *International Conference on Applications and Techniques in Cyber Security and Intelligence* (pp. 611–616). Springer International Publishing.

Zamani, H., Dumais, S., Craswell, N., Bennett, P., & Lueck, G. (2020, April). Generating Clarifying Questions for Information Retrieval. *WWW '20: Proceedings of the Web Conference 2020* (pp. 418–428). https://dl.acm.org/doi/abs/10.1145/3366423.3380126

Zhao, W. X., Liu, J., Ren, R., & Wen, J. R. (2024). Dense Text Retrieval Based on Pretrained Language Models: A Survey. *ACM Transactions on Information Systems, 42*(4), 1–60.

7

AI for Human and Misinformation Interactions

A Case of Social Media

Nannan Huang, Xiuzhen Zhang, and Jia Tina Du

7.1 Introduction

The widespread use of the internet and social networks has provided a platform for social media users to create social bonds irrespective of where they are physically located. It also acts as a breeding ground for misinformation propagation online. Research shows that social media users play a central role in spreading this misinformation online by falsely believing it (Vosoughi et al., 2018). Because of social distancing and restrictions, many social media users relied on social networking to obtain information during the early stages of COVID-19. Lack of knowledge about this new virus also facilitated the related misinformation to spread over the internet, especially when there were limited scientific studies available. Misinformation has caused harm to the general public during the pandemic. For example, Forati and Ghose (2021) revealed that locations with posted high numbers of misinformation later experienced a rise in the number of cases. Studies have also found that those with beliefs in conspiracies about the virus were more likely to reject expert, authoritative information (Uscinski et al., 2020) and had a higher hesitancy against the vaccine (Freeman et al., 2022). Allington et al. (2021) also revealed a negative relationship between COVID-19 conspiracy beliefs and health-protective behaviours, and such behaviours may have been caused by using social media as a source of information. Therefore, understanding human behaviour around health-related misinformation is crucial to combat relevant misinformation online.

Significant computational studies have concentrated on misinformation identification and mitigation to help control the spread of misinformation online. Despite the evidence showing that social media users play an important role in the spread of misinformation on social media (Vosoughi et al., 2018), limited studies have focused on examining how users interact with misinformation socially and what factors drive these social behaviours. By expressing opinions, social media users find other like-minded individuals online and create social bonds in a virtual environment. Through the appraisal framework (Martin & White, 2003) studies such as Inwood and Zappavigna (2021) have modeled social bonding behaviour in a virtual setting using the ambient affiliation social semiotic approach by leveraging fine-grained linguistic patterns in writing. Understanding social bonding behaviour is crucial for identifying the root cause of the spread of misinformation. Users are the key players in misinformation spreading by falsely believing the misinformation. In Zhou et al. (2022) the authors investigated the spread of misinformation behaviour from a social media user's intentional perspective. They found that users may have unintentionally shared misinformation on social networking sites. Using such signals and incorporating them into the model design improved the performance of their misinformation identification model. This result indicates that incorporating human information interaction signals from a social perspective can enhance model design and performance. Therefore, leveraging social bonding behaviour may aid future research in developing more effective systems to combat the spread of misinformation. This chapter investigates two research questions:

(1) How do social media users bond around misinformation?
(2) What is the relationship between emotions and social bonding behaviour?

We adopt the Stimuli–Organism–Response (SOR) framework (Mehrabian & Russell, 1974) to explore online social bonding behaviour surrounding misinformation spread through the lens of emotions. We view information exposure as *stimuli*, social media users' emotions as an *organism*, and social bonding behaviour as a *response*. Using a public COVID-19 dataset – CoAID (Cui & Lee, 2020) from X, formerly known as Twitter – we explicitly explored online social bonding behaviour around COVID-19 misinformation in our study. We analyzed conversations from X to characterize social connections and attitudes toward misinformation. We randomly sampled 330 X conversations using CoAID (Cui & Lee, 2020) and manually annotated the social bonding behaviour expressed in the reply posts. Deepmoji (Felbo et al., 2017) and the Multidimensional Lexicon of Emojis (MLE) (Godard & Holtzman, 2022) were applied to extract emotion intensities from the reply posts. More details about emotion intensity extraction are covered in Section 7.3.4. Once emotion intensities were computed, we investigated how they differed for varying levels of information veracity. This is followed by quantifying how these emotions contribute to users' attitudes toward the information mentioned in the source post. The attitude intensity of an individual decides how the social bond is formed and leads to different online social bonding behaviours.

Similar to Vosoughi et al. (2018), who found that emotion and the intensities of emotion among different information veracities are different, we found that social bonding behaviours are different around true information and misinformation. Further analysis in our study showed that, for misinformation, the emotion of surprise significantly contributes to supporting the misinformation. Anticipation, on the other hand, significantly contributes to rejecting the misinformation. In contrast, when users are exposed to true information, the emotions of anger and sadness significantly contribute to its support, unlike fear, which significantly contributes to rejecting true information.

7.2 Literature Review

7.2.1 Misinformation and Human–Information Interaction

Studies such as Soroya et al. (2021) and Ke et al. (2021) examined how social media users interacted with information during the COVID-19 event. They examined how information influences user behaviour, from seeking to avoiding information. Humans are prone to seeking knowledge when faced with uncertainties. However, it also has the drawback of making individuals feel overwhelmed by information – information overload – which makes them try to avoid it. Significant efforts have also been put into studying human–information interaction around misinformation. Vosoughi et al. (2018) discuss the spread of true and false information online from various perspectives. They discovered that false information spreads faster, deeper, and more widely on online social networks. They also found that misinformation is more novel compared to the truth. The novelty of misinformation could be the reason why it receives more attention from users and is shared more often. Weeks (2015) evaluated misperceptions of misinformation and how they affect users' judgments of misinformation from various elements. The author found that emotion, partisanship, and correction play an important role in affecting judgment accuracy in misinformation. However, in the study, the emotions are limited to anger and anxiety. This limitation is due to previous studies finding that these negative emotions contribute to human misperceptions.

7.2.2 Emotions and User Behaviours

Human behaviours are affected by emotions, consciously or unconsciously, and numerous studies have examined the effects of emotions on various user behaviours. For example, Dunn and Schweitzer (2005) examined different emotional states and how they affect an individual's trust. They found that positive emotions such as happiness increase the likelihood of an individual trusting an event, whereas negative emotions such as anger have the opposite impact. Moving this to an online setting, Wang et al. (2009) found that positive emotions have a greater impact than negative emotions when it comes to perceived belief in internet applications.

It is widely acknowledged that the inclusion of emotion as a feature in user behaviour prediction computation models is beneficial. Many studies have discovered that the design of models containing information about emotions improves model accuracy (Calvo & D'Mello, 2010; Pak & Paroubek, 2010). The improved effectiveness of the models also demonstrated that emotion is a powerful predictor of user behaviour. For instance, Chen et al. (2017) showed that their model benefits from incorporating the emotion signal when modeling the behaviour of users who repost content. User emotions have also been adapted in false information modeling to improve modeling performance (Li et al., 2016).

7.2.3 User Behaviours based on the SOR Framework

The Stimulus–Organism–Reaction (S-O-R) framework (Mehrabian & Russell., 1974) in psychology aids in understanding human behaviour and its underlying causes. Therefore, it is frequently used when the goal of a study is to identify the main factors influencing a particular behaviour. It has been heavily used in studying customer behaviour (Arora et al., 2020; Gatautis et al., 2016). For example, using the SOR framework, Sherman et al. (1997) explained how the store environment affects the emotions of customers and how that leads to different purchasing behaviours, whereas Slama and Tashchian (1987) did a case study on how consumer involvement would affect shampoo purchasing behaviour as the response.

Although it is traditionally used to study consumer behaviour, in recent years, information studies have also applied this framework to unpack the information behaviour of social media users. Soroya et al. (2021) studied how users move from information seeking to information avoidance online. Using the SOR framework, they found that information avoidance behaviour was caused by information seeking, as the stimulus drives users to experience information overload. From these affected users' internal states of information anxiety as the organism and finally becoming information avoidance as the outcome, Xiao and Su (2022) revealed a relationship between users who were incidentally exposed to misinformation and had different misperceptions as organisms and ended up sharing the misinformation as a result of their misperceptions.

The SOR framework is also widely used to investigate COVID-19-related health misinformation. For instance, Li et al. (2022) used this framework to explain how the COVID-19 risk, as a stimulus for individuals, affects their emotions as an organism and leads to different responses in terms of sharing COVID-19-related misinformation online. The framework was used by Wu (2022) to demonstrate how an individual's social and information dependency leads to positive and negative effects on them. They found the positive effect has a greater influence on users' sharing of misinformation on social media platforms as the outcome. Similarly, Sampat and Raj (2022) demonstrated, based on the COVID-19 event, how many personal characteristics influence information sharing behaviour on social media.

7.3 Methodology and Data

7.3.1 Dialogic Social Affiliation Text

Limited attention has been paid to how values are communicated and how bonds are formed on social media from a social behaviour perspective. Introduced by Knight (2008; 2010; 2013) and summarized in the ambient affiliation framework (Inwood & Zappavigna, 2021), the dialogic affiliation system is designed to evaluate how the recipient negotiates the bond introduced in the initial communication. This system first identifies the bond from a linguistic standpoint using the ideation and attitude pairs and then observes how the bonds communicate in social networks. To identify the attitude, the system leverages the appraisal framework (Martin & White, 2003). The appraisal framework (Martin & White, 2003), a semiotic social framework, is a tool that helps understand an individual's attitude and appreciation toward others through written messages. The appraisal framework contains three dimensions of evaluation, including attitude, graduation, and engagement. Since the social bonding behaviour is what we are focusing on rather than the actual bond itself, in our study, therefore, upon identifying bonds in the source post, we identify the attitude only from the appraisal framework. The attitude dimension includes effect (emotions felt, e.g., happy, sad, interested), judgment (assessing an individual's behaviour, e.g., right, wrong, irresponsible), and appreciation (valuing an object, e.g., yummy, nice, fantastic). Applying this framework to social media platform conversations helps identify the underlying bonds in the posts. Using the dialogic affiliation system targeted to evaluate social bond negotiation at an online conversation level, we can also understand how an individual would bond with the information. Figure 7.1 provides a graphic representation of how the dialogic affiliation system

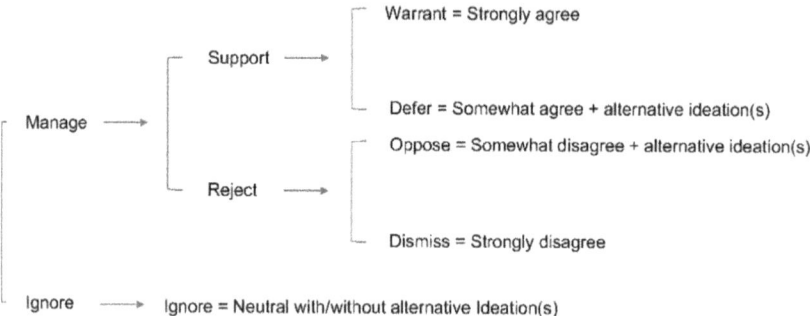

Figure 7.1 Dialogic affiliation system

functions. Under this framework, a user manages or ignores the bond that was indicated in the source post by dividing their bonding behaviour into the first and second levels. If the user is managing the bond, it can be further divided into accepting or rejecting the proposed bond. Finally, these behaviors can be classified into four groups based on how users negotiate social bonds in an online setting. We apply the framework in our study to analyze social media users' behaviour and how bonds are formed around misinformation.

According to the social bond theory (Pratt et al., 2011), one of the factors determining how strongly one will bond with the environment or other individuals is belief – that is, the value and attitude of an individual. In an online environment, this could refer to whether the information aligns with their values and whether they agree or disagree with the information. From there, users decide whether to socially bond with the information. In other words, how an individual would bond could also be determined by how much the information aligns with their values, as reflected by their attitude expressed through writing. It also acts as an indication of whether they agree with the information presented or not. In our study, we are using direct mapping of social bonding behaviour and attitude intensity, as shown in Table 7.1. It reflects whether users agree with the provided information through their social behaviour.

7.3.2 SOR Model for Information Veracity and Social Bonding Behaviors

The Stimulus–Organism–Reaction (S-O-R) framework is frequently used to understand and explain human behaviors in response to different cues in the environment and how they are triggered by different external factors (Arora

Table 7.1 *Mapping between online social bonding behaviors and attitude intensity*

Social bonding behaviour	Attitude intensity	
Support warrant	Strongly agree	2
Support defer	Somewhat agree	1
Ignore	Neutral	0
Reject oppose	Somewhat disagree	−1
Reject dismiss	Strongly disagree	−2

et al., 2020; Gatautis et al., 2016; Sherman et al., 1997; Slama & Tashchian, 1987). It is also widely used to explain how individuals react to false information and how they use information about the recent COVID-19 pandemic (Li et al., 2022; Sampat & Raj, 2022; Slama & Tashchian, 1987; Soroya et al., 2021; Wu, 2022; Xiao & Su, 2022). It has been proven to be a useful tool to describe results caused by individuals' internal states. The SOR framework has supported and directed numerous studies on human behaviour about information and health-related misinformation. We therefore apply it in our study to understand what social bonding behaviors are presented and the underlying causes for them.

Misinformation, according to earlier research, significantly affects users' emotions (Vosoughi et al., 2018; Wang et al., 2019). Therefore, information veracity was included and acted as a stimulus in our study. Information veracity as the stimuli affect users' internal states by triggering different emotional intensities in them. Hence, applying the model, the emotion intensities captured are the organisms users reveal when facing different information realities. Existing literature has revealed that emotions have an impact on their associated behaviors (Dunn & Schweitzer, 2005; Wang et al., 2009). Therefore, users' online social bonding behaviors would be affected by their emotions. In summary, applying the SOR framework to our study (Figure 7.2), the external stimuli are the veracity of the source information. The emotion experienced by users is that of the organism as it mirrors internal human states. We used the chi-square test of independence to determine whether there is a relationship between information's veracity and how users negotiate social bonds online. The null hypothesis of the test is that there is no relationship between information's veracity and how users develop social bonds online. The alternative hypothesis is that the veracity of information and how users negotiate bonds are not independent, meaning that, for different information veracity, users negotiate bonds differently in an online situation. This helps answer when the stimuli are different and whether the responses differ as well. It helps lay the groundwork before we investigate further.

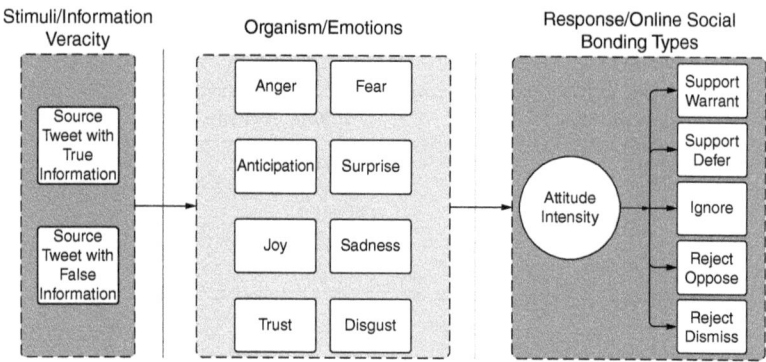

Figure 7.2 The conceptual SOR model

7.3.3 Data

After reading the truth or the misinformation, users may develop different affections and emotions toward the presented information. Users would then react and respond to their feelings when posting their opinions on various topics online. This behaviour can be understood as a user's attempt to negotiate social bonds in an online environment.

We used the COVID-19 related misinformation dataset – CoAID (Cui & Lee, 2020) – to study how users negotiate social bonds around COVID-19 misinformation. This is a dataset containing COVID-19 healthcare misinformation together with users' social engagement with the misinformation. COVID-19 is one of the major events around the globe in recent years. Using a relevant dataset (Cui & Lee, 2020) with social engagement containing a significant number of online conversations allows us to investigate how users communicate bonds around misinformation.

The dataset contains over 8,000 pairs of conversations on X through replying to a source post related to misinformation and over 127,000 pairs related to true information. The dataset provided the source and reply post IDs, so we could obtain the conversations using the IDs. The dataset also contains labels for whether the information mentioned in the source post is true or false, together with labels for whether it is a claim or news that the original post mentions.

Source posts containing facts are mostly official accounts with announcements or information URLs. There are two major types of accounts posting misinformation: private accounts and posts combating misinformation from official accounts or users from the fact-checking community, clarifying that the

AI For Human and Misinformation Interactions 161

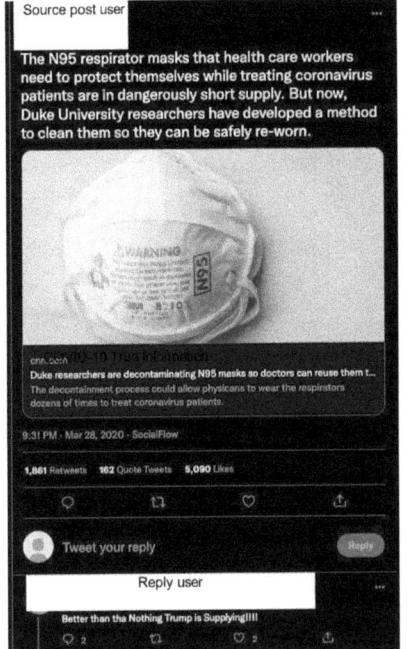
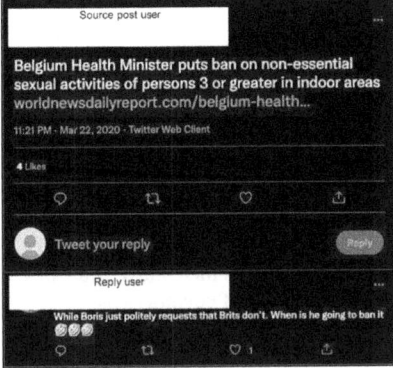

Figure 7.3 Example source and reply posts

underlying message is false. The reply posts are generally from private accounts expressing their opinions on the topic discussed in the source post. Examples of truth and misinformation source posts and their replies can be found in Figure 7.3. The source and replies were obtained using the official X API using the provided post IDs. We then filtered out any non-English conversations and randomly selected 175 conversations related to true information and 175 conversations related to misinformation. Lastly, we performed annotation using the dialogic affiliation framework, as shown in Figure 7.1, on the selected subset of X conversations.

The annotations were completed by three individuals; one is the author of this chapter, and the other two are independent researchers. Guidelines were provided to assist annotators with their annotations. They were instructed to first identify bonds using the ideation and attitude pairs in the source post. This is leveraging the appraisal framework (Martin & White, 2003), as in Inwood and Zappavigna (2021). After bonds were identified, they read the replies and used the dialogic affiliation framework to label how users negotiated bonds. Some examples of annotation are provided in Table 7.2.

Table 7.2 *Examples for annotation of social bonding*

Source Post	Reply	Social Bonding
Misinformation		
More **funny math** from @USER: (1) All non-US countries have done about 25 million tests; (2) US: about 5.9M (through Apr. 28); (3) Trump: "We've tested more than every country COMBINED"	More lies from our Lying King.	Support warrant
Royal Palace confirms **Queen Elizabeth tests positive** for coronavirus – UCR World News – Will **oil prices** fall again next week? The price $20 would be seen? I opened buy at $23.14 and didn't stop loss in time yesterday **thanks** to busy works [Face with Tears of Joy]	Let's see what news comes till tomorrow [Grinning Face with Smiling Eyes]	Support defer
CDC recommends men **shave their beards** to **protect against coronavirus**	Don't worry about Coronavirus, put a lime in it	Ignore
CDC recommends men **shave their beards** to **protect against coronavirus**	No way. I would suit up instead	Reject oppose
First **volunteer** in UK coronavirus vaccine trial has **died**	Fake news	Reject dismiss
Truthful information		
The **UK is supporting Somali government** to set up hand washing stations to **prevent the spread of Coronavirus**. The first went operational in Lower Shabelle **not far from** Mogadishu yesterday with more to follow	Job well done	Support warrant
If the **Government wants to help kids** with their education during this crisis, **instead of pushing** to send them back to unsafe schools, he could start by **ensuring** all children have the resources – like books and computers – that they need to learn at home	Why doesn't the @USER donate their educational equipment lol [Face with Tears of Joy][Rolling on the Floor Laughing]	Support defer
We know what to do but clearly aren't all doing it: wash hands, social distance, mask when you can't, stay home if you are sick	@USER The test are rigged for positive results. Investigate	Ignore
Experts call on UK to not use contact tracing app for surveillance – Business Insider @URL	@USER This would be madness don't take it out on the public ...	Reject oppose
"**Worst nightmare**": **Fauci warns** that coronavirus pandemic '**isn't over yet**'	@USER This guy changes his mind more than the weather!	Reject dismiss

The ideation and attitude pairs are in bold. @USER and @URL indicate user mention and external link, and [] represents an emoji.

Once the annotators finished the annotation, a majority vote was taken among the three sets of annotations. We discarded any sample without a majority vote. This might be due to the conflicting interpretations of the post's message (Clark, 1985; Day & Gentner, 2007), which would make coming to an agreement or comprehending its contents challenging. After removing instances without a majority vote, we had 330 annotations left, which were made up of 162 truths and 168 misinformation-related conversations.

7.3.4 Emotion Intensity

To understand how users feel after reading the information, we can evaluate the emotions extracted from their written text. By analyzing the emotion scores across various online social bonding types when exposed to truth and misinformation, we can learn what emotions might potentially affect a user's reaction to bonds.

Prior studies have concentrated on getting word counts for Plutchik's eight basic emotions (Plutchik, 1980) using the NRC Word-Emotion Association Lexicon (Mohammad & Turney, 2013) to measure the emotions in text. One of the disadvantages of this method is that it is bound by vocabulary and relies on exact word matching to extract meaning. It also failed to consider the use of negation to generate contradictory emotions. Numerous prior studies have discovered that general misinformation induces different types of negative emotions when presented to users (Vosoughi et al., 2018). It has been demonstrated that false information about COVID-19 also causes negative emotions (Leng et al., 2021). However, when we used NRC (Mohammad & Turney, 2013) to assess emotions in the chosen dataset, we discovered that it did not work well at capturing emotion intensity in the chosen dataset.

The ability of emojis to convey emotions in written text, on the other hand, is well recognized. According to Gülşen (2016), emojis can be used to represent emotions. In contrast to words, emojis, which are symbols that represent faces, can indicate one or many emotions in contrast to words (Jaeger & Ares, 2017). When compared to regular text usage, Ai et al. (2017) show that it has a greater semantic meaning. Emojis have also been suggested for use in psychometric scales to gauge emotions and personalities in several psychology studies, such as Marengo et al. (2017) and Phan et al. (2019), with promising results.

Therefore, to overcome the disadvantage of using exact word matching, we decided to first project the text message to a space represented by an emoji by applying Deepmoji (Felbo et al., 2017). This is a neural model that projects text into five distinct emojis, which are used to represent underlying emotions

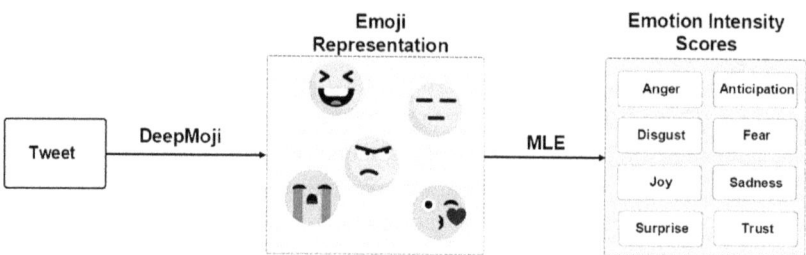

Figure 7.4 The overall process of obtaining emotion intensity scores

more comprehensively. To look up the emotional intensity of each of the emoji representations, we use the Multidimensional Lexicon of Emojis (MLE) (Godard & Holtzman, 2022). MLE comes with emotion intensity scores for 359 emojis. The emotion intensity score from MLE is calculated using over 3 million inputs. X posts and emotion ratings were provided by 2,230 individual raters. This allows direct mapping of emoji content to the intensity of Plutchik's eight emotions (Plutchik, 1980). We use MLE to map the emojis with their corresponding emotion scores after projecting the emotions into the emoji space. For each of the eight emotions, we add the scores for the five anticipated emojis and their corresponding scores. The full process of mapping the emotions and obtaining the final emotion scores is presented in Figure 7.4.

The Kolmogorov-Smirnov (K-S) test is used to analyze the distribution of emotions related to the veracity of the information. When combined with the mean and standard deviation of the emotion score, this helps to confirm whether there are any variances in the eight emotions' levels of intensity when information veracity varies. The result from the K-S test helps us answer whether the stimuli cause variance in the organism (i.e., under different information veracity, whether the emotion intensities would be different).

To determine if emotions have different impacts on social bonding types when information veracity varies, ordinary least squares regression is used to model such a relationship. Using a linear combination of the emotion intensity scores, we can estimate the users' likelihood to believe and create social bonds with the provided information. We can also quantify the potential effect each emotion has on how likely they believe and how likely they are to bond with the source post. The output of the model is used as an indication of which emotion contributes the most to how users would like to bond based on whether they believe the information or not.

As mentioned in Section 7.3.2, based on the theory of social bonding (Pratt et al., 2011), where alignment with personal value can determine how much a user would like to bond, we mapped the online social bonding type to a numerical value indicating the users' attitude, as shown in Table 7.1. This is to make the attitude of a user and how one would like to bond a quantifiable, measurable variable. Once the attitude intensity is quantifiable, then it is feasible to use the variable to model the relationship between the emotion intensity scores and how they contribute to how a user would like to bond. This is to answer the last question of our conceptual SOR model: to examine the relationship between the organism (emotion) and the response (user bonding types).

7.4 Results

7.4.1 Social Bonding Type Distribution

Using our annotated data, we can observe from Figure 7.5 that, when true information is presented to users, they tend to support the proposed bond by warranting or deferring to an alternative bond. In contrast, when

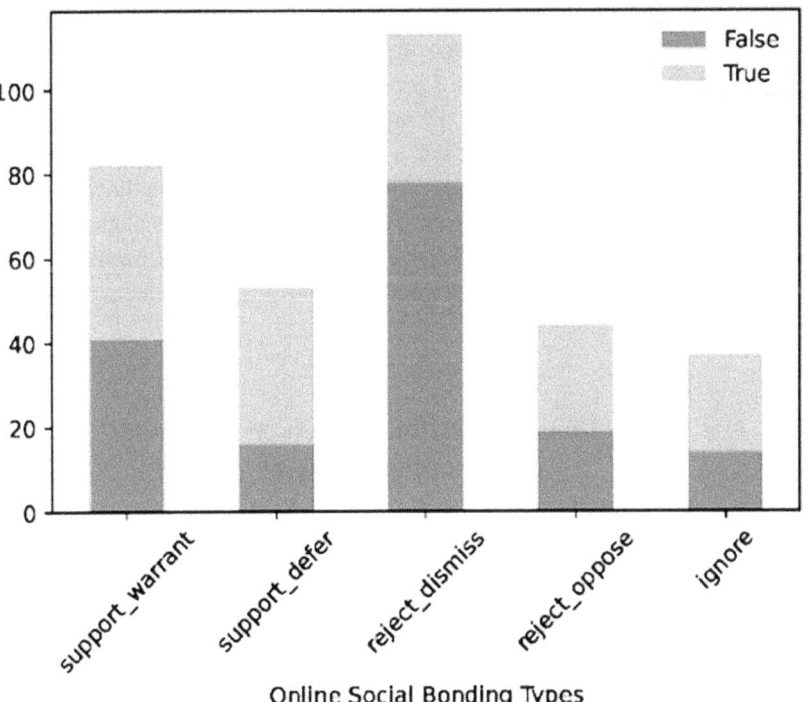

Figure 7.5 Online social bonding behaviours distribution by information veracity

misinformation is presented to users, they tend to reject the bond by dismissing or opposing it and suggesting an alternative bond. We can see that dismissal is the most common type of online social bonding when misinformation is presented to users. More users are ignoring the proposed bond when true information is presented. From the distribution, we believe that the veracity of the information affects how users negotiate bonds in an online environment. Further analyses are done in Sections 7.4.2–7.4.4 to validate that this is the case.

7.4.2 Association between Information Veracity and Negotiation of Social Bonds

As previously mentioned, we are determining whether or not the information's veracity and the type of online social bonding are independent of each other using the chi-square test of independence. This lays the foundation for further investigation into the connection between them. In the chi-square test of independence, the null hypothesis assumes that online social bonding behaviours are independent of the veracity of information. We then check whether the chi-square statistic is over the critical value. From the chi-square test result (p-value = 0.003), at a 1 percent confidence level, we can reject the null hypothesis and accept the alternative hypothesis to conclude that the veracity of the information and the way that users negotiate bonds are not independent. This is also coherent with our previous observation in Section 7.4.1. Given that these two variables are not independent of each other, we can further investigate using the SOR framework (Mehrabian & Russell., 1974) to identify the relationships between information veracity and how users choose to negotiate the bond.

7.4.3 Emotion Distribution between Different Information Veracity

To determine whether and how the veracity of the information affects users' emotions, for both the truth and misinformation, we used all the data we collected using the provided post IDs and we performed the Kolmogorov-Smirnov (K-S) test on the emotion intensity scores derived from the replies. The results can be found in Table 7.3. This is to test whether the emotional intensity distribution among the two types is the same. When the distribution is different, we can infer that the emotional intensity for that particular emotion is different among the types, which is caused by the veracity of the information.

Table 7.3 *Mean and standard deviation of emotions among different information veracities, all p-values < 0.001*

Emotion	Mean		Std		KS Test D statistic
	True	False	True	False	
Anger	0.2773	0.2799	0.0940	0.0853	0.1027
Anticipation	0.4970	0.4679	0.0792	0.0716	0.1535
Disgust	0.2061	0.2109	0.0782	0.0712	0.1222
Fear	0.2954	0.2938	0.0846	0.0773	0.0752
Joy	0.4641	0.4235	0.1214	0.0997	0.1489
Sadness	0.2731	0.2721	0.0795	0.0727	0.0836
Surprise	0.2454	0.2297	0.0360	0.0335	0.1624
Trust	0.5547	0.5229	0.0799	0.0788	0.1760

To have a better understanding of which type has the higher intensity score for each emotion, the mean and standard deviation are also calculated for the emotion intensity scores. The intensity scores for all emotions are significantly different (p-value < 0.01). With true information, emotions such as anticipation, joy, sadness, surprise, and trust are higher. With misinformation, on the other hand, emotions such as anger and disgust are higher. These results are consistent with a prior study (Vosoughi et al., 2018), with a subtle difference. Broadly, true information triggers more positive emotions, while misinformation triggers more negative emotions. Users' emotions are impacted by the veracity of information.

7.4.4 Ordinary Least Squares Regression Model on Emotion and How Users Negotiate Bonds Using Social Media

The result of an ordinary least squares regression predicting attitude intensity or online social bonding types is reported in Table 7.4. The model is applied to different types of information and is analyzing how and what emotions are affecting social bonding behaviours. Using the ordinary least squares regression model, we depicted how users prefer to connect with the information as their attitude intensity toward the provided information. We quantified what and how emotions contribute to how users bond on social media platforms under different information veracities.

From the result, we found that, when users are exposed to true information, anger, fear, and sadness contribute significantly to how they connect and bond with the information. Anger and sadness contribute significantly to positive attitude intensity and bond with the true information. Fear, on the other hand,

Table 7.4 *Ordinary least square regression model on emotion and online social bonding behaviours*

Emotion	True information	False information
Anger	87.15 (43.26)*	39.06 (50.48)
Anticipation	−40.69 (24.71)	−86.78 (28.14)**
Disgust	−69.51 (38.80)	−86.98 (51.38)
Fear	−113.39 (47.21)*	−6.55 (50.235)
Joy	13.19 (12.40)	16.96 (26.41)
Sadness	72.65 (29.50)*	33.49 (33.61)
Surprise	−0.81 (35.64)	105.14 (42.21)*
Trust	33.49 (21.615)	16.56 (24.46)

Notes: Unstandardized regression coefficients reported. Standard error is listed in parentheses. *p*-values are two-tailed. * $p < 0.05$. ** $p < 0.01$.

significantly contributes to negative attitude intensity and rejects true information. In contrast, when users are exposed to misinformation, anticipation and surprise are significant factors in determining how users bond with misinformation, while anticipation significantly contributes to a more positive attitude intensity and supports misinformation. Surprise, on the other hand, significantly contributes to rejecting the misinformation. Overall, we found that the relationship between different information veracity and the importance of different emotions in how users bond is different.

The Chi-square test result indicates that, for different information veracity, the social bonding behaviour initiated by users is different. It lays the groundwork for us to further investigate the potential factors contributing to such an outcome. This is consistent with what we saw in Figure 7.5, where users prefer to believe the truth by supporting or deferring the bond and rejecting the bond by dismissing behaviour, indicating whether the information being provided is true or not.

7.5 Discussion

We found that, when exposed to the truth and misinformation, emotion intensities as an internal state of users are different. Our findings are consistent with those of Vosoughi et al. (2018). With true information, users have higher levels of anticipation, joy, sadness, and trust. Disgust has a higher intensity when misinformation is presented to users. This also aligns with Vosoughi et al. (2018). However, a subtle difference in surprise is observed in our analysis. The intensity of surprise is higher when true information is presented but lower in Vosoughi et al. (2018). We suspect this is a case-specific observation since the dataset we used for our analysis was published during the early stages of COVID-19, when the general public still had limited knowledge on this topic. Hence, revealing a higher intensity of surprise when true information is presented is reasonable. This is also supported by the novelty hypothesis from Vosoughi et al. (2018), where information that is more novel would receive greater attention and surprise. Similarly with fear, since this is an unknown event, it is reasonable for users to feel fear even when true information is presented.

We found an association between emotions, users' attitude intensity, and social bonding behaviour when users are exposed to different information veracity. We found that, when users are exposed to misinformation, anticipation and surprise are key factors that contribute significantly to social bonding behaviour. The anticipation emotion contributes significantly to bond rejection. This is no surprise since the more anticipatory a user is, the less likely he or she will believe misinformation. However, the surprise emotion contributes significantly to supporting the misinformation. We suspect there are two reasons for this observation. Firstly, surprise as an emotion would intensify the feelings of other emotions, according to Mellers et al. (2013). Secondly, when an individual is more emotional, they are more likely to behave irrationally (Pham, 2007), in our case by falsely believing in misinformation. In contrast, when users are exposed to true information, the anger, fear, and sadness emotions contribute significantly to how they bond socially. Anger and sadness play an important role in social bonding around the truth. While fear emotions may lead people to reject factual information, we believe that encountering true information can also trigger anger and sadness when this information aligns with our observations and those reported by Vosoughi et al. (2018). Hence, these emotions have a greater contribution to attitude intensity, which is understandable. Similarly, it is understandable that fear and emotion can lead individuals to refuse or reject bonding with the truth. Especially in the case of COVID-19, true information could contain messages about the seriousness of the virus. In addition, there were uncertainties about this virus, and fear of the unknown could also cause individuals to withdraw or disassociate themselves from the information. We also suspect the distribution of bonding types can be a cause of the subtle differences between the contributions of emotion intensity and bonding behaviour. As depicted in Sections 7.4.1 and 7.4.2, bonding distributions are different under different veracity.

In an earlier study, Weeks (2015) examined information behaviour in a political context. Their study only examined two types of emotions and other factors that may influence individuals' judgments on political-related misinformation. The author found that anger, as an emotion, motivates the evaluation of uncorrected misinformation. Hence, the positive relationship between anger and belief level in our study can be explained by this. In Weeks (2015), they discovered that anxiety, the second type of emotion they are investigating, promotes initial belief, allowing individuals to believe in the information presented more easily. In our study, when users are exposed to misinformation with a higher intensity of surprise, they are more easily convinced by and believe misinformation. These are two distinct emotions that have similar outcomes when it comes to misinformation. A common factor among anxiety and surprise is the possible unknown in the future (Grupe & Nitschke, 2013). We suspect this is the reason why these two emotions come to the same conclusion. The other factors discussed in their study are case-dependent, such as political standpoints, and they do not apply to our study. Lastly, it is no surprise that, when users experience negative emotions such as fear, they prefer to withdraw rather than bond with the information.

We believe our study examining individuals' social bonding behaviors from a social perspective will help design mitigation mechanisms to counteract the spread of misinformation. The emotional signals in misinformation can be leveraged to design automatic misinformation mitigation systems. It is based on the understanding that when users are exposed to true information, anger, sadness, and fear are key contributors to socially bonding with the information. Where anger and sadness encourage a bond with true information and fear encourages a rejection bond, we may include more words related to anger and sadness to promote their propagation. In contrast, words related to fear should be minimized since they push users away from creating social bonds with the truth. With misinformation, surprise should be minimized since it leads users to falsely believe in misinformation and bond with the misinformation. Anticipation words, on the other hand, could be promoted to encourage users to disconnect from misinformation.

7.6 Conclusion

In this chapter, we applied the Stimuli–Organism–Response (SOR) framework to examine the relationship and the effect between misinformation, emotions, and social bonding behaviour in an online environment. We found that, with different information veracity, the triggered emotion intensities are different. When exposed to true information, more anger and disgust were triggered, whereas, when exposed to misinformation, higher intensities of anticipation, fear, joy, sadness, surprise, and trust were triggered. Furthermore, we found that, with different information veracity, the key contributing factors to social behaviour are different. Anger and sadness trigger social bonding reactions that support true information. The fear emotion, on the other hand, promotes rejection of true information. When exposed to misinformation, anticipation promotes rejection, and surprise promotes behaviour to support the misinformation. We believe these findings could help future research to include such signals and improve the computational model design and performance in identifying and mitigating misinformation online. Future research can examine ways to leverage such signals in model development to help design models with better performance when incorporating social signals. Our study examining individuals' social bonding behaviors from a social perspective may help future misinformation identification and mitigation studies design models that better capture misinformation from a more human-understandable perspective.

Acknowledgments

This research was supported in part by the Australian Research Council Discovery Project DP200101441.

References

Ai, W., Lu, X., Liu, X., Wang, N., Huang, G., & Mei, Q. (2017). Untangling Emoji Popularity through Semantic Embeddings. *Eleventh International AAAI Conference on Web and Social Media*.

Allington, D., Duffy, B., Wessely, S., Dhavan, N., & Rubin, J. (2021). Health-protective Behaviour, Social Media Usage and Conspiracy Belief during the COVID-19 Public Health Emergency. *Psychological Medicine, 51*(10), 1763–1769.

Arora, S., Parida, R. R., & Sahney, S. (2020). Understanding Consumers' Showrooming Behaviour: A Stimulus–Organism–Response (SOR) Perspective. *International Journal of Retail & Distribution Management, 48*(11), 1157–1176.

Calvo, R. A., & D'Mello, S. (2010). Affect Detection: An Interdisciplinary Review of Models, Methods, and Their Applications. *IEEE Transactions on Affective Computing, 1*(1), 18–37.

Chen, J., Liu, Y., & Zou, M. (2017). User Emotion for Modeling Retweeting Behaviors. *Neural Networks, 96*, 11–21.

Clark, L. F. (1985). Social Knowledge and Inference Processing in Text Comprehension. *Advances in Psychology, 29*, 95–114.

Cui, L., & Lee, D. (2020). CoAID: COVID-19 Healthcare Misinformation Dataset [arXiv preprint]. arXiv:2006.00885.

Day, S. B., & Gentner, D. (2007). Nonintentional Analogical Inference in Text Comprehension. *Memory & Cognition, 35*(1), 39–49.

Dunn, J. R., & Schweitzer, M. E. (2005). Feeling and Believing: The Influence of Emotion on Trust. *Journal of Personality and Social Psychology, 88*(5), 736.

Felbo, B., Mislove, A., Søgaard, A., Rahwan, I., & Lehmann, S. (2017). Using Millions of Emoji Occurrences to Learn Any-domain Representations for Detecting Sentiment, Emotion and Sarcasm. *Proceedings of the 2017 Conference on Empirical Methods in Natural Language Processing* (pp. 1615–1625).

Forati, A. M., & Ghose, R. (2021). Geospatial Analysis of Misinformation in COVID-19 Related Tweets. *Applied Geography, 133*, 102473.

Freeman, D., Waite, F., Rosebrock, L., Petit, A., Causier, C., East, A., Jenner, L., Teale, A.-L., Carr, L., Mulhall, S., Bold, E., & Lambe, S. (2022). Coronavirus Conspiracy Beliefs, Mistrust, and Compliance with Government Guidelines in England. *Psychological Medicine, 52*(2), 251–263.

Gatautis, R., Vitkauskaite, E., Gadeikiene, A., & Piligrimiene, Z. (2016). Gamification as a Mean of Driving Online Consumer Behaviour: SOR Model Perspective. *Engineering Economics, 27*(1), 90–97.

Godard, R., & Holtzman, S. (2022). The Multidimensional Lexicon of Emojis: A New Tool to Assess the Emotional Content of Emojis. *Frontiers in Psychology, 13*, 921388.

Grupe, D. W., & Nitschke, J. B. (2013). Uncertainty and Anticipation in Anxiety: An Integrated Neurobiological and Psychological Perspective. *Nature Reviews Neuroscience, 14*(7), 488–501.

Gülşen, T. T. (2016). You Tell Me in Emojis. In T. Ogata & T. Akimoto (eds.), *Computational and Cognitive Approaches to Narratology* (pp. 354–375). IGI Global.

Inwood, O., & Zappavigna, M. (2021). Ambient Affiliation, Misinformation and Moral Panic: Negotiating Social Bonds in a YouTube Internet Hoax. *Discourse & Communication, 15*(3), 281–307.

Jaeger, S. R., & Ares, G. (2017). Dominant Meanings of Facial Emoji: Insights from Chinese Consumers and Comparison with Meanings from Internet Resources. *Food Quality and Preference, 62*, 275–283.

Ke, Q., Du, J. T., & Ji, L. (2021). Towards a Conceptual Framework of Health Crisis Information Needs: An Analysis of COVID-19 Questions in a Social Q&A Website. *Journal of Documentation, 77*(4), 851–870.

Knight, N. K. (2008). "Still Cool ... and American Too!": An SFL Analysis of Deferred Bonds in Internet Messaging Humour. *Systemic Functional Linguistics in Use, Odense Working Papers in Language and Communication, 29*, 481–502.

Knight, N. K. (2010). Wrinkling Complexity: Concepts of Identity and Affiliation in Humour. In M. Bednarek & J. R. Martin (eds.), New Discourse on Language: Functional Perspectives on Multimodality, Identity, and Affiliation (pp. 35–58). Continuum.

Knight, N. K. (2013). Evaluating Experience in Funny Ways: How Friends Bond through Conversational Humor. *Text & Talk, 33*(4–5), 553–574.

Leng, Y., Zhai, Y., Sun, S., Wu, Y., Selzer, J., Strover, S., Zhang, H., Chen, A., & Ding, Y. (2021). Misinformation during the COVID-19 Outbreak in China: Cultural, Social and Political Entanglements. *IEEE Transactions on Big Data, 7*(1), 69–80.

Li, M.-H., Chen, Z., & Rao, L.-L. (2022). Emotion, Analytic Thinking and Susceptibility to Misinformation during the COVID-19 Outbreak. *Computers in Human Behavior*, *133*, 107295.

Li, Y., Feng, X., & Zhang, S. (2016). Detecting Fake Reviews Utilizing Semantic and Emotion Model. In *2016 3rd International Conference on Information Science and Control Engineering (ICISCE)* (pp. 317–320). IEEE.

Marengo, D., Giannotta, F., & Settanni, M. (2017). Assessing Personality Using Emoji: An Exploratory Study. *Personality and Individual Differences*, *112*, 74–78.

Martin, J. R., & White, P. R. (2003). *The Language of Evaluation*, Vol. 2. Springer.

Mehrabian, A., & Russell, J. A. (1974). *An Approach to Environmental Psychology*. MIT Press.

Mellers, B., Fincher, K., Drummond, C., & Bigony, M. (2013). Surprise: A Belief or an Emotion? *Progress in Brain Research*, *202*, 3–19.

Mohammad, S. M., & Turney, P. D. (2013). Crowdsourcing a Word–Emotion Association Lexicon. *Computational Intelligence*, *29*(3), 436–465.

Pak, A., & Paroubek, P. (2010). Twitter as a Corpus for Sentiment Analysis and Opinion Mining. *Proceedings of the International Conference on Language Resources and Evaluation, LREC*, May 17–23, Valetta, Malta.

Pham, M. T. (2007). Emotion and Rationality: A Critical Review and Interpretation of Empirical Evidence. *Review of General Psychology*, *11*(2), 155–178.

Phan, W. M. J., Amrhein, R., Rounds, J., & Lewis, P. (2019). Contextualizing Interest Scales with Emojis: Implications for Measurement and Validity. *Journal of Career Assessment*, *27*(1), 114–133.

Plutchik, R. (1980). A General Psychoevolutionary Theory of Emotion. In R. Plutchik & H. Kellerman (eds.), *Theories of Emotion* (pp. 3–33). Academic Press.

Pratt, T. C., Gau, J. M., & Franklin, T. W. (2011). Key Idea: Hirschi's Social Bond/Social Control Theory. In *Key Ideas in Criminology and Criminal Justice* (pp. 55–69). Sage Publications.

Sampat, B., & Raj, S. (2022). Fake or Real News? Understanding the Gratifications and Personality Traits of Individuals Sharing Fake News on Social Media Platforms. *Aslib Journal of Information Management*, *74*(5), 840–876.

Sherman, E., Mathur, A., & Smith, R. B. (1997). Store Environment and Consumer Purchase Behavior: Mediating Role of Consumer Emotions. *Psychology & Marketing*, *14*(4), 361–378.

Slama, M. E., & Tashchian, A. (1987). Validating the SOR paradigm for consumer involvement with a convenience good. *Journal of the Academy of Marketing Science*, *15*(1), 36–45.

Soroya, S. H., Farooq, A., Mahmood, K., Isoaho, J., & Zara, S. E. (2021). From Information Seeking to Information Avoidance: Understanding the Health Information Behavior during a Global Health Crisis. *Information Processing & Management*, *58*(2), 102440.

Uscinski, J. E., Enders, A. M., Klofstad, C., Seelig, M., Funchion, J., Everett, C., Wuchty, S., Premaratne, K., & Murthi, M. (2020). Why Do People Believe COVID-19 Conspiracy Theories? *Harvard Kennedy School Misinformation Review*, *1*(3). https://misinforeview.hks.harvard.edu/article/why-do-people-believe-covid-19-conspiracy-theories/

Vosoughi, S., Roy, D., & Aral, S. (2018). The Spread of True and False News Online. *Science, 359*(6380), 1146–1151.

Wang, C. Y., Seng-cho, T. C., & Chang, H. C. (2009). Emotion and Motivation: Understanding User Behavior of Web 2.0 Application. *2009 Sixth International Conference on Information Technology: New Generations* (pp. 1341–1346). IEEE.

Wang, Y., McKee, M., Torbica, A., & Stuckler, D. (2019). Systematic Literature Review on the Spread of Health-related Misinformation on Social Media. *Social Science & Medicine, 240*, 112552.

Weeks, B. E. (2015). Emotions, Partisanship, and Misperceptions: How Anger and Anxiety Moderate the Effect of Partisan Bias on Susceptibility to Political Misinformation. *Journal of Communication, 65*(4), 699–719.

Wu, M. (2022). What Drives People to Share Misinformation on Social Media during the COVID-19 Pandemic: A Stimulus-Organism-Response Perspective. *International Journal of Environmental Research and Public Health, 19*(18), 11752.

Xiao, X., & Su, Y. (2022). Stumble on Information or Misinformation? Examining the Interplay of Incidental News Exposure, Narcissism, and New Media Literacy in Misinformation Engagement. *Internet Research*.

Zhou, X., Shu, K., Phoha, V. V., Liu, H., & Zafarani, R. (2022). "This Is Fake! Shared It by Mistake": Assessing the Intent of Fake News Spreaders. *Proceedings of the ACM Web Conference 2022* (pp. 3685–3694).

8

Effective Human–AI Collaborative Intelligence

Zhuoren Jiang and Xiaozhong Liu

8.1 Introduction

8.1.1 The Data Challenge in AI

Artificial Intelligence (AI) systems, especially those driven by machine learning (ML), thrive on the availability of high-quality data. Data serves as the cornerstone for model training, evaluation, and, ultimately, the effectiveness of AI in real-world applications. However, achieving this high-quality data for AI remains a significant challenge. While iterative optimization of model architectures can effectively enhance performance, the benefits derived solely from structural improvements are gradually diminishing. More attention needs to be directed toward the quality, availability, and management of data, which is vital for sustained AI advancement.

The data-for-AI pipeline, which encompasses data acquisition, integration, cleaning, and annotation, is often a bottleneck in AI development. Without systematic approaches to improving data quality, inaccuracies and inconsistencies can emerge, leading to unreliable models and increased costs. As defined by the ISO/IEC 25012 standard, high-quality data is characterized by "Accuracy," "Completeness," "Consistency," "Credibility," and "Currentness" (Gualo et al., 2021). Achieving these qualities is particularly challenging due to the dynamic nature of data sources, especially in real-time systems, where data continuously evolves (Rahm & Do, 2000; Reddy, 2023). In this context, managing and maintaining data quality across diverse, dynamic sources has become a critical aspect of AI system development (Madnick et al., 2009; Pipino et al., 2002).

Beyond technical considerations, fairness and bias in data represent another significant challenge for AI (Mehrabi et al., 2022). As AI systems become more integrated into critical sectors such as healthcare and finance, biased training data can lead to harmful consequences. For instance, computer vision models for diagnosing malignant skin lesions have been shown to perform significantly worse on dark skin compared to light skin, with an AUROC (Area Under the Receiver Operating Curves) score that dropped by 10–15 percent (Liang et al., 2022). This gap resulted from biased data and annotation errors. Addressing these issues by improving annotations and ensuring diverse, representative datasets effectively mitigated the performance disparity, highlighting the importance of data diversity and fairness in AI.

Additionally, AI systems face pressing ethical concerns regarding data privacy. Techniques such as model inversion (Fredrikson et al., 2015) and membership inference attacks (Hu et al., 2022) have shown that even anonymized data can reveal sensitive information about individuals. The aggregation of data from multiple sources, particularly in international contexts where privacy regulations vary, further amplifies these risks (Casalini et al., 2021). Strong data governance is essential to ensure privacy protection, particularly in sectors like finance and e-commerce where the exposure of personal data could have serious ramifications (Panian, 2010).

As these challenges illustrate, the complexities surrounding data quality are only part of the larger issue in AI development. Equally important are the significant costs and time constraints involved in acquiring and preparing the necessary data, which further complicates the efficient deployment of AI systems. The process of data labeling, for instance, can range from simple tasks – such as categorizing social media posts as positive, negative, or neutral – to more complex activities, like designing graphical interfaces for drawing bounding boxes around objects in video footage. These more advanced tasks often require substantial engineering resources, further driving up costs (Monarch, 2021).

Human error is another critical factor that complicates data acquisition. In some cases, such as analyzing broad consumer trends, errors may have a minor impact. However, in high-stakes applications like autonomous vehicles, even small mistakes in data labeling can lead to catastrophic outcomes, such as the failure to detect pedestrians. While some machine learning algorithms can tolerate minor noise, significant human errors often introduce biases that are difficult to rectify later in the training process, emphasizing the importance of high-quality training data (Monarch, 2021).

Data preparation itself is a resource-intensive task. Surveys reveal that data scientists spend approximately 80 percent of their time on tasks like data collection, cleaning, and labeling – far more than on model development (Press, 2022). Annotation, the process of adding labels to raw data to make it suitable for training machine learning models, often consumes more time and effort than model-building (Chai & Li, 2020; Monarch, 2021). Furthermore, enterprises continue to face data-related challenges, with 96 percent of organizations reporting difficulties in handling data (Dimensional Research, 2019), and 40 percent of them expressing concerns over data quality (Forrester Consulting, 2020).

In summary, data is a fundamental component of AI systems, particularly those driven by machine learning, serving as the foundation for training, evaluation, and real-world performance. However, acquiring and maintaining high-quality data presents significant challenges. Issues such as data quality, fairness, and privacy, along with the labor-intensive processes of data acquisition, annotation, and preparation, complicate the AI development pipeline. Human errors, biases in data, and ethical concerns regarding data privacy further exacerbate these challenges. Ultimately, overcoming these obstacles is critical for the successful deployment of AI systems in practical, high-stakes environments.

8.1.2 Leveraging Human Expertise in AI: Strategies for Effective Collaboration

Given these challenges, relying solely on automated machine learning methods may no longer be sufficient to address the complexities of real-world scenarios. To further enhance AI system performance and tackle data-related issues, leveraging human expertise and skills, particularly through human–AI collaboration at critical stages, has become essential for the development of efficient intelligent systems. By integrating effective human–AI collaborative intelligence techniques (Aldoseri et al., 2023; Chai & Li, 2020; X. Wu et al., 2022), we can improve AI's ability to learn from diverse, high-quality data, enabling it to adapt to complex environments and address challenges related to data quality, fairness, and privacy. This approach paves the way for building systems that are not only high-performing but also fair, reliable, and ethically sound, accelerating AI's advancement in practical applications.

In the context of AI development, integrating human expertise into machine learning frameworks allows prior knowledge to be embedded into the learning process, enhancing the model's ability to make informed decisions even when data is limited (Diligenti et al., 2017). Table 8.1 outlines the key stages where human expertise can be effectively integrated into the machine learning workflow (Dimensional Research, 2019):

In these key stages, a series of strategies can be employed to effectively integrate human knowledge and achieve an efficient combination of human intelligence with machine learning (Monarch, 2021). The strategies outlined by Chai and Li (2020) emphasize different approaches to improving machine

Table 8.1 *Key stages for integrating human expertise in the machine learning workflow*

Stages	Description
Data Extraction	Converting unstructured data into structured forms using human-provided rules or machine learning models.
Data Integration	Merging structured data from various sources, with human intervention resolving complex cases such as deduplication or schema alignment.
Data Cleaning	Identifying and correcting errors in datasets, with human involvement handling complex issues like missing values or duplicate data.
Data Annotation and Iterative Labeling	Iteratively labeling data, focusing human effort on critical samples to reduce annotation costs.
Model Training and Inference	Combining human insights with machine learning techniques, such as deep learning or hybrid methods, to improve model performance.

learning systems. Quality improvement relies on human input to fine-tune outcomes and adjust task distribution for optimal results. Cost reduction is achieved through crowdsourcing and efficient management of human resources, minimizing overall expenses. Latency reduction tackles the slower response times associated with human involvement by implementing efficient machine learning models. Active learning directs human annotation efforts toward the most informative samples, maximizing model performance within budget constraints. Lastly, weak supervision allows for the semi-automatic generation of a large volume of useful labels, ensuring high accuracy while maintaining cost-effectiveness. These diverse strategies together enhance machine learning efficiency across multiple dimensions.

This chapter will delve into the technical foundations and practical applications of human–AI collaboration, providing a comprehensive understanding of how these systems are built, refined, and applied across various domains. We begin by exploring the core technical frameworks that support effective collaboration, including human-in-the-loop systems, active learning, crowdsourcing, and interactive machine learning, with a focus on their definitions, principles, quality control mechanisms, and cost considerations. This is followed by an in-depth examination of real-world applications and case studies, illustrating how these collaborative models are transforming industries. Finally, we turn to future directions, highlighting continuous learning from human experts, advancements in human–AI interfaces, the integration of large language models, and the ethical implications and societal impacts of these evolving technologies.

8.2 Technical Foundations of Human–AI Collaboration

8.2.1 Human-in-the-Loop (HITL) Systems

Definition and Principles

Human-in-the-Loop (HITL) systems represent a powerful framework that allows for the seamless collaboration between human intelligence and machine learning processes. The essence of HITL lies not just in improving machine learning performance, but also in enhancing human efficiency by enabling dynamic, real-time interaction with AI models throughout the learning process. By embedding human expertise, intuition, and contextual knowledge into various stages of data processing, HITL systems unlock the potential for a more symbiotic relationship between human oversight and automation (Monarch, 2021).

At its core, HITL systems engage humans in tasks like data preprocessing, annotation, and interactive labeling, where human insight is crucial for optimizing the quality and context of data that machines learn from. This direct involvement ensures that the strengths of human cognition – such as pattern recognition, domain expertise, and creative problem-solving – complement the raw processing power of machine learning algorithms (X. Wu et al., 2022).

In domains like Natural Language Processing (NLP) and Computer Vision (CV), where training data often requires nuanced interpretation, the HITL paradigm can significantly enhance both the accuracy and efficiency of AI models. By iteratively incorporating human feedback into the learning cycle, these systems mitigate the limitations posed by sparse, ambiguous, or noisy data, fostering the development of AI that is not only technically proficient but also adaptable to complex real-world scenarios (Mosqueira-Rey et al., 2023). The ultimate goal of HITL is to integrate the strengths of both humans and machines, leveraging the precision of machines and the adaptability of humans to accelerate AI innovation and improve decision-making across various domains.

The foundational principles of Human-in-the-Loop Machine Learning (HITL-ML) are as follows (Monarch, 2021):

- Improving Model Accuracy: One of the core objectives of HITL-ML is to enhance the accuracy of machine learning models by incorporating human feedback during key stages of the learning process. Human insight, particularly in tasks like annotation and validation, adds critical value to data quality, thereby refining model predictions.
- Accelerating Target Accuracy: HITL systems aim to expedite the process of reaching desired accuracy levels for machine learning models. By involving

humans in the iterative learning loop, the model can achieve optimal performance more quickly through targeted corrections and guidance.
- Maximizing Combined Intelligence: HITL synergistically combines human intuition and machine precision to maximize accuracy. By leveraging the strengths of both human decision-making and automated learning, these systems can overcome limitations inherent in either component alone.
- Enhancing Human Efficiency with AI Assistance: Another fundamental principle of HITL is to increase human efficiency by automating routine and labor-intensive tasks. Machine learning algorithms assist in handling large-scale data and repetitive tasks, freeing human experts to focus on higher-level decision-making and strategic oversight.

Benefits and Limitations

As with any system, HITL systems come with their inherent advantages and challenges.

The benefits of HITL systems include:

(1) Improved Accuracy in Sparse Data Contexts: One of the most significant benefits of HITL systems is their ability to excel in situations where data is scarce. By integrating human a priori knowledge, especially in data-limited fields such as clinical diagnosis, HITL systems can enhance model accuracy. In cases where high-quality labeled data is not readily available, human expertise fills the gap, ensuring that models perform optimally despite data constraints (X. Wu et al., 2022).

(2) Enhanced Model Performance through Minimal Feedback: Another key benefit of HITL is its ability to improve model performance with minimal human input. Cognitive science research shows that even small datasets of human feedback can lead to substantial improvements in machine learning outcomes. HITL systems leverage this principle, allowing better training outcomes even with limited human engagement, thus increasing efficiency (X. Wu et al., 2022).

(3) Increased Interpretability and Usability: Traditional machine learning models can often be difficult to interpret, leading to hesitancy in their adoption. HITL systems address this issue by incorporating human input into the learning process, which not only improves the interpretability of the results but also makes the models more usable in real-world applications. This human–AI interaction builds trust and allows practitioners to better understand and utilize AI-generated insights.

(4) Tailored Learning through Human Preferences: HITL systems offer the unique advantage of aligning AI models more closely with human preferences. By incorporating datasets reflecting human preferences, such as

preferred summaries, HITL systems employ supervised learning to develop reward models that predict outcomes aligned with human choices. Reinforcement learning can then be applied to maximize these predictions, ensuring models meet user expectations (Ziegler et al., 2020).

While HITL systems offer numerous advantages, several challenges remain. These potential constraints highlight areas where further research and refinement are necessary.

(1) One of the key challenges in HITL systems is how to efficiently and effectively embed human expertise and knowledge into machine learning models. Current approaches often rely heavily on manual data annotation (X. Wu et al., 2022), but this limits the system's ability to learn from human experience on a broader scale. Additionally, maintaining system robustness while integrating human input is a critical issue.

(2) Another significant limitation is the absence of standardized evaluation benchmarks for HITL systems (X. Wu et al., 2022). Determining which key samples to use and how to construct appropriate evaluation metrics remains unclear. This becomes particularly important in scenarios such as active learning, where learners request human labeling. Ensuring the questions are presented in a clear and understandable manner is crucial, making the usability features – such as clarity, consistency, and efficiency – highly relevant in these systems (Mosqueira-Rey et al., 2023).

(3) As HITL systems increasingly involve human input, ethical considerations such as fairness, transparency, and interpretability become more pressing. While HITL aims to make machine learning more understandable and reliable, integrating these human aspects into AI systems requires careful thought and ongoing development to ensure equitable and transparent outcomes (Mosqueira-Rey et al., 2023).

8.2.2 Active Learning

Definition and Principles

Active Learning (AL) is a machine learning approach where the learner plays an active role in selecting data for human annotation (Monarch, 2021). The learner requests an oracle, typically a human expert, to label ambiguous or informative examples that will contribute significantly to improving the model (Mosqueira-Rey et al., 2023). This method is designed to address the challenge of the labeling bottleneck by iteratively presenting unlabeled instances to be annotated by the oracle (Burr, 2009; Schröder & Niekler, 2020). Active Learning aims to reduce the amount of data that requires human labeling while maintaining or even enhancing the overall model performance (Schröder &

Niekler, 2020). Through selective data sampling, AL allows for more efficient learning, leveraging both labeled and unlabeled data in the process (P. Liu et al., 2022; Monarch, 2021).

Active learning has already been widely applied in various fields, including collaborative filtering recommender systems, supervised remote sensing image classification, text classification using deep neural networks, and medical image analysis (P. Liu et al., 2022).

The following core principles guide the operation of Active Learning systems:

- Learner Control Over Data: In Active Learning, the learner actively controls which data to query. The learner can request a knowledgeable entity, often a human expert, to annotate selected unlabeled examples, thereby focusing on the most informative data (Mosqueira-Rey et al., 2023).
- Iterative and Incremental Annotation Process: Active Learning follows an iterative, cyclic process in which the learner employs a query strategy to request labels for specific examples. These labeled examples are then used to refine and improve the model incrementally (Mosqueira-Rey et al., 2023).
- Combination of Labeled and Unlabeled Data: AL effectively operates as a form of semi-supervised learning, combining both labeled and unlabeled data. This approach is particularly valuable when labeled data is costly or scarce, enabling efficient use of available resources (Burr, 2009).
- Query Strategy for Effective Sampling: A critical aspect of AL is the query strategy (X. Wu et al., 2022), which determines which examples the learner requests for labeling. Common strategies include:
  (a) Membership Query Synthesis: The learner may generate and request labels for any instance, even synthetic ones.
  (b) Stream-based Selective Sampling: The learner evaluates instances one at a time, choosing whether to query or discard each.
  (c) Pool-based Sampling: The learner evaluates a pool of data to select the most informative examples for labeling.
- Focus on Informative Instances: The ultimate goal of Active Learning is to select the most informative or uncertain examples for annotation. This approach maximizes the efficiency of the labeling process, leading to faster model improvement and reduced reliance on large labeled datasets.

Quality Control and Cost Consideration

Active learning's quality control is centered on selecting the most valuable samples for labeling, assuming that human experts provide accurate annotations. The design of the selection process, whether model-driven or data-driven, plays a critical role. Key factors influencing quality include (P. Liu et al., 2022):

(1) Data: Representativeness, diversity, and other characteristics influence the quality of samples. Sample distribution is an inherent property of data, and there are at least three primary methods to leverage it: representativeness, diversity, and core-set selection. These methods connect sample selection to distribution from different angles, as a metric is still required to make choices, even when the distribution is well understood.
   (a) Representativeness: Selecting samples that effectively represent the overall data distribution, ensuring that the chosen samples reflect the key characteristics of the entire dataset.
   (b) Diversity: Selecting samples that exhibit a broad range of variability within the sample space, capturing more distinctions and reducing model bias.
   (c) Core-set: Identifying a set of influential samples that can maximally summarize the information contained in other samples, thus simplifying the learning process.
(2) Model Attributes: Metrics such as gradient length and Fisher information are used to assess how much influence unlabeled data can have on the model (Chaudhuri et al., 2015; Sourati et al., 2017).
(3) Metrics: Includes adversarial metrics and uncertainty measures to guide sample selection.
   (a) Best-versus-Second Best (BvSB): Compares the probabilities of the top two predictions to identify the most uncertain samples (Joshi et al., 2009).
   (b) Multiple Peak Entropy (MPE): Measures the entropy in the model's predictions, selecting samples that reflect multiple uncertainty modes (B. Liu & Ferrari, 2017).
   (c) Query by Committee (QBC): Uses a committee of models to assess disagreement among them, selecting samples where the models exhibit the most uncertainty (Kee et al., 2018).

Cost considerations are an essential part of active learning. While annotating data is typically expensive, active learning helps mitigate these costs by minimizing the number of labeled samples required for effective learning. Some costs that may need to be considered in research and practice include:

- Decision Cost: In active learning, decision cost considers both the expense of labeling data and the potential cost of future misclassification. This requires balancing the cost of annotation with the risk of errors if the

instance is used in training. For example, researchers suggest summing labeling costs, assumed to be proportional to instance length, with expected misclassification costs (Kapoor et al., 2007). While practical, this approach requires both costs to be expressed in the same currency, which can be challenging for some applications.
- Model Training Costs: In active learning, sample selection can be computationally expensive, as each iteration typically requires re-evaluating the informativeness of every data point. This iterative process can be time-consuming.
- Expert Availability: In active learning, expert availability is a critical cost, particularly in specialized fields like medical image analysis, where labeling requires a high level of expertise (Budd et al., 2021). The limited availability of qualified experts can slow down the annotation process and increase costs.
- Annotation Time: In active learning, annotation time could be a key cost, as the time spent labeling data can significantly impact the overall efficiency of the process. The design of the user interface and the size of the labeled set also play crucial roles in managing this cost. For example, researchers used active learning for morpheme annotation in rare language documentation, employing two human oracles to reduce both annotation time and corpus size (Baldridge & Palmer, 2009). Similarly, a study highlights that the interface design can be just as important as the active learning strategy itself in reducing time and cost, with the size of the labeled set directly influencing overall expenses (Druck et al., 2009).

Benefits and Limitations

Active learning offers significant benefits, particularly in terms of cost efficiency and managing scenarios with limited data. By focusing on selecting only the most informative samples, it reduces the number of labeled instances required, leading to significant cost savings while maintaining high-quality annotations (Mosqueira-Rey et al., 2023). This is especially valuable in domains where labeled data is scarce or expensive to obtain, such as rare disease detection, clinical decision-making, or specialized medical image analysis (Budd et al., 2021). For instance, in radiology reports (Hoi et al., 2006; Nguyen & Patrick, 2014) or biological research (Luo et al., 2005), active learning enables models to achieve high accuracy with fewer labeled examples, minimizing annotation costs. Moreover, active learning is highly effective in addressing data limitations, such as class imbalance or constrained annotation budgets. In such cases, it enhances the performance of pre-trained models (PTMs) and large language models (LLMs) by optimizing sample selection in imbalanced datasets, making it a powerful tool for maximizing efficiency in resource-limited settings (Dor et al., 2020).

However, active learning is not without limitations (Donmez & Carbonell, 2008; Settles, 2011). The assumption that human oracles are infallible and always available may not hold in practice (Mosqueira-Rey et al., 2023). Human annotators can experience fatigue, and labeling quality may vary over time. Additionally, querying samples one at a time can be inefficient, leading to batch querying methods, which, while more efficient, may still not fully address the variability in labeling quality. Furthermore, the cost of obtaining new labels is often assumed to be fixed, yet in real-world scenarios, this cost can vary depending on the complexity of the data. Lastly, in situations where data distributions or model classes change, active learning systems must be adaptable enough to incorporate new knowledge and adjust accordingly.

8.2.3 Crowdsourcing

Definition and Principles

Crowdsourcing refers to an online, distributed problem-solving and production model (Brabham, 2008), where tasks are outsourced to a large group of people – often through platforms like Amazon Mechanical Turk (Paolacci et al., 2010). The term was first coined in 2006 by Jeff Howe and Mark Robinson to describe how businesses were leveraging the Internet to "outsource work to the crowd" (Howe, 2006). This approach has since become integral to machine learning, advancing key areas such as data generation, model evaluation, hybrid human–AI systems, and behavioral experiments that enhance our understanding of human interaction with AI technologies (Sheng & Zhang, 2019; Vaughan, 2018). By harnessing the complementary strengths of humans and machines, crowdsourcing enables the expansion of AI capabilities through collaborative intelligence.

Crowdsourcing operates on several key principles:

(1) Collective Intelligence: The concept of the "wisdom of crowds" suggests that large groups of people, when working together, can often solve problems or make judgments more effectively than individual experts (Kameda et al., 2022). This collective intelligence is fundamental to crowdsourcing, where the input from many contributors can lead to more accurate or creative solutions.
(2) Task Submission and Contribution: Crowdsourcing involves two main groups: requesters, who submit tasks to a crowdsourcing platform, and workers, who form the crowd that contributes to solving these tasks. The

output is the result of this collective effort, and its quality often depends on the diversity and volume of contributions.

(3) Evaluation and Rewards: Requesters may evaluate the quality of the outputs and provide rewards based on performance. In some cases, quality control is delegated to the crowdsourcing platform, where outputs are evaluated and rewarded automatically. Rewards can vary, ranging from monetary compensation to gifts, reputation badges, or other incentives (Daniel et al., 2019).

These principles ensure that crowdsourcing initiatives, regardless of their specific application, follow a structured process that leverages collective human intelligence to enhance AI systems (Lease, 2011).

Quality Control and Cost Consideration

When implementing crowdsourcing, two primary concerns are cost efficiency and quality control. The challenge lies in ensuring that data labels and prediction models derived from crowdsourced work maintain high quality, especially given the varied skills and motivations of the workers (Daniel et al., 2019; Sheng & Zhang, 2019).

From a quality model perspective, several key factors affect the final output quality (Daniel et al., 2019):

- Data: The quality of both input (e.g., images, text) and output (e.g., labeled data, translated text) is crucial. High-quality data output is vital for the broader acceptance and effectiveness of crowdsourcing systems.
- Task Design: How a task is described, structured, and managed significantly impacts worker engagement, output quality, and overall performance. Clear descriptions, user-friendly interfaces, and well-designed incentives (whether intrinsic, like status, or extrinsic, such as financial rewards) contribute to task efficiency. Additionally, terms and conditions, including privacy, intellectual property rights, and ethical standards, influence worker participation and compliance. Effective resource management is also important, ensuring that the quantity of useful work completed aligns with the resources consumed, thus sustaining productivity in crowdsourcing initiatives.
- People: Both the requesters (who submit tasks and evaluate outputs) and workers (who complete tasks) play critical roles. Characteristics such as fairness, communication, and worker motivation affect the overall success of crowdsourcing tasks. Additionally, group dynamics, such as collaborative teams or the larger crowd, influence task performance and quality.

Table 8.2 outlines various methods used to evaluate outputs in crowdsourcing from a quality assessment perspective.

Table 8.2 *Quality assessment methods in crowdsourcing*

Stages	Description
Individual Assessment	Involves individuals (workers, experts, or requesters) evaluating outputs, such as rating the accuracy of specific data or reviewing completed tasks.
Group Assessment	Uses the input of multiple people to arrive at a collective judgment, as seen in methods like voting or peer review.
Computation-based Assessment	Uses automated processes, such as comparing outputs to a predefined ground truth, to assess quality without human involvement.

To effectively manage crowdsourcing quality control, researchers should focus on several key strategies: incorporating more labeled data, integrating hybrid systems, targeting uncertain or diverse data, and conducting ongoing assessments. Additionally, using on-demand evaluations and creating more benchmarks can help minimize the need for reusing data (Lease, 2011).

Benefits and Limitations

Crowdsourcing offers several significant benefits that make it a valuable tool in human–AI collaboration:

- Lowered Costs and Improved Speed: Crowdsourcing allows for faster and more cost-effective data collection by tapping into a diverse workforce. This flexibility helps accelerate data gathering and reduces the financial burden on organizations (Vaughan, 2018).
- Improved Quality: By leveraging the collective intelligence of a diverse group of contributors, crowdsourcing can handle tasks that are difficult for computers alone. Human workers bring common sense, practical knowledge, and real-world experience to the table, leading to more nuanced and accurate outputs (Gomes et al., 2011).
- Increased Flexibility: Crowds can provide dynamic data for training machine learning algorithms. The ability to generate and aggregate potentially noisy labels has spurred research into methods for improving label accuracy, making crowdsourcing an effective tool for training AI models (Zhang et al., 2016).
- Promoting Diversity: Crowdsourcing encourages input from a broad range of contributors, leading to diverse perspectives and insights, which can enhance the quality and breadth of solutions (Vaughan, 2018).
- Data Generation and Evaluation: Crowdsourcing platforms are particularly adept at generating large datasets and evaluating machine learning models,

for example, evaluating the coherence of topic models and enhancing the interpretability of predictions in supervised learning (Chang et al., 2009; Ribeiro et al., 2016).
- Hybrid Intelligence Systems: Crowdsourcing supports hybrid intelligence systems that combine human reasoning with machine learning. These systems, drawing on human common sense, subjective beliefs, and life experiences, can outperform traditional AI in specific tasks that require flexible reasoning (Chang et al., 2009; Ribeiro et al., 2016).

Despite these advantages, crowdsourcing comes with notable limitations:

- Impact on Product Quality: The inclusion of unqualified participants can lead to a significant number of low-quality or unusable contributions (Eapen et al., 2023). To mitigate errors, employers often rely on multiple workers to complete the same task, which increases both time and costs (Ipeirotis et al., 2010).
- Motivation and Engagement: It can be difficult to maintain consistent engagement and motivation among crowd participants. Varying levels of dedication can result in inconsistent contribution quality, affecting overall outcomes.
- Cultural and Contextual Differences: Differences in cultural background and context among contributors may lead to misunderstandings or inconsistencies in contributions, posing a challenge for maintaining uniform quality.
- Information Overload: The large volume of data generated through crowdsourcing can create challenges in filtering, managing, and processing information effectively.
- Data Security and Privacy Concerns: Crowdsourcing tasks may inadvertently expose sensitive personal information, such as when workers input private data like business card details or share location information through certain tasks, raising concerns over privacy and security (Deng et al., 2013).

8.2.4 Interactive Machine Learning

Definition and Principles

Interactive Machine Learning (IML) refers to a learning paradigm where humans are actively involved in the machine learning process. Unlike classical machine learning (CML), which operates in a passive, offline manner, IML allows users – whether experts or non-experts – to interactively guide, correct, and refine models as they are being trained. This iterative process ensures that the human agent can adjust the learning process to meet specific needs, optimizing the performance and relevance of the models (Fails & Olsen, 2003; Porter et al., 2013; Ware et al., 2001).

IML systems enable humans to perform tasks that are complex for machines, such as refining classification boundaries or providing annotations in image segmentation. The human role can vary, from providing input at the beginning (e.g., initial data labeling) to intervening at the end (e.g., validating machine outputs). This interaction allows for a dynamic collaboration between humans and machines, enabling each to focus on the tasks they perform best (Porter et al., 2013; Ramos et al., 2020).

Several key principles underpin IML systems:

- Humans in the ML Loop: In IML, humans play an active role in the learning loop, performing tasks that require their expertise, such as labeling or correcting outputs. The inclusion of human agents makes IML particularly valuable in domains where uncertainty and complexity prevail, such as health informatics (Holzinger, 2016).
- Incremental and Iterative Learning: IML is characterized by an incremental and iterative learning process. Human input is continuously integrated as the model evolves, ensuring that the system adapts to real-time feedback and improves over time (Dudley & Kristensson, 2018).
- Multiple Human Roles: The individuals involved in IML can assume various roles, from machine learning experts and data scientists to crowdsource workers or domain specialists. The diversity of human roles influences both the interaction and the outcomes of the system (Ramos et al., 2020).
- User-Friendly Interfaces: The design of the user interface is critical in IML systems, as it determines how users interact with the model and influences the overall learning outcome. Well-designed interfaces can empower non-experts to effectively contribute to the model-building process (Q. Yang et al., 2018).

In IML, quality control and cost considerations go beyond traditional metrics like accuracy. IML involves subjective evaluations that account for factors such as cost, confidence, and task complexity. Unlike classical approaches, IML adopts a human-centered perspective, placing emphasis on the model's utility and effectiveness for end-users.

Quality Control and Cost Consideration

Quality control in IML integrates both algorithm-centered evaluations, which are typical in Active Learning, and human-centered assessments (Fiebrink et al., 2011). This dual approach helps to address the "black-box" nature of machine learning algorithms, offering deeper insights into the model's performance and making it more interpretable and accessible to users (Boukhelifa et al., 2018). Ultimately, this ensures that IML systems are not only accurate but also practical, efficient, and user-friendly.

The cost considerations in IML include the time and resources required for human involvement. Since humans are actively engaged in the iterative learning process – either by providing annotations or refining models – the cost of human labor becomes a significant factor. However, by focusing on tasks where human input is essential, IML can optimize resource usage while still producing high-quality outcomes that meet the needs of its users.

Benefits and Limitations

IML offers several key benefits, contributing to its robustness, trustability, and lower resource demands (Wondimu et al., 2022):

- Robustness: IML enhances the robustness of models by allowing users to understand how variations in input data affect predictions. This transparency helps in creating more resilient models that can perform reliably across different scenarios and datasets.
- Trustability: By providing clear explanations for the model's decisions, IML builds trust among users and stakeholders. When people can comprehend and verify the reasoning behind predictions, they are more likely to accept and rely on the model's outcomes.
- Low Resource Requirements: IML often requires fewer computational resources than traditional machine learning models. This makes it suitable for low-resource environments, enabling the deployment of interpretable models in diverse applications, especially where computational power is limited.

Despite its benefits, IML also presents certain limitations (Mosqueira-Rey et al., 2023):

- Increased Development Complexity: IML combines machine learning with human–computer interaction, which significantly increases the complexity of developing such systems. Each IML application needs to be carefully designed and studied, complicating the overall development process.
- Dependency on Human Expertise: While IML reduces computational demands and enhances learning efficiency, it relies heavily on human expertise. The system's effectiveness can be limited by the availability and attention of human experts, as well as the varying levels of expertise, which can introduce inconsistencies and impact performance.

8.2.5 Interconnections as High-Level Paradigms

Human-in-the-Loop (HITL) serves as the overarching framework that connects various methods of human–AI collaboration, emphasizing the essential

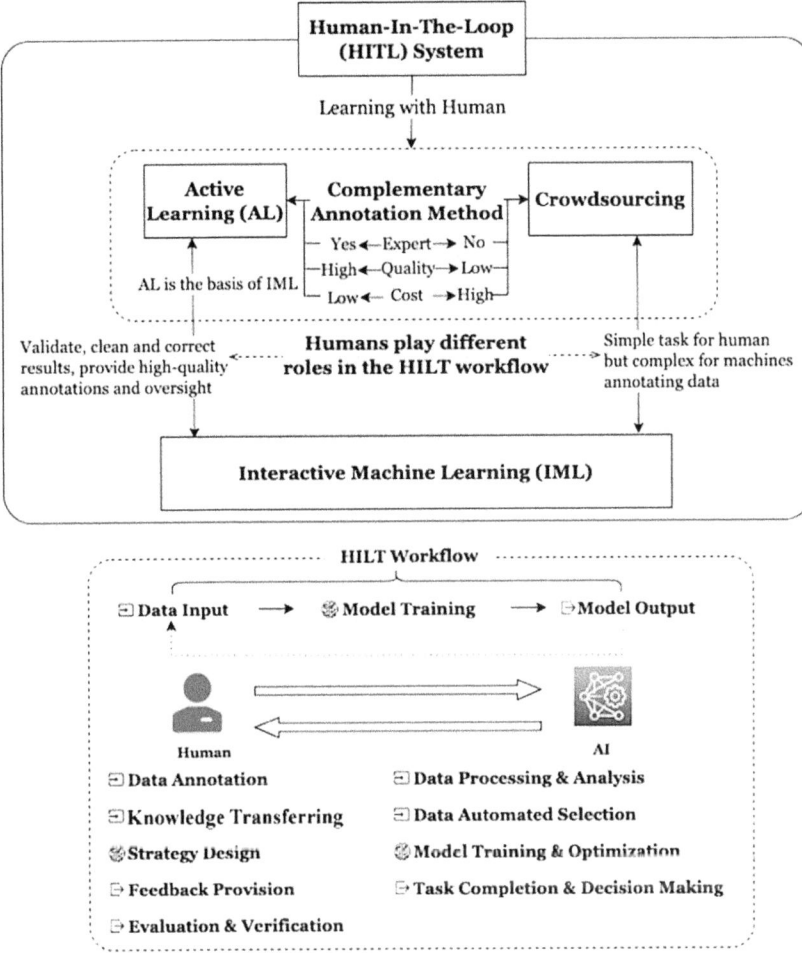

Figure 8.1 Overview of technical concepts in effective human–AI collaborative intelligence

role of human involvement in machine learning processes. HITL, along with Interactive Machine Learning (IML), Active Learning (AL), and Crowdsourcing, forms a set of high-level paradigms that offer complementary approaches to integrating human intelligence with AI systems. Each method contributes to refining the learning process by leveraging different aspects of human engagement, as illustrated in Figure 8.1.

(1) Active Learning (AL): AL focuses on the strategic selection of data points that are most valuable for annotation. By asking humans to label only the

most uncertain or informative data, AL reduces the number of required annotations, making the training process more efficient. As shown in Figure 8.1, AL is foundational to IML by enabling a more streamlined human–AI interaction, where the machine retains control while using humans as oracles for data labeling.

(2) Crowdsourcing: Crowdsourcing leverages the collective effort of nonexperts to gather labeled data at lower costs. This approach complements AL by reducing the cost of annotation while utilizing a large pool of contributors. However, as indicated in Figure 8.1, crowdsourcing often requires robust quality control due to the variable skill levels of contributors. The interplay between AL and crowdsourcing is crucial, as AL helps minimize the number of annotations, while crowdsourcing reduces the per-annotation cost, thereby substantially lowering the overall cost of creating training datasets (Mosqueira-Rey et al., 2023).

(3) Humans in the HITL Workflow: As illustrated in Figure 8.1, humans play different roles and responsibilities throughout the various stages of the machine learning process. From providing high-quality annotations to validating, cleaning, and correcting results, humans ensure that the model continually improves. These diverse roles – annotators, validators, strategists – are critical in the HITL paradigm. This dynamic feedback loop enables humans to interact in real-time, enhancing both AL and IML processes.

(4) Interactive Machine Learning (IML): IML benefits from the synergy between AL and crowdsourcing, but it differs in its approach to human interaction. In IML, humans and machines share control, with humans performing tasks beyond simple labeling, such as refining classification boundaries or providing strategic input. As Figure 8.1 shows, IML emphasizes the continuous exchange of tasks between humans and machines, with humans taking on roles in data annotation, knowledge transfer, strategy design, and model evaluation. IML systems also incorporate Human–Computer Interaction (HCI) techniques, ensuring that the user experience is optimized for nonexperts and experts alike (Mosqueira-Rey et al., 2023).

(5) Dynamic Feedback and Task Segmentation: Figure 8.1 also demonstrates how the HITL workflow facilitates real-time feedback and task segmentation between humans and AI systems. Humans handle tasks that are complex for machines, such as data annotation and model validation, while AI focuses on tasks like automated data selection, model optimization, and decision-making. This dynamic partnership between human input and machine learning drives continual model improvement and ensures a balance between efficiency and effectiveness in the learning process.

The interconnections between these paradigms are crucial for achieving a more robust, efficient, and cost-effective approach to machine learning:

- Active Learning and Crowdsourcing: Active learning minimizes annotation needs by strategically selecting samples, while crowdsourcing lowers annotation costs by distributing tasks to nonexperts. Together, they substantially reduce the costs and efforts involved in building large training datasets (Mosqueira-Rey et al., 2023).
- Active Learning and Interactive Machine Learning: Active learning serves as the foundation for interactive machine learning, but the difference lies in how control is distributed. In active learning, the model controls the learning process and uses the human as an oracle for specific tasks, while interactive machine learning involves a closer, interactive relationship between the human and the learning system, with control shared between them. Additionally, interactive machine learning incorporates HCI techniques, enhancing user interaction in more flexible and less structured environments (Mosqueira-Rey et al., 2023).

In summary, these paradigms – human-in-the-loop, active learning, interactive machine learning, and crowdsourcing – form a cohesive framework for integrating human and AI intelligence. Human-in-the-loop serves as the foundation, with active learning, interactive machine learning, and crowdsourcing contributing complementary techniques for improving learning outcomes, enhancing model robustness, and reducing costs. The continuous interaction between humans and machines ensures that these systems remain adaptive, effective, and responsive to real-world challenges.

8.3 Practical Applications and Case Studies

8.3.1 Practical Applications across Various Domains

Human–AI collaboration has shown transformative potential in numerous fields by combining advanced AI capabilities with human expertise. These efforts have significantly enhanced efficiency, accuracy, and decision-making across various domains.

Healthcare

In the healthcare domain, human–AI collaborative intelligence has become a pivotal force in advancing medical practices, improving patient outcomes, and enhancing overall system efficiency. A prominent example is medical imaging, which plays a critical role in clinical decision-making across multiple areas, including detection, diagnosis, and treatment planning (Tajbakhsh et al., 2020). While traditional methods for analyzing medical images, such as manual segmentation, are often time-consuming and labor-intensive, human–AI collaboration offers new avenues for improvement. One such approach is interactive segmentation, where clinicians can refine AI-generated initial segmentations. For instance, researchers introduced a dual-CNN-based framework that allows user interaction to correct model inaccuracies, significantly reducing the time needed for precise image segmentation in applications like brain tumor and fetal MRI imaging (G. Wang et al., 2019).

Active learning is another crucial application. In cancer pathology, where extracting key details from reports can be tedious, AI systems can assist by flagging challenging cases for human annotators, thereby reducing the manual workload (De Angeli et al., 2021). This hybrid method has shown impressive results, achieving similar performance to traditional methods while requiring fewer labeled data. Furthermore, in heart disease prediction, models that solicit expert feedback for the most relevant data points can reduce costs and enhance accuracy (El-Hasnony et al., 2022). Human experts also play an essential role in preprocessing medical data, ensuring that the AI system receives high-quality inputs. Such collaboration leads to improved outcomes, as seen in the classification of oral cancer tissues (Folmsbee et al., 2018) and radiology reports (Nguyen & Patrick, 2014).

Maintaining effective human–AI collaboration remains essential in healthcare, where the accuracy and reliability of AI systems must meet the stringent requirements of patient safety (Budd et al., 2021).

Finance

Human–AI collaboration is increasingly transforming the financial domain, combining AI's computational power with human expertise to enhance efficiency, accuracy, and decision-making. In the lending domain, artificial intelligence is being employed to streamline loan processing and ensure responsible lending decisions. However, machines alone are not sufficient for decision-making. For instance, a human–AI collaborative method was introduced to evaluate multiple independent and conflicting pieces of evidence in loan applications (Sachan et al., 2024). By comparing expert underwriters' judgments with AI-generated results, the system learns human decision tendencies, optimizing decision quality through continuous human–AI interaction. In international maritime trade, algorithms automatically gather data to generate transaction tables, but human data scientists play a crucial role in reviewing and refining these outputs. Their feedback enhances algorithm performance and adaptability over time (Gronsund & Aanestad, 2020). Moreover, active learning approaches in stock market sentiment analysis allow machines to query human experts for labels, significantly improving the model's predictive performance (Smailovic et al., 2014). This iterative process ensures that the AI continues to improve through expert guidance.

In summary, human–AI collaboration is essential for addressing complex financial challenges. This evolving synergy will continue to drive innovation and ensure fairness in financial services.

Agriculture

Human–AI collaboration has made significant advancements in the agricultural sector by improving efficiency in tasks such as crop monitoring and pest detection. For instance, in crop yield analysis, AI can detect and analyze cereal crops like wheat and sorghum, focusing on panicle density, a critical factor in evaluating yield. Researchers have introduced an automated system that combines weak and strong labeling methods to reduce annotation time and improve accuracy (Chandra et al., 2020). This approach allows human annotators to collaborate with AI in a more efficient workflow, producing high-quality data with less manual effort. Similarly, distinguishing crops from weeds is another complex task where human expertise complements AI. Scientists have developed a model to identify samples requiring labeling, which are then manually annotated by experts. This method minimizes human workload while maintaining high classification accuracy (Sheikh et al., 2020). In pest classification, research has demonstrated that cleaning redundant public datasets can reduce data size while achieving similar classification results, showcasing the power of human-guided data optimization (J. Yang et al., 2022).

In essence, human–AI collaboration significantly advances agricultural practices by improving efficiency and accuracy, minimizing manual workload and leading to more effective and precise agricultural solutions.

Education

Human–AI collaboration has transformed personalized learning and education. Researchers have developed a system in which AI classifies student profiles, enabling human experts to customize learning experiences. This synergy between AI's data processing capabilities and human expertise facilitates personalized feedback and content adjustments, leading to improved learning outcomes (De Melo et al., 2014). In the realm of scientific reading, human–AI collaboration is critical for helping students comprehend complex documents. Researchers have proposed a collaborative PDF reader powered by Open Educational Resources (OERs), which uses machine learning to analyze reader behaviors, such as highlighting and questioning, and recommends relevant OERs like videos and slides. Readers provide feedback, allowing the system to refine its recommendations based on user interactions (Jiang et al., 2016; X. Liu et al., 2015). For complex mathematical content, the system suggests a Formula Evolution Map that tracks formula development and recommends related OERs (Jiang et al., 2018). Human feedback is crucial, refining the system's recommendations to ensure greater accuracy and contextual relevance. This collaboration between humans and AI improves understanding of complex concepts, making STEM (Science, Technology, Engineering, and Mathematics) reading more efficient and personalized.

Overall, human–AI collaboration in education leverages AI's strength in data processing and the human ability to provide customized learning experiences. This partnership enhances personalized feedback, improves comprehension of scientific materials, and facilitates understanding of complex concepts through adaptive content recommendations and user interaction.

Misinformation Control and Cybersecurity

Human–AI collaboration has been applied in tackling misinformation and enhancing cybersecurity. For instance, researchers have used semi-supervised and active learning to detect camouflaged Chinese spam content, integrating human annotations with AI insights. This collaboration improves the accuracy of spam detection, making it more adaptable to evolving text camouflage and data imbalance challenges (Jiang et al., 2020). Similarly, a security system has been developed by integrating AI with crowdsourced human feedback to combat online misinformation (Demartini et al., 2020), while a human-centric vulnerability analysis system was created for cybersecurity (Shoshitaishvili et al., 2017).

These examples show how human–AI collaboration addresses complex challenges in information security, improving both the accuracy of threat detection and decision-making processes.

Law

The legal domain has embraced human–AI collaboration for tasks such as case classification and legal consultation. For instance, researchers have proposed a system where human analysts refine AI decision-making processes by adding new factors and adjusting the algorithm, ensuring flexible and informed legal decisions (Odekerken & Bex, 2020). Similarly, another legal model employs Positive-Unlabeled Reinforcement Learning (PURL) to dynamically generate diagnostic legal questions. By integrating AI insights with human expertise, this model provides accurate, context-sensitive legal advice (Y. Wu et al., 2024).

Generally, human–AI collaboration in the legal domain enables more flexible, informed, and context-sensitive decision-making by integrating AI's analytical capabilities with human expertise, optimizing multiple legal processes.

Expanding Human–AI Collaboration in Other Domains
Human–AI collaboration also extends into other domains. For example, a human–machine interactive image search method was introduced by Kovashka et al. (2015), while human-in-the-loop semi-supervised learning has been applied for random gene regulation (Wrede & Hellander, 2019). These efforts demonstrate the adaptability and scalability of human–AI collaboration across diverse industries, ensuring continuous innovation and improvement in performance.

As AI systems evolve, human oversight remains crucial for ensuring transparency, fairness, and efficiency. The integration of human expertise and AI drives innovation, improves decision-making, and enhances accuracy across various applications. These systems foster natural, efficient human–machine interactions, accelerating digital transformation and delivering smarter solutions across diverse industries.

8.3.2 Representative Case Studies

Case 1: Education Domain: Scaffolding with Open Educational Resources (OER)

An exemplary case of effective human–AI collaborative intelligence in the education field is demonstrated through the development of the OER-based Collaborative PDF Reader (OCPR). This system showcases how AI and human intelligence can work together to enhance the comprehension of complex scientific literature for students and junior scholars (Jiang et al., 2016, 2018; X. Liu et al., 2015).

A typical interface of the OCPR system is shown in Figure 8.2. The system integrates advanced text mining and heterogeneous graph mining algorithms to recommend relevant Open Educational Resources (OERs), such as videos, slides, source code, and Wikipedia pages, based on students' interactions with scientific publications. By leveraging human actions, such as highlighting and asking questions, and, most importantly, feedback on the recommended content, the system dynamically adjusts its recommendations, enabling students to better grasp complex concepts.

This human–AI collaboration enables the AI to respond to the emerging information needs of students, while allowing human oversight and

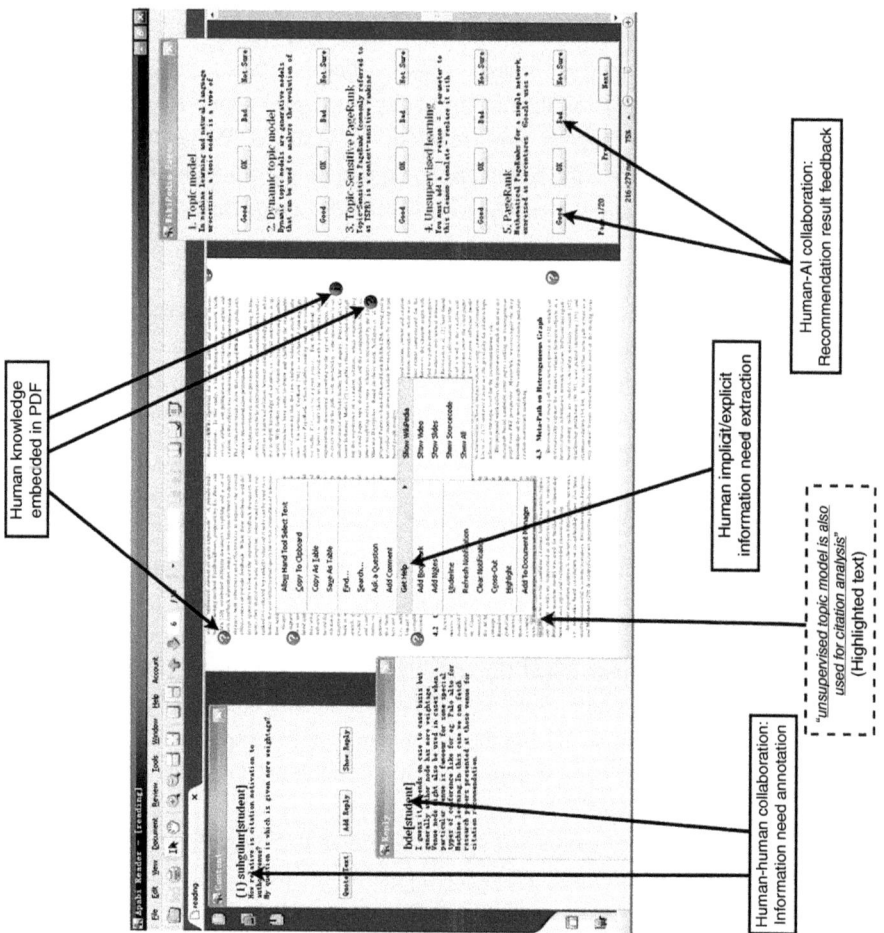

Figure 8.2 OER-based collaborative PDF reader system

intervention to refine the system's suggestions. The integration of human judgment with AI-driven recommendations creates a learning environment where complex materials are made more accessible, promoting deeper engagement and understanding.

This case highlights the power of human–AI collaboration in educational settings, where the ability of AI to scaffold learning is enhanced by human input, illustrating the future of personalized, intelligent education.

Case 2: Legal Domain: Knowledge-infused Legal Wisdom

One notable example of effective human–AI collaborative intelligence in the legal field is the development of the D3LM (Diagnostic Legal Large Language Model) framework (Y. Wu et al., 2024). This system illustrates how combining human oversight and AI can transform legal case analysis. As shown in Figure 8.3, the core innovation of D3LM lies in its ability to generate

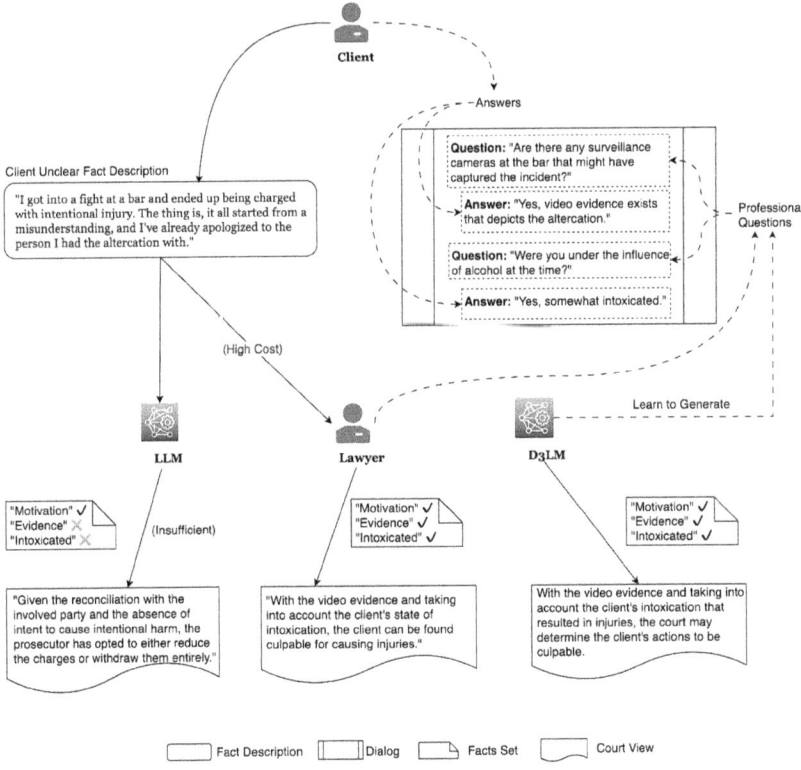

Figure 8.3 Comparison of legal service methodologies, focusing on traditional LLMs, lawyer consultations, and the D3LM model

lawyer-like diagnostic questions that guide users in formulating their legal queries more accurately. By incorporating human knowledge through targeted questioning, D3LM extracts crucial case details, which significantly improves the AI's understanding and predictive capabilities.

Unlike traditional LLMs that passively respond to user inputs, D3LM actively engages with users to gather missing or overlooked information. It utilizes the Positive-Unlabeled Reinforcement Learning (PURL) algorithm to dynamically adapt its questioning strategy, making it an example of Human-in-the-Loop systems where humans enhance AI's performance through ongoing interaction. This collaboration results in more accurate legal predictions, enriched by human guidance.

This case highlights how human–AI collaboration can empower individuals without legal expertise to receive professional-quality assistance at a fraction of the cost. Moreover, it demonstrates the potential of integrating human knowledge with advanced AI technologies to bridge gaps in domains where precise and detailed understanding is essential.

8.4 Future Directions

8.4.1 Continuous Learning from Human Experts

Model Robustness and Efficiency

The continuous integration of human expertise into AI models offers a promising pathway to enhancing their robustness and efficiency but it also presents significant challenges. As AI systems undergo iterative training cycles driven by human feedback, issues such as catastrophic forgetting may arise, where models struggle to retain previously learned information when exposed to new data. Addressing this requires strategies like active learning, which ensures models selectively query the most informative data, thereby optimizing learning while maintaining robustness (Bartolo et al., 2020; Budd et al., 2021). Incorporating human rationales into these models can further bolster both performance and stability, reducing the chances of losing acquired knowledge over time (Arous et al., 2021).

Another significant challenge in continuous learning from human experts is the efficiency of data annotation, particularly for complex tasks. Manual annotation is labor-intensive and time-consuming. While innovations like self-annotation frameworks and deep reinforcement active learning have shown potential to streamline the process (Le et al., 2020; Z. Liu et al., 2019), further advancements are needed to minimize the dependency on large-scale labeled data. For instance, some frameworks improve model robustness by integrating active learning with adversarial examples, which significantly reduces the need for annotations while boosting performance (Guo et al., 2021).

Balancing Expertise and Ensuring Feedback Quality
Balancing expertise and feedback quality is another critical factor. While nonexperts can contribute valuable insights in some cases, tasks requiring specialized knowledge demand domain experts for accuracy (Fan et al., 2019). Establishing clear guidelines for differentiating tasks suitable for nonexperts from those requiring expert input is essential for improving feedback quality. Additionally, variability in annotator expertise can lead to uneven feedback, which may negatively impact model performance (Jwo et al., 2021; Z. Liu et al., 2021). Thus, developing improved methods for evaluating and filtering human feedback is essential, particularly in complex, high-stakes domains where consistent and reliable input is critical (He et al., 2016). For instance, techniques that employ adversarial learning and knowledge graphs have proven effective in tackling these challenges by improving feedback quality and maximizing the utility of human input, even in highly imbalanced datasets (Jiang et al., 2020).

Real-World Applications and Generalization
Finally, ensuring that AI systems can generalize effectively across real-world scenarios requires robustness to domain shifts and the handling of out-of-distribution samples. Real-world environments often introduce complexities such as inconsistent data quality and ambiguous tasks (Kreutzer et al., 2021; Ziegler et al., 2020). Research has already begun addressing these challenges, for instance, by using inconsistency-based sample selection to guide human experts in annotating the most uncertain and inconsistent samples, thereby improving model accuracy and reducing labeling costs (Guo et al., 2022). Future research should focus on developing domain-agnostic models that adapt flexibly to diverse scenarios without extensive retraining (Xu et al., 2023; Ziegler et al., 2020), enhancing the scalability and applicability of human–AI collaborative systems across various domains.

8.4.2 Advancements in Human–AI Interfaces

Advancements in human–AI interfaces are essential for improving collaborative systems that rely on seamless interaction between humans and AI. A critical aspect of this improvement lies in creating more intuitive and user-friendly interfaces, which facilitate better communication between users and AI models. Human-centered design approaches can significantly enhance the quality of feedback from users, leading to improved model performance. For instance, visualizations that clarify what the model has learned play a pivotal role in improving interpretability. This allows non-experts to contribute effectively to model refinement by making the AI's decision-making process more transparent (Lee et al., 2017; Z. J. Wang et al., 2021).

Future developments in this area should focus on building interfaces that not only collect feedback but also guide users in providing targeted and actionable input. Systems that assist users in offering more precise input can significantly enhance the learning process. Furthermore, interfaces that allow users to track the evolution of AI models over time help increase transparency, fostering greater trust and long-term collaboration between humans and AI (Smith et al., 2018; Wallace et al., 2019). Human-centered designs in crowdsourcing annotation systems have been shown to enhance the quality of feedback and improve active learning model performance, highlighting the importance of intuitive interface design in optimizing human–AI collaboration (Dong et al., 2023).

Another area of focus is the growing demand for interactive tools that enable users to dynamically explore data and influence AI outputs in real-time (Patil et al., 2022). These tools allow for immediate, informed adjustments, aligning human feedback more closely with AI decision-making, particularly in complex scenarios (Shraga, 2022). In high-demand environments, interactive data cleaning tools play a crucial role in optimizing real-time human–AI interactions, further improving the system's overall effectiveness (Räth et al., 2023).

8.4.3 Integration with Large Language Models

The integration of Large Language Models (LLMs) into human–AI collaborative systems is becoming increasingly prevalent, significantly enhancing both the efficiency and accuracy of AI-driven tasks. Recent active learning frameworks, which combine human annotations with LLM-driven text classification, have demonstrated the effectiveness of techniques like uncertainty sampling in prioritizing and annotating the most informative data points. These approaches help reduce the annotation workload while maintaining or even improving model accuracy, offering a promising method for optimizing machine learning workflows (Rouzegar & Makrehchi, 2024). For instance, a recent study exemplifies how LLMs can be dynamically integrated with active learning to iteratively improve model performance, especially in few-shot learning scenarios, while reducing computational costs (C. Liu et al., 2024).

However, LLMs are not without limitations. Their inherent biases and lack of human-like decision-making capabilities pose significant challenges, especially in high-stakes or sensitive applications. In such environments, eliminating human oversight entirely is neither feasible nor advisable. Human involvement remains essential in safety-critical systems to ensure that AI-driven decisions are safe, reliable, and ethically sound (Xiao et al., 2023).

The future of LLM integration in human–AI collaborative systems will involve finding the right balance between automation and human intervention. While LLMs can complement human expertise in many tasks, they cannot fully replace human judgment in complex or ethically sensitive areas. Ongoing research is focused on developing more interactive and adaptable systems that can manage real-world complexities while ensuring that human oversight remains central to critical decision-making processes.

8.4.4 Ethical Implications and Societal Impact of Human–AI Collaboration

As human–AI collaboration continues to evolve, addressing the ethical concerns associated with these advancements is crucial. A significant risk is that AI systems trained on human feedback could be misused, potentially manipulated to influence beliefs, spread radical ideologies, or facilitate fraudulent activities (Stiennon et al., 2020). In particular, distinguishing between LLM-generated and human-written content has become increasingly difficult, raising concerns about trustworthiness in human–AI collaboration. While domain-specific content, such as scientific writing, may exhibit subtle differences, LLMs are still capable of propagating biased or ideologically influenced content, posing substantial risks to society (Ma et al., 2023; X. Zhou et al., 2023). These risks highlight the importance of developing trustworthy AI systems that embed ethical principles, ensuring transparency, fairness, and accountability, and include safeguards against malicious use, thus preventing unintended harm.

Another critical challenge lies in the vulnerability of machine learning algorithms to adversarial attacks, where malicious actors can compromise training data, threatening the integrity and security of AI models (Rožanec et al., 2024). Detecting and preventing such attacks will be essential in maintaining the reliability of AI-driven systems, ensuring they remain secure and beneficial. The next stage of AI development must therefore balance technological progress with strong ethical considerations, guaranteeing that AI systems operate in a way that is transparent, fair, and aligned with human values (Mosqueira-Rey et al., 2023).

As human–AI collaborative systems are increasingly integrated into various industries, their societal impact must be closely monitored. Research should focus on ensuring the equitable distribution of AI technologies and their application for the greater good, continuously addressing the evolving ethical challenges that emerge from their widespread use.

8.5 Conclusion

In this chapter, we first addressed the critical role of high-quality data in AI development and the challenges of data acquisition, management, and fairness. Machine learning systems depend heavily on accurate, diverse, and timely data, but ensuring this remains a key hurdle. Human errors and biases, alongside ethical concerns like privacy, further complicate this process. To tackle these issues, human expertise plays a crucial role in stages such as data extraction, cleaning, annotation, and model training. By leveraging strategies like active learning and weak supervision, human-AI collaboration enhances system performance, fairness, and scalability.

In Section 8.2, we explored the technical foundations of human–AI collaboration, focusing on Human-in-the-Loop (HITL) systems, active learning, crowdsourcing, and interactive machine learning. HITL systems enhance model accuracy and decision-making by integrating human expertise, but face challenges in embedding input effectively and ensuring robust evaluation. Active learning reduces labeling workload by selecting the most informative data points, balancing efficiency with annotation quality and cost concerns. Crowdsourcing accelerates data generation with collective intelligence, requiring strong quality control to handle varied contributor skill levels. Interactive machine learning fosters real-time human–AI collaboration, improving adaptability but increasing complexity and reliance on human expertise. These paradigms together optimize human–AI collaboration, balancing human oversight with machine automation for better outcomes.

In Section 8.3, we explored the practical applications and case studies of human–AI collaboration across various domains. In healthcare, AI aids in medical imaging and pathology, while human expertise ensures precision and reliability, improving efficiency in areas like cancer detection and heart disease prediction. In finance, AI supports decision-making in lending and stock analysis, with human oversight refining outcomes to enhance quality and fairness. In agriculture, AI assists in crop monitoring and pest detection, with human feedback improving accuracy and reducing manual effort. In education, AI personalizes learning experiences and human input guides content recommendations for better learning outcomes. In misinformation control and cybersecurity, AI models, combined with human feedback, improve threat detection and response. In law, AI supports legal consultation, with human oversight refining diagnostic processes for more accurate decisions. In the case of the OER-based Collaborative PDF Reader, human feedback refines AI content recommendations, while, in the case of the D3LM Legal Model, human oversight enhances AI's legal question generation. These examples illustrate the transformative power of human–AI collaboration across diverse fields, optimizing efficiency, decision-making, and accuracy.

In Section 8.4, we explored the future directions of human–AI collaborative intelligence, focusing on several key areas. Continuous learning from human experts emphasizes improving model robustness and efficiency through human feedback, while addressing challenges like catastrophic forgetting and optimizing annotation processes. Advancements in human–AI interfaces will prioritize transparency, intuitive design, and dynamic feedback to foster trust and improve collaboration. The integration of LLMs highlights their growing role in enhancing tasks like text classification, but maintaining human oversight is essential for ensuring safety and ethical AI use. Finally, the ethical implications and societal impact of human–AI collaboration require attention to issues such as bias, adversarial attacks, and manipulation, with a focus on developing transparent, fair, and secure AI systems that benefit the whole society.

References

Aldoseri, A., Al-Khalifa, K. N., & Hamouda, A. M. (2023). Re-thinking Data Strategy and Integration for Artificial Intelligence: Concepts, Opportunities, and Challenges. *Applied Sciences*, *13*(12), 7082.

Arous, I., Dolamic, L., Yang, J., Bhardwaj, A., Cuccu, G., & Cudré-Mauroux, P. (2021). Marta: Leveraging Human Rationales for Explainable Text Classification. *Proceedings of the AAAI Conference on Artificial Intelligence*, *35*(7), 5868–5876.

Baldridge, J., & Palmer, A. (2009). How Well Does Active Learning Actually Work? Time-based Evaluation of Cost-reduction Strategies for Language Documentation. *Proceedings of the 2009 Conference on Empirical Methods in Natural Language Processing*, 296–305.

Bartolo, M., Roberts, A., Welbl, J., Riedel, S., & Stenetorp, P. (2020). Beat the AI: Investigating Adversarial Human Annotation for Reading Comprehension. *Transactions of the Association for Computational Linguistics*, *8*, 662–678.

Boukhelifa, N., Bezerianos, A., & Lutton, E. (2018). Evaluation of Interactive Machine Learning Systems. In J. Zhou & F. Chen (eds.), *Human and Machine Learning* (pp. 341–360). Springer International Publishing.

Brabham, D. C. (2008). Crowdsourcing as a Model for Problem Solving: An Introduction and Cases. *Convergence: The International Journal of Research into New Media Technologies*, *14*(1), 75–90.

Budd, S., Robinson, E. C., & Kainz, B. (2021). A Survey on Active Learning and Human-in-the-Loop Deep Learning for Medical Image Analysis. *Medical Image Analysis*, *71*, 102062.

Burr, S. (2009). *Active Learning Literature Survey*. University of Wisconsin-Madison Department of Computer Sciences.

Casalini, F., González, J. L., & Nemoto, T. (2021). Mapping Commonalities in Regulatory Approaches to Cross-border Data Transfers. *OECD Trade Policy Papers.*

Chai, C., & Li, G. (2020). Human-in-the-Loop Techniques in Machine Learning. *IEEE Data Engineering Bulletin, 43*(3), 37–52.

Chandra, A. L., Desai, S. V., Balasubramanian, V. N., Ninomiya, S., & Guo, W. (2020). Active Learning with Point Supervision for Cost-effective Panicle Detection in Cereal Crops. *Plant Methods, 16*(1), 34. https://doi.org/10.1186/s13007-020-00575-8

Chang, J., Gerrish, S., Wang, C., Boyd-Graber, J., & Blei, D. (2009). Reading Tea Leaves: How Humans Interpret Topic Models. *Advances in Neural Information Processing Systems, 22*, 288–296.

Chaudhuri, K., Kakade, S. M., Netrapalli, P., & Sanghavi, S. (2015). Convergence Rates of Active Learning for Maximum Likelihood Estimation. *Advances in Neural Information Processing Systems, 28*, 1090–1098.

Daniel, F., Kucherbaev, P., Cappiello, C., Benatallah, B., & Allahbakhsh, M. (2019). Quality Control in Crowdsourcing: A Survey of Quality Attributes, Assessment Techniques, and Assurance Actions. *ACM Computing Surveys, 51*(1), 1–40.

De Angeli, K., Gao, S., Alawad, M., Yoon, H.-J., Schaefferkoetter, N., Wu, X.-C., Durbin, E. B., Doherty, J., Stroup, A., Coyle, L., Penberthy, L., & Tourassi, G. (2021). Deep Active Learning for Classifying Cancer Pathology Reports. *BMC Bioinformatics, 22*(1), 113. https://doi.org/10.1186/s12859-021-04047-1

De Melo, F. R., Flôres, E. L., De Carvalho, S. D., De Teixeira, R. A. G., Loja, L. F. B., & de Sousa Gomide, R. (2014). Computational Organization of Didactic Contents for Personalized Virtual Learning Environments. *Computers & Education, 79*, 126–137.

Demartini, G., Mizzaro, S., & Spina, D. (2020). Human-in-the-Loop Artificial Intelligence for Fighting Online Misinformation: Challenges and Opportunities. *IEEE Data Engineering Bulletin, 43*(3), 65–74.

Deng, D., Shahabi, C., & Demiryurek, U. (2013). Maximizing the Number of Worker's Self-selected Tasks in Spatial Crowdsourcing. *Proceedings of the 21st ACM SIGSPATIAL International Conference on Advances in Geographic Information Systems*, 324–333.

Diligenti, M., Roychowdhury, S., & Gori, M. (2017). Integrating Prior Knowledge into Deep Learning. *2017 16th IEEE International Conference on Machine Learning and Applications (ICMLA)*, 920–923.

Dimensional Research. (2019). What Data Scientists Tell Us About AI Model Training Today. *Alegion.* https://cdn2.hubspot.net/hubfs/3971219/Content%20Offers/Drafts/Alegion_SurveyNarrative.pdf

Dong, J., Kang, Y., Liu, J., Sun, C., Fan, S., Jin, H., Wu, D., Jiang, Z., Niu, X., & Liu, X. (2023). Human-centred Design on Crowdsourcing Annotation towards Improving Active Learning Model Performance. *Journal of Information Science*, doi: 10.1177/01655515231204802

Donmez, P., & Carbonell, J. G. (2008). Proactive Learning: Cost-sensitive Active Learning with Multiple Imperfect Oracles. *Proceedings of the 17th ACM Conference on Information and Knowledge Management*, 619–628.

Dor, L. E., Halfon, A., Gera, A., Shnarch, E., Dankin, L., Choshen, L., Danilevsky, M., Aharonov, R., Katz, Y., & Slonim, N. (2020). Active Learning for BERT: An Empirical Study. *Proceedings of the 2020 Conference on Empirical Methods in Natural Language Processing (EMNLP)*, 7949–7962.

Druck, G., Settles, B., & McCallum, A. (2009). Active Learning by Labeling Features. *Proceedings of the 2009 Conference on Empirical Methods in Natural Language Processing*, 81–90.

Dudley, J. J., & Kristensson, P. O. (2018). A Review of User Interface Design for Interactive Machine Learning. *ACM Transactions on Interactive Intelligent Systems*, 8(2), 1–37.

Eapen, T., Finkenstadt, D. J., Folk, J., & Venkataswamy, L. (2023). How Generative AI Can Augment Human Creativity. *Harvard Business Review*, 101(4), 56–64.

El-Hasnony, I. M., Elzeki, O. M., Alshehri, A., & Salem, H. (2022). Multi-Label Active Learning-Based Machine Learning Model for Heart Disease Prediction. *SENSORS*, 22(3), 1184. https://doi.org/10.3390/s22031184

Fails, J. A., & Olsen, D. R. (2003). Interactive Machine Learning. *Proceedings of the 8th International Conference on Intelligent User Interfaces*, 39–45.

Fan, X., Li, C., Yuan, X., Dong, X., & Liang, J. (2019). An Interactive Visual Analytics Approach for Network Anomaly Detection through Smart Labeling. *Journal of Visualization*, 22(5), 955–971.

Fiebrink, R., Cook, P. R., & Trueman, D. (2011). Human Model Evaluation in Interactive Supervised Learning. *Proceedings of the SIGCHI Conference on Human Factors in Computing Systems*, 147–156.

Folmsbee, J., Liu, X., Brandwein-Weber, M., & Doyle, S. (2018). Active Deep Learning: Improved Training Efficiency of Convolutional Neural Networks for Tissue Classification in Oral Cavity Cancer. *2018 IEEE 15th International Symposium on Biomedical Imaging (ISBI 2018)*, 770–773. https://webofscience.clarivate.cn/wos/alldb/summary/8b3794b9-2bc2-4ba9-bb93–84b37012273a-0108175925/relevance/1

Forrester Consulting. (2020). *Overcome Obstacles to Get to AI at Scale*. IBM. www.ibm.com/downloads/cas/VBMPEQLN

Fredrikson, M., Jha, S., & Ristenpart, T. (2015). Model Inversion Attacks that Exploit Confidence Information and Basic Countermeasures. *Proceedings of the 22nd ACM SIGSAC Conference on Computer and Communications Security*, 1322–1333.

Gomes, R., Welinder, P., Krause, A., & Perona, P. (2011). Crowdclustering. *Advances in Neural Information Processing Systems 24 (NIPS 2011)*.

Gronsund, T., & Aanestad, M. (2020). Augmenting the Algorithm: Emerging Human-in-the-Loop Work Configurations. *Journal of Strategic Information Systems*, 29(2), 101614. https://doi.org/10.1016/j.jsis.2020.101614

Gualo, F., Rodríguez, M., Verdugo, J., Caballero, I., & Piattini, M. (2021). Data Quality Certification using ISO/IEC 25012: Industrial Experiences. *Journal of Systems and Software*, 176, 110938.

Guo, J., Kang, Y., Duan, Y., Liu, X., Tang, S., Zhang, W., Kuang, K., Sun, C., & Wu, F. (2022). Collaborative Intelligence Orchestration: Inconsistency-Based Fusion of Semi-Supervised Learning and Active Learning. *Proceedings of the 28th ACM SIGKDD Conference on Knowledge Discovery and Data Mining*, 2935–2945.

Guo, J., Shi, H., Kang, Y., Kuang, K., Tang, S., Jiang, Z., Sun, C., Wu, F., & Zhuang, Y. (2021). Semi-supervised Active Learning for Semi-supervised Models: Exploit Adversarial Examples with Graph-based Virtual Labels. *Proceedings of the IEEE/CVF International Conference on Computer Vision*, 2896–2905.

He, L., Michael, J., Lewis, M., & Zettlemoyer, L. (2016). Human-in-the-Loop Parsing. *Proceedings of the 2016 Conference on Empirical Methods in Natural Language Processing*, 2337–2342.

Hoi, S. C. H., Jin, R., Zhu, J., & Lyu, M. R. (2006). Batch Mode Active Learning and Its Application to Medical Image Classification. *Proceedings of the 23rd International Conference on Machine Learning: ICML'06*, 417–424.

Holzinger, A. (2016). Interactive Machine Learning for Health Informatics: When Do We Need the Human-in-the-Loop? *Brain Informatics*, 3(2), 119–131.

Howe, J. (2006). The Rise of Crowdsourcing. *Wired Magazine*, 14(6), 176–183.

Hu, H., Salcic, Z., Sun, L., Dobbie, G., Yu, P. S., & Zhang, X. (2022). Membership Inference Attacks on Machine Learning: A Survey. *ACM Computing Surveys*, 54(11s), 1–37.

Ipeirotis, P. G., Provost, F., & Wang, J. (2010). Quality Management on Amazon Mechanical Turk. *Proceedings of the ACM SIGKDD Workshop on Human Computation*, 64–67.

Jiang, Z., Gao, L., Yuan, K., Gao, Z., Tang, Z., & Liu, X. (2018). Mathematics Content Understanding for Cyberlearning via Formula Evolution Map. *Proceedings of the 27th ACM International Conference on Information and Knowledge Management*, 37–46. https://doi.org/10.1145/3269206.3271694

Jiang, Z., Gao, Z., Duan, Y., Kang, Y., Sun, C., Zhang, Q., & Liu, X. (2020). Camouflaged Chinese Spam Content Detection with Semi-supervised Generative Active Learning. *Proceedings of the 58th Annual Meeting of the Association for Computational Linguistics*, 3080 3085.

Jiang, Z., Liu, X., Gao, L., & Tang, Z. (2016). Community-based Cyberreading for Information Understanding. *Proceedings of the 39th International ACM SIGIR Conference on Research and Development in Information Retrieval*, 789–792. https://dl.acm.org/doi/abs/10.1145/2911451.2914744

Joshi, A. J., Porikli, F., & Papanikolopoulos, N. (2009). Multi-class Active Learning for Image Classification. *2009 IEEE Conference on Computer Vision and Pattern Recognition*, 2372–2379.

Jwo, J.-S., Lin, C.-S., & Lee, C.-H. (2021). Smart Technology-driven Aspects for Human-in-the-Loop Smart Manufacturing. *The International Journal of Advanced Manufacturing Technology*, 114(5–6), 1741–1752.

Kameda, T., Toyokawa, W., & Tindale, R. S. (2022). Information Aggregation and Collective Intelligence beyond the Wisdom of Crowds. *Nature Reviews Psychology*, 1(6), 345–357.

Kapoor, A., Horvitz, E., & Basu, S. (2007). Selective Supervision: Guiding Supervised Learning with Decision-theoretic Active Learning. *IJCAI'07 Proceedings of the 20th International Joint Conference on Artificial Intelligence*, 877–882.

Kee, S., Del Castillo, E., & Runger, G. (2018). Query-by-Committee Improvement with Diversity and Density in Batch Active Learning. *Information Sciences*, 454, 401–418.

Kovashka, A., Parikh, D., & Grauman, K. (2015). WhittleSearch: Interactive Image Search with Relative Attribute Feedback. *International Journal of Computer Vision*, 115(2), 185–210. https://doi.org/10.1007/s11263-015-0814-0

Kreutzer, J., Riezler, S., & Lawrence, C. (2021). Offline Reinforcement Learning from Human Feedback in Real-World Sequence-to-Sequence Tasks. *Proceedings of the 5th Workshop on Structured Prediction for NLP (SPNLP 2021)*, 37–43.

Le, T.-N., Sugimoto, A., Ono, S., & Kawasaki, H. (2020). Toward Interactive Self-annotation for Video Object Bounding Box: Recurrent Self-learning and Hierarchical Annotation based Framework. *Proceedings of the IEEE/CVF Winter Conference on Applications of Computer Vision*, 3231–3240.

Lease, M. (2011). On Quality Control and Machine Learning in Crowdsourcing. *Workshops at the Twenty-Fifth AAAI Conference on Artificial Intelligence*.

Lee, T. Y., Smith, A., Seppi, K., Elmqvist, N., Boyd-Graber, J., & Findlater, L. (2017). The Human Touch: How Non-expert Users Perceive, Interpret, and Fix Topic Models. *International Journal of Human–Computer Studies*, *105*, 28–42.

Liang, W., Tadesse, G. A., Ho, D., Fei-Fei, L., Zaharia, M., Zhang, C., & Zou, J. (2022). Advances, Challenges and Opportunities in Creating Data for Trustworthy AI. *Nature Machine Intelligence*, *4*(8), 669–677.

Liu, B., & Ferrari, V. (2017). Active Learning for Human Pose Estimation. *Proceedings of the IEEE International Conference on Computer Vision*, 4363–4372. http://openaccess.thecvf.com/content_iccv_2017/html/Liu_Active_Learning_for_ICCV_2017_paper.html

Liu, C., Zhao, F., Kuang, K., Kang, Y., Jiang, Z., Sun, C., & Wu, F. (2024). Evolving Knowledge Distillation with Large Language Models and Active Learning. *Proceedings of the 2024 Joint International Conference on Computational Linguistics, Language Resources and Evaluation (LREC-COLING 2024)*, 6717–6731. https://aclanthology.org/2024.lrec-main.593/

Liu, P., Wang, L., Ranjan, R., He, G., & Zhao, L. (2022). A Survey on Active Deep Learning: From Model Driven to Data Driven. *ACM Computing Surveys*, *54*(10s), 1–34.

Liu, X., Jiang, Z., & Gao, L. (2015). Scientific Information Understanding via Open Educational Resources (OER). *Proceedings of the 38th International ACM SIGIR Conference on Research and Development in Information Retrieval*, 645–654. https://doi.org/10.1145/2766462.2767750

Liu, Z., Guo, Y., & Mahmud, J. (2021). When and Why a Model Fails? A Human-in-the-Loop Error Detection Framework for Sentiment Analysis. *Proceedings of the 2021 Conference of the North American Chapter of the Association for Computational Linguistics: Human Language Technologies: Industry Papers*, 170–177.

Liu, Z., Wang, J., Gong, S., Lu, H., & Tao, D. (2019). Deep Reinforcement Active Learning for Human-in-the-Loop Person Re-identification. *Proceedings of the IEEE/CVF International Conference on Computer Vision*, 6122–6131.

Luo, T., Kramer, K., Goldgof, D. B., Hall, L. O., Samson, S., Remsen, A., Hopkins, T., & Cohn, D. (2005). Active Learning to Recognize Multiple Types of Plankton. *Journal of Machine Learning Research*, *6*(4), 589–613.

Ma, Y., Liu, J., Yi, F., Cheng, Q., Huang, Y., Lu, W., & Liu, X. (2023). AI vs. Human: Differentiation Analysis of Scientific Content Generation [arXiv preprint]. arXiv:2301.10416. http://arxiv.org/abs/2301.10416

Madnick, S. E., Wang, R. Y., Lee, Y. W., & Zhu, H. (2009). Overview and Framework for Data and Information Quality Research. *Journal of Data and Information Quality*, *1*(1), 1–22.

Mehrabi, N., Morstatter, F., Saxena, N., Lerman, K., & Galstyan, A. (2022). A Survey on Bias and Fairness in Machine Learning. *ACM Computing Surveys*, *54*(6), 1–35.

Monarch, R. M. (2021). *Human-in-the-Loop Machine Learning: Active Learning and Annotation for Human-centered AI*. Simon and Schuster.

Mosqueira-Rey, E., Hernández-Pereira, E., Alonso-Ríos, D., Bobes-Bascarán, J., & Fernández-Leal, Á. (2023). Human-in-the-Loop Machine Learning: A State of the Art. *Artificial Intelligence Review*, *56*(4), 3005–3054.

Nguyen, D. H., & Patrick, J. D. (2014). Supervised Machine Learning and Active Learning in Classification of Radiology Reports. *Journal of the American Medical Informatics Association*, *21*(5), 893–901.

Odekerken, D., & Bex, F. (2020). Towards Transparent Human-in-the-Loop Classification of Fraudulent Web Shops. In S. Villata, J. Harašta, & P. Křemen (eds.), *Frontiers in Artificial Intelligence and Applications* (pp. 239–242). IOS Press. https://doi.org/10.3233/FAIA200873

Panian, Z. (2010). Some Practical Experiences in Data Governance. *World Academy of Science, Engineering and Technology*, *62*(1), 939–946.

Paolacci, G., Chandler, J., & Ipeirotis, P. G. (2010). Running Experiments on Amazon Mechanical Turk. *Judgment and Decision Making*, *5*(5), 411–419.

Patil, Y., Amer-Yahia, S., & Subramanian, S. (2022). Designing the Evaluation of Operator-enabled Interactive Data Exploration in VALIDE. *Proceedings of the Workshop on Human-In-the-Loop Data Analytics*, 1–7. https://doi.org/10.1145/3546930.3547509

Pipino, L. L., Lee, Y. W., & Wang, R. Y. (2002). Data Quality Assessment. *Communications of the ACM*, *45*(4), 211–218.

Porter, R., Theiler, J., & Hush, D. (2013). Interactive Machine Learning in Data Exploitation. *Computing in Science & Engineering*, *15*(5), 12–20.

Press, G. (2022, April 14). Cleaning Big Data: Most Time-Consuming, Least Enjoyable Data Science Task, Survey Says. *Forbes*. www.forbes.com/sites/gilpress/2016/03/23/data-preparation-most-time-consuming-least-enjoyable-data-science-task-survey-says/

Rahm, E., & Do, H. H. (2000). Data Cleaning: Problems and Current Approaches. *IEEE Data Engineering Bulletin*, *23*(4), 3–13.

Ramos, G., Meek, C., Simard, P., Suh, J., & Ghorashi, S. (2020). Interactive Machine Teaching: A Human-centered Approach to Building Machine-learned Models. *Human–Computer Interaction*, *35*(5–6), 413–451.

Räth, T., Onah, N., & Sattler, K.-U. (2023). Interactive Data Cleaning for Real-Time Streaming Applications. *Proceedings of the Workshop on Human-In-the-Loop Data Analytics*, 1–3. https://doi.org/10.1145/3597465.3605229

Reddy, D. (2023). Data Engineering Challenges in AI Automation. *2023 International Conference on Computing, Electronics & Communications Engineering (iCCECE)*, 107–112.

Ribeiro, M. T., Singh, S., & Guestrin, C. (2016). "Why Should I Trust You?": Explaining the Predictions of Any Classifier. *Proceedings of the 22nd ACM SIGKDD International Conference on Knowledge Discovery and Data Mining*, 1135–1144.

Rouzegar, H., & Makrehchi, M. (2024). Enhancing Text Classification through LLM-Driven Active Learning and Human Annotation. *Proceedings of the 18th Linguistic Annotation Workshop (LAW-XVIII)*, 98–111.

Rožanec, J. M., Montini, E., Cutrona, V., Papamartzivanos, D., Klemenčič, T., Fortuna, B., Mladenić, D., Veliou, E., Giannetsos, T., & Emmanouilidis, C. (2024). Human in the AI Loop via xAI and Active Learning for Visual Inspection. In J. Soldatos (ed.), *Artificial Intelligence in Manufacturing* (pp. 381–406). Springer Nature Switzerland. https://doi.org/10.1007/978-3-031-46452-2_22

Sachan, S., Almaghrabi, F., Yang, J.-B., & Xu, D.-L. (2024). Human–AI Collaboration to Mitigate Decision Noise in Financial Underwriting: A Study on FinTech Innovation in a Lending Firm. *International Review of Financial Analysis, 93*, 103149. https://doi.org/10.1016/j.irfa.2024.103149

Schröder, C., & Niekler, A. (2020). A Survey of Active Learning for Text Classification using Deep Neural Networks [arXiv preprint]. arXiv:2008.07267. http://arxiv.org/abs/2008.07267

Settles, B. (2011). From Theories to Queries: Active Learning in Practice. *Active Learning and Experimental Design Workshop in Conjunction with AISTATS 2010*, 1–18.

Sheikh, R., Milioto, A., Lottes, P., Stachniss, C., Bennewitz, M., & Schultz, T. (2020). Gradient and Log-based Active Learning for Semantic Segmentation of Crop and Weed for Agricultural Robots. *2020 IEEE International Conference on Robotics and Automation (ICRA)*, 1350–1356. https://ieeexplore.ieee.org/abstract/document/9196722/

Sheng, V. S., & Zhang, J. (2019). Machine Learning with Crowdsourcing: A Brief Summary of the Past Research and Future Directions. *Proceedings of the AAAI Conference on Artificial Intelligence, 33*(1), 9837–9843.

Shoshitaishvili, Y., Weissbacher, M., Dresel, L., Salls, C., Wang, R., Kruegel, C., & Vigna, G. (2017). Rise of the HaCRS: Augmenting Autonomous Cyber Reasoning Systems with Human Assistance. *Proceedings of the 2017 ACM SIGSAC Conference on Computer and Communications Security*, 347–362. https://doi.org/10.1145/3133956.3134105

Shraga, R. (2022). HumanAL: Calibrating Human Matching beyond a Single Task. *Proceedings of the Workshop on Human-In-the-Loop Data Analytics*, 1–8. https://doi.org/10.1145/3546930.3547496

Smailovic, J., Grcar, M., Lavrac, N., & Znidarsic, M. (2014). Stream-based Active Learning for Sentiment Analysis in the Financial Domain. *Information Sciences, 285*, 181–203. https://doi.org/10.1016/j.ins.2014.04.034

Smith, A., Kumar, V., Boyd-Graber, J., Seppi, K., & Findlater, L. (2018). Closing the Loop: User-Centered Design and Evaluation of a Human-in-the-Loop Topic Modeling System. *23rd International Conference on Intelligent User Interfaces*, 293–304. https://doi.org/10.1145/3172944.3172965

Sourati, J., Akcakaya, M., Leen, T. K., Erdogmus, D., & Dy, J. G. (2017). Asymptotic Analysis of Objectives based on Fisher Information in Active Learning. *Journal of Machine Learning Research, 18*(34), 1–41.

Stiennon, N., Ouyang, L., Wu, J., Ziegler, D., Lowe, R., Voss, C., Radford, A., Amodei, D., & Christiano, P. F. (2020). Learning to Summarize with Human Feedback. *Advances in Neural Information Processing Systems, 33*, 3008–3021.

Tajbakhsh, N., Jeyaseelan, L., Li, Q., Chiang, J., Wu, Z., & Ding, X. (2020). Embracing Imperfect Datasets: A Review of Deep Learning Solutions for Medical Image Segmentation. *Medical Image Analysis, 63*, 101693. https://doi.org/10.1016/j.media.2020.101693

Vaughan, J. W. (2018). Making Better Use of the Crowd: How Crowdsourcing Can Advance Machine Learning Research. *Journal of Machine Learning Research, 18*(193), 1–46.

Wallace, E., Rodriguez, P., Feng, S., Yamada, I., & Boyd-Graber, J. (2019). Trick Me If You Can: Human-in-the-Loop Generation of Adversarial Examples for Question Answering. *Transactions of the Association for Computational Linguistics, 7*, 387–401.

Wang, G., Zuluaga, M. A., Li, W., Pratt, R., Patel, P. A., Aertsen, M., Doel, T., David, A. L., Deprest, J., Ourselin, S., & Vercauteren, T. (2019). DeeplGeoS: A Deep Interactive Geodesic Framework for Medical Image Segmentation. *IEEE Transactions on Pattern Analysis and Machine Intelligence, 41*(7), 1559–1572. https://doi.org/10.1109/TPAMI.2018.2840695

Wang, Z. J., Choi, D., Xu, S., & Yang, D. (2021). Putting Humans in the Natural Language Processing Loop: A Survey. *Proceedings of the First Workshop on Bridging Human–Computer Interaction and Natural Language Processing*, 47–52. https://aclanthology.org/2021.hcinlp-1.8/

Ware, M., Frank, E., Holmes, G., Hall, M., & Witten, I. H. (2001). Interactive Machine Learning: Letting Users Build Classifiers. *International Journal of Human–Computer Studies, 55*(3), 281–292.

Wondimu, N. A., Buche, C., & Visser, U. (2022). Interactive Machine Learning: A State of the Art Review [arXiv preprint]. arXiv:2207.06196. http://arxiv.org/abs/2207.06196

Wrede, F., & Hellander, A. (2019). Smart Computational Exploration of Stochastic Gene Regulatory Network Models Using Human-in-the-Loop Semi-supervised Learning. *Bioinformatics, 35*(24), 5199–5206.

Wu, X., Xiao, L., Sun, Y., Zhang, J., Ma, T., & He, L. (2022). A Survey of Human-in-the-Loop for Machine Learning. *Future Generation Computer Systems, 135*, 364–381.

Wu, Y., Wang, C., Gumusel, E., & Liu, X. (2024). Knowledge-Infused Legal Wisdom: Navigating LLM Consultation through the Lens of Diagnostics and Positive-Unlabeled Reinforcement Learning. *Findings of the Association for Computational Linguistics 2024*.

Xiao, R., Dong, Y., Zhao, J., Wu, R., Lin, M., Chen, G., & Wang, H. (2023). FreeAL: Towards Human-Free Active Learning in the Era of Large Language Models. *Proceedings of the 2023 Conference on Empirical Methods in Natural Language Processing*, 14520–14535. https://aclanthology.org/2023.emnlp-main.896/

Xu, W., Dainoff, M. J., Ge, L., & Gao, Z. (2023). Transitioning to Human Interaction with AI Systems: New Challenges and Opportunities for HCI Professionals to Enable Human-Centered AI. *International Journal of Human–Computer Interaction, 39*(3), 494–518.

Yang, J., Lan, G., Li, Y., Gong, Y., Zhang, Z., & Ercisli, S. (2022). Data Quality Assessment and Analysis for Pest Identification in Smart Agriculture. *Computers and Electrical Engineering, 103*, 108322.

Yang, Q., Suh, J., Chen, N.-C., & Ramos, G. (2018). Grounding Interactive Machine Learning Tool Design in How Non-Experts Actually Build Models. *Proceedings of the 2018 Designing Interactive Systems Conference*, 573–584.

Zhang, J., Wu, X., & Sheng, V. S. (2016). Learning from Crowdsourced Labeled Data: A Survey. *Artificial Intelligence Review, 46*(4), 543–576.

Zhou, X., Wang, Q., Wang, X., Tang, H., & Liu, X. (2023). Large Language Model Soft Ideologization via AI-Self-Consciousness [arXiv preprint]. arXiv:2309.16167. http://arxiv.org/abs/2309.16167

Ziegler, D. M., Stiennon, N., Wu, J., Brown, T. B., Radford, A., Amodei, D., Christiano, P., & Irving, G. (2020). Fine-Tuning Language Models from Human Preferences [arXiv preprint]. arXiv:1909.08593. http://arxiv.org/abs/1909.08593

9

Human–AI Collaboration for Identifying Health Information Wants

Zhuochun Li, Zhimeng Luo, Ning Zou, Bo Xie, and Daqing He

9.1 Introduction

Patients living with serious and/or clinical diseases such as cancer or Alzheimer's disease and related dementias (ADRD) require extensive care, often by family members (Alzheimer's Association, 2022; Kent et al., 2016). This can be challenging and, thus, stressful for family caregivers because they do not have formal training on patient care (Reid & O'Brien, 2021). Although they can seek advice from healthcare professionals during visits, it is often not sufficient as caregiving questions and needs can happen at any time (Peterson et al., 2016; Soong et al., 2020), and current forms of advice are static and not tailored to caregivers' specific needs (González-Fraile et al., 2021).

Unprepared caregivers often seek information and support online to fulfill their changing needs (Reifegerste et al., 2021). As caregivers increasingly take on more active roles in health care, the Internet has become a prominent source of health information to guide their decision-making and self-management (Zhao et al., 2022). Yet, despite the great potential of the Internet, about 63 percent of users who seek health information on the web have reported feeling overwhelmed by the vast amount of unfiltered information and unqualified to determine the quality, veracity, and relevance of the information (Ferraris et al., 2023). Reasons behind this finding include that the search for health information is different from general information-seeking behaviors; looking for health information requires caregivers to master certain domain-specific knowledge, especially when they encounter resources full of domain-specific terminology (Chi et al., 2020). Although online health communities can serve as an important online source that provides caregivers with personal support and social engagement, there are issues related to the interactions and the quality of information that caregivers may gain from online communities (Chi et al., 2022).

Recently, Artificial Intelligence (AI) systems have been developed to be equipped with some level of relevant knowledge on diseases (Hui et al., 2024; Thaker et al., 2024; Y. Wang et al., 2024; Z. Wang et al. 2021), such that dynamic, tailored information can be provided to caregivers for better support. Within such AI systems, the critical first step of a tailored response is to accurately recognize and classify a caregiver's expressed needs (Z. Wang et al., 2021).

Identifying the category of the information needs expressed in a text is a classic text classification problem in AI and natural language processing. Both traditional statistical and more recent deep learning models have been employed to perform this task (Z. Wang et al., 2021; Zou, Ji et al., 2023; Zou, Thaker, & He, 2023), but an adequate amount of annotated training data is required so that supervised models that provide highly accurate classification performance can be developed (Z. Wang et al., 2021).

However, caregiving as a healthcare topic is still not sufficiently studied, and studies on caregivers' needs have been conducted even less. For example, in a systematic literature review, Xie et al. (2018) found that caregivers' information preferences are typically not assessed before or during the implementation of interventions; no intervention has assessed caregivers' preferences for what information they want to receive or when or how they want to receive it. Shin and Habermann (2022) also found that ADRD caregivers reported a greater level of lack of support from healthcare professionals and unmet needs for knowledge and resources.

This poses two important problems for the development of AI systems to classify caregivers' needs:

(1) AI systems rely on domain experts to pass on domain knowledge via organized classes and descriptions of caregivers' needs and annotated data for each category of needs, but domain experts such as clinicians often lack developed, comprehensive knowledge of caregiving and issues associated with diseases such as ADRD. It is difficult for domain experts to provide AI systems with a comprehensive and representative knowledge of caregivers' needs.
(2) AI systems can help domain experts improve their knowledge of caregivers' needs if they can reliably identify relevant information for each category of needs, but AI systems are not trained enough to complete such work accurately. So, they are not yet useful to help domain experts.

These two issues are intertwined. Domain experts can provide AI systems with better domain knowledge if they can get help from AI systems, and AI systems can better help domain experts if they have more domain knowledge from domain experts. Consequently, it makes great sense to study how human experts and AI systems collaborate to address this task.

In this chapter, we present our work in classifying caregivers' needs through collaboration between human experts and AI systems. We use ADRD caregiving as our example domain. Dementia has become a major public health challenge (Shu & Woo, 2021), and persons with dementia require extensive care, often provided by family members, who frequently report their challenges and stress (Reid & O'Brien, 2021). AI can support caregivers, but research is needed to understand the ways in which AI might be effective (Ji et al., 2022).

We first proposed and developed this use of AI in our earlier research (Z. Wang et al., 2021), in which ADRD domain experts worked with an interactive machine learning system to develop and revise a framework to address the health information wants (HIWs) – the types of care-related information that caregivers of those with ADRD wish to have. This ADRD framework represents caregivers' needs. Our methods can significantly reduce the amount of annotated data typically required for traditional ML models.

Large language models (LLMs) such as ChatGPT (Wu, He et al., 2023) and GPT-4 (Open AI et al., 2023) can comprehend and interpret users' needs, and they can generate outputs that meet users' requirements (Brown et al., 2020; Moor et al., 2023). Compared with traditional few-shot learning methods in clinical natural language processing (Z. Li et al., 2023), LLMs can generate high-quality responses to dementia caregivers' questions to help them overcome the challenges that they face (Aguirre et al., 2024).

In this chapter, we present our human–AI collaboration approach, in which an LLM is employed to generate simulated text, which is then validated by human experts. The validated data are subsequently treated as gold examples in in-context learning to enhance the LLM's classification performance. Through this human–AI collaboration, human experts can leverage the assistance of LLMs to gain deeper insights into caregivers' HIWs and provide more informed and tailored suggestions for them.

The set of research questions we explore are as follows:

- At which stage of the HIW classification process can a human individual and AI collaborate?
- What instructions (prompts) can we use to gain the best possible classification results from LLMs?
- What machine learning concepts developed in the past can be applied to further improve LLMs' performance?

To address these questions, we first review relevant literature on human–AI collaboration in healthcare and the application of AI including LLM technology in healthcare, with implications for our work. Then, we consider the background of ADRD-HIWs and our earlier exploration of expert–machine co-development. We outline our experimental design and present results from various classification experiments. Given these findings, we analyze and discuss our human–AI collaboration's effectiveness and suggest potential directions for future research.

9.2 Literature Review

9.2.1 Human–AI Collaboration in Healthcare

Human–AI collaboration can be defined as AI systems working jointly with humans as teammates or partners to solve problems (Lai et al., 2021). As D. Wang et al. (2020) have said, human–AI collaboration is not a new concept. Symbiotic computing, proposed by J. C. Licklider (1960) in his seminal article "Man–Computer Symbiosis," clearly presented the partnership of humans and machines. Different from the design of fully automatic AI systems, which are "black boxes" to humans, human-centered design is rooted in the design of algorithms and the implementation of applications with human–AI collaboration as a paradigm (D. Wang et al., 2020). This is the basis of human–computer interaction (Shneiderman & Plaisant, 2009).

Healthcare is an important domain for the use of AI (Jiang et al., 2017; Shaheen, 2021) because AI can mitigate the shortage of qualified healthcare workers, assist overworked medical professionals, and improve the quality of healthcare services (Lai et al., 2021). Healthcare is therefore a critical context for human–AI collaboration (Markus et al., 2021).

Researchers working on human–AI collaboration have long viewed it as a socio-technical ensemble, where respective strengths of humans and AI can extend each other's capability limits, resulting in superior task outcomes (Bansal et al., 2021). This is particularly since healthcare requires deep domain knowledge and the outcomes are critical to humans' wellbeing.

Lai et al. (2021) searched five major databases for publications in disciplines such as computer science, information systems, health informatics, and medicine, in order to review the literature on human–AI collaboration in healthcare. Their initial searches yielded 1,019 publications, but, after several rounds of filtering and full text examination, only 28 relevant studies remained. They found that research with human–AI collaboration in healthcare was increasing but the number of studies was still limited; most articles were about generic use cases, with cancer and dementia as common disease cases; most research focused on treatment, surgery and diagnosis; and the studies involved healthcare professionals, patients, and clinical researchers with AI systems.

Hemmer and his colleagues (2022) conducted semi-structured interviews and employed inductive coding to examine the factors influencing the adoption of human–AI collaboration in clinical decision-making. They found six factors, which can be summarized into one sentence "Professionals state the need for a *complementary AI* that communicates its insights *transparently* and *adapts* to the users to enable *mutual learning* and *time-efficient* work with a final *human agency*" (Hemmer et al., 2022, p. 2).

9.2.2 AI in Health Information Need Identification

With the huge amount of health information available on the internet, health consumers such as patients and caregivers actively use the internet for satisfying their health information needs (Chi et al., 2020). Despite the benefits of being confidential and anonymous, and providing emotional and social support by engaging others in online social platforms, seeking health information online can also be challenging due to the inherent complexity and uniqueness of health issues (Chi et al., 2020). Besides the health information needs of patients, there have been works on examining caregivers' needs too (Zou, Thaker, & He, 2023), which showed that their needs also evolve throughout the disease trajectory.

With rapid developments in computational capabilities, many AI techniques, such as statistical machine learning models (Habehh & Gohel, 2021) and deep learning models (Esteva et al., 2019), have been applied to healthcare. Besides the common applications on clinical decision-making (Z. Li et al., 2024; Magrabi et al. 2019), x-ray imaging (Adams et al., 2021), we also see recommender systems developed to support patients in satisfying their needs (Thaker et al., 2024).

Online social platforms provide attractive places for patients and caregivers seeking answers to their health information needs, where the support is not only information oriented but can be emotional and social (Zou, Thaker, & He, 2023). Xie et al. (2020) examined ADRD caregivers' information needs on Reddit. Zou, Thaker, and He (2023) provided a systematic review on studies that apply AI for processing ADRD caregivers' social media posts. Their initial search on ACM Digital Library, IEEE Xplore Digital Library, and PubMed generated 324 articles, but, after three rounds of screening, only 18 papers were selected for analysis. Their results show that the research in this area is still in its infancy, and much work still focuses on characterizing ADRD caregivers' behaviors on social media and predicting ADRD related activities was the focus of using AI technologies in the majority of these studies.

9.2.3 LLMs in Healthcare

Remarkable performance improvements have been demonstrated by training LLMs on general domain data, which make domain-specific pretraining unnecessary. For instance, Kung et al. (2023) evaluated GPT-3.5's responses to the United States Medical Licensing Exam (USMLE) questions. Their results were achieved at or near the passing threshold even if the LLM was not specifically trained in related fields. Similarly, Nori et al. (2023) proved that GPT-4 exceeded the USMLE passing score by more than twenty points using simple 5-shot prompting. Additionally, DeID-GPT (Liu et al., 2023) has utilized high-quality prompts to ensure privacy and summarize essential information in medical data, outperforming relevant baseline methods. Sivarajkumar and Wang (2023) proposed a prompt-based clinical natural language processing framework HealthPrompt, which improved performance in clinical NLP tasks by exploring different prompt templates without requiring extra training data.

Furthermore, several studies have focused on text classification tasks within health-related fields. Guo et al. (2024) employed data augmentation using GPT-4 alongside relatively small human-annotated datasets to train lightweight supervised classification models, achieving superior results compared to using human-annotated data alone. C. Wu et al. (2023) explored the complex task of medical Chinese text categorization by leveraging the complementary strengths of three different sub-models. Their experimental results, obtained through a voting mechanism, demonstrated that the proposed method could achieve an accuracy of 92 percent. De Santis et al. (2024) compared LLMs like Mistral and GPT-4 with traditional methods such as BERT and SVM. Their findings indicated that Mistral-7B is the optimal choice as an algorithm within a decision support system for monitoring users in sensitive medical discourses. GPT-4 also showed strong in-context learning capabilities, particularly in zero-shot settings, making it a viable option for medical text classification. Additionally, Song et al. (2024) proposed an LLM-based privacy data augmentation method for medical text classification, and their experimental results outperformed other baselines across different dataset sizes in text classification tasks.

In summary, human–AI collaboration is a topic that has lots of potential in the healthcare domain, but there is still a gap in studying how human–AI collaboration can be designed for helping caregivers involved in healthcare, particularly using the latest AI technologies like LLMs for performing human–AI collaboration.

9.3 Background

9.3.1 From HIWs to ADRD-HIWs

The shared decision-making model holds that patients (and, in the case of ADRD patients, their caregivers) should be expected and encouraged to stay informed and collaborate with medical professionals to make decisions (Charles et al., 1999; Epstein et al., 2004). This paradigm has generated much interest in individual preferences for health information and participation in decision-making (Benbassat et al., 1998). However, prior research has typically measured only a limited range of individual preferences for information and decision-making that reflects what physicians think their patients need (Beisecker & Beisecker, 1990; Ende et al., 1989) despite poor correlations between what physicians think their patients need and what patients really want to know (Xie 2009). Thus, the validity of prior research is questionable (Hubbard, 2008). Existing interventions, which typically base their content on theoretical constructs from behavior change theories (Harrington & Noar, 2012) do have their merits, but they are top-down, driven by what researchers think participants need to know, rather than what participants may want to know.

To address these limitations, Xie (2009) developed the Health Information Wants (HIW) framework that emphasizes "health information that one would like to have and use to make important health decisions that may or may not be directly related to diagnosis or standard treatment" (p. 510). The HIW framework promotes an understanding of preferences from the health consumer's perspective, rather than the provider's, by emphasizing a wide range of information and decision-making autonomy that health consumers want to have (Xie 2009). Guided by the HIW framework, Xie and her colleagues developed the HIW Questionnaire (Xie et al., 2010), which was validated among older and younger Americans, with excellent validity and reliability. The HIW framework is highly adaptable to specific populations' unique circumstances, evidenced by its successful adaptations to and validations among individuals with diabetes (Nie et al., 2016) and cancer patients and their families (Xie et al., 2017). More recently, Zou, Thaker, and He (2023) examined HIWs for caregivers of ovarian cancer patients, and Tang and colleagues (2023) studied HIWs of ADRD caregivers expressed on social media.

Given the generalizability of the HIW framework, we developed the ADRD-HIW framework (Z. Wang et al., 2021). Specifically, we adopted the HIW framework to ADRD caregiving scenarios with three rounds of development and revision. The final outcome of the ADRD-HIW framework has seven general categories that show the types of health information typically wanted by ADRD caregivers: (1) treatment/medication/prevention, (2) characteristics of/experience with the health condition/diagnostic procedures, (3) daily care for a patient at home/caregiver self-care, (4) practical information about care transition and coordination and end-of-life care, (5) psychosocial aspects of caregiving, (6) resources/advocacy/scientific updates/research participation, and (7) legal, financial, or insurance related information.

In our earlier work examining information exchange within online dementia care communities (Ji et al., 2022; Z. Wang et al., 2021; Zou, Thaker, & He, 2023), we identified that information related to the HIW category "daily care for patient at home/caregiver self-care" is among the most sought categories by ADRD caregivers. Similarly, prior review work examining past decades studies of ADRD caregiving have underscored that the majority of ADRD caregivers express a desire for support in helping daily care while balancing their caregiving role and their own personal well-being (Bressan et al., 2020). Therefore, the clinicians in our team have developed a daily care framework to organize this specific type of ADRD-HIW into seven categories, with a total of thirty-two subcategories (for details, see Table 9.1).

9.3.2 Our Earlier Effort in Expert–Machine Co-development

As part of developing our HIW-ADRD framework and analyzing caregivers' online posts, we developed the expert–machine co-development process (Z. Wang et al., 2021).

As shown in Figure 9.1, this process aims to enable human experts to collaborate with machine learning algorithms in developing the HIW framework, at the same time improving the automatic classification of online posts. Empowered by their own domain knowledge (the HIW framework and clinical knowledge), human experts generate the initial data to train the machine algorithms. The machine algorithms then provided data-driven feedback to human experts, allowing the experts to learn from the feedback to update their domain knowledge, which resulted in revising the HIW framework with data-driven evidence. The change of the HIW framework triggered experts to change the data that was fed to the machine algorithms. This co-development process can be iterative between the experts and the machine algorithms so that both the experts' clinical knowledge and the HIW framework, as well as the

Table 9.1 *ADRD-HIW daily care category and the corresponding subcategories*

Daily care category	Subcategories
1. Personal care	1.1 Bathing 1.2 Dressing 1.3 Toileting/incontinence 1.4 Transferring 1.5 Feeding/nutrition 1.6 Dental care
2. Household management	2.1 Meal preparation 2.2 Housekeeping chores 2.3 Laundry
3. Safety	3.1 Driving safety 3.2 Medication safety 3.3 Financial safety 3.4 Level of supervision 3.5 Self-neglect 3.6 Safe phone use
4. Mood and behavior management	4.1 Aggression and anger 4.2 Anxiety and agitation 4.3 Depression 4.4 Hallucinations 4.5 Memory loss and confusion 4.6 Repetition 4.7 Sleep issues 4.8 Suspicious and delusions 4.9 Wandering
5. Activities	5.1 Planning daily activities 5.2 Choosing daily activities 5.3 Conducting daily activities
6. Communication strategies	6.1 Communication with a person with dementia 6.2 Communication with other family members
7. Working with healthcare providers	7.1 What to do prior to a visit 7.2 What to do during a visit 7.3 What to do after a visit

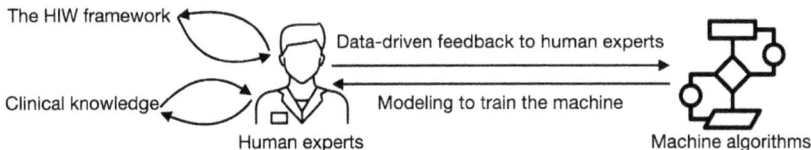

Figure 9.1 The expert–machine co-development (EMC) process (extracted from Z. Wang et al., 2021)

algorithm's effectiveness of classification, can be continuously improved. This process utilizes interactive machine learning.

9.4 Human–AI Collaboration for HIW Identifications

In our study, we rely on real posts from online social media, such as Reddit, to highlight the caregivers' health information wants (HIWs). Therefore, the classification task involves categorizing a real post into one category of the HIW framework. This task imposes a heavy workload on clinicians due to the large volume of posts. While AI such as LLMs can assist, it struggles to classify posts accurately using plain prompts alone.

To overcome this challenge and facilitate collaboration between professional clinicians and LLM, we expanded our expert–machine co-development process to human–AI collaboration: human experts have general domain knowledge to offer in the collaboration so they are good at differentiating on-topic posts for a given HIW from other off-topic ones, whereas capable AI systems such as LLMs have the ability to generate simulated text for a given requirements or instructions, even in large quantity but they might hallucinate with wrong information. Consequently, rather than having clinicians manually annotate the massive dataset of real posts, we instructed the LLM with the definition of each HIW as part of the prompt to generate five simulated posts for each HIW category. These simulated posts were then reviewed and validated by clinicians, who ensured their accuracy. The verified posts were used as examples within the prompts (thus perform few-shot in-context learning (Z. Li et al., 2023)) to guide the LLM in categorizing real posts. This method significantly reduced the manual annotation workload for clinicians, while the LLM benefited from the expert-validated examples, enhancing its performance through in-context learning. Our human–AI collaboration allows both parties to benefit from each other, resulting in improved classification accuracy.

Furthermore, we found it common for multiple possible categories to be returned after the initial classification, which led us to introduce a second round of classification to determine the most likely category based on the initial set. In the second round of classification, the LLM is prompted to select the most probable category based on the set of categories identified in the first round.

Our approach offers a new way of combining human expertise with AI to optimize task outcomes, and the results confirm the effectiveness of this collaborative method. Figure 9.2 explains the overall human–AI collaboration process between our clinicians and LLM. The details of Step 4 "the classification" is explained in Figure 9.3.

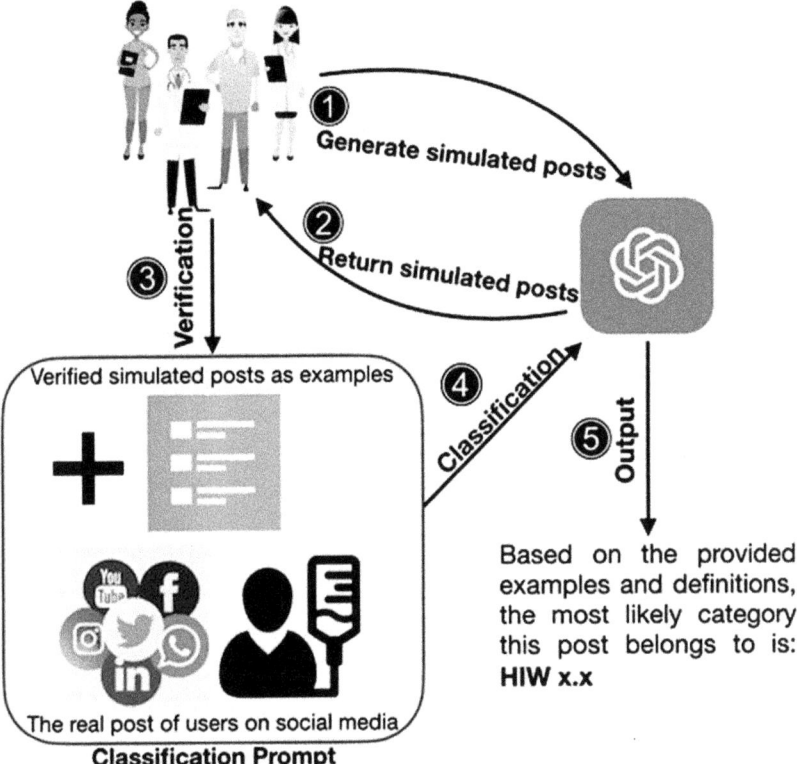

Figure 9.2 The human–AI collaboration in our classification task

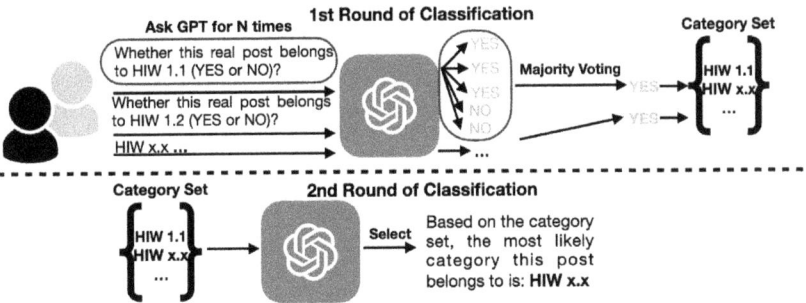

Figure 9.3 The two-round classification framework

9.5 Experiments

To demonstrate and examine our proposed human–AI collaboration for HIW classification, we conducted a series of experiments. In the remainder of this section, we will cover the datasets, LLMs, and methods.

9.5.1 Datasets

We collected real posts from a social media platform, Reddit. Reddit was chosen due to its prevalence among individuals sharing dementia-related challenges (Tang et al., 2023; Zou, Thaker, & He, 2023). The abundance of relevant posts, facilitated by the Reddit API, has enabled earlier research to identify and examine caregivers' health information wants (HIWs). In total, 14,884 posts were collected from five subreddits: "AgingParents," "Alzheimers," "dementia," "AlzheimersCanada," and "AlzheimersSupport," which cover from 2010 to 2022. Two clinicians, each with at least fifteen years of experience with persons living with dementia and their family caregivers, iteratively identified typical posts as seeds, then located similar posts using a snowball sampling technique (Goodman, 1961), and finally annotated the identified twenty posts in each of three HIW categories: "3.1 driving safety," "4.1 aggression and anger," and "4.5 memory loss and confusion." Consensus was reached through discussion. These three HIWs were selected because they represent common asked questions from ADRD caregivers.

9.5.2 LLMs

In our experiments, we exclusively use LLMs developed by OpenAI for its strong in-context learning capabilities compared to other LLMs, which makes them optimal options for medical text classification (De Santis et al., 2024). Specifically, we used the LLM GPT-4o to conduct all experiments. For parameter settings, we set the temperature as 0.8 for more varied outputs during the majority voting process. All the other parameters remained the same as default values in the official document.

9.5.3 Experiment Design

To answer the RQs mentioned in Section 9.1, we designed a set of experiments to establish baselines, explore model parameters, and conduct final assessments. In all the experiments, we model the task as the scenario in which a caregiver expresses their caregiving situations and asks one or multiple questions as their expressed needs and the AI system (LLM) automatically classifies the post to one of the HIWs in our ADRD-HIW framework.

Baseline Experiments

We established two baselines in our experiments. The first one views the task as a multi-class classification task where the input post is classified to one of the thirty-two HIW categories, where GPT-4o was used as the classifier, and the category definition for each of the thirty-two categories is used to represent the category. This baseline represents the simplest and most straightforward classification setup. It provides a foundational comparison for subsequent experiments where we will explore more optimized methods for improving the classification accuracy of the LLM in identifying caregivers' HIWs.

Since thirty-two categories are a large number to perform multi-class classification, we explore another baseline where we model the class organization hierarchically rather than flat. For example, suppose we aim to classify a post with the true category of "3.1 driving safety," which has been shown in Table 9.1. First, we attempt to classify the post into one of seven general HIWs. If the post is correctly labeled under the "Daily Care" category, we proceed to classify it into the categories within "Daily Care." Next, if the post is classified into the appropriate category, "3. Safety" within "Daily Care," we continue further classifying it into the final specific subcategory, choosing among the subcategories 3.1 to 3.6 within "3. Safety." In this setting, only the posts correctly classified in the previous hierarchy will be fed into the next level of classification. We also include this hierarchical classification as one baseline and explore further refinement to improve overall accuracy.

Experiments on Exploring Classification Techniques

In designing our classifier, we learned two things from the baselines presented in the previous subsection. First, the definition of each HIW category alone did not work well, we should also give GPT-4o posts as the examples belong to the HIW category, thus we will perform few-shot in-context learning on LLMs (Dong et al., 2022). Second, the baselines showed that multi-class classification on thirty-two HIW categories at once may be too challenging for GPT-4o. We thus convert the classification task to a series of binary classifications. Specifically, GPT-4o was asked a yes–no question for a given post on whether it belongs to a particular HIW category (one of the thirty-two HIW categories). This binary classification was repeated thirty-two times to cover all categories, which will identify all applicable categories for each post. To decrease the complexity during our exploration of parameters, we only performed binary classification on the three target categories in our dataset (3.1, 4.1, and 4.5).

In the exploration of the first parameter, we focused on *real posts* vs *simulated posts*. We performed one experiment of selecting three real posts from each target category to perform three binary classifications with few-shots in-context learning on GPT-4o. Then we utilized the simulated post to replace the real posts for few-shots in-context learning.

The simulated posts were generated through our human–AI collaboration. First, we asked GPT-4o to generate five simulated posts for each category, ensuring they aligned with the category definitions. Then, these simulated posts were reviewed and verified by professional clinicians, who selected the most representative ones. This process was repeated if the required number of simulated posts were not selected after the verification.

The second parameter we explored was around *majority voting*. Majority voting is an important technique in ensemble learning, and Huang et al.'s (2022) demonstrated that it works in LLMs. During our experiments, we also observed that GPT-4o can produce different answers even when asked the same questions at different times. To ensure more reliable and consistent final answers, we adopted the majority voting method: by asking the LLM to answer the same question multiple times, we can gather responses and select the final answer based on the most frequent outcome. This majority voting approach leverages the self-consistency of the LLM, helping to increase the confidence in the final answer. In our model, we set the number of repeating questions asking the same question for majority voting as $N = 5$.

The third parameter we explored focuses on *system prompt*. Previous research indicated that different system prompts, which define the roles that LLM can take could influence LLM behavior (Z. Li et al., 2024; Zheng et al., 2023). We changed the system prompt from the default "You are a helpful assistant." to "You are an experienced clinician specialized in dementia care." We assume the more specific role on ADRD may help LLM gain background knowledge and enhance the results.

We present one specific prompt for HIW "3.1 driving safety" here:

> **System prompt:** *You are an experienced clinician specialized in dementia care.*
>
> *I'm doing a research study to understand the challenges experienced by caregivers when caring for family members living with dementia and the types of information caregivers may want that can help them manage those challenges. I have categorized one of those types of information that caregivers might want as "driving safety" and defined it as "information about how to manage driving, e.g., when, and how to get a person living with dementia to stop driving."*
>
> *Meanwhile, I recognize that many dementia caregivers have posted their challenges on Reddit. Their posts often indicate what types of information they want to have that may help them manage those challenges. I have already composed five*

representative posts for this category of "driving safety." Now, I will give you these five representative posts; your task is to first learn the patterns in these representative posts and then to decide whether a new post that I give you belongs to this same category (YES or NO) and why. The five representative posts are:

Post 1:

Title: Need Advice on Managing Driving for Mom with Early Dementia

Content: Hi everyone, I'm feeling overwhelmed about the driving situation with my mom. She's been diagnosed with early-stage dementia and I'm not sure how to approach the topic of her stopping driving. She loves her independence but has had a couple of minor incidents recently. Does anyone have tips or resources on how to handle this gently?

Post 2:

Title: When Is It Time to Stop Driving?

Content: My dad's dementia is progressing and I'm starting to worry about his driving. He hasn't had any accidents yet, but he gets confused easily. How did you all decide it was time for your loved one to give up the keys? Looking for guidance and personal experiences that could help.

Post 3:

Title: Resources for Driving Assessments

Content: Hello, does anyone know of any reliable assessments for driving ability in seniors with cognitive impairments? My aunt has been showing signs of forgetfulness and it's getting concerning. I think a professional evaluation might help, but I don't know where to start. Any recommendations?

Post 4:

Title: Strategies for Discussing Driving with a Dementia Patient

Content: Need some advice here. My grandmother has moderate dementia and it's clear she shouldn't be driving anymore. Every time we bring it up, she gets very defensive and upset. Has anyone else dealt with this? What strategies worked for you in having this difficult conversation?

Post 5:

Title: Alternatives to Driving for Dementia Patients

Content: My spouse has been advised to stop driving due to his dementia. He's struggling with losing his independence and I want to make this transition as smooth as possible. What alternatives have worked for your loved ones? Any tips on introducing new modes of transport?

The new post that I need you to decide if it belongs to this same category is:

Title: {Filled with real post title}

Content: {Filled with real post content}

Optimized Experiment on Thirty-Two HIW Classifications

Finally, after exploring the parameters of our model, we conducted experiments on classifying against all thirty-two categories to assess our classification model. Due to the large number of categories and the complexity of real posts, we observed that our classifier often indicated "yes" for multiple categories. To address this and ensure that the most likely category is returned, we implemented a second round of classification. The detail of this two-round classification framework has been illustrated in Figure 9.3.

9.6 Results

In this section, we will present classification results corresponding to the experiments designed in Section 9.5.

9.6.1 Baseline Results

The baseline experiment results are presented in Tables 9.2 and 9.3, respectively. Table 9.3 also shows the ratio of correctly classified posts after each hierarchical classification. Only the posts that survive the current hierarchical classification will be fed into the next hierarchical classification. For example, only six out of twenty posts with the true label "3.1 driving safety" are correctly classified into "Daily Care," which is one of the seven general HIWs. Then only five among these six posts are classified into "3. Safety," which is one of the seven categories in the general HIW "Daily Care" that "3.1 driving safety" belongs (see Table 9.1).

The results in Tables 9.2 and 9.3 show that flat multi-class classification baseline performed better than the hierarchical multi-class classification baseline (0.65 vs 0.12). Although fewer classes are considered in each step of hierarchical classification, the accumulated errors in each step still have a big

Table 9.2 *Baseline results of thirty-two multiclass classifications*

	Correct Prediction	Accuracy
3.1 Driving safety	16/20	0.80
4.1 Aggression and anger	14/20	0.70
4.5 Memory loss and confusion	9/20	0.45
Total	39/60	0.65

Table 9.3 *Baseline results of thirty-two hierarchical multiclass classifications*

	7 General HIWs	7 Categories in "Daily Care"	32 Subcategories in "Daily Care"	Overall Correct Prediction (Accuracy)
3.1 Driving safety	6/20 (0.30)	5/6 (0.83)	5/5 (1.0)	5/20 (0.25)
4.1 Aggression and anger	3/20 (0.15)	2/3 (0.67)	2/2 (1.0)	2/20 (0.10)
4.5 Memory loss and confusion	5/20 (0.25)	3/5 (0.60)	0/3 (0)	0/20 (0)
Total	14/60 (0.23)	10/14 (0.71)	7/10 (0.7)	7/60 (0.12)

Table 9.4 *Results of human–AI collaboration and different classification techniques*

	Correct Prediction (Accuracy)			
	3.1 Driving safety	4.1 Aggression and anger	4.5 Memory loss and confusion	Total
Real posts	17/20 (0.85)	15/20 (0.75)	14/20 (0.70)	46/60 (0.77)
Simulated posts	18/20 (0.90)	18/20 (0.90)	17/20 (0.85)	53/60 (0.88)
+Majority voting	19/20 (0.95)	19/20 (0.95)	20/20 (1.00)	58/60 (0.97)
+System prompt	19/20 (0.95)	18/20 (0.90)	20/20 (1.00)	57/60 (0.95)

impact on the final results. Thus, dividing the thirty-two multiclasses into smaller hierarchical multiclasses is not an appropriate solution for this task.

9.6.2 Results of Human–AI Collaboration and Different Classification Techniques

Table 9.4 presents the outcomes of our human–AI collaboration method and different parameters in our classification model.

First, the results show that adding sample posts on top of definitions of HIW categories can help LLM classify posts more effectively. The classification with real posts improved the average accuracy for the three categories by 12 percent compared to the baselines in Table 9.2 (0.77 vs 0.65). Furthermore, employing simulated posts can further improve the average accuracy by another 11 percent (0.88 vs 0.77). We hypothesized that simulated posts generated by GPT-4o typically focus on more relevant content to the HIW category and contain less irrelevant information compared to real posts.

The review of our clinicians on the simulated posts and real posts confirmed our hypothesis. Consequently, our approach of using LLMs to generate simulated posts provides an important insight into obtaining sample data for performing few-shot in-context learning with LLMs. Simulated and verified data is better training data for LLMs, which are much cheaper and less time-consuming to obtain. Human–AI collaboration can be very helpful here.

Second, adding the majority voting method greatly improved the performance. The accuracy nearly reaches 100 percent across all three categories. Notably, the improvement in category 4.5, "Memory loss and confusion," is significant, achieving 100 percent accuracy. This is particularly remarkable because category 4.5 consistently had the lowest accuracy in earlier experiments, making it the most challenging category to classify. The success of the majority voting method highlights its ability to reduce randomness and leverage the self-consistency of LLMs to refine the final decision.

Third, the last row of Table 9.4 shows that the accuracy of using a task-specific role in system prompt slightly dropped compared to the default role that LLM takes (0.95 vs 0.97). Nonetheless, it would be premature to conclude that system prompts have no impact on classification tasks. The extremely high accuracy already achieved in the previous experiment might leave little room for further improvement. More extensive studies are needed to better understand the impact of system prompts on related tasks in the future.

9.6.3 Optimized Results of Thirty-Two Multiclass Classifications

Finally, Table 9.5 presents the practical scenario where we used thirty-two category definitions as input and conducted the two classifications, incorporating simulated posts and majority voting. This approach posed significantly more difficulty than our previous experiments in Table 9.4, where we focused on just three target categories.

Table 9.5 *Results of thirty-two independent binary classifications with simulated posts, majority voting = 5*

	Correct Prediction	Accuracy
3.1 driving safety	20/20	1.00
4.1 aggression and anger	19/20	0.95
4.5 memory loss and confusion	14/20	0.70
Total	53/60	0.88

First, Table 9.5 shows that the parameters we selected based on experiments on three HIW categories can still have a significant impact on the classification tasks performed on all thirty-two categories. Table 9.5 shows that the overall accuracy performed on thirty-two independent binary classifications with simulated posts and majority voting showed great improvement compared to the baseline in Table 9.2 (0.88 vs 0.65), particularly on 3.1 Driving safety (20/20) and 4.1 Aggression and anger (19/20). We also performed statistical tests on these three categories and calculated p-values of 0.033, 0.021, and 0.047, indicating statistically significant differences between the results in Tables 9.2 and 9.5. This confirms that breaking down a complex multiclass classification task into multiple independent binary classifications, using simulated posts as ICL examples, and applying majority voting can be effective classification techniques.

Notably, the results for "3.1 Driving safety" (20/20) and "4.1 Aggression and anger" (19/20) are excellent, even comparable to the simpler three-category classification experiments, which demonstrates the effectiveness of our method.

However, we observed a decrease in accuracy for "4.5 Memory loss and confusion" (14/20) compared to prior results. Upon careful review, we found that, while the target category was consistently included in the initial set, the second round of classification often failed to correctly select it as the most likely category. A potential explanation is that "4.5 Memory loss and confusion" is inherently a challenging category, as many ADRD posts contain varying degrees of information related to memory issues, making it difficult to distinguish this category. Future studies could explore advanced techniques to improve the second round of classification, particularly for complex categories like this one.

9.7 Discussions

9.7.1 Insights

Our experiments demonstrated the importance of having data (such as posts) to describe caregivers' needs, especially in the few-shot in-context learning with LLMs. Even though domain experts can provide an accurate definition for each HIW category, having posts that describe caregivers' situations and needs can greatly help the classification.

But our study showed that real posts from caregivers can be problematic to obtain and use. First, it is not difficult to obtain real posts for HIW categories that are common but some HIW categories are rare, so real posts matching to that category can be difficult to obtain. Obtaining simulated posts via human–AI collaboration and using LLMs is a great solution to this problem. Our study showed that it is much cheaper and less time consuming to obtain simulated posts even though human experts still need to verify the simulated posts for their accuracy in content.

Second, our experiments also show that simulated posts can be better examples to be used in few-shot in-context learning for LLMs to perform HIW classification because the verified simulated posts typically focus on more relevant content to the HIW category and contain less irrelevant information compared to real posts. This character of simulated posts again highlights the importance of human–AI collaboration for HIW classification.

Third, given the complexity of the categories we defined, asking the LLM to perform direct multiclass classification on a large number of categories is challenging. Our work offers an alternative approach by breaking down the single multiclass classification task into multiple independent binary classification tasks. Although this method may take more time to run and gather predictions from each task, binary classification tasks are more manageable for LLMs and often result in better overall performance.

Our final insight centers around the randomness and self-consistency in the outputs from LLMs. The literature reported that LLMs can generate different outcomes with the same input, and yet LLMs can show a certain degree of consistency among the variations of its outcomes (Huang et al., 2022). The majority voting idea implemented in our model takes advantage of this feature of LLMs and makes it a technique to further improve our HIW classification. Our experiment demonstrated the effectiveness of this technique and is consistent with the literature.

9.7.2 Limitations and Future Work

Although our method has demonstrated effectiveness in the ADRD-HIWs classification task, this technique has several limitations. First, because of the significant cost of manual annotation, our dataset has only three HIWs with twenty annotated posts for each category. Due to the limited dataset size, the evaluation performance was less conclusive than it would have been with a larger dataset. Future research would greatly benefit from a larger sample of posts that cover a broader range of HIWs caregivers may encounter. Secondly, our methods only explored limited variations in majority voting (n = 5) and system prompts. Future work could investigate adjusting the number of majority votes and experimenting with different system prompts. Thirdly, the classification performance on certain categories, like "4.5 Memory loss and confusion," as shown in Table 9.5, was unsatisfactory. Thus, more advanced classification techniques could be incorporated into the second round of classification to improve performance.

9.8 Conclusions

In this chapter, we introduce a human–AI collaboration approach for identifying caregivers' Health Information Wants (HIWs) in the context of dementia care. We establish an interactive collaboration pipeline that allows human experts to leverage the capabilities of advanced AI techniques. Specifically, we employ GPT-4o as the LLM to extract domain-specific health knowledge for constructing a HIWs classification system. A key innovation of our work is the use of simulated posts generated by GPT-4o, which are then verified by professional clinicians to create example templates. This novel approach to human–AI collaboration enables our experts to benefit from high-quality AI-generated content, significantly reducing the manual effort required for annotation, and verified posts can help LLM improve classification accuracy in return. Additionally, we explore methods such as in-context learning, majority voting, customized system prompts, and dividing complex multiclass classification tasks into multiple independent binary classifications. Through a series of experiments, we demonstrate the effectiveness of these combined methods in improving classification performance. Our findings provide valuable insights into human–AI collaboration, particularly in health-related domains, offering a promising framework for future research in this area.

Acknowledgements

Research reported in this publication was supported by the National Institute on Aging of the National Institutes of Health under Award Number R56AG075770. The content is solely the responsibility of the authors and does not necessarily represent the official views of the National Institutes of Health. The authors wish to thank Dr. Robin Hilsabeck from the University of Texas Health Science Center at San Antonio, Alyssa Aguirre in the Dell Medical School at the University of Texas at Austin, Dr. Catherine Cubbin from the Steve Hicks School of Social Work at University of Texas at Austin for developing the ADRD-HIW daily care framework and helping identify relevant social media posts, and Dr. John Bellquist from the Cain Center for Nursing Research in the School of Nursing at the University of Texas at Austin for his professional editing assistance.

References

Adams, S. J., Henderson, R. D., Yi, X., & Babyn, P. (2021). Artificial Intelligence Solutions for Analysis of X-ray Images. *Canadian Association of Radiologists Journal, 72*(1), 60–72.

Aguirre, A., Hilsabeck, R., Smith, T., Xie, B., He, D., Wang, Z., & Zou, N. (2024). Assessing the Quality of ChatGPT Responses to Dementia Caregivers' Questions: Qualitative Analysis. *JMIR Aging, 7*, Article e53019.

Alzheimer's Association (2022). 2022 Alzheimer's Disease Facts and Figures. *Alzheimer's & Dementia, 18*(4), 700–789.

Bansal, G., Nushi, B., Kamar, E., Horvitz, E., & Weld, D. S. (2021, May). Is the Mmost Accurate AI the Best Teammate? Optimizing AI for Teamwork. *Proceedings of the AAAI Conference on Artificial Intelligence, 35*(13), 11405–11414.

Beisecker, A. E., & Beisecker, T. D. (1990). Patient Information-seeking Behaviors when Communicating with Doctors. *Medical Care, 28*(1), 19–28.

Benbassat, J., Pilpel, D., & Tidhar, M. (1998). Patients' Preferences for Participation in Clinical Decision Making: A Review of Published Surveys. *Behavioral Medicine, 24*(2), 81–88.

Bressan, V., Visintini, C., & Palese, A. (2020). What Do Family Caregivers of People with Dementia Need? A Mixed-method Systematic Review. *Health and Social Care in the Community, 28*(6), 1942–1960.

Brown, T. B., Mann, B., Ryder, N., Subbiah, M., Kaplan, J. D., Dhariwal, P., Neelakantan, A., Shyam, P., Sastry, G., Askell, A., Agarwal, S., Herbert-Voss, H., Krueger, G., Henighan, T., Child, R., Ramesh, A., Ziegler, D. M., Wu, J., Winter, C., ... Amodei, D. (2020). Language Models Are Few-shot Learners. In H. Larochelle, M. Ranzato, R. Hadsell, M. F. Balcan, & H. Lin (eds.), *NIPS'20: Proceedings of the 34th International Conference on Neural Information Processing Systems* (pp. 1877–1901). Curran Associates.

Charles, C., Gafni, A., & Whelan, T. (1999). Decision-making in the Physician–Patient Encounter: Revisiting the Shared Treatment Decision-making Model. *Social Science & Medicine, 49*(5), 651–661.

Chi, Y., He, D., & Jeng, W. (2020). Laypeople's Source Selection in Online Health Information-seeking Process. *Journal of the Association for Information Science and Technology, 71*(12), 1484–1499.

Chi, Y., Thaker, K., He, D., Hui, V., Donovan, H., Brusilovsky, P., & Lee, Y. J. (2022). Knowledge Acquisition and Social Support in Online Health Communities: Analysis of an Online Ovarian Cancer Community. *JMIR Cancer, 8*(3), Article e39643.

De Santis, E., Martino, A., Ronci, F., & Rizzi, A. (2024). From Bag-of-Words to Transformers: A Comparative Study for Text Classification in Healthcare Discussions in Social Media. *IEEE Transactions on Emerging Topics in Computational Intelligence, 9*(1), 1063–1077.

Dong, Q., Li, L., Dai, D., Zheng, C., Ma, J., Li, R., Xia, H., Xu, J. Wu, Z., Chang, B., Sun, X., Li, L., & Sui, Z. (2022, June 18). A Survey on In-context Learning [arXiv preprint]. arXiv:2301.00234.

Ende, J., Kazis, L., Ash, A., & Moskowitz, M. A. (1989). Measuring Patients' Desire for Autonomy: Decision Making and Information-Seeking Preferences among Medical Patients. *Journal of General Internal Medicine, 4*, 23–30.

Epstein, R. M., Alper, B. S., & Quill, T. E. (2004). Communicating Evidence for Participatory Decision Making. *JAMA, 291*(19), 2359–2366.

Esteva, A., Robicquet, A., Ramsundar, B., Kuleshov, V., DePristo, M., Chou, K., ... & Dean, J. (2019). A Guide to Deep Learning in Healthcare. *Nature Medicine, 25*(1), 24–29.

Ferraris, G., Monzani, D., Coppini, V., Conti, L., Pizzoli, S. F. M., Grasso, R., & Pravettoni, G. (2023). Barriers to and Facilitators of Online Health Information-seeking Behaviours among Cancer Patients: A Systematic Review. *Digital Health, 9*, Article 20552076231210663.

González-Fraile, E., Ballesteros, J., Rueda, J.-R., Santos-Zorrozúa, B., Solà, I., & McCleery, J. (2021). Remotely Delivered Information, Training and Support for Informal Caregivers of People with Dementia. *Cochrane Database of Systematic Reviews*. https://doi.org/10.1002/14651858.CD006440.pub3.

Goodman, L. A. (1961). Snowball Sampling. *The Annals of Mathematical Statistics, 32*, 148–170.

Guo, Y., Ovadje, A., Al-Garadi, M. A., & Sarker, A. (2024). Evaluating Large Language Models for Health-related Text Classification Tasks with Public Social Media Data. *Journal of the American Medical Informatics Association, 31*(10), 2181–2189.

Habehh, H., & Gohel, S. (2021). Machine Learning in Healthcare. *Current Genomics, 22*(4), 291–300.

Harrington, N. G., & Noar, S. M. (2012). Reporting Standards for Studies of Tailored Interventions. *Health Education Research, 27*(2), 331–342.

Hemmer, P., Schemmer, M., Riefle, L., Rosellen, N., Vössing, M., & Kühl, N. (2022). Factors That Influence the Adoption of Human–AI Collaboration in Clinical Decision-making [arXiv preprint]. arXiv:2204.09082.

Huang, J., Gu, S. S., Hou, L., Wu, Y., Wang, X., Yu, H., & Han, J. (2023, December). Large Language Models Can Self-Improve. In *Proceedings of the 2023 Conference on Empirical Methods in Natural Language Processing* (pp. 1051–1068).

Hubbard, P. (2008). Here, There, Everywhere. The Ubiquitous Geographies of Heteronormativity. *Geography Compass, 2*(3), 640–658.

Hui, V., Wang, Y., Kunsuk, H., Donovan, H., Brusilovsky, P., He, D., & Lee, Y. J. (2024). Towards Building an e-Librarian System: Exploring Recommendation System Preferences among Ovarian Cancer Patients and Caregivers. In G. Strudwick, N. R. Hardiker, G. Rees, R. Cook, & Y. J. Lee (eds.), Studies in Health Technology and Informatics: Vol. 315. Innovation in Applied Nursing Informatics (pp. 746–747). IOS Press.

Ji, Y., Zou, N., Xie, B., He, D., & Wang, Z. (2022). Automatic Classification of ADRD Caregivers' Online Information Wants: A Machine Learning Approach. *Innovation in Aging, 6*(Suppl. 1), 485.

Jiang, F., Jiang, Y., Zhi, H., Dong, Y., Li, H., Ma, S., Wang, Y., Dong, Q., Shen, H., & Wang, Y. (2017). Artificial Intelligence in Healthcare: Past, Present and Future. *Stroke and Vascular Neurology, 2*(4), 230–243.

Kent, E. E., Rowland, J. H., Northouse, L., Litzelman, K., Chou, W.-Y. S., Shelburne, N., Timura, C., O'Mara, A., & Huss, K. (2016). Caring for Caregivers and Patients: Research and Clinical Priorities for Informal Cancer Caregiving. *Cancer, 122*(13), 1987–1995.

Kung, T. H., Cheatham, M., Medenilla, A., Sillos, C., De Leon, L., Elepaño, C., ... & Tseng, V. (2023). Performance of ChatGPT on USMLE: Potential for AI-assisted Medical Education Using Large Language Models. *PLoS Digital Health*, *2*(2), e0000198.

Lai, Y., Kankanhalli, A., & Ong, D. C. (2021). Human–AI Collaboration in Healthcare: A Review and Research Agenda. In T. X. Bui (ed.), *Proceedings of the 54th Hawaii International Conference on System Sciences* (pp. 390–399). University of Hawaii at Manoa, Department of IT Management.

Li, T., Ma, X., Zhuang, A., Gu, Y., Su, Y., & Chen, W. (2023). Few-shot In-context Learning for Knowledge Base Question Answering [arXiv preprint]. arXiv:2305.01750.

Li, Y., Zhao, W., Dang, B., Yan, X., Gao, M., Wang, W., & Xiao, M. (2024, June). Research on Adverse Drug Reaction Prediction Model Combining Knowledge Graph Embedding and Deep Learning. In *2024 4th International Conference on Machine Learning and Intelligent Systems Engineering (MLISE)* (pp. 322–329). IEEE.

Li, Z., Thaker, K., & He, D. (2023, October). SiaKey: A Method for Improving Few-shot Learning with Clinical Domain Information. In *2023 IEEE EMBS International Conference on Biomedical and Health Informatics (BHI)* (pp. 1–4). IEEE.

Li, Z., Xie, B., Hilsabeck, R., Aguirre, A., Zou, N., Luo, Z., & He, D. (2024, April 5). Effects of Different Prompts on the Quality of GPT-4 Responses to Dementia Care Questions. In *2024 IEEE 12th International Conference on Healthcare Informatics (ICHI)* (pp. 412–417). IEEE.

Licklider, J. C. R. (1960). Man–Computer Symbiosis. *IRE Transactions on Human Factors in Electronics*, *HFE-1*(1), 4–11.

Liu, Z., Huang, Y., Yu, X., Zhang, L., Wu, Z., Cao, C., ... & Li, X. (2023). Deid-gpt: Zero-shot Medical Text De-identification by Gpt-4 [arXiv preprint]. arXiv:2303.11032.

Magrabi, F., Ammenwerth, E., McNair, J. B., De Keizer, N. F., Hyppönen, H., Nykänen, P., ... & Georgiou, A. (2019). Artificial Intelligence in Clinical Decision Support: Challenges for Evaluating AI and Practical Implications. *Yearbook of Medical Informatics*, *28*(1), 128–134.

Markus, A. F., Kors, J. A., & Rijnbeek, P. R. (2021). The Role of Explainability in Creating Trustworthy Artificial Intelligence for Health Care: A Comprehensive Survey of the Terminology, Design Choices, and Evaluation Strategies. *Journal of Biomedical Informatics*, *113*, Article 103655.

Moor, M., Banerjee, O., Abad, Z. S. H., Krumholz, H. M., Leskovec, J., Topol, E. J., & Rajpurkar, P. (2023). Foundation Models for Generalist Medical Artificial Intelligence. *Nature*, *616*(7956), 259–265.

Nie, L., Xie, B., Yang, Y., & Shan, Y. M. (2016). Characteristics of Chinese m-Health Applications for Diabetes Self-management. *Telemedicine and e-Health*, *22*(7), 614–619.

Nori, H., King, N., McKinney, S. M., Carignan, D., & Horvitz, E. (2023). Capabilities of GPT-4 on Medical Challenge Problems [arXiv preprint]. arXiv:2303.13375

Open AI, Achiam, J., Adler, S., Agarwal, S., Ahmad, L., Akkaya, I., Aleman, F. L., Almeida, D., Altenschmidt, J., Altman, S., Anadkat, S., Avila, R., Babuschkin, I.,

Balaji, S., Balcom, V., Baltescu, P., Bao, H., Bavarian, M., Begum, J., ... Zoph, B. (2023, March 15). Gpt-4 Technical Report [arXiv preprint]. arXiv:2303.08774.

Peterson, K., Hahn, H., Lee, A. J., Madison, C. A., & Atri, A. (2016). In the Information Age, Do Dementia Caregivers Get the Information They Need? Semi-structured Interviews to Determine Informal Caregivers' Education Needs, Barriers, and Preferences. *BMC Geriatrics, 16*, Article 164.

Reid, B., & O'Brien, L. (2021). The Psychological Effects of Caring for a Family Member with Dementia. *Nursing Older People, 33*(6), 21–27.

Reifegerste, J., Meyer, A. S., Zwitserlood, P., & Ullman, M. T. (2021). Aging Affects Steaks More Than Knives: Evidence That the Processing of Words Related to Motor Skills Is Relatively Spared in Aging. *Brain and Language, 218*, Article 104941.

Shaheen, M. Y. (2021, September 25). Applications of Artificial Intelligence (AI) in Healthcare: A Review [ScienceOpen Preprints].

Shin, J. Y., & Habermann, B. (2022). Caregivers of Adults Living with Alzheimer's Disease or Dementia in 2020: A Secondary Analysis. *Journal of Gerontological Nursing, 48*(9), 15–25.

Shneiderman, B., & Plaisant, C. (2009). *Designing the User Interface: Strategies for Effective Human–Computer Interaction*, 5th ed. Addison-Wesley.

Shu, S., & Woo, B. K. P. (2021). Use of Technology and Social Media in Dementia Care: Current and Future Directions. *World Journal of Psychiatry, 11*(4), 109–123.

Sivarajkumar, S., & Wang, Y. (2023, April). HealthPrompt: A Zero-shot Learning Paradigm for Clinical Natural Language Processing. In *AMIA Annual Symposium Proceedings* (Vol. 2022, p. 972).

Song, Y., Zhang, J., Tian, Z., Yang, Y., Huang, M., & Li, D. (2024, February 26). LLM-based Privacy Data Augmentation Guided by Knowledge Distillation with a Distribution Tutor for Medical Text Classification [arXiv preprint]. arXiv:2402.16515.

Soong, A., Au, S. T., Kyaw, B. M., Theng, Y. L., & Car L. T. (2020). Information Needs and Information Seeking Behaviour of People with Dementia and Their Non-professional Caregivers: A Scoping Review. *BMC Geriatrics, 20*, Article 61.

Tang, A. Y., Kwak, J., Xiao, L., Xie, B., Lahiri, S., Flynn, O. A., & Murugadass, A. (2023). Online Health Information Wants of Caregivers for Persons with Dementia in Social Media. *SAGE Open, 13*(4), 21582440231205367.

Thaker, K., Rahadari, B., Hui, V., Luo, Z., Wang, Y., Brusilovsky, P., He, D., Donovan, H., & Lee, Y. J. (2024). HELPeR: Interface Design Decision and Evaluation. In G. Strudwick, N. R. Hardiker, G. Rees, R. Cook, & Y. J. Lee (eds.), *Studies in Heath Technology and Informatics: Vol. 315. Innovation in Applied Nursing Informatics* (pp. 750–751). IOS Press.

Wang, D., Churchill, E., Maes, P., Fan, X., Shneiderman, B., Shi, Y., & Wang, Q. (2020, April). From Human–Human Collaboration to Human–AI Collaboration: Designing AI Systems That Can Work Together with People. In *CHI EA'20: Extended Abstracts of the 2020 CHI Conference on Human Factors in Computing Systems*. Association for Computing Machinery.

Wang, Y., Thaker, K., Hui, V., Brusilovsky, P., He, D., Donovan, H., & Lee, Y. J. (2024). Utilizing Digital Twin to Create Personas Representing Ovarian Cancer

Patients and Their Families. In G. Strudwick, N. R. Hardiker, G. Rees, R. Cook, & Y. J. Lee (eds.), *Studies in Health Technology and Informatics: Vol. 315. Innovation in Applied Nursing Informatics* (pp. 754–756). IOS Press.

Wang, Z., Zou, N., Xie, B., Luo, Z., He, D., Hilsabeck, R. C., & Aguirre, A. (2021). Characterizing Dementia Caregivers' Information Exchange on Social Media: Exploring an Expert–Machine Co-development Process. In K. Toeppe, H. Yan, & S. K. W. Chu (eds.), *Diversity, Divergence, Dialogue: 16th International Conference, iConference 2021, Beijing, China, March 17–31, 2021, Proceedings,* Part I (pp. 47–67). Springer-Verlag.

Wu, C., Fang, W., Dai, F., & Yin, H. (2023, October). A Model Ensemble Approach with LLM for Chinese Text Classification. In H. Xu, Q. Chen, H. Lin, F. Wu, L. Liu, B. Tang, T. Hao, Z. Huang, J. Lei, Z. Li, & H. Zong (eds.), *CHIP 2023: Communications in Computer and Information Science,* Vol 2080 (pp. 214–230). Springer Singapore.

Wu, T., He, S., Liu, J., Sun, S., Liu, K., Han, Q.-L., & Tang, Y. (2023). A Brief Overview of ChatGPT: The History, Status Quo and Potential Future Development. *IEEE/CAA Journal of Automatica Sinica, 10*(5), 1122–1136.

Xie, B. (2009). Older Adults' Health Information Wants in the Internet Age: Implications for Patient–Provider Relationships. *Journal of Health Communication, 14*(6), 510–524.

Xie, B., Berkley, A., Kwak, J., Fleischmann, K. R., Champion, J. D., & Koltai, K. (2018). End-of-Life Decision Making by Family Caregivers of Persons with Advanced Dementia: A Literature Review of Decision Aids. *SAGE Open Medicine, 6,* 1–9.

Xie, B., Su, Z., Liu, Y., Wang, M., & Zhang, M. (2017). Health Information Sources for Different Types of Information Used by Chinese Patients with Cancer and Their Family Caregivers. *Health Expectations, 20*(4), 665–674.

Xie, B., Wang, M., Feldman, R., & Zhou, L. (2010, November). Health Information and Decision-making Preferences in the Internet Age: A Pilot Study Using the Health Information Wants (HIW) Questionnaire. In *Proceedings of the 1st ACM International Health Informatics Symposium* (pp. 610–619).

Xie, B., Wang, Z., Zou, N., Luo, Z., Hilsabeck, R., & Aguirre, A. (2020). Detecting ADRD Caregivers' Information Wants in Social Media: A Machine Learning-Aided Approach. *Innovation in Aging, 4*(Suppl 1), 656.

Zhao, Y. C., Zhao, M., & Song, S. (2022). Online Health Information Seeking Behaviors among Older Adults: Systematic Scoping Review. *Journal of Medical Internet Research, 24*(2), Article e34790.

Zheng, M., Pei, J., & Jurgens, D. (2023, November 16). Is "A Helpful Assistant" the Best Role for Large Language Models? A Systematic Evaluation of Social Roles in System Prompts [arXiv preprint]. arXiv:2311.10054, 8.

Zou, N., Ji, Y., Xie, B., He, D., & Luo, Z. (2023, March). Mapping Dementia Caregivers' Comments on Social Media with Evidence-based Care Strategies for Memory Loss and Confusion. In *CHIR'23: Proceedings of the 2023 Conference on Human Information Interaction and Retrieval* (pp. 362–367).

Zou, N., Thaker, K., & He, D. (2023). A Preliminary Study of Ovarian Cancer Caregivers' Health Information Seeking on Social Media. *Proceedings of the Association for Information Science and Technology, 60*(1), 1230–1232.

10

Human–AI Collaboration for Scientific Discovery

Shuo Zhao, Yang Liu, Jiayu Wan, Tan Tang, and Xin Li

10.1 Introduction

10.1.1 Introduction of Artificial Intelligence

Artificial intelligence (AI) is defined as "the science and engineering of making intelligent machines" (McCarthy et al., 2006). It is a branch of computer technology that enables machines to simulate human intelligence and problem-solving capabilities. The concept of AI first emerged in Alan Turing's renowned article (Turing, 1950), where he introduced the term "machinery intelligence." The formal terminology was established during the Dartmouth Conference in 1956 (McCarthy et al., 2006), an event recognized as the birth of AI.

Over the decades, AI technology has undergone several cycles of hype and setbacks. In its early stage (1950s–1960s), foundational algorithms were developed that laid the groundwork for many of today's advancements in AI. These algorithms can be broadly classified into two categories: symbolism and connectionism (Smolensky, 1987). Symbolism, also known as symbolic AI, represented knowledge through symbols and rules, using logic and formal reasoning to manipulate these symbols. This approach excelled in tasks requiring clear and structured knowledge, such as theorem proving and game playing. On the other hand, connectionism, or connectionist AI, sought to model the interconnected neurons in brains and aimed to create artificial neural networks (NNs) capable of learning from data.

During this stage, AI technologies were often criticized for addressing what were deemed as "toy problems." As a famous example, the early connectionism model cannot learn the XOR function (Minsky & Papert, 1969). Such critical limitations led to skepticism about the general capabilities of AI. For instance, the Automatic Language Processing Advisory Committee (ALPAC) of the United States stated in its 1966 report that "fully automatic high-quality machine translation was not going to be realized for a long time" (Pierce & Carroll, 1966). AI at this stage was akin to human childhood, with its capabilities constrained by limited computational resources and immature reasoning abilities.

In the 1980s, expert systems, a pinnacle of symbolic AI, experienced a significant rise in popularity as the first truly commercial application of AI research and development. Unlike earlier symbolic AI, which relied solely on formal logical expressions, expert systems incorporated expert knowledge by encoding it into a set of rules and heuristics applicable to specific tasks (Waterman, 1985). Utilizing inference engines, these systems could reason through complex problems and provide solutions based on accumulated knowledge. At this stage, AI functioned like a specialist, capable of handling domain-specific applications with a high degree of expertise while being limited in other areas.

As a major limitation of expert systems, they can only solve "well-defined" problems within a narrow domain. Namely, if a human expert can articulate the steps of reasoning to solve a problem, an expert system can replicate this process. However, if the reasoning cannot be explicitly explained, the expert system cannot be applied to the problem effectively. To overcome this limitation, data-driven approaches, particularly NNs, have been adopted. NNs mimic the structure and function of human brains, consisting of interconnected layers of nodes (i.e., neurons). Each node processes input data and passes the result to the next layer, gradually refining the information through multiple layers and eventually producing the final output. Unlike expert systems, NNs can learn from large datasets, identifying patterns and making predictions without the need for any explicit rule-based programming.

Although the idea of NNs was proposed much earlier – such as the basic model of a single neuron developed in 1958 (Rosenblatt, 1958) and the backpropagation algorithm for optimizing parameters in multi-layer networks derived in 1982 (Werbos, 1994) – it did not gain extreme popularity until the 2010s. The surge in its popularity was driven by dramatic advancements in computing capabilities and the availability of large-scale datasets. These conditions enabled deep NNs (DNNs), which consist of hundreds of layers and billions of parameters. As a result, NNs began to achieve superior performance over humans across various domains, including object detection, speech recognition, language processing, etc., thereby leading to the advent of the era of deep learning (DL), which continues to thrive today.

Despite the remarkable advancements in DL technologies, the emergence of large language models (LLMs) stands out as the most exciting accomplishment in recent years. These models are trained in an auto-regressive manner on large-scale corpora, predicting the next word in a sentence based on the context of preceding words. Its training process is enhanced by reinforcement learning from human feedback (RLHF), where human evaluators provide feedback to refine the model responses, aligning them closely with human expectations (Ouyang et al., 2022). As a result, LLMs can understand given instructions and generate human-like text with impressive accuracy. The capabilities of LLMs extend far beyond basic text generation. They can perform a wide range of natural language processing NLP tasks such as translation, summarization, question-answering, and even creative writing and coding. Their ability to understand context and generate coherent and contextually appropriate responses makes them incredibly versatile tools. Moreover, LLMs hold significant potential in the pursuit of artificial general intelligence (AGI). Their comprehensive cognitive abilities showcase the remarkable progresses toward machines that can understand, learn, and apply knowledge across a wide range of tasks at a level comparable to human intelligence.

10.1.2 Model Architectures and Learning Schemes

To explore human–AI collaboration for scientific discovery, it is essential to understand the popular AI model architectures and various learning schemes. Such knowledge allows us to appreciate how AI can be leveraged in scientific research and how these technologies can be tailored to address specific scientific problems. Given that DL dominates AI applications today, we will focus on the relevant topics for DL in this section.

A number of popular architectures have emerged as the foundational models in the DL era, each designed to address specific tasks. Convolutional neural networks (CNNs) are widely used for image and video processing due to their ability to capture spatial hierarchies through convolutional layers (LeCun et al., 1989). Recurrent neural networks (RNNs) are designed for sequential data (Pearlmutter, 1989), such as time series or natural language, and can retain information across long sequences, making them ideal for tasks like language modeling and translation. Graph neural networks (GNNs) excel in handling graph-structured data (Scarselli et al., 2008), consisting of nodes and edges, allowing for effective processing of relationships and interactions within data points, which is particularly useful in social network analysis and molecular biology (Li et al., 2022).

Self-attention-based models, particularly the transformer architecture, have revolutionized NLP technologies (Vaswani et al., 2017). Transformers utilize self-attention mechanisms to weigh the importance of different words in a sentence when making predictions, allowing for the modeling of long-range dependencies and the parallel processing of sequences. This has led to highly versatile and powerful language models, such as generative pretrained transformers (GPTs). Additionally, self-attention has been adapted into vision transformers (ViTs) for image recognition, demonstrating superior performance over traditional CNNs in standard benchmarks (Dosovitskiy et al., 2021).

Diffusion models represent another innovative architecture (Sohl-Dickstein et al., 2015), particularly in the field of generative modeling. These models simulate the process of data generation through a sequence of steps that gradually add and then remove noises from the data, effectively "diffusing" and then "denoising" the data to generate new samples. Diffusion models have shown remarkable success in generating high-quality images and have been applied to other areas such as audio and video generation. Their ability to model complex data distributions makes them powerful tools for a variety of generative tasks.

In addition to the various architectures of AI models, a variety of powerful learning schemes enable machines to learn from a vast amount of data and make intelligent decisions. These schemes are classified based on the nature of the training data and the learning objectives, distinguishing them into different categories such as supervised, unsupervised, semi-supervised, reinforcement, and transfer learning (LeCun et al., 2015). Supervised learning involves training an AI model on a labeled dataset, where the input data is paired with the correct output. It is highly effective for tasks like classification and regression. Unsupervised learning, on the other hand, deals with unlabeled data, allowing an AI model to identify patterns and relationships within the data on its own, which makes it suitable for clustering and dimensionality reduction tasks. Semi-supervised learning combines both supervised and unsupervised learning by using a small amount of labeled data alongside a large amount of unlabeled data to improve learning efficiency and accuracy. Transfer learning leverages pre-trained models for new tasks, saving time and resources. Additionally, reinforcement learning is a unique scheme where an AI agent learns by interacting with its environment, receiving rewards or penalties based on its actions, which makes it particularly powerful for sequential decision-making problems and tasks that require long-term planning. These schemes collectively empower AI models to tackle a wide array of complex problems, from image and speech recognition to NLP and beyond.

10.1.3 Early Human–AI Collaboration in Science

Scientific discovery is one of the most exhilarating and profoundly creative endeavors of human intelligence. It demands a profound mastery of existing knowledge, meticulous observation of natural phenomena or experimental data, strong and insightful cognition of new facts and boundless imagination to conceive underlying mechanisms. The integration of AI into scientific research is a powerful testament to the extreme capabilities and potential of AI technologies. This journey has a rich history, full of triumphs and breakthroughs. In this section, we delve into the landmark achievements of the pre-DL era (before the 2010s), celebrating the milestones that paved the way. The revolutionary cases from the DL era will be further explored in Section 10.1.4.

As mentioned previously, early AI (1950s~1960s) had quite limited capabilities. The primary efforts to apply AI in scientific research during this period focused on theorem proving. The first theorem-proving program, Logic Theorist, was developed in 1956 (Siekmann & Wrightson, 2012). It proved propositional logic theorems by using axioms and inference rules. It worked not only for numeric expressions but also for symbolic formulas, with proof searching guided by heuristics. Impressively, Logic Theorist proved thirty-eight out of fifty-two theorems in chapter 2 of *Principia Mathematica*. The achievement was further advanced in 1960 when all 350 theorems across nine chapters of *Principia Mathematica* were proved (Wang, 1960).

The 1960s through the 1980s witnessed the rise of expert systems. Expert systems like DENDRAL (Feigenbaum et al., 1970) and MYCIN (Davis et al., 1977) demonstrated the potential of AI to replicate human expertise in specific domains. DENDRAL, developed in the 1960s, was one of the first expert systems designed to assist chemists in identifying unknown organic molecules. MYCIN, developed in the 1970s, was used to diagnose bacterial infections and recommend treatments. These systems relied heavily on symbolic AI and rule-based reasoning, encoding expert knowledge into a set of if–then rules.

Despite the success of expert systems, the reliance on symbolic AI posed significant challenges, particularly the knowledge engineering bottleneck which refers to the labor-intensive process of manually encoding domain-specific knowledge into the system. As scientific knowledge became more complex and dynamic, the limitations of symbolic AI were more pronounced. The need for more scalable and adaptable AI approaches led to the exploration of other alternative methods.

The 1990s marked a paradigm shift in AI research with the emergence of connectionist AI technologies. Unlike symbolic AI, which required explicit programming of rules, connectionist AI enabled systems to learn from data. Techniques such as decision trees, support vector machines, and early NNs began to gain traction in the scientific community. These techniques were applied to deal with the specific steps in a wide range of problems, including genomics (Libbrecht & Noble, 2015), drug discovery (Gertrudes et al., 2012), and so on.

In the pre-DL era, AI was primarily used as a tool to address specific steps in scientific research. Researchers provided explicit instructions for solving domain-specific problems and AI tools operated under human guidance, demonstrating limited autonomy and creativity. The output from AI was generally expected by the researchers. While effective within their constrained domains, these early AI systems lacked the ability to generalize and adapt to broader and complex tasks.

10.1.4 Human–AI Collaboration in Modern Scientific Research

Since 2010, we have been amid an explosive surge in AI technologies, driven by enhanced computing power and large-scale training data. This empowered AI has the capacity to delve deeper and explore broader horizons than human intelligence alone, revolutionizing scientific research across various disciplines. In mathematics, for instance, AI technologies have been harnessed to generate creative code solutions for challenging open problems, offering innovative approaches that were previously unimaginable (Romera-Paredes et al., 2024). These initial solutions are further refined and optimized using genetic algorithms, a process that mimics natural evolution. The aforementioned AI techniques have yielded groundbreaking results, surpassing human achievements on longstanding open mathematical challenges such as the capset problem and the bin-packing problem.

In addition to its capabilities to solve complex problems, AI can also significantly enhance efficiency in scientific research. A notable example is AlphaFold, an AI tool developed by DeepMind, which predicts the 3D structure of proteins (Jumper et al., 2021). Proteins are essential to life, and understanding their structure is crucial for elucidating their function. Traditionally, determining protein structures required years of experimental work using techniques like X-ray crystallography or cryo-electron microscopy. Despite these efforts, only around 100,000 unique protein structures had been determined, representing a small fraction of the billions of known protein sequences. AlphaFold revolutionized this field by providing highly accurate predictions of protein structures within a short time period, dramatically accelerating the pace of biological research. The latest database release by AlphaFold contains over 200 million entries. This breakthrough not only saves time and resources but also opens new possibilities for drug discovery and understanding diseases at a molecular level (Goenka et al., 2022).

The emergence of LLMs has significantly broadened the scope of AI applications in scientific research. Previously, AI algorithms were typically accessed and utilized through programming, limiting their use to technical processes such as data processing and result analysis. However, LLMs enable researchers to interact with AI using natural language, making AI technologies more accessible and extending their utility beyond technical tasks. LLMs can assist with labor-intensive tasks like literature reviews, and even contribute to more creative endeavors, such as proposing hypotheses and designing experiments (Zhao et al., 2024).

In summary, AI has evolved from a mere tool into a vital assistant that supports researchers at every stage of their work. AI systems can rapidly process a vast amount of information, identify patterns that might be challenging for humans to detect, and suggest new avenues for investigation. With the assistance by AI, human researchers can tackle more complex problems, generate deeper insights, and drive scientific innovations more effectively. By combining AI with human intuition and expertise, the human–AI partnership enhances the depth and breadth of scientific research, enabling more innovative and impactful discoveries (Wang et al., 2023).

In the following sections of this chapter, we will explore AI applications across various disciplines, including mathematics, physics, chemistry, and life sciences. These examples will showcase AI technologies in scientific research and illustrate how they can be effectively integrated with human expertise in different fields.

10.2 Human–AI Collaboration in Mathematics

The intersection of AI technology and mathematics represents a transformative collaboration that has significantly accelerated the pace and depth of mathematical discoveries. In this section, we explore how AI aids scientists in mathematical research, highlighting key methodologies, notable achievements, and the evolving dynamics of this partnership.

10.2.1 Automated Theorem Proving

Since the birth of computers, there has been a longstanding desire to make them reason at the level of human thought. This aspiration led to the emergence of automated theorem proving (ATP) systems in the early 1950s, which reached their peak during the 1960s (Russell & Norvig, 2016). These ATP systems are designed to assist, augment, or even independently carry out the process of proving mathematical theorems.

ATP systems operate by converting mathematical premises and proofs into a formal language, such as first-order logic or higher-order logic (Loveland,

2016), that computers can process. These languages provide precise syntax and semantics, allowing unambiguous representation of mathematical ideas. The core of ATP systems, inference engines, then applies logical rules to explore the space of possible proofs that can derive desired conclusions from these premises. Various strategies, such as resolution, term rewriting, and model checking, can be employed at this stage. To navigate through this vast space, sophisticated algorithms, often involving heuristic search techniques like depth-first search, breadth-first search, and A* search, are used. Once a proof is found, ATP systems verify its correctness by checking each logical step against the rules of the formal system, ensuring that the proof is error-free and adheres to mathematical standards.

The focus of ATP systems is on proving the existing theorems. These systems not only ensure rigor but also handle the complexity of lengthy proofs that might be error-prone if done manually. For instance, the proof of the Kepler Conjecture, a centuries-old problem about the densest arrangement of spheres, was formally verified using the HOL Light proof assistant (Harrison, 2013). This collaboration exemplifies how AI can handle the intricate details of mathematical proofs, allowing human mathematicians to focus on higher-level insights and strategies.

10.2.2 Discovery of New Mathematical Conjectures

With the advancement of AI technology, AI can not only provide the proof of existing mathematical theorems, but also propose new conjectures that require validation by human researchers.

Mathematical conjectures are propositions or hypotheses based on limited evidence but have not yet been proven or disproven. They hold significant meanings as they can lead to profound discoveries and advancements in mathematical theory. Famous examples of conjectures include the Goldbach Conjecture, which asserts that every even integer greater than two is the sum of two prime numbers, a conjecture that remains unresolved. Another well-known conjecture is Fermat's Last Theorem, which claims that there are no three positive integers a, b, and c that satisfy the equation $a^n + b^n = c^n$ for any integer value of n greater than two; this conjecture remained unproven for over 350 years until it was finally resolved in 1994 (Wiles, 1995). Such conjectures not only challenge mathematicians but also drive the development of new methods and theories in mathematics.

Conjectures often arise from patterns observed in data and serve as steppingstones for further exploration and proof within the mathematical community. This data-driven aspect is where modern AI technology comes into play.

In light of this, DeepMind, a leading AI research lab, has developed an AI-based framework for discovering new mathematical conjectures (Davies et al., 2021). This framework aims to identify relationships between two mathematical objects, such as whether two properties $X(z)$ and $Y(z)$ associated with a given variable z satisfy a relationship f, formally expressed as $f(X(z)) = Y(z)$.

To achieve this, data samples $(X(z), Y(z))$ are computed and collected. AI models are then trained with $X(z)$ as input and $Y(z)$ as output to learn the relationship f. When the learned relationship $\hat{f}$ is more accurate than what would be expected by chance, it suggests that a valid relationship may exist, warranting further exploration. This framework has successfully been applied to discover new connections in algebraic and geometric structures of knots in Knot Theory and to propose new resolutions for long-standing open conjectures in Representation Theory.

In these cases, AI acts as a creative partner, generating promising conjectures that mathematicians can rigorously test and prove. This collaboration effectively blends human intuition with machine computational power, enhancing the research process.

10.2.3 Optimization of Solutions

The optimization capabilities of AI are another crucial aspect of its collaboration with mathematicians. Problems in number theory, combinatorics, and other fields often require extensive computation to test hypotheses or explore large solution spaces. AI algorithms, particularly those in evolutionary computation and reinforcement learning, excel at optimizing solutions and searching through vast, complex landscapes.

FunSearch (short for "searching in the function space") exemplifies this kind of innovative approaches (Romera-Paredes et al., 2024). Designed for combinatorics problems, FunSearch addresses challenging problems that are difficult to optimize but easy to evaluate. For example, the famous cap set problem involves finding the largest possible set of n-dimensional lattice points such that no three points are collinear. For a large n, brute force methods become impractical due to the exponential growth in the number of possible combinations. However, evaluating whether a given set satisfies the cap set constraint is straightforward by checking the rank of a matrix composed of these points.

To solve the cap set problem, mathematicians have proposed heuristics to decide how to add points to a cap set without violating the constraints. Different heuristics can lead to different solutions, and there is no consensus on what the optimal heuristic should be.

To efficiently explore this vast heuristic space, FunSearch leverages LLMs to generate code that calculates the priority of adding a point to the set. The effectiveness of different priority functions is then evaluated based on the size of the resulting set. Evolutionary algorithms are employed to select the best programs and feed back to the LLMs, generating increasingly improved priority functions. By iterating this process, FunSearch can discover superior solutions that outperform those found by human researchers.

The aforementioned collaboration targets solving problems with unknown optimal solutions. Human experts pinpoint the critical aspects of the problem (i.e., the heuristics), while AI takes on the arduous task of generating new heuristics. Guided by human expertise, AI uses evaluation metrics and evolutionary algorithms to refine its output continuously. This dynamic partnership produces scalable and innovative solutions, pushing the boundaries of what can be achieved in mathematical problem-solving.

10.2.4 Summary

In this section, we review how AI assists mathematicians across various problem types: (1) proving existing theorems with known conclusions, (2) proposing new conjectures, and (3) optimizing solutions for problems with unknown optimality. AI serves not only as a computational and verification tool but also as a means to visualize mathematical structures and explore high-dimensional data, thereby enhancing the mathematical intuition for researchers. It can also offer new perspectives and suggests unconventional approaches, inspiring mathematicians to think beyond traditional paradigms. Currently, human intervention is needed to establish rules, generate training data, and provide guidance. However, as AI continues to advance, future systems may autonomously generate and prove theorems, potentially revolutionizing the field.

10.3 Human–AI Collaboration in Physics

The discovery process in physics traditionally consists of several phases: hypothesis formulation, experimental design, data analysis, and result interpretation. In the conventional research paradigm, each phase relies heavily on human expertise. For instance, the formulation of hypotheses has depended on the intuition and experience of scientists, while experimentation is often complex and resource-intensive, requiring meticulous consideration of numerous variables.

The landscape of physical sciences is undergoing a revolutionary transformation with the emergence of AI. The advancement driven by AI is not confined to any single phase of the scientific discovery process; rather, AI is permeating every stage. AI is enhancing the precision, efficiency, and scope of scientific research, enabling discoveries that were previously unimaginable (Karagiorgi et al., 2022; Karniadakis et al., 2021).

10.3.1 Efficient Data Analysis and Interpretation

One of the primary ways AI assists scientists is through advanced data analysis and interpretation. Physical sciences often involve complex datasets that are challenging to analyze manually. AI algorithms excel at sifting through these large datasets to uncover hidden patterns and correlations.

The discovery of Higgs boson (Chatrchyan et al., 2012) is a notable example of how AI played a crucial role in physics research. The Higgs boson, also referred to as the "God particle," is a fundamental particle associated with the Higgs field, which gives other particles their mass. Studying particles like the Higgs boson requires colliding them at extremely high energies to reveal the fundamental components of matter and the forces that govern their interactions. By analyzing the particles produced in these high-energy collisions, physicists can test and validate theoretical models, explore the properties of elementary particles, and uncover new physics beyond the Standard Model.

One of the most significant tools for this research is the Large Hadron Collider (LHC), the world's largest and most powerful particle accelerator, located at European Organization for Nuclear Research (CERN). Within seconds of a collision at LHC, data from millions of sensors are recorded. The data rate – over sixty terabytes per second – is too great to be entirely written to disk. To manage this challenge, a trigger system is employed to keep only the data events that are interesting enough, targeting specific configurations of particles consistent with a physics process of interest. At the high-level trigger stage, RNNs are used to predict the physical quantity of the particles based on the spatial and temporal signals collected from sensors. If the prediction matches the predefined criteria for events of interest, the data is deemed interesting enough to keep. As such, the overwhelming majority of events produced during the collision can be rejected.

Despite this filtering, analyzing the remaining data manually would still be an overwhelming task due to its sheer volume and complexity (Andreassen et al., 2020). Detecting the Higgs boson involved identifying a very specific set of collision events among the remaining immense amount of data. To achieve this, a special clustering algorithm, named particle flow, was designed to sift through the vast quantities of collision data and identify patterns and events that might indicate the presence of new particles or unusual phenomena.

Furthermore, GNNs have emerged as a powerful tool for further data interpretation (DeZoort et al., 2023). Events recorded by the sensors of LHC can be naturally represented as graphs, where nodes correspond to individual particles or detector hits, and edges represent the spatial or temporal relationships between them. GNNs leverage this graph structure to effectively capture the complex dependencies and interactions inherent in collision data. By using GNNs, researchers can enhance the accuracy of particle tracking and identification, improve the resolution of reconstructed events, and distinguish between signals of interests and background noises with greater precision. For example, GNNs can be applied to track reconstruction tasks, where they help to connect discrete hits into coherent particle trajectories, even in densely populated environments.

As exemplified by the applications of AI at the LHC, its strong computational power and high efficiency enable the effective analysis and interpretation of large-scale experimental data. This allows researchers to focus on innovative tasks, such as discovering new particles, thereby driving scientific innovations and breakthroughs.

10.3.2 Optimized Experimental Design

In addition to the labor-intensive aspects of data analysis, AI can further significantly enhance other intelligent tasks, such as experimental design for scientific discoveries in physics. Take nuclear fusion as an example. Nuclear fusion is a process where two light atomic nuclei combine to form a heavier nucleus, releasing a tremendous amount of energy. It is the same reaction that powers the sun and stars, making it a potentially limitless and clean source of energy. Fusion offers significant advantages over nuclear fission, which involves splitting heavy atomic nuclei and is currently used in nuclear power plants. Unlike fission, fusion produces minimal radioactive waste, poses no risk of catastrophic meltdowns, and uses abundant fuel sources like hydrogen isotopes.

In the context of nuclear fusion, plasma – the fourth state of matter consisting of charged particles – plays a central role. Plasma must be confined and controlled within a fusion reactor to sustain the fusion reactions. It is crucial to control plasma shapes for optimizing the performance and stability of the fusion reaction. However, maintaining the high-temperature plasma within a tokamak – a device essential for confining plasma using magnetic fields – poses a significant challenge. Traditional methods involve controlling multiple time-varying, non-linear variables and precomputing a set of feedforward coil currents and voltages to manage plasma position, current, and shape. While effective, this method demands extensive design effort and expertise, especially when being applied to new plasma configurations.

Recent advancements have shown that AI, specifically deep reinforcement learning (RL), can revolutionize this process (Degrave et al., 2022). The RL-based approach uses an NN to represent the controlling policy, which is essentially a strategy for managing the magnetic coils in response to the state of the plasma. The training is guided by a reward system designed to maintain the desired plasma shapes, achieving stable confinement and optimizing performance. Through a process known as trial and error, the NN interacts with the simulation environment. It takes actions, observes results, receives rewards or penalties, and adjusts its policy to improve performance. Once the NN has been sufficiently trained by the simulator, its control policies are transferred to an actual tokamak. Experiments conducted on the actual tokamak showcased the efficacy of the RL controller in achieving accurate plasma control across a variety of configurations.

Such applications of AI not only optimize experimental design but also push the boundaries and accelerate the long journey of physical discoveries. As one plasma physicist noted, "AI would enable us to explore things that we wouldn't explore otherwise, because we can take risks with this kind of control system we wouldn't dare take otherwise."

10.3.3 Summary

In summary, AI has woven itself into every stage of physical discovery, from the intricate design of experiments to the analysis of vast datasets, and the interpretation of results. Its remarkable advancements have transformed the landscape of scientific research, dramatically enhancing the precision and efficiency with which we handle and interpret complex data. Yet, despite these technological strides, AI cannot replace the ingenuity of physicists, particularly in the creative and intuitive process of hypothesis formulation. This stage remains deeply rooted in human insight and imagination, areas where AI still has limited capabilities. The synergy between AI and physicists not only accelerates scientific progress and uncovers new frontiers but also highlights the irreplaceable value of human expertise in steering and shaping research.

10.4 Human–AI Collaboration in Chemistry

Chemistry fundamentally relies on meticulous experimentation and analysis. In the traditional research paradigm, chemists have spent countless hours in laboratories conducting experiments, analyzing results, and drawing conclusions to further their understanding of chemical processes and phenomena. However, human labor, while indispensable, is prone to errors and inconsistencies. Furthermore, the sheer volume and complexity of data generated in modern chemical research can overwhelm human capacity for accurate and efficient analysis.

The integration of AI into the field of chemistry has revolutionized the research paradigm. By leveraging AI, chemists can automate data collection and analysis, enhance predictive modeling, and optimize experimental workflows (Rohrbach et al., 2022; Sanchez-Lengeling & Aspuru-Guzik, 2018; Segler et al., 2018). This not only reduces the risk of human error but also significantly accelerates the pace of discovery (Baum et al., 2021). In this section, we explore the various ways in which scientists collaborate with AI to advance chemistry discoveries.

10.4.1 Automated Data Collection

Datasets are the cornerstone of chemistry research, providing the essential information needed to understand chemical reactions, properties, and behaviors. Comprehensive and accurate datasets enable chemists to identify patterns, validate hypotheses, and predict outcomes, driving scientific discovery and innovation.

Chemical data can originate from a variety of sources, including laboratory experiments and computational simulations. These data are ultimately recorded in the literature, such as scientific articles and reports. Collecting and curating the valuable information from dispersed sources is time-consuming and resource-intensive. Furthermore, human errors in manual data entry, measurement inconsistencies, and variations in experimental conditions can result in unreliable datasets.

AI attacks many of these challenges by automating the data collection process and enhancing the quality and comprehensiveness of datasets. One notable example is the use of NLP techniques to extract chemical synthesis procedures from millions of materials science papers (Kononova et al., 2019). In this text-mining pipeline, paragraphs related to solid-state synthesis are first identified from a vast number of articles using a random forest classifier, which is trained on topics extracted by unsupervised learning. Once these relevant paragraphs are pinpointed, a bi-directional long-short term memory (BiLSTM) NN, designed for processing text sequences, is adopted to recognize the material entities within them. Next, the synthesis operations mentioned in these paragraphs are classified into six categories – such as mixing, heating, and drying – using NNs and sentence dependency tree analysis. Operation conditions like temperature, time, and atmosphere are then extracted by using a regular expression matching approach. Finally, all these components are synthesized into a coherent chemical formula.

This automated pipeline has generated a dataset containing about 20,000 synthesis records from over 4 million papers, a task that would take humans decades to accomplish manually. It, in turn, illustrates the transformative power of AI in streamlining data collection. Under the meticulous guidance of human-designed processes, AI can handle the labor-intensive work of information extraction efficiently and accurately.

10.4.2 Enhanced Predictive Modeling

Molecular prediction in chemistry refers to the process of forecasting the properties and behaviors of molecules before they are physically synthesized and tested. Accurate molecular prediction is essential for guiding experimental work, reducing the time and cost associated with chemical research, and facilitating the discovery of new compounds with desired properties. By predicting how molecules will behave, chemists can make informed decisions and design more effective and efficient experiments.

Chemists often rely on empirical rules and heuristic models for molecular prediction, drawing on accumulated knowledge and observed patterns from previous experiments. For instance, group contribution methods (Constantinou & Gani, 1994) predict properties by summing the contributions of individual molecular fragments. While these methods are straightforward and quick to apply, they may lack the precision and flexibility needed for more complex molecules and reactions. To address this challenge, computational chemistry is introduced, employing computer algorithms to solve complex equations that describe molecular interactions and reactions. Techniques such as quantum mechanics, including density functional theory (DFT) (Vignale & Rasolt, 1987), allow chemists to calculate electronic structures and predict reactivity with high accuracy. Although these methods can be highly precise, they are often computationally expensive and time-consuming.

The advancement of AI technology has opened new avenues for accurate and efficient molecular predictions. Early studies utilized non-NN AI technologies to predict molecular properties based on manually crafted features. For example, a kriging method (Fletcher et al., 2014), a type of Gaussian process regression, is introduced to predict the electrostatic energies and polarization effects of aromatic amino acids. This approach involves training kriging models with geometries distorted via normal modes of vibration, which significantly reduces computational cost while maintaining accuracy. However, a major limitation of these non-NN AI methods lies in their reliance on the quality of manually extracted features, which requires extensive domain expertise.

To address this challenge, NNs, particularly GNNs, are now widely used to represent molecules more effectively. In GNNs, atoms are treated as nodes and chemical bonds as edges, enabling the training of models to predict various molecular properties without the need for manually crafted numerical descriptors. These models are applied to predict a range of molecular properties, including coordinates (Mansimov et al., 2019), mass spectra (Park et al., 2024), toxicity (Cremer et al., 2023), etc. A compact review can be found in the literature (Wieder et al., 2020).

These AI-based prediction models reduce the reliance on trial-and-error methods, allowing chemists to focus on the most promising compounds. This accelerates the discovery of new materials, pharmaceuticals, and chemicals with specific functionalities.

10.4.3 Automated Synthesis and Experimentation

Building on the advancements in automated data collection and predictive modeling, AI-powered robots are transforming the way chemists approach experimental tasks. These robots are designed to free chemists from repetitive and laborious experimental activities across different scenarios, including materials handling, synthesis, and characterization (Coley et al., 2019, 2020).

For example, solubility screening is a crucial step in understanding whether molecular compounds dissolve in a particular solvent. Traditionally, this process is time-consuming and labor-intensive, requiring periodic measurements throughout the experiment. Inspired by how human chemists visually assess solutions, CNN can be employed to automate this process (Pizzuto et al., 2022). An autonomous robot takes photos of the samples of interest, and the CNN segments the sample from the images to determine whether it has fully dissolved in the solvent. This AI-driven approach not only automates the solubility screening process but also ensures consistent and accurate assessments.

AI algorithms are also used to optimize experimental configurations during autonomous experimentation. The outcome of chemical experiments depends on various variables, including time, temperature, and atmosphere. As the number of variables increases, the experimental complexity scales exponentially. To efficiently search for the optimal configuration, a regression model is often fitted based on historical experimental data (Burger et al., 2020). This model predicts the portfolio of acquisition functions for different values of variables, narrowing the search space to configurations that are most likely to yield successful outcomes. This approach accelerates the identification of optimal experimental conditions, reducing the time and resources needed for experimentation.

Beyond individual tasks, integrated AI systems can manage entire materials discovery workflows. Traditionally, this process involves slow, laborious, iterative cycles of design, synthesis, testing, and analysis. An AI-driven robotic system can revolutionize this approach by starting with the generation of candidate materials through screening a vast array of possibilities for desirable properties. It then uses computer-aided synthesis planning to propose reaction pathways and finally synthesizes and characterizes the most promising candidates using a chemical robot assistant (Koscher et al., 2023). This integration streamlines the discovery process, enabling faster and more efficient development of new materials.

10.4.4 Summary

In this section, we briefly discuss the transformative trends in collaboration between humans and AI for chemical research, specifically in data collection, predictive modeling, and automated experimentation. The integration of AI enhances accuracy and efficiency, reduces the time and effort required by human researchers, and enables rapid synthesis and analysis of new materials.

Current AI technology still requires meticulous guidance from human experts to accommodate specific data formats, molecular mechanisms, and experimental specifications. However, the future of AI in chemistry is bright, with potential for even greater breakthroughs as AI technologies continue to evolve. As AI advances, its role in chemistry will undoubtedly expand, driving further innovation and enabling scientists to tackle increasingly complex challenges.

10.5 Human–AI Collaboration in Life Science

Life science encompasses a broad range of scientific disciplines focusing on the studies of living organisms, from the molecular and cellular levels to the entire ecosystems. It includes various fields such as biology, genetics, biochemistry, pharmacology, and medicine, all of which aim to understand the complex processes that govern life. Life sciences are integral to advancing our knowledge of health, disease, and mechanism of evolution, providing the foundation for innovations in healthcare, disease treatment, and enhancing the quality of life.

Traditionally, research in life sciences has relied heavily on empirical methods, where scientists conduct experiments to test hypotheses derived from observations. This approach, often described as the "hypothesis-driven" paradigm, involves formulating a question, designing experiments, collecting data, and analyzing the results to draw conclusions. While this method has led to significant discoveries, it is often limited by the sheer complexity of biological systems, the scale of data, and the time-intensive nature of experimental work. Moreover, the vast amount of data generated in modern life sciences, particularly with the advent of high-throughput technologies like genomics and proteomics, have outpaced the capacity of traditional analytical methods (Holzinger et al., 2023).

These challenges make life sciences well-suited to the transformative power of AI. With its ability to process vast datasets, detect patterns, and make predictions, AI provides a powerful complement to traditional research methods. By integrating AI into their work, scientists can not only accelerate the pace of discovery but also explore new and complex areas that were previously inaccessible. Given the extensive body of work on AI applications in life sciences, this section highlights key examples that showcase AI's strengths in pattern recognition and predictive modeling.

10.5.1 Sequencing and Analyzing Genetic Information

The advent of genomic sequencing has revolutionized our understanding of biology, unlocking the code of life written in DNA. However, the sheer volume and complexity of genetic data present significant challenges. Sequencing technologies, like next-generation sequencing (NGS), generate massive datasets that require sophisticated analysis to extract meaningful insights. This is where AI steps in, offering powerful tools to decode genetic information, identify genetic variants, and understand their implications for health and disease (Dias & Torkamani, 2019).

One of the critical challenges in genomic sequencing is to ensure the accuracy of large-scale DNA sequence data. Errors can occur during the sequencing process, leading to incorrect base calls, which can skew downstream analyses. AI algorithms, particularly DL models, have been developed to improve the accuracy of sequencing reads. By training on large datasets of correctly sequenced DNA, these AI models can learn to distinguish between true genetic variants and sequencing errors, enhancing the reliability of the data produced.

For instance, DeepVariant, developed by Google, is a deep learning tool that has been widely recognized for its ability to call genetic variants with higher accuracy than traditional methods (Yun et al., 2020). It uses CNNs, similar to those used in image recognition, to analyze raw sequencing data and identify variants, reducing the error rate and improving the quality of genomic data.

Once the raw DNA sequence is obtained, the next step is variant calling – identifying differences between the sequenced genome and a reference genome. These variants can range from single nucleotide polymorphisms (SNPs) to larger structural variations. AI plays a pivotal role in this process by automating the detection and classification of genetic variants.

AI-driven tools like GATK (Genome Analysis Toolkit) use machine learning algorithms to improve the accuracy and speed of variant calling (Lin et al., 2022). These tools can handle a vast amount of data generated by NGS and identify variants with high precision. Moreover, AI algorithms can prioritize variants based on their potential impact on gene function, guiding researchers toward the most biologically relevant differences.

Beyond variant calling, AI is also essential in interpreting the functional implications of these genetic variants. Machine learning models can analyze vast databases of known gene functions, protein structures, and clinical data to predict how a particular variant might affect an individual's health. For example, AI tools can predict whether a variant is likely to be pathogenic, helping clinicians make informed decisions about diagnosis and treatment.

A groundbreaking example is the collaboration between the Broad Institute and Google, where AI was used to improve the accuracy and efficiency of genomic data processing (Genome Analysis Toolkit). The partnership led to the development of deep learning models that could analyze terabytes of sequencing data in a fraction of the time required by traditional methods, paving the way for faster and more accurate genomic studies.

Additionally, AI has been instrumental in large-scale projects such as the UK Biobank (Bycroft et al., 2018), where AI-driven analyses are helping researchers understand the genetic determinants of health and disease in a population of over 500,000 participants. The insights gained from such projects are expected to lead to new diagnostics, treatments, and preventive strategies tailored to individual genetic profiles.

10.5.2 Drug Discovery and Development

The process of drug discovery and development has traditionally been a lengthy, expensive, and complex journey, often taking over a decade and costing billions of dollars to bring a new drug to market. This journey involves identifying potential drug candidates, testing their safety and efficacy, and navigating through a rigorous regulatory approval process. The challenges of this process are compounded by the high rate of failure, with many promising compounds falling short during clinical trials. However, the advent of AI has begun to revolutionize this field, offering new tools and approaches that significantly enhance the efficiency and effectiveness of drug discovery (Mak et al., 2023).

One of the first steps in drug discovery is to identify a biological target – typically a protein or gene associated with a disease – that a drug can modulate. AI technologies have proven to be invaluable in this phase (Pun et al., 2023). By analyzing large datasets from genomics, proteomics, and other omics technologies, AI can identify potential drug targets that may not be obvious through traditional methods. For example, AI algorithms can sift through a vast amount of genetic data to pinpoint mutations or expressions linked to specific diseases, helping researchers identify new targets for drug development.

Once a target has been identified, the next step is to find chemical compounds that can interact with it effectively. Traditionally, this involved screening large libraries of compounds in the lab – a time-consuming and costly process (Han et al., 2023). AI has dramatically accelerated this process through virtual screening, where machine learning models predict how different compounds will interact with the target. These models can rapidly filter out compounds that are unlikely to be effective, allowing scientists to focus on the most promising candidates.

In addition to screening, AI is also used in lead optimization, where the chemical properties of a compound are refined to improve its efficacy, reduce toxicity, and enhance its pharmacokinetic properties. AI-driven models can predict how modifications to a compound's structure might impact its behavior in the body, helping scientists design more effective drugs (Vora et al., 2023). For instance, companies like Insilico Medicine and Atomwise use AI to predict the biological activity of molecules, optimizing them for better performance before they even reach the laboratory.

The success of a drug in clinical trials is often the make-or-break point of drug development (Urbina et al., 2022). AI is increasingly being used to improve the design and execution of these trials. Predictive modeling, powered by AI, can analyze patient data to identify which populations are most likely to respond to a new treatment, enabling more targeted and efficient trials. This approach not only increases the likelihood of success but also reduces costs by minimizing the number of participants needed and shortening the trial duration.

Moreover, AI can monitor and analyze data in real-time during clinical trials, identifying potential issues or trends that might otherwise go unnoticed. This capability allows for adaptive trial designs, where protocols can be adjusted based on interim results, further increasing the chances of success.

A striking example of AI for drug discovery is the development of IBM Watson for Drug Discovery, a platform that uses AI to analyze a vast amount of scientific literature and data (Visan & Negut, 2024). In one notable instance, Watson helped researchers at Barrow Neurological Institute identify five new genes linked to amyotrophic lateral sclerosis (ALS), a breakthrough that could lead to new treatment avenues. Similarly, the British AI company BenevolentAI used its technology to identify an existing drug, baricitinib, as a potential treatment for COVID-19, which subsequently received emergency use authorization during the pandemic.

10.5.3 Summary

The integration of AI into life sciences has revolutionized the way research is conducted, enhancing both the speed and accuracy of scientific discoveries. By integrating AI into the research process, scientists can enhance their ability to uncover new insights, accelerate discoveries, and address questions that were previously too complex to tackle. AI not only augments human expertise but also opens up new avenues for exploring the intricacies of life, making it an invaluable partner in the pursuit of scientific discovery in the life sciences.

10.6 Summary

AI has undeniably become a transformative force in scientific discovery, fundamentally changing how researchers approach problems, analyze data, and generate insights. This chapter has explored the dynamic partnership between human researchers and AI systems, emphasizing the powerful synergy that drives scientific progress across various disciplines. In this summary, we delve deeper into this collaboration by highlighting the crucial role of human guidance in applying AI technologies, examining AI's influence on the core components of scientific discovery, and addressing the ethical considerations that emerge from this evolving relationship.

10.6.1 Impacts of AI on Scientific Discovery

Scientific discovery generally unfolds in three key steps: (i) hypothesis generation and selection, (ii) the design of methods to validate or disprove the hypothesis, and (iii) the derivation of insights from interpreting the results. AI influences each of these components to varying degrees.

The generation of hypotheses is a critical first step in scientific enquiry, traditionally driven by human intuition, experience, and creativity. This intuition is often rooted in a deep understanding of a specific scientific domain and is sparked by human intellect. AI, with its unparalleled ability to process vast amounts of information, can be harnessed to explore extensive hypothesis spaces, pinpointing those that align with existing knowledge. However, it is widely recognized that while AI excels at synthesizing and organizing existing knowledge, it still struggles to generate truly novel insights.

Once a hypothesis is formed, the next step involves developing methods to test it. This task typically falls to human experts who specialize in the relevant scientific field. AI systems can enhance this process by optimizing experimental designs, simulating various scenarios, and reducing reliance on trial and error. This not only minimizes resource use but also accelerates the path to discovery.

The final stage of scientific discovery involves interpreting results and drawing meaningful insights. This is where AI truly shines in its capacity to validate or disprove hypotheses. AI excels at processing and analyzing large datasets, identifying trends, anomalies, and subtle patterns that might elude human analysts. For example, AI can analyze complex genetic data to uncover interactions that contribute to specific traits or diseases, offering insights that could lead to new therapeutic approaches.

10.6.2 Human Guidance to AI for Scientific Discovery

While AI is increasingly embedded in every facet of scientific research, significantly reducing human labor, the success of AI in this domain still hinges on crucial human guidance. For AI to reach its full potential in scientific discovery, expert human intervention is indispensable. This guidance is vital for navigating the complexities of three key areas: (i) acquiring and preparing datasets to train AI models, (ii) designing AI models that are precisely tailored to the chosen datasets, and (iii) developing effective training schemes that enable AI models to learn meaningful patterns from the data. Each of these elements demands a deep understanding of both the scientific domain and the unique capabilities of AI technology.

Dataset Acquisition and Preparation

The success of any AI model hinges on the quality and relevance of the dataset used for training. Human expertise is essential in acquiring datasets that accurately represent the problem domain and ensuring that these datasets are comprehensive, unbiased, and appropriately curated. In scientific discovery, this often involves collecting data from various sources, such as literature, experimental results, and numerical simulation, to create a robust and representative dataset.

Although AI technology can automate many aspects of this process, such as using NLP to extract chemical equations from literature or deploying AI-powered robots to conduct experiments, human guidance remains indispensable. Expertise is essential in addressing issues like missing values, noise, and outliers, which require a deep understanding of the scientific context to ensure the data fed into the AI model is both accurate and meaningful. Without meticulous human oversight at this stage, AI models risk learning patterns from misleading datasets that are irrelevant to the research problem, potentially undermining the integrity of the scientific discovery process.

Model Design and Customization

The design of AI models must be meticulously tailored to the dataset's specific characteristics and the scientific questions being addressed. Different data types require distinct model architectures: for example, image data typically benefits from CNNs, sequential data like genomic sequences are often best processed with RNNs or transformers, and molecular structures are most effectively analyzed using GNNs.

While these guidelines provide a foundation for selecting AI models, human expertise is essential in crafting models that not only perform well on a given dataset but also adhere to the underlying scientific principles. The goal is to create a model that can effectively capture the nuances of the data without overfitting or underfitting, which requires a balance between model complexity and generalization ability. Human judgment is also crucial in ensuring that the model's outputs are interpretable and aligned with scientific goals, as the ability to explain and validate predictions is fundamental to advancing knowledge and making credible discoveries.

Training Scheme Development

The choice of a training scheme is closely tied to the nature of the task and the annotation status of the dataset. For tasks involving the identification of patterns or the prediction of continuous values, classification and regression training schedules are typically employed. These approaches often require a substantial volume of well-annotated data samples. While manual annotation is possible, it can be incredibly labor-intensive. A more efficient alternative is to generate data labels from experimental results or numerical simulations guided by expert-defined rules.

On the other hand, when the goal is to optimize a problem with limited labeled data but clear criteria for evaluating outcomes, reinforcement learning and genetic algorithms are often the preferred methods. These approaches excel in scenarios where the model learns by interacting with the environment and progressively improving based on feedback or evolving solutions to find the best outcome.

Training AI models to learn patterns from data is a complex process that demands strategic human oversight. Human intervention is crucial for embedding domain knowledge into the training process, such as incorporating scientific constraints or directing the model's attention to key data features. This not only enhances the model's performance but also ensures that the AI system yields scientifically valid and actionable insights, paving the way for meaningful discoveries.

10.6.3 Ethical Considerations in Human–AI Collaboration for Scientific Discovery

Human–AI collaboration in scientific discovery holds immense potential, but it also raises significant ethical concerns that must be addressed to ensure that this partnership benefits society without unintended harm. One of the most pressing issues is the potential for bias in AI systems. AI models are trained on existing data and, if that data reflects historical biases – whether related to gender, race, or other factors – the AI could perpetuate and even amplify these biases in scientific research. This could lead to skewed results, misrepresentation of certain populations, or biased scientific conclusions, ultimately affecting the fairness and credibility of scientific discoveries.

Another ethical concern is the transparency and interpretability of AI-driven research. AI systems, particularly complex models like deep neural networks, often operate as "black boxes," making decisions that are difficult for even experts to fully understand or explain. This lack of transparency can pose significant risks in scientific discovery, where understanding the rationale behind a finding is crucial for its validation and acceptance. If scientists rely too heavily on AI without demanding interpretability, there is a danger of accepting results that cannot be independently verified, leading to a potential erosion of trust in scientific outcomes.

Moreover, the power dynamics in human–AI collaboration also raises ethical questions. As AI systems become more integrated into scientific research, there is a risk that the role of human scientists may be diminished or that decision-making power may shift disproportionately toward those who control the AI systems. This could create inequalities within the scientific community, where certain groups or individuals have more influence over research outcomes due to their access to or control over AI technologies. Ensuring equitable access to AI tools and maintaining a balance in human–AI collaboration is essential to prevent the concentration of power and to foster inclusive scientific progress.

The ethical implications of AI-driven discoveries also extend to the potential consequences of these discoveries themselves. AI has the capability to accelerate the pace of research, leading to breakthroughs that could have profound societal impacts – both positive and negative. For instance, AI could uncover new drugs or therapies at an unprecedented speed, but it could also be used to develop harmful technologies or exacerbate existing inequalities. The scientific community must therefore engage in ongoing ethical reflection and dialogue to consider the broader implications of their work and to ensure that AI-driven discoveries are aligned with societal values and contribute to the common good.

Finally, the integration of AI into scientific research raises questions about accountability. When AI systems are involved in generating hypotheses, designing experiments, or interpreting data, it becomes more challenging to determine who is responsible for the outcomes, particularly if those outcomes are harmful or erroneous. Establishing clear guidelines for accountability in human–AI collaborations is crucial to address this issue. This includes not only holding developers and users of AI systems accountable but also ensuring that there are mechanisms in place to correct or mitigate any negative impacts resulting from AI-driven research.

In conclusion, while the collaboration between humans and AI in scientific discovery holds great promise, it also presents a complex landscape of ethical challenges. Addressing these issues requires a proactive and multidisciplinary approach, involving ethicists, scientists, policymakers, and the public in ongoing discussions to guide the responsible development and use of AI in science. By doing so, we can harness the full potential of AI to advance knowledge while safeguarding the ethical foundations of scientific inquiry.

References

Andreassen, A., Komiske, P. T., Metodiev, E. M., Nachman, B., & Thaler, J. (2020). OmniFold: A Method to Simultaneously Unfold All Observables. *Physical Review Letters, 124*(18), 182001.

Baum, Z. J., Yu, X., Ayala, P. Y., Zhao, Y., Watkins, S. P., & Zhou, Q. (2021). Artificial Intelligence in Chemistry: Current Trends and Future Directions. *Journal of Chemical Information and Modeling, 61*(7), 3197–3212.

Burger, B., Maffettone, P. M., Gusev, V. V., Aitchison, C. M., Bai, Y., Wang, X., ... & Cooper, A. I. (2020). A Mobile Robotic Chemist. *Nature*, *583*(7815), 237–241.

Bycroft, C., Freeman, C., Petkova, D., Band, G., Elliott, L. T., Sharp, K., ... & Marchini, J. (2018). The UK Biobank Resource with Deep Phenotyping and Genomic Data. *Nature*, *562*(7726), 203–209.

Chatrchyan, S., Khachatryan, V., Sirunyan, A. M., Tumasyan, A., Adam, W., Aguilo, E., ... & Damiao, D. D. J. (2012). Observation of a New Boson at a Mass of 125 GeV with the CMS Experiment at the LHC. *Physics Letters B*, *716*(1), 30–61.

Coley, C. W., Eyke, N. S., & Jensen, K. F. (2020). Autonomous Discovery in the Chemical Sciences Part II: Outlook. *Angewandte Chemie International Edition*, *59*(52), 23414–23436.

Coley, C. W., Thomas III, D. A., Lummiss, J. A., Jaworski, J. N., Breen, C. P., Schultz, V., ... & Jensen, K. F. (2019). A Robotic Platform for Flow Synthesis of Organic Compounds Informed by AI Planning. *Science*, *365*(6453), eaax1566.

Constantinou, L., & Gani, R. (1994). New Group Contribution Method for Estimating Properties of Pure Compounds. *AIChE Journal*, *40*(10), 1697–1710.

Cremer, J., Medrano Sandonas, L., Tkatchenko, A., Clevert, D. A., & De Fabritiis, G. (2023). Equivariant Graph Neural Networks for Toxicity Prediction. *Chemical Research in Toxicology*, *36*(10), 1561–1573.

Davies, A., Veličković, P., Buesing, L., Blackwell, S., Zheng, D., Tomašev, N., ... & Kohli, P. (2021). Advancing Mathematics by Guiding Human Intuition with AI. *Nature*, *600*(7887), 70–74.

Davis, R., Buchanan, B., & Shortliffe, F. (1977). Production Rules as a Representation for a Knowledge-based Consultation Program. *Artificial Intelligence*, *8*(1), 15–45.

Degrave, J., Felici, F., Buchli, J., Neunert, M., Tracey, B., Carpanese, F., ... & Riedmiller, M. (2022). Magnetic Control of Tokamak Plasmas through Deep Reinforcement Learning. *Nature*, *602*(7897), 414–419.

DeZoort, G., Battaglia, P. W., Biscarat, C., & Vlimant, J. R. (2023). Graph Neural Networks at the Large Hadron Collider. *Nature Reviews Physics*, *5*(5), 281–303.

Dias, R., & Torkamani, A. (2019). Artificial Intelligence in Clinical and Genomic Diagnostics. *Genome Medicine*, *11*(1), 70.

Dosovitskiy, A., Beyer, L., Kolesnikov, A., Weissenborn, D., Zhai, X., Unterthiner, T., ... & Houlsby, N. (2021). An Image Is Worth 16x16 Words: Transformers for Image Recognition at Scale. *International Conference on Learning Representations*, *9*, 1–21.

Feigenbaum, E. A., Buchanan, B. G., & Lederberg, J. (1970). *On Generality and Problem Solving: A Case Study using the DENDRAL Program* (No. NASA-CR-123182).

Fletcher, T. L., Davie, S. J., & Popelier, P. L. (2014). Prediction of Intramolecular Polarization of Aromatic Amino Acids using Kriging Machine Learning. *Journal of Chemical Theory and Computation*, *10*(9), 3708–3719.

Gertrudes, J. C., Maltarollo, V. G., Silva, R. A., Oliveira, P. R., Honorio, K. M., & Da Silva, A. B. F. (2012). Machine Learning Techniques and Drug Design. *Current Medicinal Chemistry*, *19*(25), 4289–4297.

Goenka, S. D., Gorzynski, J. E., Shafin, K., Fisk, D. G., Pesout, T., Jensen, T. D., ... & Ashley, E. A. (2022). Accelerated Identification of Disease-causing Variants with Ultra-rapid Nanopore Genome Sequencing. *Nature Biotechnology*, *40*(7), 1035–1041.

Han, R., Yoon, H., Kim, G., Lee, H., & Lee, Y. (2023). Revolutionizing Medicinal Chemistry: The Application of Artificial Intelligence (AI) in Early Drug Discovery. *Pharmaceuticals, 16*(9), 1259.

Harrison, J. (2013). The HOL Light Theory of Euclidean Space. *Journal of Automated Reasoning, 50*, 173–190.

Holzinger, A., Keiblinger, K., Holub, P., Zatloukal, K., & Müller, H. (2023). AI for Life: Trends in Artificial Intelligence for Biotechnology. *New Biotechnology, 74*, 16–24.

Jumper, J., Evans, R., Pritzel, A., Green, T., Figurnov, M., Ronneberger, O., ... & Hassabis, D. (2021). Highly Accurate Protein Structure Prediction with AlphaFold. *Nature, 596*(7873), 583–589.

Karagiorgi, G., Kasieczka, G., Kravitz, S., Nachman, B., & Shih, D. (2022). Machine Learning in the Search for New Fundamental Physics. *Nature Reviews Physics, 4*(6), 399–412.

Karniadakis, G. E., Kevrekidis, I. G., Lu, L., Perdikaris, P., Wang, S., & Yang, L. (2021). Physics-informed Machine Learning. *Nature Reviews Physics, 3*(6), 422–440.

Kononova, O., Huo, H., He, T., Rong, Z., Botari, T., Sun, W., ... & Ceder, G. (2019). Text-mined Dataset of Inorganic Materials Synthesis Recipes. *Scientific Data, 6*(1), 203.

Koscher, B. A., Canty, R. B., McDonald, M. A., Greenman, K. P., McGill, C. J., Bilodeau, C. L., ... & Jensen, K. F. (2023). Autonomous, Multiproperty-driven Molecular Discovery: From Predictions to Measurements and Back. *Science, 382*(6677), eadi1407.

LeCun, Y., Bengio, Y., & Hinton, G. (2015). Deep Learning. *Nature, 521*(7553), 436–444.

LeCun, Y., Boser, B., Denker, J. S., Henderson, D., Howard, R. E., Hubbard, W., & Jackel, L. D. (1989). Backpropagation Applied to Handwritten Zip Code Recognition. *Neural Computation, 1*(4), 541–551.

Li, M. M., Huang, K., & Zitnik, M. (2022). Graph Representation Learning in Biomedicine and Healthcare. *Nature Biomedical Engineering, 6*(12), 1353–1369.

Libbrecht, M. W., & Noble, W. S. (2015). Machine Learning Applications in Genetics and Genomics. *Nature Reviews Genetics, 16*(6), 321–332.

Lin, Y. L., Chang, P. C., Hsu, C., Hung, M. Z., Chien, Y. H., Hwu, W. L., ... & Lee, N. C. (2022). Comparison of GATK and DeepVariant by Trio Sequencing. *Scientific Reports, 12*(1), 1809.

Loveland, D. W. (2016). *Automated Theorem Proving: A Logical Basis.* Elsevier.

Mak, K. K., Wong, Y. H., & Pichika, M. R. (2024). Artificial Intelligence in Drug Discovery and Development. In: H. G. Vogel (ed.), *Drug Discovery and Evaluation: Safety and Pharmacokinetic Assays* (pp. 1461–1498). Springer.

Mansimov, E., Mahmood, O., Kang, S., & Cho, K. (2019). Molecular Geometry Prediction using a Deep Generative Graph Neural Network. *Scientific Reports, 9*(1), 20381.

McCarthy, J., Minsky, M. L., Rochester, N., & Shannon, C. E. (2006). A Proposal for the Dartmouth Summer Research Project on Artificial Intelligence, August 31, 1955. *AI Magazine, 27*(4), 12.

Minsky, M., & Papert, S. (1969). *Perceptrons*, MIT Press.

Ouyang, L., Wu, J., Jiang, X., Almeida, D., Wainwright, C., Mishkin, P., ... & Lowe, R. (2022). Training Language Models to Follow Instructions with Human Feedback. *Advances in Neural Information Processing Systems, 35*, 27730–27744.

Park, J., Jo, J., & Yoon, S. (2024). Mass Spectra Prediction with Structural Motif-based Graph Neural Networks. *Scientific Reports, 14*(1), 1400.

Pearlmutter. (1989, June). Learning State Space Trajectories in Recurrent Neural Networks. In *International 1989 Joint Conference on Neural Networks* (pp. 365–372). IEEE.

Pierce, J. R., & Carroll, J. B. (1966). *Language and Machines: Computers in Translation and Linguistics*. National Academy of Sciences/National Research Council.

Pizzuto, G., De Berardinis, J., Longley, L., Fakhruldeen, H., & Cooper, A. I. (2022, July). Solis: Autonomous Solubility Screening using Deep Neural Networks. In *2022 International Joint Conference on Neural Networks (IJCNN)* (pp. 1–7). IEEE.

Pun, F. W., Ozerov, I. V., & Zhavoronkov, A. (2023). AI-powered Therapeutic Target Discovery. *Trends in Pharmacological Sciences, 44*(9), 561–572.

Rohrbach, S., Šiaučiulis, M., Chisholm, G., Pirvan, P. A., Saleeb, M., Mehr, S. H. M., ... & Cronin, L. (2022). Digitization and Validation of a Chemical Synthesis Literature Database in the ChemPU. *Science, 377*(6602), 172–180.

Romera-Paredes, B., Barekatain, M., Novikov, A., Balog, M., Kumar, M. P., Dupont, E., ... & Fawzi, A. (2024). Mathematical Discoveries from Program Search with Large Language Models. *Nature, 625*(7995), 468–475.

Rosenblatt, F. (1958). The Perceptron: A Probabilistic Model for Information Storage and Organization in the Brain. *Psychological Review, 65*(6), 386.

Russell, S. J., & Norvig, P. (2016). *Artificial Intelligence: A Modern Approach*. Pearson.

Sanchez-Lengeling, B., & Aspuru-Guzik, A. (2018). Inverse Molecular Design using Machine Learning: Generative Models for Matter Engineering. *Science, 361*(6400), 360–365.

Scarselli, F., Gori, M., Tsoi, A. C., Hagenbuchner, M., & Monfardini, G. (2008). The Graph Neural Network Model. *IEEE Transactions on Neural Networks, 20*(1), 61–80.

Segler, M. H., Preuss, M., & Waller, M. P. (2018). Planning Chemical Syntheses with Deep Neural Networks and Symbolic AI. *Nature, 555*(7698), 604–610.

Siekmann, J., & Wrightson, G. (eds.). (2012). *Automation of Reasoning: 2: Classical Papers on Computational Logic 1967–1970*. Springer Science & Business Media.

Smolensky, P. (1987). Connectionist AI, Symbolic AI, and the Brain. *Artificial Intelligence Review, 1*(2), 95–109.

Sohl-Dickstein, J., Weiss, E., Maheswaranathan, N., & Ganguli, S. (2015, June). Deep Unsupervised Learning using Nonequilibrium Thermodynamics. In *International Conference on Machine Learning* (pp. 2256–2265). PMLR.

Turing, A. M. (1950). Computing Machinery and Intelligence. *Mind, 59*(236), 433.

Urbina, F., Lentzos, F., Invernizzi, C., & Ekins, S. (2022). Dual Use of Artificial-Intelligence-Powered Drug Discovery. *Nature Machine Intelligence, 4*(3), 189–191.

Vaswani, A., Shazeer, N., Parmar, N., Uszkoreit, J., Jones, L., Gomez, A. N., ... & Polosukhin, I. (2017). Attention Is All You Need. *Advances in Neural Information Processing Systems, 30*, 5998–6008.

Vignale, G., & Rasolt, M. (1987). Density-Functional Theory in Strong Magnetic Fields. *Physical Review Letters, 59*(20), 2360.

Visan, A. I., & Negut, I. (2024). Integrating Artificial Intelligence for Drug Discovery in the Context of Revolutionizing Drug Delivery. *Life, 14*(2), 233.

Vora, L. K., Gholap, A. D., Jetha, K., Thakur, R. R. S., Solanki, H. K., & Chavda, V. P. (2023). Artificial Intelligence in Pharmaceutical Technology and Drug Delivery Design. *Pharmaceutics, 15*(7), 1916.

Wang, H. (1960). Proving Theorems by Pattern Recognition I. *Communications of the ACM, 3*(4), 220–234.

Wang, H., Fu, T., Du, Y., Gao, W., Huang, K., Liu, Z., ... & Zitnik, M. (2023). Scientific Discovery in the Age of Artificial Intelligence. *Nature, 620*(7972), 47–60.

Waterman, D. A. (1985). *A Guide to Expert Systems*. Addison-Wesley Longman Publishing Co., Inc.

Werbos, P. J. (1994). *The Roots of Backpropagation: From Ordered Derivatives to Neural Networks and Political Forecasting* (Vol. 1). John Wiley & Sons.

Wieder, O., Kohlbacher, S., Kuenemann, M., Garon, A., Ducrot, P., Seidel, T., & Langer, T. (2020). A Compact Review of Molecular Property Prediction with Graph Neural Networks. *Drug Discovery Today: Technologies, 37*, 1–12.

Wiles, A. (1995). Modular Elliptic Curves and Fermat's Last Theorem. *Annals of Mathematics, 141*(3), 443–551.

Yun, T., Li, H., Chang, P. C., Lin, M. F., Carroll, A., & McLean, C. Y. (2020). Accurate, Scalable Cohort Variant Calls using DeepVariant and GLnexus. *Bioinformatics, 36*(24), 5582–5589.

Zhao, S., Chen, S., Zhou, J., Li, C., Tang, T., Harris, S. J., ... & Li, X. (2024). Potential to Transform Words to Watts with Large Language Models in Battery Research. *Cell Reports Physical Science, 5*(3), 101844.

11

Challenges of Generative AI on Human–AI Interaction and Collaboration

Shaobo Liang and Yiting Cai

11.1 User-level Challenges

11.1.1 Trust Building

Trust and comprehension of AI systems are essential components of effective human–AI collaboration and interaction. The degree of trust that users place in AI significantly influences their perceptions of AI-generated content and serves as a critical psychological factor that impacts their adherence to system recommendations. The decision-making processes employed by AI are inherently complex and present certain technical challenges, which can hinder users' understanding of how AI-generated content is created. Furthermore, users often lack the capacity to modify system recommendations, which complicates their ability to lower their defenses against generative AI. Currently, strategies such as enhancing users' decision-making control and elucidating the decision-making mechanisms of AI systems are frequently implemented to foster trust. Nevertheless, these approaches also present limitations, as they raise questions regarding the extent to which AI systems should offer explanations.

Research indicates that excessive elaboration on the reasoning processes of AI may heighten users' perceptions of task complexity, resulting in cognitive overload and a subsequent decline in trust toward generative AI systems (Westphal et al., 2023). This phenomenon may adversely affect users' favorable assessments of human–AI interactions. According to cognitive load theory, human working memory has inherent limitations, and effectively managing cognitive load intensity is essential for facilitating successful learning outcomes. For individuals with lower cognitive abilities who encounter difficulties with complex tasks, an excess of task-related information can overwhelm their cognitive processing capacities, thereby hindering their ability to understand and adhere to the intended applications of generative AI.

Furthermore, trust in AI systems is a dynamic construct, with users' comprehension of AI performance and reliability evolving gradually as familiarity and individual cognitive capabilities improve. Given that human–AI collaboration and interaction represent emerging technologies, it is reasonable to expect that the development of trust will occur at a gradual pace.

In the context of fostering trust between users and generative AI, it is essential to recognize that factors extending beyond users' subjective influences are also significant. These include advancements in emotional contagion pathways and the humanization of AI. Generative AI systems are required to process various types of data while simultaneously providing feedback and facilitating interaction (Lukyanenko et al., 2022). Products such as Character AI, Janitor.AI, and Pi have garnered substantial user engagement, underscoring the critical role of emotional companionship that AI models can offer in the realm of human–AI collaboration and interaction. It is imperative for AI systems to effectively manage the degree of emotional transmission to engage users and cultivate their trust. Nevertheless, the extent of humanization must be judiciously calibrated. While enhancing the human-like qualities of AI systems can improve user-friendliness, excessive humanization may provoke skepticism and potentially erode users' trust in the professionalism of the AI.

11.1.2 Algorithm Aversion

Some people in society demonstrate a pronounced aversion to content generated by AI, which is often manifested through behaviors such as reluctance to utilize AI products and dismissal of AI-generated outputs. This resistance impedes the potential for collaboration between generative AI systems and their users (Cheng et al., 2022). The psychological factors underlying this algorithmic aversion can be classified into three distinct categories: a perceived competition with AI, a desire for transparency and control in decision-making processes, and a bias against the creative capabilities of AI.

Generative AI represents a culmination of significant technological advancements, and the collaboration and interaction between humans and AI have substantially transformed both daily life and production processes. In light of these profound changes, users have expressed concerns regarding potential job displacement and have experienced anxiety related to technology, resulting in the emergence of algorithmic aversion.

Even when AI models can provide more accurate and higher-quality responses than their human counterparts, users frequently exhibit a preference for human references. This phenomenon is referred to as "algorithmic aversion, a tendency to favor human input over AI" (Mariadassou et al., 2024, p. 2).

Research indicates that artworks produced through the collaboration of human creators and AI are often perceived as more aesthetically pleasing. Furthermore, the involvement of AI can enhance the creativity of human-generated works (Hitsuwari et al., 2023). The interaction and collaboration between humans and AI present significant opportunities in the realm of artistic creation; however, algorithmic aversion remains a substantial obstacle to its advancement. There is a prevailing belief that works created by humans possess greater beauty and are infused with a sense of humanistic care. The increasing prevalence of AI-generated artworks, coupled with the challenges associated with distinguishing between human and AI creations, has, in certain respects, undermined the dominance of human creators, thereby exacerbating negative perceptions and evaluations of AI-generated content.

Although people may dislike the label of "algorithm" or "AI," they often express appreciation for the actual outputs generated by generative AI. For example, when the origin of content is ambiguous, users often exhibit a more favorable response to jokes suggested by algorithms than to those proposed by humans. In the context of emotional support, content generated by ChatGPT is perceived as more attentive and is rated higher in terms of emotional value. This suggests that users are not inherently opposed to the content generated by algorithms; rather, it is their reluctance toward the labels "AI" and "algorithm" that hinders the wider acceptance of generative AI technologies (Elyoseph et al., 2023; Yeomans et al., 2019).

11.1.3 Acceptability

Individual differences among users significantly contribute to the varying levels of acceptance of generative AI. Factors such as cultural context and patterns of emotional expression play a crucial role in shaping these differences. To effectively meet the needs of a diverse user base, generative AI must integrate appropriate frameworks that account for emotional expression and cultural contexts. This necessity poses challenges for the localization strategies and cultural sensitivity of AI systems.

Firstly, linguistic and behavioral preferences are critical factors that influence the adoption of generative AI. AI systems must conduct extensive research on local dialects, semantics, and accents within the fields of speech recognition and natural language processing to achieve objectives related to language comprehension, language generation, and multilingual prediction. Moreover, in the context of product design, it is imperative to consider the usage habits and requirements of users from various regions to enhance the overall user experience (Khurana et al., 2023).

Secondly, users' perceptions of fairness regarding generative AI play a crucial role in its acceptance. The challenges associated with racial and cultural biases present in existing generative AI models remain inadequately addressed (Gilliard, 2022). When these biases are applied in critical domains such as healthcare, employment, and security governance, they have the potential to exacerbate discrimination and reinforce power imbalances, thereby diminishing users' trust in generative AI.

11.2 Algorithm Optimization Challenges

11.2.1 Theoretical Gaps

Generative AI is a significant advancement in technological development; however, there exist notable gaps in the emerging theories surrounding human–AI interaction. Specifically, there is a lack of clarity regarding the advantages of AI and the application of these theories to enhance the usability and acceptability of AI systems. A discernible disconnect persists between theoretical research on generative AI and the rapid pace of practical advancements in the field. In recent years, generative AI and AI-driven self-service systems have experienced swift progress and have been implemented in critical domains such as autonomous driving, healthcare, and legal services. On one hand, generative AI has emerged as a reliable tool for improving human efficiency and accuracy, facilitating human–AI interaction and collaboration, and alleviating individuals from repetitive tasks. Conversely, there remains a lack of consensus on the allocation of responsibility in tasks that involve generative AI and automated systems. The inherent complexity of AI models complicates the ability of human agents to assume full responsibility for the outcomes generated by these systems (Königs, 2022). This situation has led critics to highlight the issue of a "responsibility gap" in the context of generative AI and human–AI collaboration, a concern that current theoretical frameworks are insufficient to address comprehensively.

Beyond the theoretical divide between generative AI and its practical applications, there exists a notable deficiency in empirical evidence that substantiates the advantages of human–AI interaction and collaboration within specific domains. In the field of education, for instance, intelligent robots and adaptive learning systems are increasingly utilized by both educators and learners (Chen et al., 2020). AI technologies facilitate personalized learning environments by customizing educational plans to align with individual learning styles and enhancing learner motivation. Furthermore, these technologies assist educators in alleviating the burden of repetitive tasks, thereby allowing for more meaningful and individualized instruction. Despite the burgeoning interest in AI within educational research, there has been a lack of concerted efforts to integrate AI technologies with established educational theories. Consequently, this gap has hindered the ability to fully articulate the essential value of AI in the educational sector.

11.2.2 Inequality and Lack of Accessibility

Fairness and accessibility are critical directions in the development of generative AI, as these technologies should serve users from diverse educational backgrounds and economic conditions equally. Currently, the human–AI interaction services provided by AI systems pose certain technical barriers, challenging the knowledge levels of users and limiting the application market for generative AI. AI systems need to reduce the difficulty for non-expert users to engage with and benefit from generative AI, expanding the user base while leveraging technology to serve society. The accessibility for users with varying health conditions is another key point that generative AI must address. At present, generative AI has not fully met the expectations of its target audience. Fairness and accessibility are essential considerations in the advancement of generative AI, as these technologies must equitably serve users from diverse educational backgrounds and socioeconomic conditions. Currently, the human–AI interaction services offered by AI systems present certain technical barriers that challenge users' knowledge levels and restrict the market applicability of generative AI. It is imperative for AI systems to mitigate the complexities that non-expert users face in engaging with and benefiting from generative AI, thereby broadening the user base and utilizing technology to serve societal needs. Additionally, addressing accessibility for users with varying health conditions is a critical aspect that generative AI must prioritize. At present, generative AI has not fully incorporated technologies to support individuals with disabilities. For example, when visually impaired users utilize screen readers to access generative AI outputs, platforms such as ChatGPT fail to provide clear indications of where the output begins and ends, nor do they label the locations of buttons for copying, editing, or rating the content.

The integration of technology to assist individuals with disabilities is crucial. For example, visually impaired users who depend on screen readers to interact with generative AI outputs may encounter challenges, as ChatGPT fails to offer clear demarcations indicating the beginning and end of the output. Additionally, it does not adequately label the locations of buttons for copying, editing, or rating the content.

The unfairness of generative AI is reflected in aspects such as race, gender, and age. Research has found that generative AI associates terms like "Africa" with "poverty" and depicts all flight attendants as female. These outputs from generative AI are not objective representations of the real world but rather amplify unfair biases (Ananya, 2024). The discriminatory inclinations of generative AI models are frequently nuanced and challenging to identify. Mitigating this issue by eliminating biased content from training datasets is both resource-intensive and difficult to execute. Consequently, it is imperative to engage in a collaborative effort among governments, researchers, and users to oversee the content produced by AI models and to swiftly rectify any inappropriate biases present in the models' reasoning.

11.2.3 Emotional Design

The emotional expressions exhibited by AI systems can significantly impact user responses to the information presented. Positive emotions conveyed by AI may influence users through two distinct pathways: the affective pathway, which can enhance trust via emotional contagion, and the cognitive pathway of expectation–disconfirmation, which may diminish trust. Users' expectations regarding the emotional expression patterns of generative AI vary based on the context and the intended purpose of the interaction.

In addition to methods of emotional expression, users' emotional requirements for AI systems differ across various application contexts and needs. Research has investigated how the type of AI and the nature of human–AI collaboration influence consumer acceptance (Peng et al., 2022). The findings indicate that when AI functions as a supportive entity for humans, there is an increase in consumer acceptance of AI services for tasks that necessitate a high degree of warmth. However, this effect is not evident when AI operates under human supervision. Consequently, it is essential to enhance the emotional design framework when developing AI systems to accommodate diverse collaboration scenarios and modes, thereby more effectively addressing user needs.

11.2.4 Cultural and Linguistic Adaptation

Generative AI training datasets are frequently derived from extensive global datasets, which typically provide superior representation of mainstream languages and cultures. However, users from underdeveloped regions who utilize minority languages or possess distinct cultural backgrounds may be marginalized by generative AI systems. Consequently, their specific needs may not be adequately recognized, resulting in challenges for these users in obtaining equivalent levels of service compared to their counterparts.

Culturally, research comparing the responses of five prominent language models – GPT-4, GPT-4 Turbo, GPT-3.5, and GPT-3 Turbo – against data from nationally representative surveys indicates the existence of cultural and linguistic biases (Tao et al., 2024). The findings suggest that the cultural values expressed by all examined language models are more closely aligned with those of English-speaking and Protestant European nations. From a linguistic perspective, many generative AI systems that are language-based depend on a restricted corpus of language data and frequently emphasize standardized language variants. This reliance can foster the perception that there exists a singular "correct" method of utilizing a specific language, thereby contributing to linguistic bias (Jenks, 2024).

While users typically perceive AI as more objective and rational than human decision-makers, AI algorithms frequently embody the subjective biases of their creators, including programmers, data scientists, and other human developers. This phenomenon hinders the advancement of generative AI and adversely affects the production of knowledge within human society.

11.2.5 Controlling the Degree of Humanization

Humanization represents a significant trend in the evolution of chatbots. Numerous studies have demonstrated that the incorporation of human-like attributes in AI systems, such as warmth and competence, can enhance user trust and positively influence user satisfaction during interactions (Han, 2021). In these contexts, generative AI affects users through various dimensions, including auditory and emotional responses, which contribute to an increase in overall interaction satisfaction. Generative AI is capable of performing tasks such as playing music, ordering products, and personalizing plans, with these human-like services directly contributing to improvements in users' life satisfaction and well-being. Nevertheless, fulfilling users' expectations for human-like services poses considerable challenges. A limited proportion of users believe that AI-based systems can deliver services that are more satisfying than those provided by humans (Zhu et al., 2023). Furthermore, frequent security and privacy breaches in human–AI interactions and collaborations adversely affect user evaluations.

As generative AI progresses, its behavior and communicative style increasingly exhibit characteristics reminiscent of human interaction. This evolution is reshaping the dynamics between humans and AI, fostering more romanticized emotional investments in these technologies. However, it is important to recognize that the social roles assumed by AI in expressing emotions are not designed to fulfill user needs; rather, they reflect the intentions of the developers through pre-programmed behaviors and responses. In light of this reality, it is imperative to evaluate and address the moral risks associated with various forms of AI companionship. When users perceive AI companionship as a source of genuine emotional support, "emotional bubbles can impede personal emotional development and diminish users' capacity to cultivate diverse social relationships, thereby complicating their interactions with individuals who possess differing emotional perspectives (Mlonyeni, 2025). Conversely, emotional bubbles may create an illusion of external validation, which poses a significant threat to societal moral standards. Consequently, the ethical development of emotional companionship functionalities within generative AI in the context of human–AI interactions presents a complex challenge that necessitates thorough examination and consideration.

11.3 Psychological Game in Human–AI Interaction and Collaboration

11.3.1 AI as a Human Workforce Substitute

Technological advancements and innovations in automation technology have progressively supplanted repetitive and standardized tasks that were traditionally performed by humans. Furthermore, with the emergence of deep learning, big data analytics, and other digital technologies, the phenomenon of "machine replacement" has expanded beyond low-skilled labor, exerting a substantial impact across various industries.

According to the World Economic Forum's report titled *The Future of Jobs Report 2020*, economic downturn resulting from the COVID-19 pandemic, in conjunction with rapid advancements in automation technology, is accelerating changes in the job market at an unprecedented rate. It is projected that automation and the evolving labor dynamics between humans and machines will disrupt approximately 85 million jobs across fifteen global industries within the next five years. The demand for technical positions, including data entry, accounting, and management services, has been significantly affected. However, the ongoing wave of industrial upgrading and the robust growth of digitalization have led to an increase in hiring demand within the AI, big data, and manufacturing sectors, thereby creating additional job opportunities. Nevertheless, this growth also intensifies job insecurity. Research indicates that sectors characterized by high levels of automation – such as agriculture, forestry, animal husbandry, fishing, mining, manufacturing, and construction – are particularly vulnerable to job displacement. Older workers with lower educational attainment are at an especially high risk of being replaced (Wang et al., 2022). Furthermore, the development and rapid proliferation of generative AI and AI models present unprecedented challenges for knowledge workers, with data analysts, product managers, and other high-level professionals potentially facing threats that may surpass those encountered by manual laborers (Dăniloaia & Turturean, 2024).

Overall, traditional mechanistic perspectives frequently interpret the coexistence of machines and humans as a zero-sum game, neglecting to evaluate the broader opportunities afforded by generative AI and human–AI collaboration from a macroeconomic standpoint (Novella et al., 2023). This situation underscores the initial disparity between humans and artificial intelligence during the early phases of technological transformation.

11.3.2 AI and Team Collaboration

The swift advancement of generative AI is reshaping the parameters of human–AI interaction and collaboration, thereby influencing team dynamics across a range of task scenarios. Empirical research suggests that the capabilities of generative AI in executing various innovative tasks have exceeded those of 90–99 percent of human participants (Haase and Hanel, 2023). It is evident that AI is poised to become an essential collaborator in future work environments.

The integration of generative AI into workplace environments is poised to effect significant transformations. Conventional systems for assessing work capabilities are becoming increasingly obsolete, necessitating a redefinition of the value that individuals contribute within teams. Although attributes such as emotional intelligence and adaptability continue to be vital, proficiency in generative AI has emerged as an essential skill that stands apart from traditional competencies (Relyea et al., 2024). In the context of evaluating individual performance within a team, the capacity to enhance task quality through AI assistance is now a more critical determinant than traditional skill sets.

In addition to affecting individual performance evaluation criteria, human–AI interaction and collaboration may have negative impacts on the overall teamwork environment. On one hand, an overreliance on AI models can lead to the phenomenon known as "social loafing," focus and motivation compared to when they are working independently (Cymek et al., 2023). This is further exemplified by the concept of "automation complacency" in autonomous driving, which indicates that the presence of automation technology can lead to distractions among workers (Li et al., 2024; Liu, 2023). Consequently, it is imperative to clearly define the boundaries of cognitive autonomy that is transferred from humans to AI within human–AI teams, and to establish appropriate interpersonal dynamics and interaction frameworks between humans and AI.

11.3.3 Security and Privacy

The swift advancement of generative AI has yielded substantial benefits across various domains, including healthcare, education, and the arts. Nevertheless, it has also engendered apprehensions regarding deepfake technology, breaches of privacy, data contamination, and the safeguarding of intellectual property. These concerns pose significant threats to user security and privacy rights. The origins of these issues can be attributed to both a deficiency in preventive awareness and the profit-driven motivations of capital, which highlight intrinsic shortcomings within the generative AI technology itself.

The advancement of generative AI and deepfake technology, which enables the production of images, audio, and video content derived from real-world materials, has raised significant concerns about misinformation and authenticity. These fabricated yet often difficult-to-detect forms of media present significant risks, including the manipulation of personal content, identity theft, and challenges associated with identity verification (Jones et al., 2018). In the digital age, personal information, such as images and life histories, can be accessed at minimal cost. Deepfake technology facilitates the generation of counterfeit content from personal photographs and audio recordings, thereby jeopardizing individual reputation and security while also enabling online fraud, extortion, and the dissemination of malicious software. Numerous identity verification methods depend on biometric data, including voice and facial characteristics, which underscores the importance of safeguarding sensitive personal information (Li et al., 2020). As detection technologies for deepfakes continue to evolve, users may experience a lack of trust in human–AI interactions, potentially hindering the acceptance and promotion of generative AI technology.

The security and privacy threats encountered by users during their interactions with generative AI are primarily attributable to the inherent limitations of the technology. Generative AI employs deep learning algorithms and sophisticated neural network models to learn from extensive datasets, with the objective of simulating human cognitive processes and providing conversational services. At its current developmental stage, generative AI lacks a genuine understanding of user needs; rather, it replicates patterns from existing datasets (Sengar et al., 2024). This limitation can result in outputs that do not correspond with user input, exhibit biases, or contain inaccuracies. Furthermore, the challenge of accurately discerning a user's true intent complicates the regulation of generative AI outputs and exacerbates regulatory difficulties. In terms of data privacy, certain generative AI tools engage in excessive data collection, often without the user's explicit consent. Additionally, during interactions with generative AI, users may inadvertently disclose substantial amounts of personal information in pursuit of more precise and customized responses. This information may subsequently be incorporated into the AI's training data and potentially shared with other users (Kaswan et al., 2023). For instance, in March 2023, multiple Twitter users reported that ChatGPT generated content that included personal information such as names, phone numbers, and email addresses belonging to others. Although OpenAI promptly addressed this issue, it adversely affected user trust and raised significant concerns regarding data security, leading some countries and organizations to impose restrictions on the utilization of generative AI.

11.4 Countermeasures

11.4.1 Providing More Transparent and Explainable Generative AI Services

To improve the explainability of generative AI, it is crucial to tackle the challenges associated with model complexity and data uncertainty. From an algorithmic standpoint, AI algorithms frequently exhibit high complexity and encompass numerous parameters, rendering their output mechanisms similar to a "black box," which diminishes their explainability. Simplifying model architectures and parameters, as well as employing more interpretable algorithms, can facilitate the development of decision models that are more comprehensible. Examples of commonly utilized algorithms that exemplify this approach include decision trees, logistic regression, linear regression, and random forests.

Numerous companies engaged in artificial intelligence development are presently concentrating on the research of generative AI systems that facilitate user comprehension of their decision-making processes. For example, OpenAI has been actively developing technologies and tools aimed at enhancing interpretability, thereby assisting users in understanding how AI models identify user requirements and generate decisions based on these attributes (Raiaan et al., 2024). By integrating visualization technologies and adopting more interpretable model architectures, complex decision-making models can be represented through intuitive visualizations and animations. This approach not only improves the explainability of the overall decision model but also fosters increased user trust in the decisions made by generative AI systems.

Training datasets that contain noise or inaccuracies can make the decision output mechanisms difficult to understand, affecting the explainability of generative AI systems. Introducing uncertainty assessment and robustness analysis can provide measures of the trustworthiness of generative AI outputs. Additionally, improving the selection and cleaning of training data helps offer more transparent and explainable services during human–AI interaction and collaboration.

11.4.2 Addressing the "Hallucination" Problem in Large Generative AI Models

In recent years, generative AI models such as ChatGPT have gained widespread adoption, generating considerable interest across multiple domains. These models, which are underpinned by large language models (LLMs), possess the capability to discern user intentions and generate engaging and accurate interactive content. This functionality not only enhances work efficiency but also offers emotional support in human–AI interactions and collaborations. Nevertheless, despite the high level of precision and fluency exhibited in these interactions, a notable challenge remains: the phenomenon known as hallucination is inherent to generative AI models (Filippova, 2020; Ji et al., 2023).

Large generative AI models, characterized by extensive training datasets and diverse application contexts, are capable of generating content that may seem coherent and plausible, despite being a product of hallucination. Consequently, the evaluation and mitigation of hallucinations in these models are essential, as they significantly influence user satisfaction in interactions and collaborations between humans and AI (Tonmoy et al., 2024).

To mitigate the adverse effects of model hallucinations, it is essential to prioritize the quality of training datasets during the pre-training phase. In the instruction fine-tuning phase, the implementation of manual data cleaning can effectively prevent hallucinations that arise from behavior cloning phenomena. Furthermore, during the reinforcement learning phase, the application of varying degrees of penalties for incorrect responses, contingent upon different tones and attitudes, can incentivize generative AI to recognize its errors. This strategy aids in circumventing hallucinations that stem from the overconfidence of the AI model.

11.4.3 Solutions for Addressing Privacy Leakage in Generative AI

To tackle privacy leakage and safeguard user security, two main approaches should be reinforced:

Enhancing Data Security Measures

Automated System Controls: Enhancing data security necessitates a proactive approach to preventing privacy breaches. The implementation of automated systems can substantially reduce the risks associated with data leakage. Cutting-edge technologies such as Robotic Process Automation (RPA), low-code development platforms, process mining, and Natural Language Processing (NLP) are leading the research efforts in this domain (Haleem et al., 2021; Ng et al., 2021). Prior to the extensive adoption of generative AI, intelligent automation had already facilitated the creation of conversational processes, wherein workflows and commands are initiated through keyword instructions. By integrating generative AI-driven automation within local or cloud-based systems, it is possible to establish an intermediary isolation layer between the user and the generative AI. This strategy enhances security in comparison to cloud-based content generation, thereby offering a superior level of data protection.

Using Synthetic Data

Synthetic Data Generation: Addressing data leakage in generative AI can be effectively accomplished through the utilization of synthetic data. Techniques such as Generative Adversarial Networks (GANs), sequence models, and data anonymization are capable of producing datasets that closely resemble real personal information while omitting actual identifiable details. Synthetic data is characterized by its high quality, efficiency, and cost-effectiveness, and its artificial generation inherently provides privacy protection (Guo & Chen, 2024). The evolution of privacy regulations is further promoting the adoption of synthetic data as a vital solution. Within the realm of generative AI, it is imperative to concentrate on enhancing the quality, authenticity, interpretability, and applicability of synthetic data to develop models that more effectively satisfy user requirements.

The implementation of these strategies can effectively mitigate the risks of privacy leakage in generative artificial intelligence, thereby ensuring the security and protection of user data.

Acknowledgements

This work was supported by the Natural Science Foundation of Hubei Province (No. 2025AFB770), and and "the Fundamental Research Funds for the Central Universities."

References

Ananya. (2024). AI Image Generators Often Give Racist and Sexist Results: Can They Be Fixed? *Nature, 627*, 722–725. https://doi.org/10.1038/d41586-024-00674-9

Chen, X., Xie, H., Zou, D., & Hwang, G. J. (2020). Application and Theory Gaps during the Rise of Artificial Intelligence in Education. *Computers and Education: Artificial Intelligence, 1*, 100002.

Cheng, X., Zhang, X., Cohen, J., & Mou, J. (2022). Human vs. AI: Understanding the Impact of Anthropomorphism on Consumer Response to Chatbots from the Perspective of Trust and Relationship Norms. *Information Processing & Management, 59*(3), 102940.

Cymek, D. H., Truckenbrodt, A., & Onnasch, L. (2023). Lean Back or Lean in? Exploring Social Loafing in Human–Robot Teams. *Frontiers in Robotics and AI, 10*, 1249252.

Dăniloaia, D. F., & Turturean, E. (2024). Knowledge Workers and the Rise of Artificial Intelligence: Navigating New Challenges. *SEA: Practical Application of Science, 12*(35).

Elyoseph, Z., Hadar-Shoval, D., Asraf, K., & Lvovsky, M. (2023). ChatGPT Outperforms Humans in Emotional Awareness Evaluations. *Frontiers in Psychology, 14*, 1199058. https://doi.org/10.3389/fpsyg.2023.1199058

Filippova, K. (2020). Controlled Hallucinations: Learning to Generate Faithfully from Noisy Data. [arXiv preprint], arXiv:2010.05873.

Gilliard, C. (2022, January 2). Crime Prediction Keeps Society Stuck in the Past. *WIRED*. www.wired.com/story/crime-prediction-racist-history/

Guo, X., & Chen, Y. (2024). Generative AI for Synthetic Data Generation: Methods, Challenges and the Future [arXiv preprint]. arXiv:2403.04190.

Haase, J., & Hanel, P. H. (2023). Artificial Muses: Generative Artificial Intelligence Chatbots have Risen to Human-level Creativity. *Journal of Creativity, 33*(3), 100066.

Haleem, A., Javaid, M., Singh, R. P., Rab, S., & Suman, R. (2021). Hyperautomation for the Enhancement of Automation in Industries. *Sensors International, 2*, 100124.

Han, M. C. (2021). The Impact of Anthropomorphism on Consumers' Purchase Decision in Chatbot Commerce. *Journal of Internet Commerce, 20*(1), 46–65.

Hitsuwari, J., Ueda, Y., Yun, W., & Nomura, M. (2023). Does Human–AI Collaboration Lead to More Creative Art? Aesthetic Evaluation of Human-made and AI-generated Haiku Poetry. *Computers in Human Behavior, 139*, 107502.

Ji, Z., Lee, N., Frieske, R., Yu, T., Su, D., Xu, Y., ... & Fung, P. (2023). Survey of Hallucination in Natural Language Generation. *ACM Computing Surveys, 55*(12), 1–38.

Jenks, C. J. (2024). Communicating the Cultural Other: Trust and Bias in Generative AI and Large Language Models. *Applied Linguistics Review, 16*(2), 787–795.

Jones, M. L., Kaufman, E., & Edenberg, E. (2018). AI and the Ethics of Automating Consent. *IEEE Security & Privacy, 16*(3), 64–72.

Kaswan, K. S., Dhatterwal, J. S., Malik, K., & Baliyan, A. (2023, November). Generative AI: A Review on Models and Applications. In *2023 International Conference on Communication, Security and Artificial Intelligence (ICCSAI)* (pp. 699–704). IEEE.

Khurana, D., Koli, A., Khatter, K., & Singh, S. (2023). Natural Language Processing: State of the Art, Current Trends and Challenges. *Multimed Tools Appl, 82*, 3713–3744. https://doi.org/10.1007/s11042-022-13428-4

Königs, P. (2022). Artificial Intelligence and Responsibility Gaps: What Is the Problem? *Ethics and Information Technology, 24*(3), 36.

Li, L., Mu, X., Li, S., & Peng, H. (2020). A Review of Face Recognition Technology. *IEEE Access, 8*, 139110–139120.

Li, M., Guo, F., Li, Z., Ma, H., & Duffy, V. G. (2024). Interactive Effects of Users' Openness and Robot Reliability on Trust: Evidence from Psychological Intentions, Task Performance, Visual Behaviours, and Cerebral Activations. *Ergonomics, 67*(11), 1612–1632.

Liu, P. (2023). Reflections on Automation Complacency. *International Journal of Human–Computer Interaction, 40*(22), 7347–7363.

Lukyanenko, R., Maass, W., & Storey, V. C. (2022). Trust in Artificial Intelligence: From a Foundational Trust Framework to Emerging Research Opportunities. *Electronic Markets, 32*(4), 1993–2020.

Mariadassou, S., Klesse, A. K., & Boegershausen, J. (2024). Averse to What: Consumer Aversion to Algorithmic Labels, but Not Their Outputs? *Current Opinion in Psychology, 58*, 101839. https://doi.org/10.1016/j.copsyc.2024.101839

Mlonyeni, P. M. T. (2025). Personal AI, Deception, and the Problem of Emotional Bubbles. *AI & Society, 40*, 1927–1938. https://doi.org/10.1007/s00146-024-01958-4

Ng, K. K., Chen, C. H., Lee, C. K., Jiao, J. R., & Yang, Z. X. (2021). A Systematic Literature Review on Intelligent Automation: Aligning Concepts from Theory, Practice, and Future Perspectives. *Advanced Engineering Informatics, 47*, 101246.

Novella, R., Rosas-Shady, D., & Alvarado, A. (2023). Are We Nearly There Yet? New Technology Adoption and Labor Demand in Peru. *Science and Public Policy, 50*(4), 565–578.

Peng, C., van Doorn, J., Eggers, F., & Wieringa, J. E. (2022). The Effect of Required Warmth on Consumer Acceptance of Artificial Intelligence in Service: The Moderating Role of AI–Human Collaboration. *International Journal of Information Management, 66*, 102533.

Raiaan, M. A. K., Mukta, M. S. H., Fatema, K., Fahad, N. M., Sakib, S., Mim, M. M. J., ... & Azam, S. (2024). A Review on Large Language Models: Architectures, Applications, Taxonomies, Open Issues and Challenges. *IEEE Access, 12*, 26839–26874.

Relyea, C., Maor, D., Durth, S., & Bouly, J. (2024, August 7). *Gen AI's Next Inflection Point: From Employee Experimentation to Organizational Transformation*. McKinsey & Company. www.mckinsey.com/capabilities/people-and-organiza

tional-performance/our-insights/gen-ais-next-inflection-point-from-employee-experimentation-to-organizational-transformation

Sengar, S. S., Hasan, A. B., Kumar, S., & Carroll, F. (2024). Generative Artificial Intelligence: A Systematic Review and Applications [arXiv preprint]. arXiv:2405.11029.

Tao, Y., Viberg, O., Baker, R. S., & Kizilcec, R. F. (2024). Cultural Bias and Cultural Alignment of Large Language Models. *PNAS Nexus*, *3*(9), 346.

Tonmoy, S. M., Zaman, S. M., Jain, V., Rani, A., Rawte, V., Chadha, A., & Das, A. (2024). A Comprehensive Survey of Hallucination Mitigation Techniques in Large Language Models [arXiv preprint]. arXiv:2401.01313.

Wang, X., Zhu, X., & Wang, Y. (2022). The Impact of Robot Application on Manufacturing Employment. *Journal of Quantitative Technology Economics*, *39*(4), 88–106.

Westphal, M., Vössing, M., Satzger, G., Yom-Tov, G. B., & Rafaeli, A. (2023). Decision Control and Explanations in Human–AI Collaboration: Improving User Perceptions and Compliance. *Computers in Human Behavior*, *144*, 107714.

Yeomans, M., Shah, A., Mullainathan, S., & Kleinberg, J. (2019). Making Sense of Recommendations. *Journal of Behavioral Decision Making*, *32*(4), 403–414.

Zhu, Y., Shi, H., Hashmi, H. B. A., & Wu, Q. (2023). Bridging Artificial Intelligence-based Services and Online Impulse Buying in E-retailing Context. *Electronic Commerce Research and Applications*, *62*, 101333.

12
Conclusion

Dan Wu, Guoye Sun, and Shaobo Liang

12.1 Key Findings in Human–AI Interaction and Collaboration

With the rapid development of artificial intelligence technology, human–AI interaction and collaboration have become important topics in the field of contemporary technology. The capabilities of AI have gradually expanded from basic task automation to complex decision support, content creation, and intelligent collaboration in high-risk scenarios. This technological evolution has provided unprecedented opportunities for industries in different fields, but also brought challenges, such as privacy protection, credibility issues, and the ethical and legal relationship between AI and humans. This book explores the role and potential of AI in human–AI interaction and collaboration from multiple dimensions and analyzes AI's performance in privacy and credibility, knowledge sharing, search interaction, false information processing, and high-risk application scenarios in detail through different chapters. This chapter will synthesize the research results of the previous chapters, summarize our main findings in the book, and put forward the importance and suggestions for academic research and industry practice, as shown in Figure 12.1. At the same time, we will also discuss the limitations of the research and look forward to future research directions.

The human-centered design concept is crucial. In Chapter 2, we proposed a theoretical framework for human–AI interaction and collaboration, and elaborated on several hot issues in the quality of human–AI interaction, such as user psychological modeling, explainable AI, trust, and anthropomorphism. The study found that the design of AI systems is not only a technical challenge, but also involves how to integrate user needs and experience as core elements into the design and implementation of AI systems. The human-centered design concept requires us to always understand the needs of the user's perspective

Conclusion

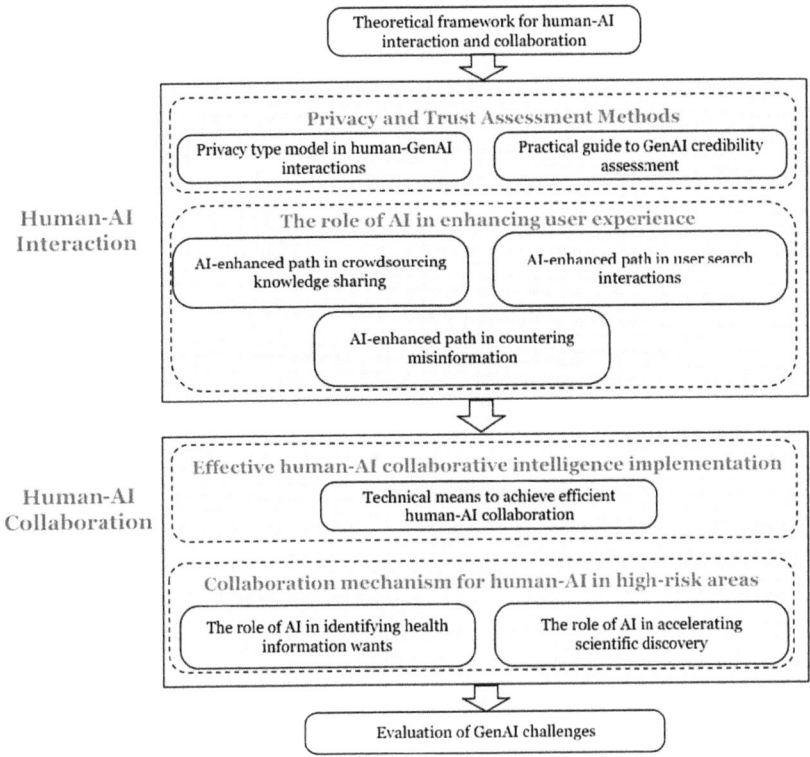

Figure 12.1 Overall key findings

during the algorithm development and application process and pay attention to the quality and method of human–machine interaction. This finding has important guiding significance for the development of future AI systems, especially in industry applications. Only on the basis of ensuring a good user experience can the potential of AI systems be fully realized.

Privacy and trust are core elements in the interaction between AI and humans. In Chapter 3, we analyzed the privacy issues of humans and generative AI and proposed a related privacy type identification framework. With the rapid development of generative AI such as large language models (LLMs), the problem of privacy leakage has become increasingly prominent. In Chapter 3, we conducted a detailed analysis of the challenges of privacy protection in generative AI and proposed a systematic privacy classification model to help developers and users better understand privacy risks and take corresponding protection measures. Due to the complex working mechanism of generative AI, privacy leakage is usually difficult for users to detect, which puts higher requirements on the establishment of user trust. Therefore, when developing generative AI, the industry should actively explore ways to strengthen privacy protection by improving pre-training data and controlling generated content. At the same time, users should be clearly informed of the working mechanism of the system and the possible privacy risks involved to enhance their awareness of privacy protection. Chapter 3 particularly emphasizes the privacy identification problem in the interaction between users and generative AI and proposes an effective privacy identification solution, which provides a reference for users to be aware of the protection of personal privacy information when interacting with AI.

Chapter 4 further explores the credibility assessment of generative AI. With the widespread application of generative AI in many fields (such as medical care, education, etc.), users have higher and higher requirements for the transparency and explainability of AI system decisions. How to find a balance between data security, privacy protection, and transparency of AI algorithms is an important direction for future research. In practical applications, credibility depends not only on the accuracy of AI, but also on whether its decision-making process is reasonable and explainable, and how to effectively manage potential errors. Chapter 4 deeply analyzes the multiple factors that affect users' trust in AI-generated content, including data, algorithms, systems, and individual characteristics of users. In order to build a trustworthy AI ecosystem, developers and researchers need to make transparency and explainability one of the core principles during the design phase to help users understand the decision-making process of AI systems. At the same time, the industry also needs to invest more resources to develop more transparent and fair evaluation methods to ensure that users can make wise decisions based on reliable information.

The role of AI in enhancing user experience and decision-making is explored in detail in Chapters 5–7. First, Chapter 5 introduces how AI promotes the effective use of crowd intelligence by supporting crowdsourced knowledge sharing. In large-scale collaboration and information sharing, AI not only improves the efficiency of information retrieval, but also helps users effectively organize and filter valuable content. AI in this crowdsourcing model is not limited to passively providing information but actively participates in the creation and sharing of user knowledge, reflecting the efficiency of human–machine collaboration. Chapter 5 demonstrates through case studies how AI-powered crowdsourcing systems can play a key role in addressing major social issues such as finding missing children. AI can not only improve the efficiency of crowdsourcing systems, but also avoid the "tragedy of the commons" phenomenon by motivating collaborative workers, improving transparency, and coordinating individual behaviors. AI-supported crowdsourcing systems have significant social value. They can not only bring together collective wisdom to solve complex problems, but also promote closer collaboration among all sectors of society, especially in issues related to public resource management such as climate change, traffic congestion, and public health. Future research should further explore how to optimize AI algorithms in crowdsourcing platforms to better motivate participants and improve overall collaboration efficiency.

Chapter 6 continues this idea and explores how AI can support search interactions and enhance user understanding. AI is not only an information retrieval tool but also an assistant that guides users' thinking. Through intelligent search and sorting methods, it helps users obtain information faster and more comprehensively, thereby improving the quality of decision-making. This enhanced search interaction mode can be seen as a combination of traditional information retrieval and deep learning technology, aiming to optimize the cognitive load in human–AI interaction. Chapter 6 examines the application of AI in information retrieval, specifically how to improve user understanding by enhancing search interactions. Through case studies and experimental analysis, AI-supported search systems have shown significant advantages in improving retrieval efficiency, reducing the number of user query modifications, and extending the time users stay on relevant pages. AI-enhanced search can not only better understand the user's query intent, but also provide more contextual results to help users obtain information more effectively. This discovery has important application value for information-intensive tasks such as academic research and business decision-making. In the future, search engine developers should focus on optimizing user interaction interfaces using AI technology to improve users' search satisfaction and usage intentions.

Chapter 7 focuses on the application of AI in dealing with false information. Currently, the proliferation of false information has a great impact on user cognition. AI can help users identify the authenticity of information through algorithm identification and filtering mechanisms, thereby establishing a healthier information dissemination environment. This is particularly important in the application of digital media and social platforms. AI can significantly reduce the spread of false information and maintain the positive development of social public opinion. In Chapter 7, we explore the impact of AI on the spread of misinformation on social media, especially its effect on user emotions and social behavior. By applying deep learning models to analyze users' online conversations during the epidemic, we found that the authenticity of different information will trigger emotional reactions of different strengths and further affect users' social connection behaviors. For example, misinformation often elicits higher emotions of expectation, fear, and surprise, thereby promoting behaviors supportive of the misinformation. Our research shows that AI can help analyze sentiment signals and provide new ideas for improving misinformation identification and mitigation strategies in online communities. Future research should further explore how to use emotional signals to optimize AI models, especially for applications on open platforms such as social media.

Effective human–machine collaborative intelligence plays a vital role in the development of AI. In Chapter 8, we explore how to achieve efficient cooperation between humans and machines through technical means. Whether it is in simple task allocation or complex decision-making, the role of AI is not only an assistant, but also an active participant.

This chapter particularly emphasizes three important characteristics of human–machine collaboration: information sharing, decision-making collaboration, and feedback mechanisms. Information sharing means that humans and AI can transfer task-related data and knowledge in real time, while decision-making collaboration means that, during the task execution process, AI can dynamically adjust decisions based on human needs or feedback. The feedback mechanism is that AI optimizes its own algorithm based on real-time feedback from humans to ensure a positive cycle in human–AI interaction.

The application of AI technology in high-risk scenarios is one of the key areas discussed in this book. In Chapters 9 and 10, the cooperation mechanism of AI in high-risk fields such as human health and scientific discovery is introduced in detail, and the application of AI in human–machine collaboration is further explored, especially in a limited data environment, and how human experts can improve the performance of AI models through collaboration with AI. Chapter 9 focuses on how AI can assist in the identification of information needs in the medical field. By collaborating with human doctors, AI can accelerate the identification and processing of patient needs, thereby improving medical efficiency. Chapter 9 particularly emphasizes the application of AI in caregiver information behavior. By combining AI with caregiver knowledge, smarter intervention measures are developed to help caregivers obtain the required health information. The advantage of human–machine collaboration is that it can optimize AI systems through continuous iteration and feedback, while allowing human experts to better use AI technology for data analysis and decision-making. Chapter 10 further expands human–machine collaboration to the field of scientific discovery and elaborates on the role of AI in accelerating scientific discovery. AI not only improves the efficiency of data analysis and predictive modeling, but also automates the experimental process, prompting a profound change in the scientific research paradigm. Through the collaboration between human experts and AI systems, scientists can discover new knowledge more quickly and make breakthroughs in many fields such as mathematics, physics, chemistry, and biology. As AI technology continues to mature, future scientific research will rely more on AI's predictive and data processing capabilities, which also provides broad prospects for interdisciplinary cooperation. However, the application of AI in scientific research also brings ethical challenges and, in the future, more attention needs to be paid to the formulation of norms and standards for the use of AI in scientific research.

In Chapter 11, we explored the challenges of generative AI in human–AI collaboration. The application of generative AI in creative tasks is gradually increasing, such as copywriting and image generation. However, this also raises many questions, such as how to define the creative boundaries of AI, how to ensure that the generated content meets ethical and legal standards, and how to balance the relationship between AI-generated content and human originality. These problems need to find effective solutions in future research and applications. In Chapter 11, we discussed the trust, transparency, and cultural sensitivity issues brought about by the rapid development of generative AI. As the complexity of AI systems interacting with humans increases, it becomes crucial to ensure the fairness and adaptability of AI systems in different cultural contexts. In addition, AI algorithms need to be optimized according to the needs of different users to achieve maximum benefits in a variety of application scenarios. Establishing and maintaining user trust in AI systems is the basis for the widespread application of AI and the industry must make long-term investments in algorithm design, user experience optimization, and ethical standards.

12.2 Future Challenges

Although this book explores the application of AI in human–machine collaboration from multiple perspectives, it faces several technical, ethical, and social challenges.

12.2.1 Technical Challenges

Explainability and Transparency

Many AI systems, particularly deep learning models, operate as "black boxes," lacking transparency in their decision-making processes. In high-stakes fields like healthcare and finance, it is crucial for AI to provide clear explanations for its decisions to build user trust and identify potential biases.

Processing and Fusion of Multimodal Data

Human cognition relies on integrating various information sources. While AI has advanced in single-modal data processing, it still needs to improve its ability to understand and combine multimodal data, such as voice, images, and text, for better collaboration.

Large-scale Data Privacy and Security

AI's performance often depends on large datasets, which may include sensitive user information. Ensuring privacy while maintaining performance will be a key challenge, necessitating technologies like federated learning and differential privacy. Securing data transmission across cloud and edge computing platforms is also essential.

12.2.2 Ethical Challenges of Human–AI Relations

Lack of Ethical Norms and Legal Frameworks

With AI's growing role in society, establishing a unified ethical and legal framework globally is urgent. Variations in national laws can lead to ethical dilemmas and conflicts, particularly concerning surveillance and privacy.

Bias and Discrimination in AI Decision-making

Data biases can lead AI systems to make unfair decisions, exacerbating social inequality. Researchers must monitor bias throughout the AI lifecycle, aiming for systems that can automatically detect and correct these biases.

Responsibility Allocation between Humans and AI

Determining responsibility in complex tasks is increasingly complex. Future legal frameworks will need to clarify the accountability of AI systems, manufacturers, and users to prevent disputes.

12.2.3 Social Challenges of Human–AI Collaboration

Impact of AI on the Job Market

While AI improves efficiency, it threatens traditional jobs, particularly in sectors like manufacturing and transportation. Societal measures, such as education reform and vocational training, will be necessary to support workforce transitions.

Redefinition of the Relationship between Man and Machine

As AI evolves from a tool to a partner, society must redefine human–AI relationships and consider when AI might gain rights or responsibilities.

Fairness of AI in Public Services

AI can enhance public services but may also deepen social inequalities. Ensuring equitable access to AI benefits for all social groups is crucial, requiring fairness to be prioritized in AI design and application.

12.3 Prospects for Coping Strategies

In order to cope with various challenges in the future development of AI, multiple fields need to make corresponding adjustments and plans.

12.3.1 Promote Multidisciplinary Cross-collaboration

The complexity of AI technology determines that its development cannot rely solely on breakthroughs in the field of computer science, but requires the joint participation of disciplines including psychology, sociology, ethics, and law. Multidisciplinary cross-collaboration can not only provide a broader perspective for the technological progress of AI but also help solve the ethical and legal issues of AI in practical applications. For example, psychologists can help design interactive systems that are more in line with human cognitive and behavioral habits, while sociologists can evaluate the impact of AI on different social groups to ensure the fairness of technology.

In the future, in-depth cooperation between academia and industry is also key. Academia can promote the development of AI technology through cutting-edge research, while industry can continuously verify and improve these technologies through practical applications. In this process, governments and international organizations also need to actively participate in promoting the establishment of global AI standards and norms to ensure that technological progress is coordinated with social development.

12.3.2 Strengthen AI Education and Public Awareness

In order for society to better adapt to the rapid development of AI technology, it is crucial to improve education and public awareness. At present, many people's understanding of AI is still limited to the one-sided reports of mass media, which leads to misunderstanding and fear of technology. In order to eliminate these misunderstandings, society needs to strengthen popular science education for the public to help people more comprehensively understand the capabilities, limitations, and application scenarios of AI.

In addition, more knowledge and courses about AI should be introduced into the education system to help the younger generation master AI technology and understand its possible impact on society. This is not only about training the next generation of AI developers, but also about letting practitioners in more fields understand how to work with AI and how to use AI to improve efficiency at work. For example, in the fields of medicine, law, finance, etc., professionals need to learn how to use AI tools to assist them in making more accurate and efficient decisions.

12.3.3 Promote the Construction of Laws and Regulations and Ethical Frameworks

In order to ensure that the development of AI has a positive impact on society, governments and international organizations must speed up the formulation of relevant laws, regulations, and ethical frameworks. This is not only to regulate the application of AI technology, but also to solve the problem of responsibility division in AI applications. The future legal framework should clearly stipulate who should be responsible for the results when AI systems fail – developers, operators, or users? This division of responsibilities needs to be formulated according to specific application scenarios to ensure that the relevant parties can bear legal responsibilities in accidents caused by technical errors or deviations.

At the same time, the construction of a global ethical framework is also crucial. Although the social and cultural backgrounds of different countries and regions are different, the application of AI is almost ubiquitous on the cross-border Internet. International cooperation and consensus are essential to establish global AI ethical norms so as to effectively respond to the transnational ethical and legal challenges brought by AI technology. For example, the application of AI in sensitive areas such as data privacy, surveillance technology, and military use must be clearly regulated within the international legal framework to avoid international conflicts and social instability caused by the abuse of technology.

12.3.4 Establish a User-centered Design Concept

The design of AI systems should not only pursue technological advancement but also attach great importance to user experience and needs. This requires that, in the design process of AI, user convenience, safety, and satisfaction should always be put first. User feedback should play a key role in the development and iteration of AI systems. By continuously obtaining users' experiences and opinions in actual use, developers can better improve the functions and interaction methods of AI systems.

The design of AI systems in the future should be more humane, especially in decision support systems and collaboration tools. AI's suggestions and outputs should be presented in a form that is easy for users to understand, so as to avoid confusion caused by complex technical details. At the same time, AI's user interface and interaction methods should also be more intuitive and friendly, so that users of different ages and cultural backgrounds can easily use it.

The future of human–AI interaction and collaboration is full of infinite possibilities. The continuous advancement of AI technology will not only change our work and lifestyle but also completely reshape the structure and function of the entire society. However, the development of technology is not isolated. It must be combined with social ethics, laws and regulations, and user needs to truly achieve sustainable innovation and progress.

This book explores the advantages, limitations, and challenges of AI technology by analyzing in detail several important issues of AI in human–AI interaction and collaboration. In the future, AI will continue to play a key role in different fields. From medical care and education to public services, AI will contribute to improving efficiency, improving decision-making, and enhancing user experience. At the same time, we must also realize that the development of AI requires the joint efforts of all parties in society, including technical researchers, policymakers, ethicists, the public, and so on, to ensure that AI technology truly benefits all mankind.

Through continuous innovation and reflection, we believe that the future of human–AI collaboration will be smarter and more humane and will bring more fairness and well-being to society on the road to technological progress.

Acknowledgment

This work was supported by the National Natural Science Foundation of China (No. 92370112) and the Innovative Research Group Project of Hubei Provincial Natural Science Foundation (No. 2023AFA012).

For EU product safety concerns, contact us at Calle de José Abascal, 56–1°, 28003 Madrid, Spain or eugpsr@cambridge.org.

www.ingramcontent.com/pod-product-compliance
Ingram Content Group UK Ltd.
Pitfield, Milton Keynes, MK11 3LW, UK
UKHW020611061125
464675UK00030B/95